More Praise for Cynthia L. Selfe and Gail E. Hawisher

"The best teachers know that writing can never be a self-enclosing practice, but must remain intimately connected to all media of expression, and thus constantly open to change. Selfe and Hawisher are the best of the best, and this book contains a rich harvest, not only of their own thinking, but also of pathbreaking work by colleagues and students. Anyone who hopes to understand the complex relationship of literacy and interactive media will find this book stimulating, challenging, and rewarding."
—Stuart Moulthrop, Professor of Information Arts and Technologies, University of Baltimore

"This text will be widely cited, as are all other of the editors' projects. Part of their popularity is due to their philosophy of inclusiveness, particularly assembling new voices. Like James Gee's work before it, *Gaming Lives in the Twenty-First Century* will also bridge a gap to understanding video games, helping us all recognize the impact of digital media technologies on a range of literacy practices—alphabetic, cultural, and critical."
—Kristine Blair, Bowling Green State University

"*Gaming*   4/08   are not
only time   ided as
coauthors   digital
environ   This
collecti   died,
especia

rsity

Previous Publications

Selfe, Cynthia L., & Hawisher, Gail E. (2004). *Literate Lives in the Information Age: Narratives of Literacy from the United States.* Mahwah, NJ: Lawrence Erlbaum.

Hawisher, Gail E., & Selfe, Cynthia L. (Eds.). (2000). *Global Literacies and the World Wide Web.* New York: Routledge.

Hawisher, Gail E., & Selfe, Cynthia L. (Eds.). (1999). *Passions, Pedagogies, and 21st Century Technologies.* Logan: Utah State University Press.

Hawisher, Gail E., & Selfe, Cynthia L. (Eds.). (1997). *Literacy, Technology, and Society: Confronting the Issues.* Upper Saddle River, NJ: Prentice Hall.

Hawisher, Gail E., LeBlanc, Paul, Moran, Charles, & Selfe, Cynthia L. (1996). *Computers and the Teaching of Writing in American Higher Education, 1979–1994: A History.* Norwood, NJ: Ablex Publishing.

Hawisher, Gail E., & Selfe, Cynthia L. (Eds.). (1991). *Evolving Perspectives on Computers and Composition Studies: Questions for the 1990s.* Urbana, IL: NCTE.

Hawisher, Gail E., & Selfe, Cynthia L. (Eds.). (1989). *Critical Perspectives on Computers and Composition Instruction.* New York: Columbia University's Teachers College Press.

Gaming Lives in the Twenty-First Century

Literate Connections

Edited by
Cynthia L. Selfe and Gail E. Hawisher

Associate Editor
Derek Van Ittersum

Foreword by
James Paul Gee

First published in 2007 by
PALGRAVE MACMILLAN™
175 Fifth Avenue, New York, N.Y. 10010 and
Houndmills, Basingstoke, Hampshire, England RG21 6XS.
Companies and representatives throughout the world.

PALGRAVE MACMILLAN is the global academic imprint of the Palgrave Macmillan
division of St. Martin's Press, LLC and of Palgrave Macmillan Ltd. Macmillan® is a
registered trademark in the United States, United Kingdom and other countries.
Palgrave is a registered trademark in the European Union and other countries.

ISBN-13: 978-1-4039-7219-4   hardcover
ISBN-10: 1-4039-7219-2   hardcover
ISBN-13: 978-1-4039-7220-0   paperback
ISBN-10: 1-4039-7220-6   paperback

Library of Congress Cataloging-in-Publication Data

Gaming lives in the twenty-first century: literate connections / edited by Cynthia L.
    Selfe and Gail E. Hawisher; foreword by James Paul Gee.
        p.cm.
    Includes bibliographical references and index.
    ISBN 1-4039-7219-2 (alk. paper)—ISBN 1-4039-7220-6 (alk. paper)
    1. Video games—Psychological aspects. 2. Video games—Social aspects.
    3. Computer games—Psychological aspects. 4. Computer games—Social aspects.
    5. Learning, Psychology of. 6. Visual literacy. I. Selfe, Cynthia L., 1951-II. Hawisher,
    Gail E.

    GV1469.3.G43 2007
    794.8—dc22   2006049826

A catalogue record for this book is available from the British Library.

Design by Macmillan India Ltd.

First edition: March 2007

10 9 8 7 6 5 4 3 2 1

Printed in the United States of America

Transferred to digital printing in 2008.

We dedicate this volume to the graduate students with whom we have worked over the years—those whose studies are in process and those who have gone on to new positions in universities across the country. As their teachers, invariably we are the ones who have learned from them and benefited from our innumerable conversations and collaborations. We thank them sincerely and wish them our very best as they continue to contribute their special wisdom to their own students, to the field, and to their many new colleagues.

Contents

Foreword

James Paul Gee

When I wrote *What Video Games Have to Teach Us about Learning and Literacy* (2003) I was fairly new to video games, but I had long had an axe to grind about literacy, learning, and the human mind. Literacy, I had argued in *Social Linguistics and Literacies* (1996), is not something that happens primarily in the privacy of people's minds; reading and writing are not just mental acts or cognitive achievements. Rather, literacy is something that happens out in the world of social, cultural, and institutional activities.

People do not just read the Bible, a physics book, a legal document, or an *anime manga*[1] as words on a page. They read, talk about, and act upon these documents in distinctive ways for distinctive purposes. You don't really know how to read these things if you don't know something about what people do with them and what it means to them when they do it. For example, a radical socialist reads a given legal decision differently than does a conservative legal historian or a crusading lawyer defending an indigent client. Literacy is at home in the world of talk, action, interaction, and values, not only in people's heads.

If all you can do when confronted with a written text is plug in something like dictionary definitions for the words on the page, all you have is a verbal understanding of the text. If, on the other hand, you can plug in, not just words for words, but, rather, images, actions, and dialogue for the words on the page, then you have what I call a "situated understanding."

This issue of situated understanding became dramatically clear to me when I started playing video games. Like a good baby boomer, but not a smart young person, when I played my first game, I initially tried to read the manual cover to cover. I understood what the manual was saying as words, but I had no idea what it really meant or how it applied. I felt that I would be unable to play the game, since it all seemed so unclear. But then I put the manual down and played. After a few hours of play, I returned to the manual and now what had seemed so unclear was completely lucid. I even had a hard time recalling why the text had seemed so hard in the beginning.

Why? Because now I could associate the words on the page with actions, images, and experiences from the game. After I had played a number of games of a similar type, I found that my growing genre knowledge—knowledge about how different types of games work—made such reading even easier. After I had eventually participated in gamer dialogue and social practices, I found such reading yet easier. Indeed, now I did not need to read the manuals cover to cover at all and could just use them for reference purposes when I wanted to check things out for my own goals.

It dawned on me that school books—for example, a high school biology book—are like those manuals. Both are technical documents. Just like the game manual, the biology book makes no real sense unless and until students have gotten to play the game, the game of biology in the case of the biology book. Things will get easier still if they get to understand the genre of the activities they are involved in by engaging with multiple examples. They will get yet easier if they get to participate in dialogue with people affiliated with and devoted to biology in some substantive, yes, even passionate, way. If all kids have in school are verbal understandings and not situated ones, then, while some of them may pass paper-and-pencil tests, few of them will be able to solve real problems in the world.

This perspective on literacy leads to a perspective on learning. Learning is not something that happens just in the privacy of people's minds. It is something that happens in the ways in which people do or do not participate in characteristic activities that other people have already invented, whether this be a fundamentalist church, a physics lab, a court of law, or a group of *anime otaku*.[2] Learning in this sense does not come just through skill and drill, it is not "decontextualized," and it is not easy to test with a piece of paper, a pencil, and an hour's worth of time. Classrooms need to be places where teachers have established coherent practices, connected to important domains that exist out in the world, wherein reading and writing are situated in the ways in which my game reading is situated in the images, actions, experiences, and dialogue I have with games and people devoted to them.

Ironically enough, these perspectives on literacy and learning are grounded in a particular perspective on the human mind and human thinking. In my view, humans think, when they are thinking at their best, through their bodies and emotions. They have experiences in the world (with those bodies) and they feel a certain way about those experiences, they evaluate or appreciate them in certain ways. In turn, they store these experiences and evaluations in their minds and use them to build mental models or simulations of what might happen before they act in the world.

Thinking is, in large part at least, a matter of having goals, intending to act, and making predictions about how to achieve these goals on the basis of models or simulations we build in our heads. These models are based on the experiences we have had in our bodies and how we have felt about them (edited them in terms of what we have focused on and paid attention to). When I wrote *The Social Mind* this was not a standard perspective on the mind. It is much closer to being so today (see, e.g., Barsalou, 1999; Glenberg, 1997; Hawkins, 2005). And, of course, video games fit well with this perspective on the mind, since they are just external simulations of experience that the player experiences through a surrogate body in the virtual world he or she finely controls.

These perspectives on literacy, learning, and mind have a bite: they immediately involve us in issues of equity and justice, issues central to my book *Situated*

Language and Learning (2004). If reading is connected to imaging, acting, experiencing, and dialogue; if learning is a matter of affiliating and participating; and if the mind is built on experiences in the world, then it matters deeply who gets to participate where and when; it matters deeply what experiences people have had or have been allowed to have.

The child who is given only a textbook in her science classroom is not on the same footing as the child who also gets to talk about and engage in science activities with her parents at home supported by a good computer and the Internet, as well as in museums and field trips, and a school full of computers and labs. One child is reading the manual without having played the game. It does not work—I can tell you, I tried it. Resources count: not economic resources per se, but experiential resources, access to experiences, images, and dialogue.

When I started playing video games—and I started because my six-year-old son, Sam, turned me on to video games and today, years later, correctly points out that I would never have ventured here without him—I saw something else. Ever since I had written the *Social Mind*, I had followed changes in the learning sciences, changing views of what constitutes optimal conditions for human learning. As I played good video games, it became obvious to me that these games incorporated good learning principles—just the sort that were showing up in cutting-edge research in the learning sciences—at a time when many of our schools were returning to a skill-and-drill regime that deserted such principles, at least for poor children.

Good video games offer pleasure from continuous learning and problem solving. They are hard and complex and their difficulty ramps up as the game proceeds. If no one could learn them, the companies that make them would go broke. By necessity, game designers have had to become learning designers as well. At the same time, a good video game is really not just the game in the box, it is also the activities of the whole group of people who interact over the game by mutual play, talk, writing (e.g., FAQs), chat rooms, and websites. In playing and learning video games, language and literacy are fully situated in images, actions, interactions, and dialogue.

I had intended, I must admit, *What Video Games Have to Teach Us about Learning and Literacy* to be a virus that used games—an appealing and controversial topic—to spread views on literacy, learning, and the mind that I already believed in. That plan did not really work. Much of the audience for the book have read it the other way round: the views on literacy, learning, and the mind have served as a carrier for spreading interest in games and gaming culture beyond the sphere of gamers. It has carried the message, as well, to gamers themselves that games are worth taking seriously outside gamer communities.

This volume you hold in your hand rectifies this matter very well, indeed. Here we see, in every chapter, how a close look at gamers of all different kinds can show us sociocultural literacy and situated learning in action in a way that goes far beyond my more theoretical take on the matter. This book is, as such, a seminal contribution to contemporary literacy studies. At the same time, it takes the empirical study of gamers and gaming in real life to a new high. Let me quickly say why.

No remark in my book has angered some of my academic colleagues more than when I wrote:

> Two issues have taken up the vast majority of writing about video games: violence (e.g., shooting and killing in games, depictions of crime) and gender (e.g., whether and how much girls play, whether and how video games depict women poorly). I have nothing whatsoever to say about these issues in this book. They are well discussed elsewhere. (p. 10)

A great deal of my previous work has been devoted to thinking critically about the political and equity implications of various literacy, learning, and school practices. However, when I wrote my video game book, I viewed video games and gaming as a fairly new phenomenon, especially for us academics, most certainly for us baby boomer academics. I knew we academics sometimes had a tendency to kill new things with critique before we got a chance to understand its full potential, for good or ill.

I also thought a good deal of the research on gender and games, and even more so the research on violence in games, was not based on deep interaction with games, gaming, and gamers. I thought if we understood this phenomenon of video gaming deeply enough—and "read" it with some charity to begin with—we could eventually deepen both our praise and critique of video games and popular culture more generally. This is the same analytic principle I apply in my work on discourse analysis, for example, in my book *An Introduction to Discourse Analysis* (1999).

I don't think the issue of gender and games is just that many games are made for boys. In fact, more and more girls are playing games and games are changing. Girls and women are the majority of the people who play *The Sims,* the best-selling computer game of all time. As far as I am concerned, an important issue is that our society takes games, technology, math, and science away from girls at just the same time, namely, during middle school. This is the time when girls are expected to serve the interests of the heterosexual crowd and not develop their technical chops. We need to give them back full access.

I do not think the issue of race and games is just that some games are racist. They are no more or less so than the U.S. media culture they give back to us, though the way they deal with race is a very important topic, since in a game like *Grand Theft Auto: San Andreas* you are not just looking at media about African Americans, you are in it and playing as an African American. However, I also think that another important issue here is the fact that while African Americans are one of the largest category of game players in every genre of computer games, poorer African American children (as well as other less-privileged children) often do not get the opportunity to have games and other digital literacies put into larger learning systems where they can be leveraged for technical and technological learning. They often do not have the opportunity to have their gaming interests, as well as their other cultural affiliations, related to school and leveraged for success in school, though this is true of many other children, as well.

What I thought was most needed after my book, the next stage, so to speak, was just the sort of book you are about to read. These authors look at real people—quite different people in every way—and ask what they actually do, think, and feel. They are not engaging in a critique of games and gaming from the outside. They are looking at what people actually do and from a position of real understanding of games and gaming, not as a monolithic thing, but as a diverse array of practices, groups, and enterprises. What they find sometimes supports my book, sometimes qualifies it, and sometimes surpasses it altogether. They engage in critique without destroying what they critique; they know how to expose points of weaknesses and still leverage potential for good.

Notes

1. Japanese animated cartoons, remembering that animation is not just for children in Japan.
2. "Obsessive," devoted and expert fan of any one particular theme or hobby.

References

Barsalou, Lawrence W. (1999). Perceptual symbol systems. *Behavioral and Brain Sciences, 22,* 577–660.

Gee, James P. (1990). *Social linguistics and literacies: Ideology in discourses.* London: Falmer, Second Edition, 1996.

Gee, James P. (1992). *The social mind: Language, ideology, and social practice.* New York: Bergin & Garvey.

Gee, James P. (1999). *An introduction to discourse analysis: Theory and method.* London: Routledge, Second Edition, 2005.

Gee, James P. (2003). *What video games have to teach us about learning and literacy.* New York: Palgrave Macmillan.

Gee, James P. (2004). *Situated language and learning: A critique of traditional schooling.* London: Routledge.

Glenberg, Arthur M. (1997). What is memory for? *Behavioral and Brain Sciences, 20,* 1–55.

Hawkins, Jeff. (2005). *On intelligence.* New York: Owl Books.

Introduction: Gaming Lives in the Twenty-First Century

Gail E. Hawisher and Cynthia L. Selfe

Gaming Lives in the Twenty-First Century: Literate Connections explores the complexly rendered relationship between computer gaming environments and literate activity by focusing on in-depth case studies of computer gamers in the United States at the beginning of the twenty-first century. Building on the popularity of James Paul Gee's book *What Video Games Have to Teach Us about Learning and Literacy* (2003), the volume examines Gee's claim that good computer games can provide better literacy and learning environments than U.S. schools. Our aim throughout the book is to tell the stories of individual gamers—using their own words and observations—and to offer historical and cultural analyses of their literacy development, practices, and values.

This book is also part of an ongoing, large-scale study of digital literacy in the United States and abroad involving life-history interviews with more than 350 participants. We have conducted these interviews over a seven-year period with people of different ages who come from a range of racial and ethnic groups and from diverse cultural, educational, and socioeconomic backgrounds. We have also published this ongoing work in a series of journal articles and, most recently, in *Literate Lives in the Information Age: Narratives of Literacy from the United States* (Selfe & Hawisher, 2004).

Continuing this line of research, *Gaming Lives* focuses more precisely on the literacies acquired, practiced, and valued within the digital environments of computer games—exploring participants' responses to a standard set of questions that detail

- demographic information;
- access to computer-based gaming environments at various times in the participants' lives (or the lack thereof);
- the nature of both the formal and informal literacy instruction participants received;
- the ways in which literacy practices and values intersect with gaming practices, values, and environments;
- patterns of acquiring these literacies (or patterns associated with why such acquisition did not happen); and
- the cultural values placed on the literacies that take place in gaming environments and on gaming itself.

This edited collection examines the responses from these gamer interviews within a context of historical, cultural, educational, political, and ideological trends that have characterized gaming over the last 30 years (Kent, 2001). The explosive growth of the computer-gaming industry ("Game Sales," 2002), for example, has many educators concerned about the amount of time young people are devoting to such pursuits and worried that computer games may serve to distract students' attention from more conventional academic studies. Gee (2003) argues persuasively that, far from distracting students from learning, many video games actually teach important concepts and principles required for learning, thinking, and literacy in today's world.

As readers probably already know, there are many different platforms for these games, and the terminology one adopts makes a difference when talking to people to find out how they engage in gaming. The most common comprehensive term seems to be "video games," and this is the term Gee (2003) adopts in his book. He tells us, for example, that some people play video games on game platforms (Play Station 2, Nintendo's GameCube and Gameboy, and Microsoft's Xbox are just a few), and others on computers with keyboards but often with handheld controllers, sometimes in the form of joysticks. He thus makes the distinction between platform games and computer games, viewing both as a type of video game. There are also, of course, the older arcade games, which several people in our earlier study (Selfe & Hawisher, 2004), who are now in their late 30s, played and sometimes still play, but today they often play the games on computers. In this book, we use the terms "video games" and "computer games" interchangeably and are primarily concerned with gaming that makes use of computer screens or even television screens. We recognize, however, that these games migrate increasingly to other platforms, and, most recently, to the screens of mobile phones.

In this particular historical and cultural context, young people's enthusiasm for video and computer gaming has proven to be an increasingly vigorous arena for public debate. On the one hand, a number of studies (e.g., Anderson & Bushman, 2001; Anderson & Dill, 2000; Fleming & Rickwood, 2001) and news stories (Ovalle, 2004) continue to focus on computer gaming as a factor in violent, aggressive, or antisocial behavior. Other researchers, however, note more positive findings:

> On several measures—including family closeness, activity involvement, positive school engagement, positive mental health, substance abuse, self-concept, friendship network, and disobedience to parents—game players scored more favorably than did peers who never played computer games. It is concluded that computer games can be a positive feature of a healthy adolescence. (Durkin & Barber, 2002, p. 376)

A recent report from the Pew Internet and American Life study site (Jones, 2003) reflects some of the complexity that brackets these debates. On the one hand, the report notes that 48 percent of student gamers feel "gaming keeps them from studying 'some' or 'a lot'" (p. 2) and that 9 percent of students play games specifically to avoid studying. On the other hand, the report indicates that 20 percent of computer gamers cited computer games as a way to "spend more time with friends," "make new friends," and "improve existing friendships" (p. 2). The report also noted that college students had positive feelings about games—describing them as both "exciting" (34 percent) and "challenging" (45 percent) (p. 2)—and noted that computer gamers posted as many hours of studying as the general student population.

The chapters in this edited collection explore the differing perspectives represented by such debates by relating the stories and experiences of individual gamers who have formed their own observations about the benefits and shortcomings of game playing in a digital world. No other book of which we are aware has taken on a life-history approach to examining this relatively new cultural pastime and its place in people's literate lives. Our hope is that this collection will be of interest to a large group of literacy scholars and graduate students in the fields of literacy; education; computers and composition; gaming; cultural studies; rhetoric and composition; and science, technology, and society. We believe that those who are interested in computer gaming as a popular cultural phenomenon will also find it timely. Finally, this book should appeal to readers of Gee's landmark book, *What Video Games Have to Teach Us about Learning and Literacy* (2003).

An additional goal for the book has been to provide literacy instructors with a methodology that they might use in their own teaching for evaluating the impact of gaming on literate lives. While a visiting scholar at the University of Louisville, one of the editors, Cynthia Selfe, used life-history interviews in a graduate class on the import of new information technologies. Using this particular methodology, which we have been developing since 1998, the graduate students were able to add a useful component to the larger research and, at the same time, explore issues related to gaming and literacy as writing instructors. The insights they gleaned could then be discussed with the college students in their own writing classes.

Hence, we have included at the end of this introduction the class assignment that the graduate students took up, the interview protocol that they used, and a sample paper by Beth Powell and her coauthors to illustrate how they carried out the assignment. By foregrounding a method focusing on life-history interviews, we hope to showcase the promise of the approach for research and pedagogy. The classroom setting provided an excellent opportunity for the graduate students to immerse themselves in a methodology focusing on life-history interviews as well as attend to possible connections between gaming and literacy.

Overview of Chapters

The 13 chapters presented here explore Gee's claims and test his theories about gaming as an environment in which individuals learn specialized knowledge and literacies. The implicit aim of each chapter is to describe how literacy practices in online gaming environments have been shaped, both directly and indirectly, by the development of the personal computer and the gaming industry.

The first of three sections, Gaming and Literacy, builds on the intimate connections between the primarily social development of literate practices and gaming behaviors. In chapter 1, Cynthia Selfe and her coauthors, Anne Mareck and Josh Gardiner, register Gee's (2003) claims that video games can provide young people with a wide range of values, skills, and understandings, among them:

- active, critical learning, and literacy practices
- opportunities to try on and practice with new and valuable identities
- intrinsic rewards for learning and practicing
- opportunities to achieve a level of mastery that extends personal confidence
- opportunities to connect texts and embodied experience

In comparing Gee's claims with the life experiences of a 13-year-old gamer, the authors also discuss why the literacies of this young man have not found their way into classrooms or onto the radar screens of composition teachers. In the second chapter, Iswari Pandey and his coauthors, Laxman Pandey and Angish Shreshtha, bring an international perspective to gaming and literacy. "Gaming, Class, Culture, and Literacy Learning" argues that we need additional studies on gaming to understand if people from a different cultural background learn, play, and interpret games—designed and manufactured primarily in the United States— differently from those who were themselves brought up in the United States. In order to explore cultural differences in gaming, the chapter analyzes the practices of two gamers who were born in Nepal but who are currently pursuing graduate studies in the United States. In chapter 3, "Found in Translation: Cultural Literacy, Language Acquisition, and Narrative Comprehension in the Advanced Gamer," Erin Smith and Eve Deitsch continue the focus on international contexts and new literacies. They examine the critical and cultural literacy of an undergraduate gamer whose avid interest in gaming and, consequently, in game development led her to learn Japanese and develop an extensive knowledge of the gaming industry. The two authors trace the complex interplay between gaming literacies and the sophisticated metalevel awareness of narrative and narrative conventions (culti- vated through gaming practice) that allowed her to critically assess the translation of the *Final Fantasy* games. In chapter 4, "Gaming, Identity, and Literacy," Daniel Keller explores the gaming practices of five players, three from the United States, one from Scotland, and one from New Zealand. In taking a detailed look at this Interactive Fiction gaming community, Keller found that these gamers are well educated, have a strong sense of community, and create and play games in a seem- ingly gender-inclusive space. Through interviews with this particular affinity group, which Gee (2003) defines as a group of people associated with a particular semiotic domain (in this case, interactive fiction), Keller demonstrates how such groups illuminate current understandings of identity, technologies, and literacy.

The second section of *Gaming Lives* includes essays that take up issues grouped under the heading Social Dimensions of Gaming. In chapter 5, "Narrative, Action, and Learning: The Stories of *Myst*," Debra Journet argues that video games make virtual experiences feel embodied or real to players through their narrative shape. For Journet, video games narrate an imagined world in which the purposive actions of players/characters have consequences, and it is in relation to this story that learning becomes situated. She also examines Gee's notion of "projective identities" (2003, p. 55), identities that players embody in game playing and that, like other conceptions of the "self," are narrative constructs. Chapter 6, "Gaming, Agency, and Imagination," looks at the experiences of a 36-year-old male rural gamer to understand the relationship between gaming, literacy, and imagination. The two authors, Deanna McGaughey-Summers and Russell Summers, attempt to move beyond dualistic thinking regarding the merits of gaming as either good or bad. More specifically, they argue through their case study that gaming can provide an opportunity for gamers to compose alternative worlds through which they negotiate social problems. In chapter 7, "Relationship Gaming and Identity," JoAnn Griffin presents a case study of a gaming couple, Stephanie and Josh. In so doing, she argues that gaming is sometimes used to complement and extend real-life relationships and that the spaces created by gaming often have a greater impact on relations among gamers than the games themselves. In the final chapter of this section, "Dungeons, Dragons, and Discretion," Stephanie Fleischer, Susan Wright, and Matthew Barnes lay out several observations about gaming and Generation X. Their case study research suggests that some gaming experiences tended to influence how their participants, now in their early 30s, became versed in traditional literacies, such as language and math skills, and also developed nontraditional literacies, such as social and ethical capacities. Taken together, these chapters make a strong case that there are no simple answers when it comes to judging the multifaceted influences of video games on literacy, learning, and the diverse social lives in which we participate.

Gaming and Difference, the third and final section of the volume, includes five essays that explore the relationship of games and gaming juxtaposed with the many differences that make us human. In chapter 9, "'A Real Effect on the Gameplay': Computer Gaming, Sexuality, and Literacy," Jonathan Alexander and his coauthors, Mack McCoy and Carlos Velez, explore how some gay and lesbian gamers use online games to probe, often for the first time, issues of sexuality. In the process, gay gamers' literacy practices in virtual worlds begin to take into account the impact of sexuality, sexual politics, gender conformity, and heteronormativity on the shaping of identity, community, and even political awareness—both in the virtual worlds of computer games and beyond. In "Learning Differences Meet Gaming Literacies," chapter 10 of this volume, Matthew Bunce, Marjorie Hebert, and J. Christopher Collins use Gee's (2003) identity and self-knowledge principles and draw upon the work of Selfe and Hawisher (2004) to argue that learning-different students can use gaming contexts as an environment in which they can learn more about their literacy potential in and outside the classroom. Through an interview with J. Christopher Collins, a video gamer and senior at St. Edward's University in Austin, Texas, they examine Collins's difficulties with reading and writing alongside his many successes in operating a complex flight simulator in a gaming environment. In chapter 11, "Racing Toward Representation," Samantha Blackmon and Daniel Terrell interrogate how children interpret race in Rockstar Games' 2002 blockbuster *Grand Theft Auto: Vice City*. Their aim is to ascertain whether or not Gee's (2003) concept of multiple routes of progress and differing learning styles can be extended to critical thought about the game environment itself. In chapter 12, "Portrait of a Gray Gamer," John

Branscum looks to his case study of Frank Quickert for insights into the gaming practices of those who are on the edge of retirement. Quickert's gaming and life experiences represent him as a gamer intent on tackling those games that revolve around strategy and long-term planning versus first-person shooter games. Unlike early research (e.g., McGuire, 1986) that portrayed computing technology as essentially therapeutic when it came to the aged, Branscum argues that today's senior citizens see other benefits to be derived from video gaming. In chapter 13, "Gender Matters: Literacy, Learning, and Gaming in One American Family," Pamela Takayoshi depicts one American family's interactions with video gaming. Through interviews, observations, and written reflections, she examines the lessons female family members have learned through video games about literacy, gender, identity, and technology. More than anything, the chapters in this section and, we would argue, in the whole book, begin to enlarge teachers' and scholars' understandings of what it means to navigate, create, and learn in the virtual worlds of gaming regardless of our differences.

Overview of Method

As an introduction to the method of several of the chapters, we include the assignment the graduate students in Cynthia Selfe's class at the University of Louisville took up as they began their research into how ordinary people engage and play video games. Following the assignment, we have incorporated the gaming interview protocol that the graduate students used and which is a modification of Selfe and Hawisher's (2004) original series of questions for their larger research project on digital literacies. And finally, we include the essay that grew out of Beth Powell's interviews with John and Mary Reeve, who are also coauthors of the piece. The other graduate students who participated in the project and the class are, in order of appearance, Iswari Pandey, Daniel Keller, Deanna McGaughey-Summers, JoAnn Griffin, Stephanie Owen Fleischer, Susan Wright, and John Branscum. Other contributors to this collection used different methods and different questions to guide their research, but all, we believe, shed light on the many connections between gaming and literacy.

In conducting research on gaming, we have come to understand that our method provides no panacea for dealing with the thorny issues entailed in the politics of representation. As hard as we and the contributors have tried to represent the participants' stories in ways that would do justice to them and to the research, we continue to stumble along the way. Thus, our method is fraught with difficulties but is also enriched by the different perspectives that the informants brought to the project. The strengths of this combination of qualitative methodological approaches lie, we believe, in their ability to capture the *ongoing* life stories of people living in a particular period of history—in great detail and in personal terms. Importantly, this approach does not purport to identify generalizable results, as the chapters well illustrate. Like Deborah Brandt (2001), however, we also found that the richness of information contained within the individual stories outweighed the limitations of our sample.

Assignment

Identify a person who plays computer games and is willing to work with you. Your goal is to produce a multimodal literacy biography of your own design, focused on the literacy of gaming, that adds to the class's understanding of literacy.

This assignment will take the form of a paper that is essentially biographical in nature, but it will also include still images that enter into some kind of dialogue with the alphabetic text. You can focus on the gamer, his/her parents, his/her teachers, his/her friends, and the game itself—among other topics.

Your essay should set the gamer's activities and life in a cultural ecology. You can construct this cultural ecology from various sources: historical timelines about what happened in the world/nation during the person's lifetime, technology timelines about how technology changed during the person's lifetime, video game timelines that show how computer/video games changed during the person's lifetime, and so on.

Ask your informant to sign a consent form that outlines the purpose of this project, and that gives you permission to use their responses for the purposes of this class. If the person is under 18, tell their parent(s) about this project and have them sign as well. You can write your own sheet or use a consent form from my project with Dr. Hawisher.

Make sure that you borrow a digital camera (from me or from a friend) and take photographs of the person you are interviewing. Download the pictures onto your computer and use them to illustrate and add information value to your paper.

Your biography should help both you and classmates learn more about literacy and gaming and about the values and practices of gamers. Your paper should help us understand how gaming as a literacy is shaped by—and shapes—micro-, medial-, and macrolevel factors within the life of an individual and within a cultural ecology of literacy.

Evaluation

Elements of cultural ecology sketchy<————> Very thorough
Comment:

Biography less than thoughtful<————> Biography very thoughtful
Comment:

Digital Photographs add little to paper<——>Photos add a great deal
Comment:

Literacy practices/values not explored<——>Thoughtfully explored
Comment:

Paper needs work (writing, scholarship, documentation mechanics)<——>Paper is terrific!

Comment:

Total points < 1———3———5———7———9———20>

Gaming Protocol

Name:

Occupation:

Nationality:

Race:

Ethnic heritage:

Real-world gender/orientation (e.g., heterosexual, gay, lesbian, bisexual, transgendered, other—only if you are comfortable answering):

Gaming gender/orientation (e.g., the gender you use in gaming situations):

Religion/denomination (only if you are comfortable answering):

Immediate family members and ages (Please list individuals and ages):

Income level (e.g., working class, middle class, upper middle class, something else):

        Growing up?

        Now?

Parents'/guardians' education and professions:

Place and date of your birth:

Where do you live? (Please list each place where you have lived and the dates you lived there.):

Schooling history (Please list each school you have gone to and the dates you attended—or at least every school you can remember):

        Elementary   College
        Secondary   Other

What was your first introduction to computers and gaming?

What kinds of computer/video games does your family play? Other kinds of games?

Briefly describe your family's attitude toward playing electronic games.

Can you tell us about the computer games you have played at different ages?

What games have you liked best and why?

What literacy skills and understandings did these games demand?

Can you tell us about how you learned to approach or solve gaming problems? To react to gaming situations?

Can you tell us stories about how you learned to respond to other gamers? To develop or interact with other characters in games?

Have computer games taught you anything about "writing" and "composing"? (Think of "writing" character descriptions, profiles, MOO/MUD descriptions. Think of "composing" rooms, characters, images, scenarios.) If so, please explain.

Have games taught you anything about learning new technologies or environments? If so, please explain.

Can you tell us how you learned to access gaming rules? Have these rules taught you anything about problem solving? If so, please explain.

Has gaming taught you anything about how to compete or collaborate with other people? If so, please explain.

Can you tell us stories about the people you played games with at various times of your life (provide dates) and why you played with them?

Have you encountered a "grammar" of gaming? A set of shared conventions that structure most games and that allow you to "read" them efficiently, even when they are new to you? What are the rules of this grammar?

Did gaming help you develop any other kinds of skills and understandings? If so, please explain.

Can you think of anything that computer gaming has helped you understand? Learn? If so, please explain.

What computer games do you have at home? Who owns them? Who bought them? Where do you keep them?

Does your family have any rules about gaming? Games?

What kinds of educational games do you play in school and at home?

What did your friends think about computer gaming at school? About your participation? Do you have any stories you can tell us that would illustrate what your friends think about computer use or attention to computer gaming at school?

What did your teachers/the school think about computers and computer gaming? Do you have any stories you can tell us that would illustrate what the educational system thinks about computers or attention to computer gaming?

Are there any rules that your school has about educational gaming? About playing other kinds of computer games in school?

Do these games or the playing of these games reveal or demonstrate any differences having to do with gender? What can they teach us, if anything, about gender, computers, and gaming?

How/when/where/why do you see yourself gaming in the future?

Anything more you would like to say about gaming and computers?

Essay

Literacy Learning in Digital Environments
Coauthors: Beth Powell, John Reeve, and Mary Reeve

"[School is a system] determined to annoy me. They write instruction manuals for games. They don't write them for school. They should" (J. Reeve, 2004).

In gaming environments, youths like John Reeve, a sixteen-year-old high school student living in Virginia Beach, Virginia, use language and other semiotic systems to create characters. A character John has created in *Final Fantasy XI*, for example, includes the black mage. John has had to learn to create and act out narratives through his character within the landscape of *Final Fantasy XI*. As he does this, however, he also constitutes his own personal identity as a literate individual who can learn, act effectively, and control his own environment.

The identities created within gaming environments and through the narratives of games are complex. The identities John creates in his gaming share characteristics with Gee's (2003) projective identity and Castell's (1997) resistance and project identities. John's gaming allows him to construct characters based on his personal likes/dislikes, constituting characteristics of projective identity, which is an identity somewhere between virtual and real identities. John's gaming also allows him to construct characters that are powerful or authoritative, constituting characteristics of resistance identity, which is constructed as a way of resisting the current position one is in within society. Finally, John's gaming helps him construct characters whose identities are constructed through the relationship one has with others (project identity). Through these characters and identity projects, John is learning by engaging in learning and literacy practices.

Youths like John transfer this learning and these literacy practices from the gaming worlds to the real world. College teachers of literacy and composition can learn from such youths what kinds of activities seem important to them. For example, John is engaged, in gaming, in the real work of becoming-through-language, and not in the faux work currently assigned in most class-rooms.

Family Influence and Evolution of Gaming
Influenced by his family's emphasis on literacy, John is a highly literate sixteen year old. His parents ensure that there is reading material available at home. His mother is a homemaker with an associate degree in art, a bachelor's degree in business, and work experience in administration. She also acted as teacher, home-schooling John for two of his junior high years. John's father is a captain in the navy. Besides having a job that focuses on communication and information, his father enjoys listening to books on tape on his long daily commute.

Also, his older sisters have careers in fields where they teach literacy and lan-guage. One sister is a first-grade teacher with a master's degree in reading. His other sister is a college composition instructor working on a PhD in rhetoric and composition. Growing up, John's family value system placed positive emphasis on traditional literate activities, and his home environment reflected this with easy access to print media: books, journals, magazines, and newspapers. Now, as a teenager, the early influences are illustrated in John's pastimes: he reads a variety of genres for pleasure and spends his leisure time at the local bookstore. He also writes his own stories on the computer.

Aside from these very traditional literacy-learning environments, John also plays video games, which likewise provide a rich environment for learning and appreciating various literacies. As with the pleasure he derives from print media, John's enjoyment of gaming stems from family influence. He says, "Well, when I first learned to play video games, it was my sisters who taught me." He remem-bers playing games such as *Duck Hunt, Mario Brothers,* and *Tetris* with his older sisters.

John's gaming has evolved with the technology that has developed steadily since his birth. He was born in 1987. A year later, Nintendo's *Super Mario Brothers 3* was released in Japan, and in 1990 Nintendo acquired *Tetris.* By 1993, his sisters, who are a great deal older, were out of the house, and he moved on to the next generation of Nintendo and Sega; this next generation produced more dynamic graphics (e.g., *Gamespot*). Now, along with PlayStation games, role-playing games (RPGs) are popular with gamers like John.

John predominantly plays the following: PlayStation games such as *Dance Dance Revolution,* computer games such as the *Sims* series, and RPGs such as *Final Fantasy XI.* While *Dance Dance Revolution* teaches John coordination (M. Reeve, 2004) and *Sims* games teach John problem solving (J. Reeve, 2004), it is the work that he does when playing *Final Fantasy XI* and other RPGs that help him to actively construct an identity.

Although his earliest memories of gaming are associated with his sisters, John also used the games as a way to amuse himself: "Well, I lived in a neighborhood with no other children, so it was a way to keep myself entertained" (J. Reeve, 2004). Conventional wisdom stereotypes the gamer as a person lacking in social skills (Betts, 2004); however, John's experiences with gaming, while serving as entertainment "in a neighborhood where there were not any small children" (M. Reeve, 2004), did not isolate him from society.

Indeed, John's gaming plays a large part in his social life today. Now that he plays online RPGs, he often plays them with his friends. In fact, the games are a way for him to continue socializing with friends. A couple of years ago, his family moved from Tennessee to Virginia Beach. Besides e-mail and instant messaging, RPGs are a way for him to keep in touch and maintain relationships with the friends he has known since primary school. Two of his close friends, for example, play *Final Fantasy XI*, and the three often "party" together (play online at the same time and on the same server).

Identities Developed through the Gaming Experience

Projective Identity

> Remember that the projective identity is the interface between one's real-world identities and the virtual identity [. . .]. The projective identity is the space in which the learner can transcend the limitations both of the virtual identity and the learner's own real-world identity. (Gee, 2003, p. 67)

John and his friends each play a different character in *Final Fantasy XI*, and those characters in a sense represent the boys' personalities while at the same time existing as complete fictions. John likes *Final Fantasy XI* because, as he states, "it's a world that's completely different from what we are pretty much and [. . .] you can create and customize your own character, so it's essentially like you have a presence in that world." His character, the black mage, is a magician specializing in attack spells. One of his friends has chosen to be a white mage, who is a magician specializing in healing and defensive magic. His other friend is a warrior; warriors specialize in close combat fighting. The game consists of missions and quests on which characters go, working together at the same time they are individually advancing in terms of class (white mage, black mage, warrior, red mage, and thief, are all professions).

The characters become more complicated with race. There are five races in *Final Fantasy XI:* Mithra, Hume, Elvaan, Galka, and Taru Taru. The combination of race and profession determines how the character will develop. John's "race" is Elvaan, and his character's goal is to get the job of summoner (one of the advanced classes in the game).

Playing the black mage, John constructs an identity similar to the projective identity described by Gee (2003) as one where John still gets to be John, but he is also a magician. Note how he describes his role as black mage in *Final Fantasy XI:*

> As a black mage, I can do massive damage, but a human with a medium-sized fly-swatter could probably take me out. [. . .] Physically I'm a wimp, but magically I'm a powerhouse.

Using the pronoun "I" indicates John's level of commitment to this character he has created.

It is this immersion in the game as a character actively engaged in constituting the world in which he is playing that appeals to John. Other games also have this appeal. For example, John likes *Sims* games because they provide a place to simulate being someone else. In fact, he compares *Sims* to *Final Fantasy XI*, which he says "is a *Sims* game in its own because you're simulating being another person." And in that simulation, a person must make choices, "like what do you want to do in the long run, who do you want to be, and how do you want to do it" (J. Reeve, 2004).

Resistance Identity

> Resistance identity: generated by those actors who are in positions/conditions devalued and/or stigmatized by the logic of domination, thus building trenches or resistance and survival on the basis of principles different from, or opposed to, those permeating the institutions of society. (Castells, 1997 p. 8)

John's gaming also allows him to construct an identity with characteristics similar to resistance identity, a concept defined by Manuel Castells (1997). As a character in an RPG, John gets to resist the role ascribed to him as a high school student still under the control of his teachers and parents. Not only does he get to view the world through the relatively powerful role of black mage, in *Final Fantasy XI*, he also plays games that allow him to explore more deviant ways of being.

One such game is *Blood Omen*, a game about vampires. The main character is a vampire, and "Well, he has motives. He's more of an anti-hero than a hero, not quite a villain, but he's working for a grander purpose" (J. Reeve, 2004). In the first game, "he's trying to restore a world that's become corrupt, but to do that he kind of has to kill people off that world so it can be remade" (J. Reeve, 2004). From this game, John has learned that "a lot of the times, villains don't see themselves as villains. They see themselves as striving for something" (J. Reeve, 2004). From playing this game and others that have similar antiheroes, he has learned that "things are rarely black and white."

Project Identity. Project identity, according to Castells (1997), is generated by resistance identity. It is defined thus: "When social actors, on the basis of whatever cultural materials are available to them, build a new identity that redefines their position in society and, by so doing, seek the transformation of overall social structure" (p. 8).

John's video gaming also helps him construct an identity with characteristics similar to project identity in that he "parties" with a group of players who collaborate to position themselves as certain characters in a virtual world. In order to successfully play games such as *Final Fantasy XI,* gamers do not play alone. John says that the different characters must work together against "monsters" in the game. He describes the process from *Final Fantasy XI:*

> When you're in a party situation, you'll go after one tough monster that you wouldn't be able to handle on your own, and warriors [. . .] and monks [. . .] are generally referred to as tanks, because they'll keep the aggression of the monster on them and keep it from hurting the mages who generally can do more damage but are more vulnerable. [. . .] And the white mage's job is to make sure the tank doesn't die and if the tank dies that the other mages don't die, and if the other mages die, to run like hell. (J. Reeve, 2004)

This description implies a collaboration between characters (and, thus, players), where each character has a specific role to gain a specific goal. John has pointed out that when a person does not pull his/her own weight, the party members will become irritated. For example, he describes a party situation in which a white mage, whose job is to make sure nobody dies, did not do anything, and "we lost three warriors."

John, as mentioned earlier, often plays with his friends from Tennessee; however, when his friends are not online, he will play with strangers. When playing with strangers, John says that he does not talk to those people about personal topics, but he talks to them "within the world" about "stuff in the game, like 'do you want to fight that worm' or that kind of thing." He considers this socializing. There can be camaraderie between players: "Whenever someone levels up, you can generally hear about five people congratulating each other even when they're not in your party." Collaborating to ensure success and to help each other out, gamers have to rely on the support of their groups (J. Reeve, 2004). However, as John points out, playing RPGs "lets you get a sense of being an individual, but not so much independence as collaboration." This teamwork aspect of gaming helps players develop identities that are constructed out of a social context (albeit, a virtual social context).

What College Literacy and Composition Teachers can Learn from Gamers
The identity principle, according to Gee (2003), states that one takes on and plays with identities while making choices (p. 67). Gee suggests that "active, critical learning" is "inextricably caught up with identity" (p. 59). Within a semiotic domain, a person can only learn if he/she is committed to the learning "in terms of time, effort, and active engagement" (p. 59). One must identify oneself as one who can find value in that semiotic domain (p. 59). This commitment gives the person the incentive to learn in that domain. The problem for teachers of literacy and language is the difficulty of getting this commitment from their students.

However, as John's comments indicate, the gaming world elicits that commitment from youths. John's gaming encourages him through various identity projects to learn certain things: as a *gamer*, to learn the rules of the game; as a *black mage* in *Final Fantasy XI* or as a *vampire* in *Blood Omen*, to act a part in that game; and as a *character* in an interactive RPG, to learn his role and responsibilities among other characters.

As a gamer, John has learned a great deal about computer technology and about the culture of gaming. For example, he has learned "cheats" for the *Sims* series. These "cheats" allow him more freedom to do what he wants in those games—he can, for instance, get more virtual money to buy virtual things. He has also learned the language of RPGs. He says, "It's like going to a separate country and immersing yourself in language." This learning came from the experience of playing and asking other players what certain acronyms (like RPG) mean.

As a character in *Final Fantasy XI,* John has also learned how to be a black mage. Again, this learning comes through practice and experience: "I'll generally hunt monsters to gain experience because I have till level 30 to become a summoner" (J. Reeve, 2004). He knows what he needs to do to become a summoner (his ultimate goal in the game).

Finally, as a member of a virtual community in *Final Fantasy XI,* John has learned how to interact as a black mage among other characters. His mother, who supports his gaming for the most part, admits that "he is learning to communicate and work in a team in the Internet games" (M. Reeve, 2004) like *Final Fantasy.*

The commitment that John has to *Final Fantasy XI* is evident in the amount of energy he puts into researching the games and gaining experience as a player. In terms of research, he looked up a lot of the characters in *Final Fantasy XI* once he realized they were from ancient mythology, because mythology is one of his personal interests. Another aspect of research is finding out how to play the games. He admits that he spends more money on instruction manuals than on the games themselves. What can teachers of literacy and language learn from this kind of commitment?

While video games provide an opening for conversation between John and his friends at school, that is where the connection between gaming and schooling ends. In fact, John's school is lacking in technology. He says,

> Well, I don't do anything on the computers at school because the school computers they have two in my classroom, and pretty much the only thing you're allowed to do on it is run typing software.

Furthermore, "They've [the school administration] never gotten around to hooking it [the Internet] up. The computer system at my school is kind of an irritation for me." Luckily, John has access to computer technology at home; however, that is not the case for all youths.

There are two issues teachers need to address: how to engage students in the kinds of learning that youths like John assume for themselves through gaming and how to make school more accessible to students like John. Students are often mystified by the demands teachers place on them. Why, students may wonder, are they asked to engage in faux work when they could be learning problem-solving skills, teamwork skills, and even computer skills in an environment where they are committed to "being" a character who must negotiate a virtual environment in order to survive in that world? Why, also, students may wonder, are they not allowed to use the dynamic technology that engages them often in more ways than print media? Students like John show teachers that learning takes place in environments where students have agency (such as being able to create one's own character) and in environments that students value, such as those places (virtual or real) where they can interact with their friends.

References

Anderson, Craig A., & Bushman, Brad J. (2001). Effects of violent video games on aggressive behavior, aggressive cognition, aggressive affect, physiological arousal, and prosocial behavior: A meta-analytic review of scientific literature. *Psychological Science, 12*(5), 353–359.

Anderson, Craig A., & Dill, Karen E. (2000). Video games and aggressive thoughts, feelings, and behavior in the laboratory and in life. *Journal of Personality & Social Psychology, 78*(4), 772–790.

Betts, Mitch. (2004). ThinkTank. [Review of the book *GOT game: How the gamer generation is reshaping business forever*]. *Computerworld, 38*(44), 42.

Brandt, Deborah. (2001). *Literacy in American lives.* Cambridge: Cambridge University Press.

Castells, Manuel. (1997). *The power of identity.* Second edition. Oxford, Blackwell Publishing.

Durkin, Kevin, & Barber, Bonnie. (2002). Not so doomed: Computer game play and positive adolescent development. *Applied Developmental Psychology, 23,* 373–392.

Final Fantasy Realm. (2002). Online Evolution Pty., Ltd. Retrieved July 25, 2005, from http://ffxi.crgaming.com/jobs/viewarticle.asp?Id=13

Fleming, Michele, & Rickwood, Debra J. (2001). Effects of violent versus non-violent video games on children's aggressive mood, and positive mood. *Journal of Applied Social Psychology, 31*(10), 2047–2071.

"Game Sales." Game Research website. (2002, January 19). Retrieved September 18, 2003, from http://gameresearch.com/business.asp

Gamespot. (2005). CNET Networks, Inc. Retrieved July 25, 2005, from http://www.gamespot.com/Gamespot.com

Gee, James Paul. (2003). *What video games have to teach us about learning and literacy.* New York: Palgrave Macmillan.

Jones, Steve. (2003). Let the games begin: Gaming technology and entertainment among college students. Retrieved January 25, 2006, from http://www.pewinternet.org/pdfs/PIP_College_Gaming_Reporta.pdf

Kent, Steven L. (2001). The ultimate history of video games: From Pong to Pokemon—The story behind the craze that touched our lives and changed the world. New York: Prima Lifestyles.

McGuire, Francis A. (Ed.). (1986). *Computer technology and the aged: Implications and applications for activity programs.* New York: Haworth Press.

Ovalle, David. (2004, January 15). Minors' access to violent games could be limited. *Miami Herald*. Retrieved January 25, 2006, from http://www.miami.com/mld/miamiherald/news/local/7713271.htm

Reeve, John. (2004, April 12). Personal interview.

Reeve, Mary. (2004, April 12). Personal interview.

Selfe, Cynthia L., & Hawisher, Gail E. (2004). *Literate lives in the information age: Narratives of literacy from the United States.* Mahwah, NJ: Erlbaum.

Part I

Gaming and Literacy

1

Computer Gaming as Literacy

Cynthia L. Selfe, Anne F. Mareck, and Josh Gardiner

> Ironically, it is often those who were, as teachers, very close to former generations of students, who now feel that the generation gap cannot be bridged and that their devotion to teaching has been betrayed by the young who cannot learn in the old ways.
>
> *(Margaret Mead, Culture and Commitment)*

> In a game you want to learn because you're playing it, and if you didn't want to learn, why would you be playing it?
>
> *(Josh Gardiner)*

Young people's enthusiasm for video and computer gaming has proven an increasingly vigorous arena for public debate. Although many decry the violence that abounds in some video games, other writers see positive outcomes:

> On several measures—including family closeness, activity involvement, positive school engagement, positive mental health, substance abuse, self-concept, friendship network, and disobedience to parents—game players scored more favorably than did peers who never played computer games. It is concluded that computer games can be a positive feature of a healthy adolescence. (Durkin & Barber, 2002, p. 376)

However, many people, parents and educators alike, continue to fear the violent socialization seemingly inherent to the compelling games. But computer gaming and violent socialization are not inextricably linked: they are discrete components of a complex culture undergoing rapid technological and social change during an era of unprecedented global transformation. The violence that parents and educators so fear may simply be one aspect of the larger world context in which the games have arisen. The principles of learning to which the games owe their popularity, often overlooked, are essential to consider.

More than a decade ago, when television was the prime media suspect in the debate on the violent socialization of youth, the educational theorist Neil

Postman (1993) made a suggestion that still seems pertinent today. Postman proposed that television and school, rather than being mutually exclusive, were in truth two competing systems of learning. He suggested that rather than ignoring, defaming, or belittling television's influence, educators would do well to closely examine television in order to better understand its relationship to learning. Television, Postman (1979) noted, was fast on its way to becoming the "first curriculum." He examined what he called a "media war" between traditional print-based classroom methods and the powerful new visual media represented at the time by television, and concluded that a sort of "collision" results when an emerging technology and its accompanying ideology begin to challenge the cultural dominance of long-established practices:

> In the United States, we can see such collisions everywhere—in politics, in religion, in commerce—but we see them most clearly in the schools, where two great technologies confront each other in uncompromising aspect for the control of students' minds. On the one hand, there is the world of the printed word with its emphasis on logic, sequence, history, exposition, objectivity, detachment, and discipline. On the other, there is the world of television with its emphasis on imagery, narrative, presentness, simultaneity, intimacy, immediate gratification, and quick emotional response. Children come to school having been deeply conditioned by the biases of television. There, they encounter the world of the printed word. A sort of psychic battle takes place, and there are many casualties—children who can't learn to read or won't, children who cannot organize their thought into logical structure even in a simple paragraph, children who cannot attend to lectures or oral explanations for more than a few minutes at a time. They are failures because there is a media war going on, and they are on the wrong side—at least for the moment. Who knows what schools will be like twenty-five years from now? (1993, p. 16)

While Postman's primary concern was for the young victims of the media war, children he described as not receiving the education they may need to survive and succeed in today's world, he took less time to consider the successful "early adaptors" of emerging technologies—young people who are fluent in the dual literacies of the old and the new ways, successful in both worlds.

Most recently, James Gee (2003), a linguist and literacy scholar at the University of Wisconsin, has weighed in on the debate. In *What Video Games Have to Teach Us about Learning and Literacy*, Gee shares his "frustrating and life enhancing" journey of "revelation," during which he became fascinated with the sophisticated learning theory embedded in the flash and glamour of the games. Gee was surprised to learn that a video game, one of the "good" ones, can take a player as many as 50–100 hours to win. A video game is "long, hard, and challenging" and, unlike schools, the manufacturers of the games keep making them harder, because that's how the kids like them. In school, if a class doesn't seem to understand a concept, the teacher keeps simplifying it until the class understands. Game designers do just the opposite. They keep making the games harder and harder to win; not unwinnable—just hard. Learning, says Gee, good learning, should be both frustrating and life enhancing, and the games are just that. In his analysis of the learning principles inherent in the "good" games, Gee identified 36 discrete elements at play. According to Gee:

> Better theories of learning are embedded in the video games many children in elementary and high school play than in the schools they attend. Furthermore, the theory of learning in good video games fits better with the modern, high-tech global world today's children and teenagers live in than do the theories (and practices) of learning they see in school. (p. 7)

In this chapter, we want to situate some of the issues located at the intersection of literacy studies and computer gaming by focusing on Josh Gardiner, a thirteen-year-old gamer from a small town in the Upper Peninsula of Michigan. This is the first of a series of case studies of gamers. Listening to what Josh has to say, we believe, can help us understand the personal values that one young person associates with the literacy practices of gaming. These values, I would argue, have to do with the formation of a commitment to personally selected, cross-cultural literacy communities, the ability to enact personal choice and political agency through and with literacy practices, and the opportunity to shape identity within literate environments. In turn, understanding these personal values may help us better appreciate and apply the powerful theories of learning underpinning the popularity of the games.

Josh Gardiner

Josh Gardiner, born in Escanaba, Michigan, in 1986, was attending Escanaba Junior High School when we first talked. Josh's parents, both of whom have a high school education, place a high value on conventional literacy and on digital literacies and consider both important aspects of social and economic prosperity.

In many ways, Josh seems a typical contemporary adolescent. In his words:

> My mom would probably say I have a little bit of an attitude. My dad would probably say I'm a good student and I try hard . . . a good kid. I don't get in much trouble, I don't go do drugs, I don't drink, maybe drink a Pepsi.

> I've . . . got my friends around Escanaba. We try to go to the movies or something like that, we try to hang out every now and then, go ride bike with each other, go fishing, just going out. . . .
>
> Boring. There's not a whole lot to do. . . . I like to go fishing late at night cause that's when the walleye come out, and the police will tell you to go home when it's like 12:00 but that's when they're just coming out.

Josh's education in the Escanaba public school system also seems fairly routine for the United States' increasingly technological culture. Attending a school where the curriculum was influenced by the explosion of technological innovation and growth in the 1980s, Josh began using computers in kindergarten—primarily playing educational games in his classes. But Josh claimed it was his grandmother who was responsible for getting him involved in computer environments as a problem solver. As he remembers it:

> She was taking classes at Bay College, but she had her address book password protected just because it had to. I think I was 6 years old when I first tried getting into it. I think it was about a year or a year and a half later that I finally got into it [the address book].

Both of Josh's parents considered his technological literacy to be a key factor in determining his future success and, in many ways, they took great pride in his digital accomplishments and expertise. Both parents, for example, rewarded Josh for good grades by contributing pieces of increasingly sophisticated computer hardware to his collection:

> He's actually just finished building his own computer . . . At Christmas he had asked his grandmother for the tower cover, and she bought him the one he wanted. He's earned different things for us with school and his good grades: "Okay, you've earned so much, which processor do you want, which card do you want for graphics. . . . He owes us for every lawn cutting for the next year, at least."

In school, however, Josh's teachers asked him to use computers in relatively limited ways—for word processing, for Web-based research projects, primarily. It is not surprising, then, that it has been gaming which really captured Josh's attention as he approached his teenage years. By the time he entered junior high school, for example, Josh was spending "about 20 hours a week . . . mainly on the weekends" playing online, first-person shooter games such as his favorite, *Counter-Strike,* one of the most popular games ever invented, a game based on the theme of counterterrorism.

In comparison with his school-based literacy and learning activities—which he considered passive and of limited interest—Josh considered the literacy he acquired in the context of gaming environments to be active, challenging, and intellectually engaging:

> In school, say you get a project that takes the average student 30 minutes, I'll get done in 10, and I'll sit there and start talking with somebody. If school was, like, you went there, you did your work and went on to your next class and you could go home, it would be a lot more fun for people and people would do a lot better, I think, because in class you sit there and listen to a teacher lecture, then you do your work. Half the time halfway through you fall asleep and you don't even know what he/she is talking about.
>
> In gaming you're always doing something. . . . I'm a visual learner, I hate reading. I mean, I like reading books every now and then, but I don't learn anything from a manual, I gotta fiddle around with it.

Chafing under what he considered to be the constraints of both school and home, Josh considered the power to make choices—about learning, about literacy, about life—increasingly important:

> Until you're 18 your parents make every decision for you. And [then] when you're 18, your boss makes your decision for you or your wife makes the decision. I don't

really think people these days get to make their own decisions like they used to, where you'd walk to a fork in the road; go right, there's a swamp, but it gets you there 20 minutes quicker, and if you go left, it's a perfect trail.

In gaming environments, Josh felt, he could make choices about what to do and what to learn—and then take responsibility for the outcome of those choices. This, he speculated, led to confident decision making and problem solving:

> I would say that it's an attribute of self-confidence. . . . You won't go play against people that are 10 times better than you if you don't think you have a slight chance to win. You gotta have a little bit of self-confidence, self respect, to be able to go do that.

Gaming also provided Josh a very real exigence for using language and other semiotic systems to communicate and collaborate with individuals and groups outside the immediate circle of people he interacted with in Escanaba. To play *Counter-Strike*, for instance, Josh had to assemble a team—or clan—of players to schedule regular practice sessions for its members, to exchange ideas about the team's strategies and collaborative approaches, and to maintain a sense of team cohesion.

When we talked to him about his *Counter-Strike* clan, Josh used these words:

> Most people in my clan, I met . . . through playing games, and a couple people I knew ahead of time, I started to know they played games.
>
> There's 7 guys and 5 girls, 12 people altogether, I think only 3 of us are from the United States. Two people are from Britain, one person's from Ireland, got another guy in the Netherlands, got a guy in Spain, got a girl in Italy. People from all over the place.
>
> Michael, he's from the Netherlands and he's 16. He's big into gaming; he's the person who helps us develop new versions of games with our little group. He's helped us set up our own server program that will tell people's computers what the server is and how many people are on there, and what game we're playing and stuff. I have another friend, Lee Arletian; he's from the UK. He's 16 and he's kind of a tech guru, he knows what's the latest technology and how to overclock your computer. His dad owns a college, so he gets to test out new software for the college, and he gets the new graphics card that just came out, so he's got 200 frames per second while we're still getting 150, so he kind of rubs it in our face. There's Emily, she's from Italy. She's 17. She's just kind of the gamer, she's kind of into the technology of setting up computers and stuff, but she pretty much just plays games with us. There's Jennifer, she's a California girl and she's 23. She's just kinda there. She doesn't do a whole lot, she just kind of plays the game. She's really good, pretty much every time we play she's got 3:1 kills; she beats everybody.

Within this social group and the *Counter-Strike* environment, Josh acquired not only gaming literacies, but also additional cultural and linguistic literacies:

> [You can] learn another language, or pick up on dialects or ethnic backgrounds, or recent events in the news. You can learn lots from gaming in my opinion. . . .
>
> I've picked up on French, not a lot of Italian, I know a little Dutch. I play with people a lot so I've picked up on a lot of their words that they use fluently over the microphone and I'll use them with them or if I'm playing so they understand me a little bit easier.

If Josh considered games to be an effective and engaging environment for learning and literacy, however, this fact was far less evident to the adults in his life. In general, as Gee (2003) and others have pointed out, these adults considered playing computer games to be a "waste of time" (p. 19). Josh's father, for instance, noted that he did not feel his son had "learned a lot from the gaming aspect" and expressed the opinion that Josh did not "really play a whole lot of games."

His mother, Josh explained:

> Thinks gaming is just a bunch of little schizophrenic maniacs . . . who are looking for a little kid to abduct and do their own little experiments like aliens and stuff on them. Just from, like, the way she reacts when I talk to her or my dad about people I've met online.
>
> The people I've met . . . a couple of them have really helped me out with emotional problems and stuff like that. . . . Well, my grandpa passed away a couple years ago. I kinda went for support with my friends online and [they said] it'll be alright, you know, it's time to go and stuff. They kinda helped me through it by saying 'let's just go play a game or something,' tried to take my mind off things.
>
> I don't know—I think games can actually help people to be less violent because they can take their aggressions against other people out on the computer rather than doing it in real life.

Josh feels that teachers, too, consider gaming to be not only dangerous, but antithetical to formal education and effective learning:

> Our school has no liking for you installing software on their computers or playing games and stuff, and I know our principal hates people that play games, cause I've tried talking to him to ask if we could get the club started, and he kind of went off on me. I got an hour lecture on why I shouldn't be playing games.

But Josh sees it differently:

> In a game you want to learn because you're playing it, and if you didn't want to learn, why would you be playing it?

Issues at the Intersection

So what does Josh's story suggest about the complex constellation of issues that rests at the intersection of literacy and computer gaming? During the course of our study of individuals such as Josh, three main issues have become apparent:

Intergenerational Disjuncture

Young people like Josh and the adults in their worlds do not necessarily share a common understanding of and appreciation for gaming as literacy. This serious intergenerational disjuncture, likely a product of the accelerated pace of technological change with its accompanying cultural transformation and at the root of the concern felt by parents and educators, may be better understood in the context provided by Margaret Mead in her 1970 book, *Culture and Commitment: A Study of the Generation Gap.* In her introduction to this volume, Mead notes:

> An essential and extraordinary aspect of man's present state is that, at this moment in which we are approaching a world-wide culture and the possibility of becoming fully aware citizens of the world . . . we have simultaneously available to us for the first time examples of the ways men have lived at every period over the last fifty thousand years . . . At the same time that a New Guinea native looks at a pile of yams and pronounces them "a lot" because he cannot count them, teams at Cape Kennedy calculate the precise second when an Apollo mission must change its course if it is to orbit the moon. . . . Some fifty thousand years of our history lie spread out before us, accessible, for this brief moment in time, to our simultaneous inspection. . . . This is a situation that has never occurred before in human history . . . [We] now share in a world-wide, technologically propagated culture.
>
> A profound disturbance is occurring in the relationships between the strong and the weak, the possessors and the dispossessed, elder and younger, and those who have knowledge and skill and those who lack them. The secure belief that those who knew had authority over those who did not has been shaken. (p. xvi)

Mead goes on to describe three distinct cultural styles, each distinguished by the ways in which children are prepared for adulthood. The first of these styles, the "post-figurative," characterizes societies in which change is largely imperceptible and the "future repeats the past." In such cultures, adults are able to pass along the necessary knowledge to children. "The essential characteristic of postfigurative cultures," Mead maintains, "is the assumption, expressed by members of the older generation in their every act, that their way of life (however many changes may, in fact, be embodied in it) is unchanging, eternally the same" (Mead, 1970, p. 14). Education within such cultures privileges the passing down of traditional values and knowledge through an adult-teacher.

The second of Mead's styles—that characterizing "co-figurative" cultures—arises when some form of disruption is experienced by a society. As Mead notes, such disruptions may result from the "development of new forms of technology in which the old are not expert . . ." (p. 39). In this kind of culture, young people look to their contemporaries for guidance in making choices rather than relying on their elders for expertise and role models in a changing world.

A third, and final, cultural style—which Mead terms the "pre-figurative"—is symptomatic of a world changing so fast that it exists "without models and without precedent" (p. xx). In prefigurative cultures, change is so rapid that "neither parents nor teachers, lawyers, doctors, skilled workers, inventors, preachers, or prophets" (p. xx) can teach children what they need to know about the world. The prefigurative cultural style, Mead argues, prevails in a world where the "past, the culture that had shaped [young adults'] understanding—their thoughts, their feelings, and their conceptions of the world—was no sure guide to the present. And the elders among them, bound to the past [can] provide no models for the future" (p. 70).

Mead made these remarks in 1970, after she had spent 45 years observing, studying, and theorizing about cultural groups around the world and well prior to the advent of the Internet. The near-future prefigurative world, in which our youth must soon survive and work and raise families, is arguably the most complex ever faced by a new generation of the human race. And our youth realize, as we may not, that the answers they need are not the ones we are offering them in school. Yet we continue to face them each day, standing at the head of the class, striving to shore up the myth of a postfigurative ideal whose time has long since passed. As Mead says:

> At this breaking point between two radically different and closely related groups, both are inevitably very lonely, as we face each other knowing that they will never experience what we have experienced and that we can never experience what they have experienced . . . Once the fact of a deep, new unprecedented, worldwide generation gap is firmly established, in the minds of both the young and the old, communication can be established again. But as long as any adult thinks he can . . . invoke his own youth to understand the youth before him, he is lost. (1970, p. 63)

Computer gaming, an intriguing offshoot of our rapidly changing culture, is a source of constant fear for Josh's parents and teachers. Like many well-intentioned adults, although they live on the wild border of a cofigurative/prefigurative era, they steadfastly abide by the mythic conventions of the postfigurative literacy yardstick by which they themselves were measured. They worry a great deal about Josh's gaming and, rather than recognizing gaming as one of the very few models for learning about life in a newly forming culture available to our youth, seem to consider it to be a distraction from more formal (postfigurative) literacy practices. As Durkin and Barber (2002) describe these concerns:

> Games' popularity among young people has been the focus of considerable lay and professional concern. Game playing can divert time from other activities, including schoolwork and sports, games often appear "mindless" and repetitive to nonplaying adults, there is the possibility that preoccupation with activities on computer screens could impede social interaction, and many games include themes of violence. (p. 374)

So far, research does not support these possibilities. After conducting a review of the literature, Bensley and Van Eenwyk (2000) concluded that "current research evidence is not supportive of a major public concern that violent video games lead to real-life violence" (p. 256). And further, the Office of the Surgeon General (2001) found that "the impact of video games on violent behavior remains to be determined" (p. 92).

A New Semiotic Domain: Multimodal Literacy

For students like Josh, their skills too often unrecognized and unappreciated by the adults around them, online gaming environments represent what Gee identifies as an important *semiotic domain* characterized by the practice and valuing of *multimodal literacies*. In the *Counter-Strike* environment, for example, Josh and his clan forge meaning and understanding not only from the alphabetic exchanges they carry on, but also from their interpersonal interactions; from the images, sounds, gestures, symbols, and movements; from their shared use of specialized knowledge, terms, processes, strategies, and approaches; and from their common set of literacy values.

Multimodality is a key feature of this semiotic domain and others, as Gee explains:

> In the modern world, print literacy is not enough. People need to be literate in a great variety of different semiotic domains . . . The vast majority of these domains involve semiotic (symbolic representational) resources besides print. (p. 18)

Those raised on and successful in print communication may find it difficult to give credence to the evidence that multimodal literacy is fast replacing traditional print literacy. As members of a highly technological culture committed to developing even more powerful technological tools, we bear daily witness to the emergence of a new literacy ideology, but that new ideology feels distinctly alien. Postman (1993) discusses the idea that in a tool-using culture, implements such as reading and writing are slowly integrated into a culture over a long period of time. Eventually, the ideology of the culture and the ideology of the tool coexist in a harmonious, unquestioned manner and conflict rarely arises. But with the advent of television and its accompanying audiovisual modes of communication, our print-based literacy ideology was challenged. Visual, interactive images are more compelling to the user. Perhaps, in some way, they are more biologically familiar to the human mind than print-based communicative modes. At this point in history, by and large, our children are raised from infancy on the compelling images of the TV set, the video game, and the computer. Alphabetic literacy for our children is often experienced as an add-on, a curious school-based task that seems to have little relevance outside the classroom.

As a culture we find comfort in harkening back to the days of the founders of the Constitution; our legal system is built on interpretation of what those founders might have intended, yet the framers of the U.S. Constitution were schooled only in print literacy. They had no television, no radio. Long-distance communication, in the form of letters, took weeks or months to complete. Decisions were tempered by the aging effect of time and rumination. And up until 1792, long after the formation of the United States of America, the concept of "grading" students on their work did not even exist:

> The idea that a qualitative value should be assigned to human thoughts was a major step toward constructing a mathematical concept of reality. If a number can be given to the quality of a thought, then a number can be given to the qualities of mercy, love, hate, beauty, creativity, intelligence, even sanity itself. (Postman, 1993, p. 13)

Today's literacy demands and the cognitive choices available to meet those demands are starkly different from those afforded by the culture in which the founders lived and worked. Even as our ability to engage in instantaneous global communication and the sudden decisions and global consequences resulting from that ability would have been beyond the imagination of the founders, so the implications of the immense literacy and communication changes taking place in our own time are often difficult for us to grasp.

Gunther Kress (1999), professor of education at the Institute of Education at the University of London, suggests that the very nature of language has already shifted: "The landscape of communication of the 1990s is an irrefutably multi-semiotic one; and the visual mode in particular has already taken a central position in many regions of this landscape" (p. 69). Yet many educators faithfully cling to the familiar educational tools of the immediate past, in which they are highly skilled, and doggedly continue to teach the rhetorical means to manipulate relatively simple alphabetic representations of reality. Rather than having an empowering, invigorating experience, our students, raised on visual media, more often than not find school irrelevant and boring—a burden to be endured in order to obtain the certificates that will enable them to pursue their goals.

Students such as Josh have learned to manage this dualism of literacies—one institutional, one cultural. While the more pressing relevancy of multimodal communication is obvious to learners like Josh, they humor their teachers by listening to lectures, writing papers, and taking tests. Diana George (2002), professor of composition, cultural, and visual studies at Michigan Technological University, writes that "for students who have grown up in a technology-saturated and an image-rich culture, questions of communication and composition will include the visual, not as attendant to the verbal but as complex communication intricately related to the world around them" (p. 32).

Affinity Groups and Learning

Young people's literacy activities in the semiotic domain of gaming may prepare them to operate, communicate, and exchange information effectively in a world that is increasingly digital and transnational—and in ways that their formal school does not.

Josh's literacy activities in the *Counter-Strike* environment, we would argue—unlike his formal literacy practices at school, which are conducted primarily in English and which focus primarily on U.S. culture—prepare him to operate effectively in digital landscapes that Manuel Castells (1996, 1997, 1998) describes as increasingly transnational. These environments are characterized by multiple languages, cultures, and interests that cut across conventional geopolitical borders. Communications in these environments, as the New London Group (1999) notes, must be increasingly multimodal to effectively cross linguistic and cultural boundaries.

Castells (1996, 1997, 1998) notes that the affinity groups which gather and communicate in these transnational computer networks—such as those formed by Josh and his gaming friends—are predicated on shared interests and literacy practices that extend beyond conventional geo-political borders. These groups, Castells contends, are where the new cultural codes—"under which societies may be re-thought, and re-established"–will be worked out in the coming decades (p. 361).

And Josh understands this. He knows that gaming environments provide the ideal setting for the set of literacy practices that he values and that he thinks will be important to him in the future. Importantly, these practices are based on a number of productive and generalizable learning principles identified by Gee (2003).

Josh communicates and works with an international "affinity group" whose members bond with one another "primarily through a common endeavor" (p. 192) and shares goals, values, understanding, knowledge, and expertise. As Gee notes:

> Much of the knowledge of an affinity group is *tacit* (embodied in members' mental, social, and physical coordination with other members and with various tools and technologies), and distributed (spread across various group members, their shared sociotechnological practices, and their tools and technologies). (p. 193)

Within his gaming clan, Josh is an "insider," a "teacher," and a "knowledge producer" (p. 197) who has the ability to shape the learning environment (p. 197) through his literacy practices—among them his daily communications with individual team members, group planning and strategy exchanges, and collaborative gaming sessions.

Because he is an insider, Josh's literate practices—the words, symbols, images, gestures, and artifacts he uses—have meanings that are specific to members of this domain, and he has had to employ his literacy practices in rhetorically appropriate ways that achieve identifiable results. In sum, Josh's literate practices help him *do* things, *accomplish* things, on which he places a positive value.

Gaming environments have provided the opportunity for Josh to reflect on those models of learning and literacy in which his parents and teachers are invested and compare them to with those models to which he himself subscribes. As Gee notes:

> Good video games have a powerful way of making players consciously aware of some of their previously assumed cultural models about learning itself. In fact good video games expose a whole set of generational models of what constitutes typical ways of learning . . . Baby-boomer models are still quite prevalent in schools as teachers, administrators, and parents. (p. 162)

Further, Josh's clan has also helped Josh understand the learning models of other cultures and places. In these transnational gaming environments, Josh is responsible for making active and critical choices about his own learning. He chooses not only the particular semiotic domain he wants to join (gaming, for instance), but he also chooses the time, place, conditions, and pace of his literate practices and his exchanges with other people affiliated with this domain. Within this semiotic domain, as Josh himself has noticed, when he makes good choices as an active learner, his self-confidence is enhanced and his identity as a literate individual and as a successful learner is reinforced (Durkin & Barber, 2002). As Gee (2003) comments further:

> All deep learning—that is, active, critical learning—is inextricably caught up with identity in a variety of different ways. People cannot learn in a deep way within a semiotic domain if they are not willing to commit themselves fully to learning in terms of time, effort, and active engagement. Such a commitment requires that they

are willing to see themselves as the *kind of person* who can learn, use, and value the new semiotic domain. In turn, they need to believe that, if they are successful learners in the domain, they will be accepted in the affinity group associated with the domain. (p. 59)

Preparing for the World of the Future

Currently, we would argue, as Josh participates in gaming environments, he is participating in a world and enacting a set of literacy practices that exists beyond the imagination of his parents and his teachers, attuned as they are to the postfigurative tradition of print. Josh is preparing himself for the world of the future, despite the fears of his caretakers. He lives in parallel universes, the illusory, predictable, postfigurative world of his parents and teachers, and the pre-cofigurative world of the present and the future—the world that he understands he and his children will inhabit. His adult caretakers do not understand his need for this preparation; he must find his tools and his answers on his own, with the help of his affinity group.

Contemporary literacy scholars—Deborah Brandt (1995, 2001), Harvey Graff (1987), James Gee (2003), and Brian Street (1995)—remind us that conceptions of literacy and literate behavior are shaped by (and shape) a constellation of complex and overdetermined social formations. As a result, we can understand literacy as a set of practices and values *only* when we properly situate these elements in a particular historical period, cultural milieu, or cluster of material conditions.

The contested nature of gaming literacies at the beginning of the twenty-first century is indicative of a historical and cultural period undergoing not only rapid change, but also the "rapid proliferation and diversification of literacy" (Brandt, 1995, p. 651). This proliferation places increasing pressure not only on Josh, but also on his parents and teachers. In such a context, successful rhetors will, we know, draw on "all available means" to communicate effectively and effect change in their own lives. For Josh and other young people like him, success in a world of rapid technological change may well depend on the ability to develop new literacy practices that prove increasingly effective in transnational digital landscapes like gaming environments.

Kurt Squire (2001), assistant professor at the University of Wisconsin in educational communications and technology and visiting research fellow at MIT, where he codirects a project investigating the educational potential of digital gaming, points out that the first generation of computer gamers is now over 30 years old. Those individuals, products of game socialization, of whom Squire is one, have quietly integrated into the society at large. While much of the debate and research about gaming tends to stubbornly focus on the teaching strength of perceived violent imagery, Squire calls our attention to the idea that

the most under-examined potential of games may be their impact as an educational medium. Playing games, I can relive historical eras (as in *Pirates!*), investigate complex systems like the Earth's chemical & life cycles (*SimEarth*), govern island nations (*Tropico*), manage complex industrial empires (*Railroad Tycoon*), or, indeed, run an entire civilization (*Civilization* series). Did I forget to mention travel in time to

Ancient Greece (*Caesar I, II, & III*), Rome (*Age of Empires I,* and *II*), relive European colonization of the Americas (*Colonization*), or manage an ant colony, farm, hospital, skyscraper, theme park, zoo, airport, or fast food chain? . . . the impact of games on millions of gamers who grew up playing best-selling games such as *SimCity, Pirates!,* or *Civilization* is starting to be felt. (2001, para 3)

Perhaps in our well-intentioned concern for our youth, we have been inclined to overlook or dismiss the positive, exciting, socially transformative developments in computer gaming—or the skillful, tactical agency that young people, themselves, can enact.

Shortly after the September 11th attacks, a *Counter-Strike* player—a woman named AnneMarie Schleiner—sickened by the World Trade Center bombing and equally disturbed by the answering violence of the war on terrorism, decided to remind players of *Counter-Strike* that the scenarios they were enacting in their virtual gaming world did not *have* to follow the same trajectory as those events that characterized the real world. Indeed, as Schleiner understood, virtual worlds can be *better* than the real world. Gamers do not have to *reinscribe* the shape and trajectory of the conflicts in the real world; they can be activists that suggest a different and a better way for things to go. Says Schleiner, "Reality is," after all, "up for grabs. The real needs to be remade by us."

To this end Schleiner formed a team of antiwar activists called *VelvetStrike. Velvet-Strike* members, many of whom played—and continue to play—*Counter-Strike,* created a series of programming hacks. *Velvet-Strike* gives these open-source hacks away for free so that they can be surreptitiously inserted in *Counter-Strike* games by players committed to bringing antiwar issues to the forefront of gamers' attention and changing the way that people think of resolving conflict. These rhetorical hacks take the semiotic form of visual *sprays*—spray-painted antiwar slogans and images conveying messages like "No bombs" and "We are all Iraqis now" and "Stop the war." Once they are secretly slipped into the program of a *Counter-Strike* scenario, these sprays randomly appear on the walls of the *Counter-Strike* palace during play.

The *Velvet-Strike* website also provides players with "recipes" for intervention. They suggest, for instance, that players enter a *Counter-Strike* scenario as a member of the Terrorist Team, but that they rescue and free the hostages they have been assigned to guard. As Schleiner has said, her real interest is *not* trying to stop people from playing *Counter-Strike*. Rather, she understands that there is something "ultimately subversive" in reminding players that *Counter-Strike* is "only a game" and that at any moment, a player can "switch sides with the 'other,' can decide to resist his or her own leaders, can imagine themselves taking action to stop violence."

The beauty of this seemingly futuristic rhetorical situation—an online military-style game played by transnational virtual soldiers and terrorists infiltrated by virtual antiwar protestors—the complexity of the communication, the intricate nature of the multimodal composition, and the breadth of literacies necessary to conceive and accomplish such a feat is astonishing.

Such is the literacy skill of many of the students who pass daily through our classroom doors and sit at the desks, halfheartedly waiting to see if we will teach them anything at all of what they will need to know not only to survive, but to thrive in their future.

References

Anderson, Craig A., & Bushman, Brad J. (2001). Effects of violent video games on aggressive behavior, aggressive cognition, aggressive affect, physiological arousal, and prosocial behavior: A meta-analytic review of scientific literature. *Psychological Science, 12*(5), 353–359.

Anderson, Craig A., & Dill, Karen E. (2000). Video games and aggressive thoughts, feelings, and behavior in the laboratory and in life. *Journal of Personality & Social Psychology, 78*(4), 772–790.

Bensley, Lillian, & Van Eenwyk, Juliet. (2000). *Video games and real-life aggression: Review of the literature.* Olympia, WA: Washington State Department of Health.

Brandt, Deborah. (1995). Accumulating literacy: Writing and learning to write in the twentieth century. *College English, 57,* 649–668.

Brandt, Deborah. (2001). *Literacy in American lives.* Cambridge: Cambridge University Press.

Castells, Manuel. (1996). *The rise of the network society.* (Volume I in *The information age: Economy, society, and culture*). Malden, MA: Blackwell.

Castells, Manuel. (1997). *The power of identity.* (Volume II in *The information age: Economy, society, and culture*). Malden, MA: Blackwell.

Castells, Manuel. (1998). *End of millenium.* (Volume III in *The information age: Economy, society, and culture*). Malden, MA: Blackwell.

Durkin, Kevin, & Barber, Bonnie. (2002). Not so doomed: Computer game play and positive adolescent development. *Applied Developmental Psychology, 23,* 373–392.

Fleming, Michele, & Rickwood, Debra J. (2001). Effects of violent versus non-violent video games on children's aggressive mood, and positive mood. *Journal of Applied Social Psychology, 31*(10), 2047–2071.

Gee, James Paul. (2003). *What video games have to teach us about learning and literacy.* New York: Palgrave Macmillan.

George, Diana. (2002). From analysis to design: Visual communication in the teaching of writing. *College Composition and Communication, 54*(1), 11–32.

Global Reach. (2003). Retrieved March 5, 2003, from http://www.glreach.com/globstats/index.php3

Graff, Harvey J. (1987). *The legacies of literacy: Continuities and contradictions in western culture and society.* Bloomington, IN: Indiana University Press.

Kress, Gunther. (1999). English at the crossroads: Rethinking curricula of communication in the context of the turn to the visual. In Gail E. Hawisher, & Cynthia L. Selfe (Eds.), *Passions, pedagogies and 21st century technologies* (pp. 66–88). Logan: Utah State University Press.

Mead, Margaret. (1970). *Culture and commitment: A study of the generation gap.* Garden City, NY: Natural History Press/Doubleday.

Office of the Surgeon General. (2001). Youth violence: A report of the Surgeon General. U.S. Department of Health and Human Services.

Ovalle, David. (January 15, 2004). "Minors' access to violent games could be limited." *Miami Herald.* Retrieved 25 January, 2006, from http://www.miami.com/mld/miamiherald/news/local/7713271.htm

Postman, Neil. (1993). *Technopoly: The surrender of culture to technology.* New York: Random House.

Postman, Neil. (1979). The first curriculum: Comparing school and television. *Phi Delta Kappan, 61*(3), 163–168.

Schleiner, Anne-Marie. (March, 2002). Velvet-Strike: Counter-Military graffiti for CS. About. Retrieved March 1, 2004, from http://www.opensorcery.net/velvetstrike/about.html

Squire, Kurt. (2001). Reframing the cultural space of computer and video games: Reframing the debate. *MIT Comparative Media Studies: Games-to-Teach Project.* Retrieved July 5, 2004, from http://cms.mit.edu/games/education/research-vision.html

Street, Brian V. (1995). *Social literacies: Critical approaches to literacy in development, ethnography, and education.* London: Longman.

The New London Group. (1999). A pedagogy of multiliteracies: Designing social futures. *Harvard Educational Review, 60*(1), 60–92.

2

Transcultural Literacies of Gaming

Iswari P. Pandey, Laxman Pandey, and Angish Shreshtha

One of the fastest-growing export industries in the global marketplace, computer and video games are now rivaling movie box office sales in the United States (Frauenfelder, 2001; "Video games," 2004), causing concerns that games may be taking over the television audience. Reporting on a recent study, CNN ("Is TV losing out," 2004) speculated that "increased video game play could be among the many factors leading to the decline in TV viewership by younger men." Educators and cultural critics have recently started to study this phenomenon in terms of its economic shift and the cultural literacy it affords. The intricate relationship between gaming and literacy learning, and the way each shapes and is shaped by the other in today's increasingly electronically mediated world, is also receiving some attention. While researchers such as Anderson and Bushman (2001), Anderson and Dill (2000), and Fleming and Rickwood (2001) found that video games, among others, contributed to aggression and violence, scholars such as James Gee (2003), Cynthia Selfe (2004), and Durkin and Barber (2002) have looked at the complex ways in which video/computer games are embedded in certain principles of learning in today's information society.

However, by and large, these studies have been based on gamers born or growing up in the postindustrial society of the United States. We need more studies to understand whether gamers from a different background play and learn from the games in the same way, and in what ways, if any, their gaming are practices wedded to other literacy practices. In other words, we are interested in questions such as, How do gamers from other geopolitical locations receive and play these games designed and manufactured primarily in the United States (or by extension in the global North) and for consumers connected to it? Similarly, what do these gamers' experiences say in the debate about gaming's tendentious relationship with learning and violence? More important, what role or place does gaming have in people's struggle to learn the grammar of living, learning, and working in cross-cultural, transnational spaces in the context of rapid global movement of people? Similarly, what can such practices tell scholars and teachers of literacy and writing?

A study of gaming practices by people who have navigated different geopolitical and cultural spaces would suggest some answers to these questions. Such an investigation could also help us develop a more robust understanding of gaming's interrelationship with learning in a broader sense. In this chapter, we look at the practices of two gamers (Angish Shrestha and Laxman Pandey) from Nepal currently in the United States, vis-à-vis their conventional print and digital literacies. By understanding Angish's and Laxman's practices, we observe the role gaming plays in developing literacies and in accessing the codes of cross-cultural citizenship in the mediated world. As Angish and Laxman credit the informal gateways of gaming for their understanding of persona, audience, and purpose they needed to perform in school/college and workplace, we hope this chapter will also help teachers and scholars of literacy and writing appreciate how reading and writing in the informal gateways of gaming are embedded in the literacy performance in college classes.

We first present the two case studies of Laxman and Angish within the broader cultural ecology of their conventional as well as digital literacy acquisition before we discuss the findings that emerged from the narratives.

Laxman Pandey

Computer games don't affect kids, I mean if Pac Man affected us as kids, we'd all be running around in darkened rooms, munching pills and listening to repetitive music.

(Marcus Brigstocke)

Laxman Pandey

Program of study:

Master of Business Administration candidate

Value of a UD education:

The learning experience at UD is more interactive and practical than back home [in Nepal]. We are introduced to a lot of real-world scenarios and often work together in teams. This helps us prepare for the future and develop our problem-solving skills.

—From the University of Dayton Graduate Admissions Office. Spotlights. Dec. 2004. Retrieved Feb 27, 2005, from

http://gradadmission.udayton.edu/spotlight/spotlight.asp?iSpotID=256

Laxman was born in Palpa of western Nepal in 1975, four years after the country had imported its first computing machine (Bhattarai, 2002) and the same year Bill Gates and Paul Allen started Microsoft ("Media History," 1996). Nepal was under the direct rule of the king for 15 years and was expecting a political uprising in four years that would lead to a referendum in 1980. Although Laxman's village still had no electricity when he was born, that same year, Namco began making video games, Atari created the "prototypical *Home Pong* unit," and Midway Games imported a "Taito game called *Gunfight,* the first game to use a microprocessor" in the United States (Kent, 2001, p. xii).

Laxman was in the second year of an MBA program at the University of Dayton, Ohio, when he was first interviewed in the spring of 2004. Prior to joining the university in the Midwest, he had a strong academic track record. He had been to Budhanilkantha, arguably Kathmandu's most prestigious English-medium school, and completed his undergraduate studies at the Tribhuvan University in Kathmandu. He was the youngest of six children and grew up in a family that was, in his own words, "very close and loving." Although his mother was barely able to read and write, his father had some college education, and they placed high premium on his literacy in both the local (Nepali, the national language of Nepal) and global (English) languages. The emphasis on the English language was "especially for my father [was] involved in politics and business for sometime." The entrepreneur father knew which language would offer his son an edge in the global marketplace. Had it not been for him, Laxman would have gone to a public school, typical for a middle-class family such as his in the Nepali mid-hills, instead of to a private English-medium school first and then the Budhanilkantha School. In a country where the official literacy rate of adult males in 2003 stood at 58 percent ("UNAIDS," n.d.), going to a public school too would be quite an opportunity, one that about half the children of his age group were denied when he started school in 1980. In his own words:

> I was fortunate to have gone to Budhanilkantha School. It was my parents who got me there, and . . . where I am now.
> I am the youngest son in the family and they wanted to give me the very best of education they could. One of my brothers was more interested in business and quit school to run a hardware store. My sister was already in a local public school and was doing okay. I was also in the same school [as my sister] but I always topped my class so I was admitted to a private school in Kathmandu, and then they had me take the entrance exam for the Budhanilkantha School. I did well and was offered 50 percent scholarship. . . .
> My parents thought I would be a doctor. I am not in medical field, but they are still happy. I have acquired the highest level of education in my family. I hope to find a good job when I finish my MBA.

His parents' support and his hard work helped Laxman stand out in his school and college. He was also active in extracurricular activities while in school and in community work after his graduation. He has been an active member of his school alumnae club, the Society of Ex-Budhanilkantha Students (SEBS) for several years, and at the time of this interview, he was engaged in fund-raising for a scholarship program run by SEBS in the remote areas of Nepal.

For Laxman, school was the gateway to digital literacy, while his home was the primary gateway to conventional print literacy in the Nepali language. In 1986, when he learned how to use a computer, he became one of the first few students to acquire the skills as part of school education in Nepal ("Budhanilkantha School History," n.d.). As Laxman recalls:

> I was in the 6th grade when they had the first computer lab in school. It was the science teacher who taught us [computer education]. He taught us basic computer use

> skills once a week. It was a new thing. We were motivated to try the new thing, but also a bit uncomfortable because the machines were so rare those days. I didn't have one at home and I knew that many of my friends were seeing it there for the first time.

However, the best thing about computers, like reading and writing, was that he liked it.

The way Laxman learned computer literacy is interesting, especially given that serious learning—whether digital literacy or conventional print literacy—is often placed in opposition to play. In Laxman's case, however, the teacher first "taught us how to play games" and so learning the rest of it came "pretty easy." All the other subjects of study were taught using the more conventional methods of lecture, discussion, or class activities. The computer class was meant to familiarize students with how to use it, and they got to do it with fun. Laxman noted that because it mixed play and learning productively, he "always looked forward to this class," which offered a real breather from the more dull routine.

Interestingly, when Laxman was learning how to use a computer in 1986, Nintendo of America released the Nintendo Entertainment System in the United States nationwide for the first time (although it had been available in Japan since 1983), Sega released its Sega Master System, and Atari released the 7800 game console ("Nintendo," 2006). Soon Laxman was playing educational games such as *Bushbuck charms* in his school. Definitely worlds apart compared to some of his counterparts in the United States in terms of access to new games and software in 1986, but when Sony released the PlayStation in the United States in 1995, Laxman played the console the same year in Nepal. This was a different world—not only because information technology and the global market system were bringing the world closer, but also because urban Nepal was now more easily connected to the digital world following the democratic movement of 1990. The new economic as well as media and communications policies of the government created an environment that was more conducive to this shift.

Laxman's encounter with gaming had a direct, even causal, relationship with his computer literacy. He learned to "use mouse and computer keyboard commands" while playing simple games like *Minesweeper* and *Solitaire*, although he was not thinking of learning computers or the value of digital literacy at the time he learned them. He was "just happy playing," as he remembers. But soon he was deeply in it, asking his teacher's permission to use the machines during free time. He started to value his computer literacy as he acquired some programming skills in his junior years at school. After he graduated from high school, he also attended a professional training course for Java programming and soon was reading more about computers and programming. One of his concentration areas in his MBA at the University of Dayton was Business Information System, which builds on his digital literacy. Overall, he considers computers integral to his learning and staying in touch with his network of family and friends.

Laxman liked digital environments most because he liked playing with texts and images he would create, as well as the games he played in between. He uses computers for as many reasons as there could possibly be: to access the Web, research and write papers, compose or edit Web pages, read news, play games online, listen to music, watch videos, see live games and updates, chat on instant messenger services, and also talk to people.

When Laxman began playing games on his own, it was basically to "kill time and enjoy," but what became clear to him later on was that he was also learning a certain set of cultural and subcultural cues through these games. His first games were educational, or what are sometimes called part of "edutainment." Some of the games he played in his high school days included activities like identifying animals, professions, or a destination city, or demanded similar other performances. One such game he liked most was the *Bushbuck charms,* in which "you must race either against the clock or a computer opponent to retrieve treasures from around the globe" ("*Bushbuck charms,*" n.d.). He "loved the challenge of treasure hunting" and liked it also for the cultural and geographical literacies it afforded.

Laxman always felt good about his programming skills and gaming. In gaming environments, he liked the way he could make choices. While such choices gave a sense of power and agency, they also gave him an added security and freedom that regardless of the outcome, his life would not be practically affected by those choices. It is not to suggest that he would not take losses or victories seriously or would not play seriously. He did. In fact, he liked the games that were within his ability or his learning range and always played with a desire to win. However, he also knew that this was "simply [a] game" and seemed to know the psychological benefit of gaming. In his own words:

> I begin with the basics first and every time I play the game I try one step higher or more difficult. I play to enjoy and so naturally when I cannot win, I feel a bit disappointed. But I also use the experience to do better next time or remind [me] that this is just a game and I have not lost my money or education.

Such metathinking about gaming demonstrates his ability to handle complex situations in life in meaningful ways. He also calls himself an optimist: "I am an always-positive-thinking man," and realized that gaming was teaching him "to be prepared for any situation"—however adverse—in life.

Laxman does not think that gaming is responsible for violence. He would rather find the gaming experience helpful to understand a little more about the causes and consequences of violence within the make-believe world. However, he notes that there might be certain games which, when played by "certain impressionable kids who could not think critically," might contribute to violent behavior in real life also. But there would be other factors as well to blame for that—games would be "just one small factor in a complex picture." Even though he played violent games only occasionally, he considered such a practice another opportunity to release his anger and also a way to know and experience how some people might be capable of acting in certain ways under given circumstances. That helped him avoid troubles in real life: "I credit it to gaming in addition to my loving family and friends that I have never had a fight or quarrel in my life. Even more important, I have always had good relationship with people at my school or work."

Most important of all, however, Laxman feels that gaming prepared him to be a fast thinker and actor, the prerequisites that he found necessary to adapt to the life of a graduate student in the United States and to the demands of professional life (as a teacher and administrator in a college) back in Nepal. He says:

> I have used various knowledges gained through games and it has been much easier for me to adapt to different situations and new cultures. It also helped me to understand the psychology of students because I could better relate to them, and I found it easy to motivate them by understanding them. I could also mix with them much easily in Nepal as well as here (the US). This has been a real life advantage of being a gamer.

Juggling different roles in the gaming environment gave Laxman an opportunity to imagine different ways of thinking and acting in real life.

Before we speculate further on the literacies of gaming, let's turn to Angish.

Angish Shreshtha

> That's what learning is, after all; not whether we lose the game, but how we lose and how we've changed because of it and what we take away from it that we never had before, to apply to other games. Losing, in a curious way, is winning.
>
> (Richard Bach)

Angish was born in Kathmandu, the capital city of Nepal, in 1981, the year Nepal imported its second computer in ten years (Bhattarai, 2002) and one year after the country's first plebiscite which, amid reports of poll rigging, made the Panchayat victorious under the king's direct rule. It was also the year Microsoft introduced MSDOS1 operating system ("Media History," 1996), and, interestingly, when Angish encountered a computer for the first time in his home in 1992, the machine ran MS DOS. Angish was born into a well-educated, upper-middle-class family with one sister and a brother. Both of his parents had a master's degree in education and were lecturers in the Tribhuvan University in Kathmandu. His mother was also a computer programmer, with some financial and instructional investment in the country's computing sector. Angish attended a private English-medium school throughout and went to St. Philomena's College of the University of Mysore, India, for his undergraduate studies. He graduated with a bachelor of commerce degree in April 2003 with accounting and computer science as majors. When Angish was first interviewed in the spring of 2004, he was a first-year MBA student at the University of Findlay, Ohio. His sister was completing her degree in dental surgery in Nepal, and his brother had just completed high school in Kathmandu. His brother was also an avid gamer and computer programmer, who, according to Angish, "has a hobby of computer programming and web page designing. . . . He has learned many computer languages, and uses Linux as well."

Angish learned basic alphabetic and numerical literacy at home with his parents, who would also tell him "stories that reflected the value of education and what it meant when making a decision, like how a literate person would react like in a situation and make choices when needed to, and how an uneducated person would act in that situation. [That] helped a lot." When he was at school, his parents constantly monitored his progress and required him to read and write a lot at home. In his own words,

> They thought learning was an important part of life, and a person would always reflect his identity by his character and education. They always encouraged me to read and write, and valued these skills as the most important part of life. . . . They also brought stuff that would increase the vocabulary and story books and different types of slates where you could write and do maths and drawings.
> . . . .
> They brought us story books and after telling us to read it, told us to write a summary and sometimes write similar stories or imagine new stories and write, etc.
> . . . .
> I read nonfiction books but I also loved to read lots of comics and war stories when I was a kid.

Like his conventional literacy, Angish's electronic literacy also began at home in 1992, the year when *Sonic the Hedgehog 2* was released (Jones, n. d.) and two years after a popular uprising brought the erstwhile absolute monarchical system within the limits of a parliamentary democracy in Nepal. As he says, "When I was 11 my mother brought a computer home; that was when I came in contact with it first. My mother used to teach me how to use it. . . . It ran DOS." The following year, his school also started running a computer class in grade six:

> I was 12 years of age and we had to take computer class which was compulsory for everybody. . . . I was especially motivated by new games and I learned fast because I really loved to play. The teachers always encouraged us, and . . . we accessed computer twice a week at school and daily at home. At school, everybody loved games. That taught us the most.

And now:

> I use computer daily to do a lot of stuff and totally depend on it to do everything. For example, to do my assignments, research, check emails, surf the Internet, and to play games.

His parents wanted him to be not only electronically literate but also "learn new programs that would help me in my professional field that I am heading towards." He specially recalls his parents telling him, before he came to the United States, "to learn database programming (Oracle) and . . . that it would help me a lot because my background is commerce, and now I can see how it is going to help me to find jobs related to my computer literacy." Angish grew up in an environment where computers were used profusely:

> My parents use it for doing their research work. My sister does all her assignments in the computer and sometimes plays games. My brother mostly plays games in the computer and also loves programming; he's always busy learning new programs; and my two nephews love to play games.

His friends also equally valued computer use:

> They take it as one of the most important parts of modern life because most of my friends are computer engineers. When I was a kid, there were very few computers. I had one but most of my friends didn't have it, so they came to my place to play games and sometimes also to use Internet and email or do other stuff.

And his school reinforced the value of electronic literacy: "In my school, computer education was a compulsory subject, and . . .we were asked to mug up facts for computer quiz. New products, programs, and software were also occasionally introduced." In such an environment, Angish and his brother felt encouraged to look for new avenues to acquire further expertise. Just out of high school in Kathmandu, they subscribed to a few computer magazines that were shared between the brothers. His familiarity with computers was so strong that he liked doing his homework only on his computer: "It was very hectic working manually without a computer." He could not imagine a workplace without computers, because the machines "make your work easier, faster, reliable and more accurate. To a large extent, it has prepared me to move a step ahead in my future, and I would not have been what I am now without the knowledge and use of computers." He spends "much time with computer because I do my assignments on it; and when I am free I play games or watch movies." Besides, he does "programming and lots of stuff like make small movies or record music and burn CDs, etc." Similarly, he uses the Net "to research, to read news (mostly sports), to email, search new games, chat . . . to listen to music and to download favorite music, songs, games, etc."

His gaming practices, as his electronic literacy, also began at home. Angish's love of gaming seems to have roots in his love of stories. By the time he left elementary school, he was not only reading a variety of narrative texts but also writing in response to those works, sometimes even conjuring up stories similar to the plot structure in the source material. Every time he plays games, he says, he uses a similar type of exercise to imagine different play structures for the given game and to write new programs and games with his brother. He says, "I'm very patient in playing games and never quit or become mad just because I can't figure out what's going on; . . . I want to learn more skills and play the game and figure it out some way or the other. I keep thinking of all the possible ways of acing it."

His patience, imagination, his academic training in management science and his familiarity with some major aspects of computer technology are all in tune with his future goal: "to become a high level manager or corporate leader." The qualities he has learned to value and develop as he grows academically and professionally are the ones that his favorite games also seem to be reinforcing. The games he played most were: *Age of Empires, Chess, Need for Speed, Soccer (FIFA), Basketball, Quake,* etc. "As I play . . . I like the difficulty level increasing with each of my moves." Angish plays "to have some fun" and spend time when he feels "bored with other things," but he feels that it is more rewarding than it may appear: "It helps me understand others, other players, and the ideas behind writing that game."

Angish ranks the games he plays according to the challenge and potential benefits they offer. His favorite games are *Chess, FIFA,* and *Age of Empires,* "because you have to use your brain, plan right strategies, and use skills to ace them." He describes the benefits of playing games thus:

> It makes you good at thinking fast to make and implement decision to play games, as much as decision making applies in real world. It helps you a lot to improve your concentration.
>
> When I play I feel I am inside a computer and the character is me. . . . I like bold, clever, fast characters. I like their styles, especially. . . . I feel relaxed when I play well. If it is a soccer and when it's a tie I like the part most when it's challenging and a situation where a golden goal comes. I usually play the striker and I would love to be striker and a game planner or captain. I would accept to be a captain in real life situation also."

As games allow projective identities, Angish usually takes the role of the protagonist, or a role that gives him "the decision-making power." For example, when he plays *FIFA,* he plays the striker. Although there is no game that he would not play, like Laxman, he has not played a lot of violent games.

For Angish, games help not only to escape the dull routine, but also provide additional ways to be mentally astute. The skills he has learned to value most at school and college—"ability to plan right and make right strategies, quick decision making, and grabbing an opportunity when I get or see one"—are those he learned more from gaming than from anywhere else. Instead of interfering with his normal routine, gaming "prepares me to be better at dealing with the world." Against the background of some complaints that popular computer games teach youngsters to be disruptive or antisocial, he snaps, "Not at all—until you do implement the gaming scenario in real life, but for that there are other things more responsible than gaming." He chooses *Age of Empires* to describe his one favorite game and explains the rationale thus:

> *Age of Empires* is not a violent game and it's a game where you can choose what time and place you want to act on . . . how to conquer the world and be the leader. It builds your planning and coordination skills. . . . It's a game based on conquering the world, so it may seem violent, but it actually is a game that needs a lot of skills and talent to play it.
>
> I have picked up lots of skills and tactics from this game. As you know, playing games and situations in real life are very different, but it helps you a lot in prompt decision making and all related stuffs. . . . I don't want to give all the credit to the game alone—there are other things, like family, friends, etc.—but I guess it (gaming) makes a big difference.

What We Can Learn

Although Angish and Laxman primarily played what Gee (2003) classifies as "good" games, in which the player controls the construction of a society or civilization, they also had some experience with other kinds of games. Looking at the gaming practices of Laxman and Angish, we can learn a lot about gaming's relationship with learning and larger sociocultural and geopolitical questions.

Observation #1

Responses to gaming practices are context-specific. In her case study of a gamer, Selfe (2004) found that parents and teachers viewed gaming unfavorably although the gamer considered his practice a positive and fun learning experience. The gaming experiences of Laxman and Angish show that their practice was not viewed negatively. While their teachers used selected games to teach computer use, their parents also embraced every part of electronic literacy. The causes could be several, one of which might include the tendency in Nepal to embrace new technology with a greater amount of enthusiasm when it is introduced. The fact that computing was first introduced in selected schools only in the late 1980s and that computers were not available widely even in urban Nepal until the late 1990s may support this inference. However, we also recognize that other issues, such as school, teachers' individual choices, economic and educational status, and the level of trust within the family, could be among other several variables.

Observation #2

Electronic literacy is clearly embedded in the family's educational and economic background. Both Angish and Laxman learned print literacy at home as they were both born into literate families; but while for Angish home was the primary gateway for gaming and digital literacy, it was at school that Laxman became acquainted with computers. Time was a factor: Laxman learned it first in 1986 when his school was offering computer education as an additional class for the first time in its history, while Angish learned it in 1992 at home when he was eleven years old. However, a family's educational and economic status clearly predicated where and when one was exposed to the new interface. After all, not even one out of a thousand people was computer literate or owned a computer in Nepal in 1991 ("UN Human Development Report," 2003).

Observation #3

Gaming environments consist of a semiotic system (Gee, 2003) generated by complex symbolic codes that are charged with meanings pertaining to complicated social issues and relations such as class, gender, ethnicity, and the nation. For gamers such as Laxman and Angish, understanding these codes also meant understanding the assumptions of the cultures that produced these games. They learned that gaming was not simply playing with the machine, but entering a complex set of relationships that assumed significance only when they took the assigned roles and played by the given rules. They learned to assume the subject oppositions offered (hero, villain, etc.). Their active interaction in the gaming environment reinforced their understanding of some of the aspects of Western culture they were learning from other sources and the media. The game scenarios carried a range of meanings with regard to gender, class, colonialism, and consumerism, as well as the relationship of the individual with the larger society. When they played and immersed themselves in the gaming environment, they also felt that they were acclimating to the Western, especially American, way of life. This resulted in their largely smooth transition to American universities, where they are performing excellently.

Observation #4

Gaming texts gave players meaningful experiences of the world through representations or images and patterns of narrative. As Angish and Laxman attest, they learned to play by the rules set up and take advantage of the opportunities that they saw in the process. However, gaming environments also enabled them to assume agency and control. They were able to use the environment as they best liked it. As Stuart Hall suggests in "Encoding/ Decoding" (1980), readers of a text can, while accepting or following the preferred "encoded" meaning, also "decode" secondary and different meanings. Thus, while the gamers used gaming to learn the meanings encoded in them, they also constructed their own meanings out of them. The process became interactive. It was no longer simply the passive sender-receiver, or producer-consumer relationship enacted in the digital interface; it was a much more complex negotiation. For example, Angish said, playing *Age of Empires* was not only fun "but also [an opportunity] to realize the importance of making right strategies . . . and also remind [me] the value of having a long term ambition and work toward attaining it."

Clearly, by playing *Age of Empires,* Angish and Laxman were learning a colonial narrative and the "ambition" of colonial empires, a narrative common in Nepalese youths. Of course, the country was never directly colonized nor did it ever colonize another country in the way modern colonialism developed, but its nationalistic history is infused with brave soldiers fighting to unify the squabbling principalities into modern Nepal and to defend the country against external invaders such as the (British) East India Company. Imbued with a glorified narrative of conquest, Angish and Laxman found it easy to identify with and play by the colonial narrative undergirding *Age of Empires* or other real-time strategy games such as *Rise of Nations* as well as its expanded version, *Rise of Nations: Thrones & Patriots,* in which they would play against others in leading a nation of their choice. Through that experience, Angish and Laxman had a chance to understand how to cope with competitive educational or corporate settings and how to succeed in a competitive Western world that depends on the colonizing power of international monopoly capitalism. It also helped them imagine leadership roles in those settings.

Observation #5

Gaming can be an important venue to acquire and immerse in cultural literacy. Angish and Laxman felt that learning to take different roles, and composing their identities accordingly prepared them to more comfortably participate in diverse roles/activities and navigate different geocultural spaces in Nepal and the United States. Gaming was one of the activities that helped them to establish special rapport with friends and colleagues of their generation in the United States. As Angish stated, it also helped him be close to some of his roommates and classmates when he first moved to Findlay, Ohio, from Nepal: "When we realized we had played the same games, we had a special relationship. Actually, the guy from Australia and I had even played the same roles most of the time." Moreover,

> We share various codes to crack down games with other games. So I came across different gamers from around the world who became good friends later in life. I was shocked and thrilled to find out gamers from other countries such as Europe, Middle East, Korea, Japan and Russia because I thought it was famous in America and Europe only. Even more, I found many teenage girls to be good gamers, who became good friends of mine. This helped me share my culture and know about their culture and background as we started to chat frequently and got acquainted with each other, wrote emails and talked about our family, culture, and food besides gaming and its thrill of winning. So it was one way to learn and teach about cultures and so on.

Laxman also had a similar experience:

> I still recall playing games in Yahoo Games with people from the US, Canada, and Australia when I was in Nepal. I eventually became very good friends with them. We used to share about our cultures and how things were done differently and how we would respond to the same thing differently. We used to teach/learn about each other's cultures and also about our school and college activities. That was one of the important things I learned through games.

Observation #6

Gamers also felt that gaming could be put to a variety of purposes ranging from active learning to passive pastime. While Angish and Laxman had a lot of learning and networking experience through gaming, they also played simply to "kill time." Similarly, they did not play many games that they would describe as violent, but thought that it should have very little, if any, impact on real-life behavior. Angish and Laxman also considered violence in gaming environments to have made them more alert to the dangers of violence in real life. In the course of the interview, Laxman said: "The gaming experience actually helped me pause and think about the results of violence in real life. I could relate to certain situations and act accordingly. That also helped to realize what could possibly go wrong using violence, and that might have helped me to better understand a situation and act." Meanwhile, however, we realize that, on the one hand, Angish's and Laxman's gaming experience with violence may not be representative in that they initially played educational games and then they started selecting games that appealed to them for escape or cultural literacy. On the other hand, they often deliberately filtered more violent games out and even when they occasionally tried them, they knew what they were doing. It is important to keep this in mind with regard to their response to violence in gaming.

Observation # 7

Gaming contributes positively not only to reading and writing but also to a greater awareness of audience and purpose. Angish and Laxman read much about their favorite games both within and without the gaming environment, and both attribute their fast reading and comprehension skills to this experience. Similarly, both of them have found the writing they do in the gaming environment to boost their actual written-communication skills. The globally homogenizing power of gaming seems to help players to switch roles appropriate to their context and perform the literacy tasks as expected in a given setting. Laxman reports a business professor's comments on one of his written projects thus:

> It was a major first project of my semester here [at the University of Dayton] and I put a lot of effort on it. The professor was known to be very strict and demanding. I did hours of research and when I wrote I decided to be as close to the task as possible. I had to write about a company and what it should do to expand its business. I had to focus on its current situation and then outline possible changes. Actually, I imagined that I was writing a game in which my professor would be intrigued to keep reading till the end. The professor was really happy with my work and even showed it to some students as a sample.

Angish also had similar experiences. He even remembers writing games while in Nepal and some of his European and American "buddies" asking him to make certain things clear. In a way, he had participated in a kind of peer-review exercise in writing and found it rewarding in his academic writing also:

> That experience [peer review] immensely helps me now as I write. I often get somebody to read my draft, but even if there is nobody I try to read it as somebody else [would] and make final revisions. Once a teacher told me, "most foreign students have problems with thesis but you seem to be fine."

As teachers of rhetoric and composition, we know how hard it is to make our students aware of their audience and purpose, and sometimes even to get them to engage productively in peer-review workshops. However, as Angish's and Laxman's experiences suggest, many of our students might have already had some experience with these practices in arenas other than school or college writing classes. We as well as our students usually suffer from a perception that what is popular outside the academy, or the "nonacademic," bears little relevance to academic tasks, especially academic writing, and we fail to build on the existing literacies that our students bring to class. If we encourage our students to think about what they understand by audience, purpose, and similar other rhetorical strategies in non-academic settings such as gaming, we are far more likely to be successful in converging their prior literacies with the ones prized in our classes and beyond.

Gaming environments certainly represent the ideas and images of play and pleasure as imagined by the producers and marketers, but as Angish's and Laxman's experiences show, they can also be a learning resource. As they understood, gaming environments also helped them to learn a set of expected actions and relationships in the given environment—or at least as the designers/producers and gamers in the West would consider to be within the "normal." As such, the games they played helped them not only to attain a larger cultural literacy of the West, where they are now, but also define and follow their learning objectives. Their experiences with the digital interface certainly enabled them to overcome the geo-politico-cultural constraints. Gaming offered the players not only a new structure of fun-filled interaction and learning, but also enhanced their reading, writing, and computer programming skills with a greater awareness of audience and purpose. At the same time, however, we also call for further investigation into the way the interactive potentials of gaming are constrained and structured by the intricate process of design, technology, and marketing and the way they produce and reproduce the dominant ideologies of capitalism and the media. However, for the time being, we want to close with Angish's observation on gaming:

> The reading and writing helped a lot. In general, to break the source code was much important for a gamer. In order to finish the game one needs a good knowledge about computer programs, and a good network and connection with other gamers is vital for a gamer. Gaming helped me hone my knowledge in computer programs and even more helped me become a good programmer as I had to learn many programs such as C++, Java, XML, and HTML and other languages (that I don't want to mention here) which were very important. Despite the time spent, it helped my progress in other study subjects by improving my concentration and also made me a fast learner. For I believe that reading and writing helps a lot in good judgments. I build a good network of friends from different countries and share experience and culture. This is not just for the sake of game codes that you want from them and they want from you, but it also builds a bond of friendship and trust. Moreover, it helps in communication with people of different ages and backgrounds. It helped me especially when I came to United States for my master's degree, I was able to communicate with everybody and was not unfamiliar with any thing because I already knew their cultures through chats, games, films, etc. and I had a lot of confidence because of that. I am very confident of my life and future.

In many respects, gaming served as a gateway through which Angish and Laxman were able to enter a new culture with less trepidation than they otherwise might have experienced. In their minds, the resulting confidence, in turn, contributed to the success of their everyday literacy encounters in their new college settings.

References

Anderson, Craig A., & Bushman, Brad J. (2001). Effects of violent video games on aggressive behavior, aggressive cognition, aggressive affect, physiological arousal, and prosocial behavior: A meta-analytic review of scientific literature. *Psychological Science, 12*(5), 353–359.

Anderson, Craig A., & Dill, Karen E. (2000). Video games and aggressive thoughts, feelings, and behavior in the laboratory and in life. *Journal of Personality & Social Psychology, 78*(4), 772–790.

Bach, Richard. (n.d.). Quotes for winning. Retrieved June 21, 2005, from_http://www.motivatingquotes.com/ winningq.htm

Bhattarai, B. (2002, February 1–7). Can Nepal do IT? *Nepali Times, 79.* Retrieved March 20, 2004, from http://www.nepalitimes.com/issue79/technology.htm

Brigstocke, Marcus. (n.d.). Pacman. Retrieved April 26, 2005, from http://www.marcusbrigstocke.com/pacman.asp

Budhanilkantha school history. (n.d.). Retrieved April 2, 2004, from http://www.bnks.edu.np/history.html

Bushbuck charms, viking ships, and dodo eggs. (n.d.). Retrieved April 17, 2004, from http://www.the-underdogs.org/ game.php?id=158

Durkin, Kevin, & Barber, Bonnie. (2002). Not so doomed: Computer game play and positive adolescent development. *Applied Developmental Psychology, 23,* 373–392.

Fleming, Michele, & Rickwood, Debra J. (2001). Effects of violent versus non-violent video games on children's aggressive mood, and positive mood. *Journal of Applied Social Psychology, 31*(10), 2047–2071.

Frauenfelder, Mark. (2001). Death match: Your guide to the box wars. Wired magazine, *9,* 05. Retrieved June 7, 2004, from http://www.wired.com/wired/archive/9.05/deathmatch.html

Gee, James P. (2003). *What video games have to teach us about learning and literacy.* New York: Palgrave Macmillan.

Hall, Stuart. (1980). Encoding/decoding. In Stuart Hall, Dorothy Hobson, Andrew Lowe, & Paul Willis (Eds.), *Culture, media, language: Working papers in cultural studies, 1972–79* (pp. 128–139). London: Hutchinson.

Is TV losing out to video games? (2004, March 8). *CNN.* Retrieved April 1, 2004, from http://www.cnn.com/2004/TECH/fun.games/03/08/tv.playstation.reut/

Jones, Randolph M. (n.d.). A timeline of events relevant to computer and video games. Retrieved July 21, 2004, from http://www.cs.colby.edu/~rjones/courses/cs398/history.html

Kent, Steven L. (2001). *The ultimate history of video games: The story behind the craze that touched our lives and changed the world.* California: Prima Publishing.

Nintendo Entertainment System. (2006). *Wikipedia, the free encyclopedia.* Retrieved January 31, 2006 from http://en.wikipedia.org/w/index.php?title=Nintendo_Entertainment_System&oldid=37451255

Selfe, Cynthia. (2004). Computer gaming as literacy. Paper presented at CCCC, San Antonio, Texas, 2004.

The media history project: Timeline. (1996). Retrieved July 21, 2004, from http://www.mediahistory.umn.edu/time/ alltime.html

UNAIDS. (n.d.). Retrieved April 12, 2004, from http://www.unaids.org/EN/Geographical+Area/by+country/nepal.asp

UN Human Development Report. (2003). Retrieved April 12, 2004, from http:www.undp.org/hdr2003/indicator/ cty_f_NPL.html

Video games: Gaming goes to Hollywood. (2004, November 21). *The Economist.* Retrieved March 25, 2004, from http://www.economist.com/business/displayStory. cfm?story_id=2541401

3

Lost (and Found) in Translation: Game Localization, Cultural Models, and Critical Literacy

Erin Smith and Eve Deitsch

I guess you could argue that I was always interested in Japanese games, I just didn't know it.

(Eve Deitsch)

In *What Video Games Have to Teach Us about Learning and Literacy* (2003), James Gee revisits concepts that have been central to the development of sociocultural literacy theories over the past two decades. As opposed to the idea that reading and writing are cognitive skills that exist independent of context, literacy as a social practice (Street, 1984) is predicated upon the notion that meaning is always situated—"local, grounded in actual practices and experiences" (Gee, 1996, p. 41). In such local contexts learners build abstract concepts as they connect them to experiences or embodied knowledge. Rather than thinking of people as either literate or not, depending upon their ability to read and write, Gee argues that we need different literacies to function in different "semiotic domains," which he defines as "any set of practices that recruits one or more modalities . . . to communicate distinctive types of meanings" (2003, p. 18). Video games, for Gee, represent a group of related semiotic domains marked by the same kinds of literate practices that might characterize successful literacy in other domains, such as school, home, or community. According to Gee, semiotic domains are reciprocally constituted by internal and external "design grammars." The internal content of a game is shaped by the external features of its play and its intelligibility within a broader community of game-playing "affinity groups," while the external context is continually shaped by the practices and desires of the individuals who play the games. Within the world of the game, learners have opportunities to test the cultural models that inform their literacy in other semiotic domains as they encounter different worlds and different approaches to learning. In these ways, video games provide an environment that can foster active learning—that is, learning that involves experience, affiliation, and the acquisition of resources for future learning (p. 23). At the same time, as Gee and others (New London Group, 2000) have argued, critical literacy is a product of learning "not only how to understand and produce meanings in a particular semiotic domain that are recognizable to those affiliated with the domain, but, in addition, how to think about the domain at a 'meta' level as a complex system of interrelated parts" (2003, p. 23).

Despite Gee's interest in external design grammars and the cultural and contextual aspects of literacy, he is surprisingly silent on the unique confluence of global economic and cultural concerns that govern the gaming industry and its relationship to the critical literacy of game players. The gaming industry provides an extraordinary example of Fredric Jameson's (1998) claim that global communication and distribution systems both constitute and are constituted by economic and cultural forces. Since its inception, the computer gaming industry has been a global industry, one that exemplifies in many ways the logic, strategies, and contradictions of an emerging economic and cultural system that strives to balance global reach with local appeal. As the New London Group observes:

> Local diversity and global connectedness mean not only that there can be no standard; they also mean that the most important skill students need to learn is to negotiate regional, ethnic, or class-based dialects; variations in register that occur according to social context; hybrid cross-cultural discourses; the code switching often to be found within a text among different languages, dialects, or registers; different visual and iconic meanings; and variations in the gestural relationships among people, language, and material objects. Indeed, this is the only hope for averting the catastrophic conflicts about identities and spaces that now seem ever ready to flare up. (2000, p. 14)

If, then, we are to talk about the cultural content of games, it is imperative that we consider the way that local and global concerns are negotiated, at both the site of game production as well as that of game play. Gee argues that within the game world and the game-playing experience, learners have opportunities to think in ways that might help broaden their awareness of other cultural models, as well as their own. While it may be true that learners can think critically about cultural models with which they are familiar, it is an extremely tricky business to discern within the game world the many permutations of culture and economic interest that forge games for the global marketplace. To what extent can we lay claim to cultural information within the world of the game without a consideration of these broader contexts?

This chapter looks at the experience of Eve Deitsch (née Eschenbacher)[1], a 24-year-old American who has been playing computer games almost literally since birth. Eve's story most certainly demonstrates that her video game literacy is, from the beginning, marked by the acquisition of both internal and external design grammars in the ways that Gee defines them. At the same time, significant aspects of Eve's critical literacy in this semiotic domain have been informed not only by internal and external design grammars, but by forces beyond these local contexts and affinity groups. Her experience as an American who learned Japanese and now works for a game localization firm in Japan bespeaks another kind of grammar, one that represents those constitutional aspects of semiotic domains that require learners—consciously or unconsciously—to negotiate their local practice with cultural or economic investments external to yet nevertheless embedded in the semiotic domain. As Eve's case demonstrates, when learners are invited to investigate the way that games come *to be* in conjunction with what they *are* when played, they become active explorers of "local diversity and global connectedness," a practice that enhances not only their game play, but their critical literacy skills as well.[2]

Semiotic Domains Reloaded

Eve Eschenbacher was born near Auburn, Michigan, a small rural town located between Midland (home of Dow Chemical) and Bay City. Her father has a degree in accounting from a state university and her mother is a high school graduate. Reading was highly valued in her home, and Eve could read by the age of four. Both parents encouraged her reading activities in different ways: "I remember that whenever I got sick, my mom would stop by the bookstore after the doctor so that I could pick out a book to read while I was recovering." By the time Eve entered school, she could already read and recalls having to amuse herself while her classmates caught up:

> I remember taking "chapter books"—kids' novels that had chapters, but still were only 50–100 pages long—to school in Kindergarten and reading them during breaktimes. During class time, the teacher was trying to teach us all how to read. I was the only one in the class who knew how already, and I got bored. Who needs "See Dick. See Jane. See Dick and Jane" when you can read novels?

Her love of reading continued throughout her years in school, and Eve recalls regularly challenging herself by choosing longer, harder books for open-book report assignments, completing her reports before the due date, and reading more books than were assigned.

While many of her reading activities were done independently, Eve credits a good deal of her reading comprehension to logic puzzles that she regularly solved with her father:

> [They contained] sentences like "Brian is neither the person who went to China, nor the person who bought the lamp," which tried to help you solve a puzzle of who did what when, or who went where and bought what, that sort of thing. I had to learn to think about a sentence carefully, several times if necessary, and even in conjunction with other sentences, in order to solve a puzzle. For example, according to the previous sentence, Brian didn't go to China, and he didn't buy a lamp. But you can also get more meaning out of that for your grid. The person who went to China didn't buy a lamp, either. Nor did the person who bought a lamp go to China. So, I learned to pull a lot of meaning from everything I read, to see it from different angles.

Computer and video games worked in concert with the logic puzzles, teaching her "that there is information everywhere, and that it's important to read carefully and be observant. . . . In adventure games, there's always something important that is said in a conversation that won't come up again until you need it in a puzzle later." Games helped Eve develop more sophisticated alphabetic reading skills and constituted a significant literacy in their own right, one marked both by her acquisition of internal and external design grammars specific to games and game technology as well as by a series of cultural or ideological factors that influenced the development of her literacy.

The story of Eve's relationship to gaming begins at a formative moment in the home computer industry. A month before Eve was born, Eve's father convinced her mother to let him buy a Commodore VIC-20. Thus, Eve and the family's first home computer arrived at roughly the same time, an occurrence anticipated by Commodore's marketing strategy for the VIC-20. The VIC-20, with its advertising tagline "the friendly computer," was marketed as the family machine in the Commodore product line (Schembri and Boisseau, 1995) and its advertisements from 1981 proudly proclaimed that it was a "true computer" and not merely a "game machine":

> Commodore's VIC 20 lets you plug in the same exciting game cartridges available on most game machines . . . but the VIC is a full featured computer and that makes a big difference.
>   Here's a simple test to help you find out whether you're buying a game machine or a computer . . . simply ask the salesperson if the device you're evaluating has these features:
>
> 1. Does it have a full size typewriter keyboard?
> 2. Can you use all 3 types of storage media?
> 3. Is full-power BASIC built-in?
> 4. Is a self-teaching instruction book included?
> 5. How many accessory ports are there?
>
> (Schembri & Boisseau, 1995)

The VIC-20 marketing brochure provides a good example of external design grammar and its role in game literacy. According to Gee (2003), external design grammars help us recognize "what is and what is not an acceptable or typical social practice and identity in regard to the affinity group associated with a semiotic domain" (p. 30). To exemplify his point, Gee turns to debates about the relative merits of platform versus computer-based gaming and how they participated in articulating norms for acceptable gaming community practice:

> Was the Xbox really a game platform? Could a real game platform have a hard drive? Perhaps the Xbox is really a computer in disguise. This is a debate over the very external design grammar of the domain: Is the pattern "video game, game platform, hard drive" acceptable within the external design grammar of the domain? Does it count as an acceptable part of valued social practices and identities in the domain? Should it? (p. 35)

In the same way, the technical features of the VIC-20 represent more than just the "brute technology" that enables certain computing practices. Rather, it shows "the ways in which external technological and material facts become social facts and values" (p. 35). Its features provide new definitions of home computing and new expectations for the literacy of home computer consumers and users.

Eve's descriptions of her early game playing demonstrate an awareness of external design factors as markers of her evolving literacy:

> It had games on these huge cartridges, as well as on cassette tapes. From as early as I can remember, my father would load in a cartridge of Pong or Kickman—you played them with these big paddle controllers where you turned a large knob, which was easy for little hands like mine to operate. He and I would compete at these games. We had a furnished room in the basement that was my dad's computer room. My mom wasn't into computer games at all. As I got older, I learned to load them myself, as well as turn the computer on myself. When I was around age 6 or so, we got a newer Commodore—a Commodore 128—I learned quickly how to type in the commands to boot the games. . . . I remember playing "Ultimate Wizard" . . . against my father for several weeks straight. It only gave you 5 lives, so we'd each play to see who could get the farthest. I think the highest I ever got was around level 20. My father got to Level 65. Neither of us ever beat it.

This story of literacy acquisition is told as much through the mastery of external design grammar as of game content itself. Eve's ability to begin game playing at such a young age is predicated on the design of the controller, which made it "easy for little hands." While the games may not always have represented a higher level of content or sophistication, Eve's development as a gamer is measured in large part by being able to turn on the computer and load tapes herself, and later by learning to type in commands on the computer. Moreover, her explicit memory of the system names itself represents another example of her entrance into the affinity group of game players.

As Eve goes on to describe her history with video games, her growing independence is reflected in her control of the game systems. As newer console systems were released, Eve would receive them as gifts for Christmas:

> I ended up getting a Nintendo, Super Nintendo, Sega Genesis, Nintendo 64, and a PlayStation, as well as a Game Boy, and a Sega Game Gear. And that's just until I went to college. . . . [Since then] I have added 3 more consoles to my collection—a Game Boy Advance, Game Boy SP, and a PlayStation 2.[3]

Ownership of these different systems represents another marker of Eve's literacy. The ability to move comfortably among different platforms depends upon a met-alevel understanding of how games work in a general way, rather than rote memorization of how to operate one particular system. Eve had some access to computers in her school, joining a "computer club" in the fourth grade and taking a computer class in the seventh grade, she describes most of her literacy activities within school as alphabetic and artistic. She took journalism and creative writing, and she was the assistant editor of her high school newspaper for two years and unofficial editor of a school literary magazine. All the coursework in her senior year of high school was in the arts and languages.

Most of Eve's gaming activities took place on her own systems outside school, and perhaps the most significant moment in the development of her critical literacy as a game player was when she recognized that every one of the gaming systems that she owned herself was made in Japan.

> I guess you could argue that I was always interested in Japanese games, I just didn't know it. Every game console system was made in Japan, until the XBox (and that was during my college years). Most people just didn't realize it, especially most kids.

In his long discussion of the Xbox in *Video Games,* Gee never mentions two very significant cultural and economic aspects of the Xbox's release to affinity groups of computer users and game players. First, as Eve notes above, Japanese companies manufactured almost every other game console on the market. Second, the release of the Xbox became part of the debate surrounding open source software and, for many advanced computer users and gamers, represented yet another attempt by Microsoft to promote proprietary systems and consolidate its monopoly to the detriment of shared programming knowledge and literacy.[4]

Although in *Video Games,* Gee identifies learning principles explicitly associated with "cultural models" and others that highlight the significance of cultural contexts to learning, his depictions of game literacy stop short of referencing economic and international contexts of game development and their relationship to literacy and learning. Principal among these is localization—the practice of preparing a product developed in one culture for consumption in another. Localization raises many more questions about the nature and content of cultural models that circulate within and around games and the ideological designs that constitute them.

Wake Up and Smell the Culture

Sony is credited with coining the phrase "global localization" or "glocalism" (*dochaku*) to describe the practice of designing and marketing products that can be adapted to local markets (or indigenized), rather than forcing local cultures to adapt to foreign products (a far less successful marketing approach) (Pieterse, 2004, p. 50). Localization practices include the process of translation, but extend in both practice and theory to a broader cultural and political arena. Localization is a critical issue for software and game developers who seek a global market for their product. Hall and Hudson (1997) identify five levels of software localization that represent different investments of resources depending on the market aspirations of the developer (see figure 3.1).

The process of "complete" localization is expensive and resource intensive as, among other things, a mistake about a geographic border or a reference to a "state" as opposed to a "region" may represent an insult or political statement to a consumer in another country.

Microsoft, for example, has created a Geopolitical Product Strategy (GPS) team to maintain and monitor a knowledge base of global developments as well as culturally and politically sensitive topics (Microsoft, 2000). The GPS is responsible for the more sensitive aspects of product localization in over 60 countries, as well as for educating game designers about the cultural and political stakes of

Localization Level	Market Aspirations
None	You offer single-country-based product only
Minimum	Your product meets basic requirements such as those demanded by local legislation
Moderate	Your product meets fundamental customer requirements to match local market competition
High	Your product meets additional market needs to establish a market leader position
Complete	Every attribute category and all user components of your product are internationalized and the product is capable of full localization in any market—this is the ideal approach if justifiable on cost grounds.

Figure 3.1 Hall and Hudson's Localization Levels.

their design choices. In a recent GameSpot News interview, Tom Edwards discussed the tensions between his team's work and that of game developer's:

> "They tell me, 'You know, everything you just told us about what not to do is stuff that we purposely try to do because it's edgy and appeals to the demographics we're trying to sell to,'" Edwards says. "Think about it. You take people like that, who may not have the best cultural and cross-cultural exposure, then you put them in a global industry, where their actions have a global reach, and they don't understand that. Then there's going to be problems. And it's almost inevitable." (Goize & Sinclair, 2004)

While productivity software such as Microsoft Office might need to concern itself with menu items and how geographic regions appear when a user selects a time zone, Edwards's comments allude to additional concerns that may face game designers who are attempting to develop compelling narratives and exciting game play for cross-cultural audiences.

Preventing mistakes in large-scale localization of software is challenging and resource-intensive work, even more so for products such as computer games, which depend on narrative and immersive environments. Functionality in games encompasses more than being able to navigate the interface and shoot things. It frequently requires both narrative comprehension and narrative pleasure, aspects of game play that can differ greatly from one culture to the next. Thayer and Kolko (2004) argue that narrative is chief among the challenges of game localization. "To ensure the functionality of games, localizers must at times undertake a process called "blending," which involves writing a new game narrative for a target culture, a narrative that will be more comprehensible within that culture than the original and that will hopefully ensure greater sales of the game" (p. 481). Thayer and Kolko claim that digital games are unique in their need for this kind of reworking in the localization process. Game developers for international markets also design games, from the outset, with localization in mind. Plotlines that will require extensive overhaul in order to become suitable for another market may be scrapped or, if developed, not released outside the country of origin.[5]

Localization practices are also affected by the cultural image of the exporting country. Decisions as to whether cultural references ought to be exported with the product frequently depend upon the relative value of cultural image on the global market. Koichi Iwabuchi observes that despite the profound influence of Japanese consumer technologies on the cultural activities of our everyday life, they have tended not to be talked about in terms of a Japanese cultural presence" (2002, p. 26). Although we might identify Japan as a leading manufacturer of consumer electronics, Iwabuchi argues, such products do not carry with them the "bodily, racial, and ethnic characteristics"—the "cultural odor"—that binds positive cultural associations to the appeal of the product (p. 28). When a cultural image is exported along with the product, the symbolic association with the culture of origin helps determine its appeal and value. For example, when McDonald's sells a Big Mac and fries, its value is enhanced by the way those products participate in the discursive construction of "Americanness" to foreign consumers. According to Iwabuchi, Japanese consumer electronics are, on the whole, "culturally odorless," in that their appeal has had little to do with the ways in which a consumer might associate them with Japan or Japaneseness. In contrast to the "odorlessness" of consumer electronics, the immense popularity of Japanese animation and computer games has led some Japanese critics to "confer a specific Japanese 'fragrance' on these cultural products" (p. 31). Pokémon, for example, has been discussed in terms of its positive cultural associations with Japan. "Japanimation" and video games have garnered fans across the world who see these cultural products as uniquely Japanese. In other words, the Japaneseness of these products adds to their value, representing for some a "Japanization" of the West.

However, Iwabuchi is skeptical about the extent to which the dissemination of Japanese cultural products actually represents either a sign of Japanese symbolic power or culture:

> It is one thing to observe that Pokémon texts . . . are influencing children's play and behavior in many parts of the world and that these children perceive Japan as a cool nation because it creates cool cultural products such as Pokémon. However, it is quite another to say that this cultural influence and this perception of coolness is closely associated with a tangible, realistic appreciation of "Japanese" lifestyles or ideas. (p. 34)

Of particular concern in this regard is the creation of characters for Japanese animation and computer games that do not look Japanese: "Such non-Japaneseness is called mukokuseki, literally meaning 'something or someone lacking any nationality,' but also implying the erasure of racial or ethnic characteristics or a context, which does not imprint a particular culture or country with these features" (p. 28). Take, for example, this passage from *Got Game: How the Gamer Generation Is Reshaping Business Forever*:

> The game generation is deeply, truly global. Don't ask how they'd do on a geography test. Give a cross-section of American business professionals an unlabeled map and ask them to fill in rivers and capitals, and our money would be on the oldest respondents. But ask them to draw a conceptual map of the business world and there's one

key thing that the gamers would certainly get right: The United States won't be alone at the center. Why would it? Any serious gamer knows the best games are from Japan. So are most of the cool platforms and devices—not to mention an awful lot of serious players. (Beck & Wade, 2004, p. 158)

As Iwabuchi predicts, the particulars of the culture or country—"rivers and capitals"—are superseded by the perception of "coolness," a profitable quality that has little to do with Japanese culture (or geography) itself.

When Eve says that she was "always interested in Japanese games," but "just didn't know it," it seems possible that she references the issue of cultural "odorlessness" raised by Iwabuchi. Reflecting on what she understood about the "Japaneseness" of the games she played, she says:

Looking back, I can't think of any ideas about Japanese culture that I had due to video games. I think this might be due to the Japanese culture being a secondary part to the games—the fantasy story was at the forefront. . . . It's funny, actually, that Japanese games don't outright teach you much about Japanese culture. There are a few games where the stories are set in Japan, and you learn bits and pieces about the culture, but most video games are set in fantasy lands with fantasy characters, and there isn't anything in them that is blatantly Japanese culture.

There is a profound contradiction, then, in the way Japanese popular culture manifests Japanese culture in that it "simultaneously articulates the universal appeal of Japanese cultural products and the disappearance of any perceptible 'Japaneseness'" (p. 33). Iwabuchi raises essential questions about the paradoxical nature of Japanese cultural products in the global marketplace. As we think about the cultural content that may or may not be found in the design and marketing of video games, it is vital that we consider the practice of game localization, its role in global game development and marketing, and its impact on the cultural form and content of video games.

Like those members of the game generation described by Beck and Wade, Eve describes her initial attraction to Japan as emanating both from her awareness that the cool games came from Japan and from more general Japanese inroads into popular culture:

In my late high school and college years, I started to realize that a lot of these games I was playing had originated in Japan, and the interest began to grow. This is also when other Japanese pop culture began gaining popularity in the US. I started looking at them in a different view, and became more and more intrigued. . . . I had an interest in Japan stemming from a lot of different things (being a kid in the US in the 80s, a Japanese man who gave a speech at my junior high, anime, video games, etc.).

Eve is quite explicit, though, that her primary interest in learning Japanese was "in order to be closer to working with computer games."

I was trying to figure out what I wanted to study. That would be when I started looking back on all those years of game playing, and thinking, "Hey, I know a lot of this stuff, I just didn't know that I knew it!" When I transferred to MTU, I thought I would program games. I soon learned that programming wasn't for me, though, and moved into a different area. I still wanted to be with my games, though, so I had to come up with a different idea.

The different idea that Eve came up with was to spend 11 months in Japan from May 2002 to April 2003, when she began studying Japanese in an intensive program.

As Eve's cultural awareness and language skills developed, she began to interact with the games on a much more meta-analytical level.

While I was studying Japanese, I picked up some video games in Japanese, and started playing them (part for fun, part for study). As my language abilities grew, I noticed more and more differences between what they were saying and what the English versions were saying. I guess that's one reason why I am where I am at now.

When Eve returned to the United States, she resumed classes at Michigan Tech and continued to work at her Japanese. When she approached a professor about doing an independent study for the spring semester, her professor suggested that she study game localization practices. Although Eve had not heard the term "localization" before, she already had a great deal of familiarity with the practices of localization from her experience of playing the games in English and Japanese, as she mentions above.

Principle 30 in Gee's *Video Games* is the "Cultural Models about the World Principle," in which "learning is set up in such a way that learners come to think consciously and reflectively about some of their cultural models regarding the world, without denigration of their identities, abilities, or social affiliations, and juxtapose them to new models that may conflict with or otherwise relate to them in various ways" (p. 166). According to Gee, cultural models "are images, story lines, principles, or metaphors that capture what a particular group finds 'normal' or 'typical' in regard to a given phenomenon" (p. 143). These models allow us to act on "auto pilot" and generally remain invisible to us until they are challenged or pushed up against different models. Gee's examples in gaming situations range from playing the role of a criminal in *Grand Theft Auto* to learning that Jewish settlers in the Syrian-made game *Under Ash* are not considered to be civilians (and can be shot like other military personnel). Often in shooter games, incurring a civilian death means losing the game or failing the mission. It is not always obvious who is classified as a civilian, and it is incumbent upon the player to make that determination based on his or her understanding of who is doing what kind of job and for what reason. Context provided in the game can provide some clues, but those clues might be ignored or misunderstood if they are underwritten by a cultural model unfamiliar to the player.

When games are localized for new markets, however, careful attention is paid to how well a game narrative will be received by a local audience based on their existing cultural models or mores. While the examples referenced by Gee offer up instances where gamers may encounter the kind of challenge that sparks reflection, the localization practice of blending may actively work to eliminate those opportunities in the game. In the research paper that Eve wrote for her independent study, she noted several examples where narratives were changed so as not to violate cultural taboos or expectations.

> There are often social settings that are changed for one reason or another. *Earthbound* and *Final Fantasy 6* both contain the most common example of a name change. Because of Nintendo's strict censorship rules, Bars were changed to Cafés. In addition, any and all references to alcohol were removed. So, you will run into several red-faced characters who tell you that they drank too much "espresso." While a child wouldn't question it, it's harder for an adult to believe. But the whole "bar changing to café" situation is interesting and complex, like other major changes in a story.

Later in her paper, Eve examines how eliminating alcohol not only effaces a particular cultural practice, but changes characterization as well as relationships between characters.

In *Final Fantasy Tactics Advance* the three main characters, Marche, Mewt, and Ritz, are walking home from school when they run into Mewt's father. In the Japanese version, Mewt's father is quite drunk. Mewt is embarrassed that his father has become an alcoholic since his mother's death. Marche snaps at him, saying, "It's good that your parents were at least together." He then leaves, and Ritz reveals that Marche does not have a father. This establishes two character relationships—the relationship between Mewt and his alcoholic father, and the relationship between Marche and Mewt. Mewt is embarrassed at his father because his father is an alcoholic. He mentions that his father has let himself go since his mother's death. This also establishes Marche's feelings about Mewt. Marche is jealous of Mewt for having a father. He is also a bit angry because Mewt is embarrassed about his father. Marche seems to think that Mewt should appreciate his father and the kind of relationship that his parents had that left his father so devastated when his mother died.

In the English version of the game, the same character relationships are established, but for different reasons. Owing to localization and censorship issues, Mewt's father is not drunk. When the three main characters encounter him, he is apologizing profusely to an unidentified gentleman. Mewt says that his father used to work at a bigger company before, but "broke down big time" following the death of his mother. This establishes Mewt's embarrassment at his father's inability to stand up for himself. Marche then mentions that "he seems nice," because "not too many parents talk to their kids like that." He also mentions "I bet you used to go out on vacations and stuff a lot." This establishes Marche's jealousy; however, it's not to the same degree. Marche just seems to be remarking about how nice it is to have a father, and he is not upset about Mewt's feelings toward his father at all. This changes the relationship that is being established between the two friends, Mewt and Marche.

In addition to the effects described by Eve above, the Japanese version suggests that Mewt should respect his father because he is his father, while the English version offers a cultural model that suggests that there are material reasons why Mewt should appreciate having a father: "I bet you used to go out on vacations and stuff a lot." The English version also offers up another cultural model—children who do not have fathers are fine—when, in fact, the Japanese version of

Marche, who is angry and jealous, might more accurately represent the feelings of a young boy in this situation. The examples provided by Eve illustrate how localization can actively remove opportunities to explore behavior that violates cultural norms and may even, at times, introduce idealized cultural models that affirm normative behavior and confirm normative values and beliefs.

Moreover, when game graphics are not changed to accompany the new story, games may teach learners to overlook obvious contradictions between the text and the images, reading past them in order to reconcile difference with their dominant cultural model. Eve describes another example in *Final Fantasy X-2*, in which Aniki has a crush on his first cousin Yuna:

> Several characters mention this, and the situation manifests in several interactions. Relationships between first cousins are accepted, but far from commonplace in Japan. In America, they are quite taboo. . . . Thus, all references are removed [from the localized English version]. . . . Because this fact was written out of the American version, all references to it had to be removed as well. At one point in the game, Aniki hears that Yuna was in trouble. He says that he is coming down right away to help. Rikku (his sister) then says to Yuna (in the Japanese version) "He really favors you." In the English version, this was changed to "What about me?"
>
> However, there is one interaction that does not fit the adapted relationship. This interaction is again, part of the movement of the characters programmed into the game. After the scene in which Aniki heads down to help Yuna, he is lying on the floor. Yuna comforts him, and he tries to make a move to kiss her. He does this in a sort of sneaky way, much like the cliché "yawn-and-put-your-arm-around-her-shoulders" move. He stretches up, with arms on either side of Yuna's shoulders. Rikku runs over and kicks him, shouting "Sicko!" This seems odd and out of place to the Americans playing the game, because there's no suggested crush or relationship between the two characters.

This example illustrates how external design grammar (i.e., aspects of design related to affinity groups) might actually override internal design grammar (which would dictate how game players connect the action in the game with the dialogue). Thus, without an awareness of how localization may create these moments of dissonance in a text, adding another level to the semiotics of the domain, members of an affinity group could agree upon meanings where visual and alphabetic/aural semiotics are actually in conflict.

"It Makes Me Wonder If You Were Playing It Blindfolded with Earplugs In"

While Eve was working on this independent study, she was also reading David Freeman's (2003) book *Creating Emotion in Games*, his guide to scriptwriting and the concept of "emotioneering." Freeman offers 300 techniques for creating and scripting characters that create emotional engagement and identification for game players. Eve was particularly critical of Freeman's depictions of the Japanese games, especially *Final Fantasy*, and sent him an e-mail telling him so. Eve's e-mail to Freeman is fascinating in that as she progresses through her critique of Freeman's *Final Fantasy* reading, her readings become progressively metalinguistic. Moreover, this progression is tied in many ways to her familiarity with Japanese culture and the production aspects of game development. The following excerpts from the e-mail are quoted at length to give a sense of the fullness of Eve's critique and the different language that she uses as she develops the different sections of her analysis. She begins with a rather impassioned opening:

> I have been reading your book, "Creating Emotion in Games," and have found it incredibly enjoyable. However, I have some disagreements regarding points that you have made in your book, and I feel it necessary to point them out. Your examples regarding American games are wonderful, and have been dead-on, from what I can tell. (I have not played all the games you mention, however.) But when you begin discussing Japanese games, namely "Final Fantasy X," you stray so far from the reality of the game that it makes me wonder if you were playing it blindfolded with earplugs in.

Eve's opening paragraph indicates the extent to which she thinks Freeman may have erred with respect to the game and, to go a bit further, provides in one sense a metaphor for the difference between reading from Eve's culturally aware position. As she proceeds through her critique she begins by clarifying some plot and character points:

> Not only do you misspell the lead character's name (Tidus, with a "d" not two "t"s), but you mention, on page 253, that Tidus is "a young man who is angry because (as far as he knows) his father deserted him." This is blatantly incorrect. Tidus never says that he is angry with his father for deserting him. In fact, Tidus was quite happy his father disappeared. It is stated several times in the game that Tidus hates his father. He is not merely angry with him, Tidus hates him. They go into this in detail later. Tidus's father, Jecht, was a star blitzball player. Jecht was very famous. However, Jecht had a drinking problem. He was an alcoholic. On top of this, whenever Jecht was home, Tidus's mother ignored Tidus, preferring to spend her time with Jecht. On top of that, Jecht was arrogant. He believed he was the best, and would state this all the time. He would always tell Tidus that he wasn't good enough, that Tidus could never do the things Jecht could do. Furthermore, Jecht would make fun of Tidus for crying. If you played the game through, you'll notice there's a set of lines that Jecht says in Flashbacks and at the end of the game when Jecht is dying. He says, "You're gonna cry. You always cry. See, you're crying."

Eve goes on to provide an example of how the problem between Tidus and Jecht was integrated into the interactive game play:

> Remember the "Jecht Shot mini-game? Where you had to try to perform the Jecht shot on the boat, by pushing directional buttons to rid yourself of Jecht's criticisms?" "You can't do it, kid!" "I'm the best!"

The first section of her comments clarifies aspects of the game text: "You misspell the lead character's name," "It is stated several times that," "You'll notice there's a set of lines," "Remember the Jecht Shot mini-game."

Eve's next set of comments, however, requires not just a clear and thorough understanding of the particulars of the plot, but an interpretation of the game's central theme, which she supports with specific examples from the game:

> My other comment/complaint is regarding the information you have on page 380 regarding connecting the story and the gameplay. You mention that "The biggest recurring story element in the game is dreams." I fail to see how this can be true. I do not understand what you think the dreams are in this game. I didn't see dreams as a recurring theme at all. The biggest recurring element I saw was faith. Yuna believed the teachings that she followed, which is why she chose to be a summoner. Wakka believed the teachings, so he became a guardian. He mentions that the teachings say that when they've atoned for their ways, that Sin will go away. Later, when they realize that Sin is the person who gave them the teachings (Yu Yevon), they have a hard time dealing with it. How would you react to finding out that the very thing you've based your life around is a lie? Can you imagine how a priest might feel if they found unquestionable proof that the bible was merely a book of fiction, and there never was a Jesus?
>
> Going back to my argument, Tidus is the only dream in the game. You find out that the Fayth, the people who turned themselves into statues (for lack of a better term—they're big rocks in the floor) in order to become powerful Aeons that you can call on to help you, have been dreaming, trapped in their statues. The power that they have to be Aeons is the same power that they use to create Tidus. The only people who have this dreaming power in the game are NPCs [non-player characters]— why should any other person in the game have it? Especially because the recurring faith aspect of the game is present anytime Yuna is used. She can "pray," or cast "holy," or summon the Aeons and control them. Tidus has a dream, yes, but he does not understand why. He does not know how anything works, and he does not learn this until late in the game. I do not see how any of the examples you gave could have been easily implemented, without seeming more like cheap thrills. Tidus did not have the power of the Fayth, he merely was who he was, able to exist because of the Fayth. He was like an Aeon in this aspect, but he was not an Aeon, because the Aeons were embodiments of the Fayth.

In the section above, Eve clearly understands that this part of her critique is centered on interpretation; thus, she refers to what she is writing in this section as "argument" and works through her interpretation of "Faith" by providing specific examples of how the different characters enact this theme. She also ties her understanding of the theme to particular things that a game player can do with a character like Yuna. Throughout this close reading of the game, Eve integrates conventional aspects of narrative analysis—looking at how elements of plot, description, and characterization support her argument about the theme—with aspects that are specific to interactive environments—what characters can do, the difference between what nonplayer characters (i.e., those characters whose responses and abilities are preprogrammed within the game) and what players can do. Moreover, she makes a distinction between activities that might be considered extraneous to the game play, the "cheap thrills," and those that are essential to the unfolding of the story and its meaning.

Finally, Eve discusses the effect of localization on the game, demonstrating her understanding of how the external realities of global product distribution can change the game despite the best efforts of game designers:

> Another argument that you could get into (that would take possibly a whole 'nother book) is that there are differences between the original Japanese version and the translated version. These differences are due to many factors—from the way the characters were voice acted, to the way the script was translated. I recall the voice actor for Tidus's character stating in an interview that the original voice actor had a passion and fire that the American actor couldn't hope to re-create, so the American actor turned the American version of Tidus into a kind of "dude." The point is that no matter how hard the original team worked to Emotioneer the game, to reveal important things through dialogue and voice acting, it could easily have been blown to hell by a bad, or even mediocre translation job.

In this final section of her analysis, Eve displays a great deal of sophistication and metalevel understanding of game design. She pulls together several different threads that highlight her multimodal literacy. Not only is she aware of how translation issues can change the versions, she understands that the reception of the game and characterization within the narrative are affected by such production elements as voice acting. Finally, she connects Freeman's concept of *emotioneering* (which she defines) to the potential effect that localization might have on it. Throughout this e-mail, Eve ties traditional practices of close reading and critical literacy to her analysis of that game, displaying the qualities that we regularly seek in the alphabetic literacy of our students.

Eve's desire to write to Freeman demonstrates her willingness not just to consume games, but to participate actively in the shaping of knowledge within the game-playing community. In response, David Freeman wrote Eve a very kind and thoughtful email, thanking her for pointing out these aspects of *Final Fantasy:*

> It's interesting that no one else has sent me similar comments. I can't believe that you're the only Final Fantasy X fan out there, but perhaps you're the first one who has read the book that carefully. (The book came out in Oct. and we've sold about 2500 copies so far.)

And, finally, Freeman—who runs national seminars for game designers and writers—asked Eve a question that speaks to the level and quality of her engagement with his book, as well as her literacy: "Besides being a game player, are you also a designer?" Although Eve is not a game designer now, shortly after this exchange with Freeman, she returned to Japan in July 2004 to take a position teaching English in Toki, Gifu. In December, she was hired by Intac, a Japanese localization firm in Tokyo, many of whose clients are game developers.

Conclusion: Globalization and Critical Literacy

Fredric Jameson (1998) argues that while globalization is celebrated for cultural pluralism rooted in difference and differentiation, its economic logic promotes "the rapid assimilation of hitherto autonomous national markets and productive zones into a single sphere . . . standardization on an unparalleled new scale" (p. 57). Globalization is not simply the proliferation of communication networks and technologies that place us in immediate contact with other cultures and give us immediate access to their commodities. It is essentially bound to practices of exporting and importing, sometimes directly for economic purposes, as with the entertainment industry and popular culture; sometimes incidentally as cultural mores and practices are embedded in the products themselves: "Whoever says the production of culture says the production of everyday life" (p. 67). While Gee has valuable insights into how social networks and game design operate within the semiotic domain, he does not account fully enough for the critical aspects of game design that may not be directly accessible in the immediate context of game play, particularly those related to game production and distribution in the global marketplace.

Throughout her life, Eve's alphabetic literacy and her literacy within the semiotic domains of game play have worked together to foster strong reading and writing skills. It seems evident, however, that the level of her critical literacy—that is, those aspects of her literacy that engage games through a metalevel understanding of them as semiotic systems—is most profoundly influenced by her understanding of the gaming industry, particularly her awareness of its global nature and cultural implications. When Eve plays games, she recognizes how they have been shaped, not just as stories or as entertainment, but as cultural products designed for specific cultural audiences. It is this awareness that enables her to notice discrepancies between what characters say and do within the game, as well as to become curious enough about the differences to want to play the game in its original form, a desire that has led her to become a fluent speaker and reader of Japanese.

The story of Eve's critical literacy supports Deborah Brandt and Katie Clinton's (2002) concerns about "the limits of the local" in their recent critique of social practice theory. Brandt and Clinton argue that social practice theory may need to pay closer attention "to the ways that 'local literates' are recruited into distant campaigns" (p. 347). By calling for a "transcontextual" approach, they point out that what we can see at the particular scene of literate practice may not give us the whole picture: "Where anyone is observed reading and writing something, it is well worth asking who else is getting something out of it; often that somebody will not be at the scene" (p. 347). As Eve's case illustrates, the global/local nexus of video game development, production, and distribution begs this question as well. To ask learners to engage these questions is to cultivate not only active engagement with video games, but also the meta-awareness that is the hallmark of critical literacy, particularly in an age of globalization. Thus, an expanded definition of what kinds of design grammars govern semiotic domains can help highlight the cultural and economic fields that surround the gaming industry, both complicating and enriching Gee's insights on what video games have to teach us about learning and literacy.

Notes

1. Throughout this chapter, we will refer to Eve in the third person. Although she is the coauthor of this chapter, she is its subject as well. Sections of her paper for an independent study on localization are quoted at length, both because they provide part of the argument about the significance of localization and because they offer evidence of the sophistication of Eve's critical thinking and how it has developed in the context of game play.
2. See Kress and Van Leeuwen (2001) for a discussion of distribution and production as significant semiotic components of multimodal discourse.
3. Eve actually has two PlayStations, one for U.S. games and one for Japanese games, because of region encoding.
4. For many serious computer users and programmers, it is a point of pride to exclude the Xbox from their list of game consoles in the same way that it means something to say that you use Linux rather than Windows. A quick Google search on the phrase "never buy an xbox" will bring up equal numbers of folks who will not buy it because of loyalty to other platform consoles and those who will not simply because it is a Microsoft product.
5. For specific examples see Thayer and Kolko (2004); Goize and Sinclair (2004); Pham and Sandell (2003).

References

Beck, John C., & Wade, Mitchell (2004). *Got game: How the gamer generation is reshaping business forever.* Boston, MA: Harvard Business School Press.

Brandt, Deborah, & Clinton, Katie. (2002). Limits of the local: Expanding perspectives on literacy as a social practice. *Journal of Literacy Research, 34*(3), 337–356.

Freeman, David (2003). *Creating emotion in games: The craft and art of emotioneering.* Indianapolis, IN: New Riders.

Gee, James P. (1996). *Social linguistics and literacies: Ideology in discourses.* London; Bristol, PA: Taylor & Francis.

Gee, James P. (2003). *What video games have to teach us about learning and literacy.* New York: Palgrave Macmillan.

Goize, Benjamin, & Sinclair, Brendan. (2004). Spot on: Singin' the localization blues. *Gamespot News.* Retrieved on February 15, 2005, from http://www.gamespot.com/xbox/action/kakutochojin/news_6105587.html

Hall, P.A.V., & Hudson, R. (1997). *Software without frontiers: A multi-platform, multi-nation, multi-cultural approach.* New York: Wiley.

Iwabuchi, Koichi. (2002). *Recentering globalization: Popular culture and Japanese transnationalism.* Durham, NC: Duke University Press.

Jameson, Fredric. (1998). Notes on globalization in a philosophical context. In Fredric Jameson & Masao Miyoshi (Eds.), *The cultures of globalization* (pp. 54–77). Durham, NC: Duke University Press.

Kress, Gunther, & Van Leeuwen, Theo. (2001). *Multimodal discourse: The modes and media of contemporary communication.* London: Arnold.

Microsoft (2000). Microsoft's Geopolitical Bug Experts. *Microsoft*. Retrieved May 15, 2005, from http://www.microsoft.com/presspass/features/2000/Dec00/12-06gps.mspx

New London Group. (2000). A pedagogy of multiliteracies. In Bill Cope & Mary Kalantzis (Eds.), *Multiliteracies: Literacy learning and the design of social futures* (pp. 9–37). London: Routledge.

Pham, Alex, & Sandell, Scott. (2003, June 9). Marketing video games in Germany is feat of skill. *Los Angeles Times*.

Pieterse, Jan N. (2004). *Globalization and culture: Global melange*. Lanham, MD: Rowman & Littlefield.

Schembri, Thierry, & Boisseau, Olivier. (1995). Commodore Vic-20. *Old-Computers.Com: The Museum*. Retrieved on February 15, 2005, from http://www.old-computers.com/museum/computer.asp?c=252&st=1

Street, Brian. (1984). *Literacy in theory and practice*. Cambridge: Cambridge University Press.

Thayer, Alex, & Kolko, Beth. (2004). Localization of digital games: The process of blending for the global games market. *Technical Communication, 51*(4), 477–488.

4

Gaming, Identity, and Literacy

Daniel Keller with Paul Ardis, Vivienne Dunstan,
Adam Thornton, Rachel Henry, and Brett Witty

Many of the games discussed in this book fall into the categories of shooter games (e.g., *James Bond* games, *Counter-Strike*), simulation/strategy (*Civilization*), or sports games. Most of these games are played on video consoles, and all of them feature graphical representations as a primary element. Neither of these qualities describes the games explored in this chapter, which deals with the genre of Interactive Fiction (IF). IF games are played only on computers and they are entirely text based. IF games trace their origins to the rise of computing and to paper-and-pencil role-playing games, such as *Dungeons and Dragons*, during the 1970s. IF's first games *Adventure* and *Zork* were also among the first computer games and led to the creation of Infocom, one of the most successful computer game companies of the 1980s. While IF games are no longer commercially viable, they are still being created, downloaded, and played by members of various Internet groups.

From Adam Cadre's *Photopia*

In the throne room

This room is just as big as the others you've seen, but unlike the others, this one contains a barnacle-encrusted object in the unmistakable shape of a chair; given the place you've found it and the fact that it's built into the floor, you can only conclude that it must be a throne. The far wall features a carved-out alcove that looks like it must have been a fireplace, though how one might go about lighting a fire underwater is anyone's guess. Mounted on the wall above the fireplace in an "X" shape are a pick-axe and a shovel.

An arched doorway leads east, but is completely blocked by debris. You can also go back the way you came.

>get shovel

You are unable to take the shovel: it's wedged behind the pickaxe.

>get pickaxe

The pickaxe clings firmly to the wall. You tug on it again and this time the handle moves a few centimeters; then you feel a distinct click. The castle begins to rumble, with the shaking most pronounced in the direction of the keep.

The shovel which was wedged behind the pickaxe clatters to the ground, and the rumbling stops. After that, the pickaxe swings back in to the place.

The Internet communities that create and share these games engage in reading and writing practices similar to those that teachers focus on in writing classrooms. In such games, player-authors become entrenched in the conventions of the genre through playing (reading) the games; familiarize themselves with the practices of the community and become a part of it, learning how to accumulate knowledge within an affinity group; and write, test, and revise games that are often beta tested (peer-reviewed) by others in the community before finally being published. Obviously, many differences exist between these IF communities and groups of students in composition classrooms, so one-to-one connections cannot be made. The goal of this chapter is to introduce readers to five IF players, and to explore their gaming and literacy practices within the context of learning principles articulated by James Gee in *What Video Games Have to Teach Us about Learning and Literacy* (2003)—specifically the principles concerning affinity groups, and the part they play in affecting genre, identity, choice, and assessment.

This chapter also aims to extend the discussion of IF to the teaching of writing. Many teachers of composition are well aware that we need to help students learn to see themselves as writers—in Gee's words, "to see themselves as the kind of person who can learn, use, and value the new semiotic domain" (p. 59). However, knowing this principle has not made teachers any better at implementing it in composition classrooms.

The five players on whom this chapter focuses all encountered IF games at early ages and, through them, gained extensive experience with digital and alphabetic literacies, which are now crucial elements of their educations and careers. Paul Ardis, for instance, is a 20-year-old computer science major at Purdue University. Similarly, Vivienne Dunstan is a 31-year-old PhD student of history at the University of Dundee, Scotland. Before turning to history studies, she was a computing undergraduate and postgraduate, with "plenty of experience of programming" in her 25 years of using computers. Rachel Henry is a 29-year-old graduate of MIT. Before becoming a full-time mom, she worked in the education department of a database software company. Adam **Thornton** is a 32-year-old Informational Technology (IT) consultant. Fluent in a **dozen** computer languages, he has been working professionally with computers **for 15 years.** Finally, Brett Witty is a 23-year-old PhD student of mathematics in **Canberra,** Australia.

Familial and Educational Gateways

Although this chapter refers to the case-study participants as "players" and "gamers," these individuals are far more than consumers and players of video games. Each has varying experience with conventional literacy, with creating IF games, and with producing digital texts. In Gee's terms, they have learned enough about their domain to make "active and critical choices" (2003, pp. 98–99) about IF and have become designers. The literacies of each contributor have been shaped by—and shaped—micro-, medial-, and macrolevel historical trends associated with digital literacy, the various social and economic contexts of literacy and gaming, and the literacy values and practices of their families and friends—among many, many other factors.

All of the contributors to this chapter, for example, felt that their parents had provided a strong level of support for their conventional alphabetic literacies. According to these five participants, their parents read widely and extensively, and encouraged their children to do the same. Brett, for example, noted that his parents put very few restrictions on his reading, encouraging him to read broadly and widely. As he recalls,

> My parents didn't mind what I read, and they encouraged me to write ever since I showed interest. My father read lots of books (mostly of the political thriller kind), and my mother read this and that (sometimes magazines, sometimes books). All throughout my life they have encouraged me to read whatever—so long as it wasn't offensive or "troublesome." I read a lot of everything (fantasy, sci-fi, real science, and various "interest" books).

Adam's parents had a similar attitude—they promoted the growth of his alphabetic print literacy in whatever form it took. Reading was reading was reading—even when it entailed "crappy" science fiction. As he explains,

> I suspect that I horrified my parents a little bit with all of the crappy SF I read, but I also devoured pretty much anything else within reach, which has led to my being, for instance, the only person under the age of sixty with Betty MacDonald's books banging around his head. I always preferred reading to pretty much any other entertainment, and my parents never really tried to restrict it. Occasionally, they'd point me in the direction of something—the *Alexandria Quartet,* Flannery O'Connor, Robertson Davies—but I also found a lot of my favorites (Baum and Tolkien among them) more or less on my own.

Like most of the gamers, Paul, too, "was always a bit of a bookworm," reading sci-fi and fantasy novels "almost exclusively, a habit which hasn't changed too much yet." His parents encouraged his reading and even modeled healthy reading habits. As he recalls:

> On a typical night, they'll both sit down in the living room and spend a couple of hours or more reading away. As a result, it was soon after I could read that I was entered in summer reading programs at the library.

Rachel and Vivienne had similar stories to tell about their family literacy values and practices. Vivienne's parents were both teachers and encouraged her "to read widely." Before she was 12, she was reading "well above" her age group, "devouring masses of books in the local public library and at home." Her school library had a "dire selection" except for "some classics." Her mother was of particular help when it came to Vivienne's voracious reading:

> As I got older I quickly outgrew the books in the children's section of the public library and my mother used to borrow books for me from the adult's section, including 1 volume at a time of *Lord of the Rings* until I'd read that.

Rachel's parents read the entire *Lord of the Rings* and *Narnia* series aloud to her before she could read on her own. Once Rachel could read by herself, her reading level quickly surpassed that of her peers, and her local library had a hard time supplying her demand. As she recalls,

> I remember reading 'chapter books' earlier than most of my peers. I would say by the time I was nine I was reading at an adult level and had exhausted the "kid books" section at the library.

Rachel's voracious reading continued through high school and college and is still a prominent part of her life. As she notes, "So far in 2004 I have read 26 novels, three non-fiction books, and listened to another three books on CD or tape."

The literacy environments that these parents established also depended, at least to some extent, on socioeconomic factors. Each family, for example, was able to provide their children with access to computers—in one form or another—when they were quite young. Paul, the child of two software engineers, remembers that he had extensive access to computers: "At home, we had two machines at any one time, and I would often glom on to one of them for hours at a time to play various computer games." He fondly recalls playing computer games with his father:

> When I first played "Colossal Cave," it was with my dad. . . . The way it worked was that we'd sit side-by-side at the computer (with me at the keyboard) and would talk about the next move before doing it. His work was quite involving at the time, so I felt a bit restricted and soon moved on to playing by myself. However, I do remember enjoying those sessions with my dad, who I've idolized since a very young age.

Brett's family, too, purchased a computer when he was relatively young. As he notes,

> We got our first proper computer—a 286—when I was about ten. I originally became proficient with the computer because I wanted to write my stories on the computer and play games.

With access to a computer, Brett quickly learned QuickBASIC and Visual Basic, programming "graphic displays, extremely basic physics models, random story writers, experiments in cryptography and the beginnings of games." In his experiments, he was always "either learning something new or trying to do something I had seen in a game."

Much like Paul and Brett, Vivienne was using a computer at home by the age of nine, and some of her fondest memories of playing games date back to that time, playing IF on a sluggish Commodore 64 and MUDs on the Internet, which caused her to rack up quite a long-distance bill:

> Usually I'd be playing IF on the Commodore 64, and IF was a very long-drawn-out experience then, typically waiting ages for the game to load, quite a pause between turns, and disk-loading of new sections. Around this time I also remember playing MUD via phone/modem through Prestel in the UK. I ran up quite a big phone bill over a couple of days, and remember getting in trouble with my parents.

Rachel and Adam had their earliest computing experiences not at home, but at friends' houses and at their parents' workplaces. Rachel, for instance, reports using "computers recreationally about as long as they have existed." Although Rachel did not have access to a computer at home, she did have access to these machines at school and at her mother's workplace. Most of her computer use, as a child, was limited to schoolwork—"writing papers, working on the school literary magazine, or something for my creative writing classes." Rachel played games at her mother's workplace as well, sometimes playing IF with her mom. As she recalls,

> When I was a kid my mom would do the typing. We both read [the screen] independently and made suggestions about what to try. Usually we kept a map that we would both add to. We solved the puzzles cooperatively.

Adam, too, played games at his dad's workplace—a Chevy dealership—and at a friend's house, using computers with now-obscure titles: PDP-11 and TI 99-4/A. From grade six through high school, Adam had an Apple II. Describing himself as "part of the generation who can code," Adam was programming games and doing "lots of (very slow) mathematical visualization" at a young age. Adam has been working professionally with computers for 15 years and is now an IT consultant. In particular, Adam realizes his good fortune at being born at the right time and in the right socioeconomic situation and to parents who did not make his computer-gaming existence too difficult:

> My parents were well-off enough to afford a computer and they didn't fuss too terribly much about the amount of time I spent playing with it. In a lot of ways I'm just lucky to be the age that I am, and that I had the opportunity to obsessively fiddle with something that ultimately turned out to be a decent career. If I were five years older, instead of being a relatively well-paid computer geek, I'd have been one of those guys in the Car Club always tinkering trying to get an extra three horsepower out of his engine, and I'd be a much-less-well-paid mechanic.

Adam's recognition of his having entered the world on the cusp of the computer age is important when considering how he and the other players became involved with IF. Because they were raised in families that encouraged reading and enabled access to computers, these players were the ideal audience for games based on the concept of interactive stories related solely through text. When Infocom formed in 1979 and released its first IF game, *Zork,* it was entering a computer game market in which graphic technology was rudimentary, allowing only for simple line drawings and a limited color palette. Even though competing games' graphics were not terribly impressive, Infocom still had to draw consumers away from such games to convince them that its offering of textual worlds was a better choice.

One of the key challenges that Infocom faced was to make the case to U.S. consumers that text-based game entertainment was not a waste of money and computer equipment. Arguably the most successful purveyor of IF, Infocom capitalized on the fact that the middle-class families—then beginning to buy computers in large numbers—were also readers. The company marketed its games accordingly, taking the unusual approach of selling its games alongside both digital texts and print texts in computer game stores *and* bookstores. In addition, the box descriptions of these games typically referenced both print and literary antecedents. *A Mind Forever Voyaging,* for instance, name-dropped Huxley and Orwell; while *The Lurking Horror* was described as part H. P. Lovecraft and part Stephen King. Infocom also involved an author in a book-to-game translation when Douglas Adams coauthored the game version of his *Hitchhiker's Guide to the Galaxy.* Whereas many game companies during this period included only a disk and an instruction manual in their game packaging, Infocom included short magazines that related to the game's story, masterfully easing readers of print texts into the environments of computer-based gaming.

Brett explains the attraction of book readers to IF in this way:

> Such people naturally adapted and were drawn to computers, but were familiar with traditional books and didn't like the arcade-style entertainment usually offered. Although off-the-beaten-track, IF offered the intellectual challenge of books and benefits of a simulated environment. I would think that such people would adapt to computers regardless of what is available. IF is just a nice niche for people like that.
>
> IF offers something novel (pardon the pun) in that you have the potential for something as literary as a novel, but as adaptive as a computer program.

Although IF games clearly involved reading and writing, the parents of the five case-study subjects were not easily convinced that their children were learning in gaming environments or that computer games were part of the equation for academic success. Almost all the parents of case-study participants viewed games as entertainment rather than education, and—perhaps more importantly—came to understand games and education as part of a play/work dichotomy. Vivienne's parents, for example, made distinctions between educational and noneducational software—and IF was not considered to be the former. As Vivienne recalls,

> My parents didn't view IF or other computer games as educational tools. Games were fun. There were more educational uses of the home computer, like learning to program or using custom-written educational software (e.g., language learning programs).

Similarly, although Adam's parents "didn't fuss too terribly much" about the extensive time he spent on computers, they did consider his computer time less valuable than the time he spent reading books. Within the hierarchy of the family's literacy values, moreover, playing video games and watching TV came at the bottom of the heap:

> While my parents encouraged reading, they were less sanguine about ridiculous computer overuse. It was difficult to make the case that the computer was somehow different than video games (which, to be fair, much of the time it wasn't), and those were down there with TV in the don't-overdo-it realm.

For Paul, at this age, games were banned entirely unless they were being played on the computer. Paul remembers that his parents "declared a moratorium on video game consoles," but not on computer games; he imagines that they made such a distinction because they wanted him to gain experience with computers, even if the experiences came from games:

> My parents disapproved of the obsessive factor of video game consoles and believed (wrongly) that such would not be duplicated on a PC. Also, though they would not likely admit to this, they both wished me to gain a strong interest in computing, since both of them are computer scientists; I did build up such an interest, after all.

In contrast, neither Brett's parents nor his teachers played a significant role in shaping the specific uses he made of time spent on the computer. His friends, however, exerted an important influence:

> My teachers had little to do with my early computer training and by the time that they were in a position to help me, I already knew as much as them. My parents weren't particularly computer literate, but some of my friends were, so I guess my friends influenced me the most with regard to computers. The friends led to playing games which led to programming.

Gee notes that "a number of the young people" he interviewed found video games to be a "fruitful precursor domain for mastering other semiotic domains tied to computers and related technologies" (2003, p. 48). This observation is supported by numerous stories of individuals who grew up as gamers later being hired by professional game-development companies (King & Borland, 2003). This pattern finds credence in the case studies on which this chapter focuses. For most of the participants featured here, games served as a primary gateway to learning programming.

At the same time, for many of these players, this important gateway proved somewhat difficult both to find and enter. Gaming was often discouraged at home and in school. The schools attended by the case-study participants, for instance, generally promoted computers only for academic uses: working on the school paper, writing essays, learning programming. Game playing, of course, was prohibited. Even in this context, however, Adam and Paul found ways around such restrictions. By the age of 12, for example, Adam was already making "menu-based text adventures for the Apple II." His school's computer lab "prohibited game playing, but programming was perfectly fine." To get around this restriction, Adam and his friends learned the programming language BASIC and used the lab's computers to write simple adventure games for each other to play.

Paul's high school also served as a gateway for his digital literacy, but, like Adam's school, this gateway was not entirely an open one. Most of Paul's teachers, for instance, instead of encouraging technological skills, set up their classrooms so that they were "independent from machines"; Paul was not even allowed to use a calculator in his calculus class. Nor was he encouraged to take a programming course—the word among students was that these courses were "slow and worthless." Paul and his classmates knew enough about computers to realize that their school curriculum was inadequate, and they knew how to get around the school's rules on the "non-academic uses" of computers in order to play games:

> The only time that I saw a computer during the school day was when my friends and I went up to the computer lab in the library to play games. The administration of my school frowned upon the computers being used for non-academic uses, so they installed a program (I forget the name) which blocked specified URLs that they would store. At the time, my friends and I liked playing games on a site that was called Virtual Arcade.

> Having seen one student go to this site, the lab admin blocked the URL http://www.virtualarcade.com, believing that this would solve the problem. However, we discovered that simply using www.virtualarcade.com (without the protocol listed) would be interpreted within the browser as correct for the site but would not be stopped by the block. Realizing (weeks later) that we had done this, the admin blocked all protocol attempts directed at www.virtualarcade.com, again thinking that the problem was solved.

> However . . . we would use URL obfuscation techniques (such as using character codes for letters) in order to get around the block. By this time, the admin had started logging all sites I (and I believe one other of my friends) visited. They would block all sites that we visited with games on them, but we found various mirror pages and alternate locations each day. In a way, it was another game that we played: annoy the admin. . . . We were always looking for new (and increasingly more obscure) ways to make the job harder.

In college the case-study participants found both their print and digital literacies to be of value. But their more formal experiences with programming and computers in college courses lacked the creative dimension of writing and programming games. As Rachel noted,

> I find myself much more motivated to figure out programming problems and algorithms if there's a game puzzle behind the problem—and much *less* motivated by the usual problems presented by regular programming classes.

Vivienne, too, was struck by the differences between her informal, self-sponsored adventures with coding and the more formal approaches to programming fostered in computer science courses. Before converting to history studies, Vivienne completed a bachelor's degree in computer science and started a PhD in it. She quickly came to the conclusion that playing and coding IF and MUDs offered a "crucial" creative outlet—and one that balanced the "very mechanical process" of her coursework:

> Go into the computing lab for the required amount of time, implement the program (having designed it beforehand), write it up, and then hand it in for marking, etc. It

was far less about being creative, and far more about implementing. [IF] was fun, something I chose to do in my spare time, and for my entertainment. Crucially, it also tapped into my imaginative side, something that my studies completely failed to address.

Brett's take on this matter has to do with the difference between the coding he did for games and that which he completed during more formal coursework. For Brett, programming classes were "essentially linear" in their approach to problem solving, while coding games were "nonlinear." In some important ways, this contrast between traditional programming and the coding that players do for games, may mirror the sharp division between how students are taught to write in many composition classes and how they choose to write when authoring self-sponsored creative works. Most college students, for instance, are asked to limit their writing in introductory composition class to nonfiction prose and to focus on a relatively narrow set of assignments and approaches. Although many of these students come to college enjoying the practice of self-sponsored creative writing—in online chat rooms and in digital gaming environments, for instance—they are discouraged from even thinking about these practices as "writing" of the kind they are asked to do in school. It does not escape the notice of students, for instance, that fictional genres are scarcely found in composition handbooks and readers. Many students, moreover, are discouraged from writing fiction and poetry except in creative writing classes. Such experiences may contribute to students' general lack of enthusiasm for college-level writing classes.

For Brett, writing IF has provided a different perspective on composing print novels as well as on coding programs. As a writer of "novels, poems, articles—both technical and fun, and (of course) IF," Brett is experienced in multiple genres and has gained an expanded awareness of print literacy. In articulating what he has gained from his IF experiences, Brett illustrates what Gee calls metalevel thinking (2003, p. 50) and the principle of intertextuality (p. 108)—both of which are crucial to learning:

> In conventional writing, most problems of plotting, pacing, point-of-view and characters aren't that difficult to deal with. But in IF, due to its nonlinear nature, you have to really think about these considerations. You also have to willingly sacrifice some of these aspects in order to have a more smooth gaming experience. For example, you can almost never calculate the pace of a game without making it run on rails [forcing the player's choices and trajectory]. In a book, you have full control over pacing and so you are obliged to worry about it. [With a book] you never have to worry about readers' personalities, whereas in IF . . . games need to be fully debugged to satisfy the poke-and-prod players, [and] they need to be well-written to satisfy the literary types.

Choice and Identity

As Gee notes, three identities are at play in a video game—virtual, real, and projective. The virtual identity is often referred to by gamers as the Player Character (PC), the character that players control in the game world. The real identity is the player's, which, as Gee notes, consists of multiple nonvirtual identities that "are filtered through" the game-playing experience and affect the player's choices. The projective identity is one that the player "projects" onto the virtual character, specifically in terms of values and goals (pp. 54–55). Given that these values and goals must operate with the predetermined (programmed) characteristics of the virtual identity, projective identity is shared between the player's real and virtual identities (p. 56), between the player and the PC. Gee further states that the involvement of the "tripartite play of identities" in video games is "at the root of active and critical learning in many other semiotic domains, including learning content actively and critically in school" (p. 59).

Many of the helpful concepts that Gee uses to explain how real, virtual, and projective identities work—identity repair (p. 61) and Eric Erickson's *psychosocial moratorium* (p. 62)—are familiar, in one form or another, to composition instructors. For instance, Gee refers to three principles associated with identity repair work that composition teachers should find, in his words, "pretty basic":

1. The learner must be enticed to try, even if he or she already has good grounds to be afraid to try.
2. The learner must be enticed to put in lots of effort even if he or she begins with little motivation to do so.
3. The learner must achieve some meaningful success when he or she has expended this effort. (pp. 61–62)

Similarly, most writing teachers will have little difficulty understanding Gee's explanation of how video-game environments make use of Erickson's concept of *psychosocial moratorium*. Gee, for instance, notes that games create "a learning space in which the learner can take risks where real-world consequences are lowered" (p. 62), a space in which there is "a relatively low cost of failure and high reward for success" (p. 63). Many composition teachers use these same concepts to structure the low-risk environments of writing classrooms.

According to the case-study participants in this chapter, the identity work that goes on in gaming has a great deal to do with *choice*—an observation also made by the participant-authors in chapter 8, Stephanie Fleischer's and Susan Wright's chapter in this book. One of the main reasons players are drawn to IF is that a well-designed game offers a range of options. Rachel, for example, plays "a lot of computer games" and thinks that some games come close to being IF, but "too often the narratives are simplistic and linear and confining, like a really bad piece of IF." She likes games in which "the player's actions should make a difference. I don't like it when the author has left only one course of action, and stops all other behaviors."

Paul, too, prefers IF to graphic-based computer games. As he notes, such games are

an interesting distraction but often not as deep or engaging as IF can be due to the lack of user interaction within the story (arcs are predefined, actions are limited to a small set of possibilities within the game rules).

Because IF games are text based, designers can more easily program multiple PC actions and game responses into the story. In graphic-based games, programming multiple options for the player becomes a phenomenal task. As Adam explains,

> Graphic games tend to be less involving, simply because the amount of effort to create as much plausible response to player choice is so much huger if you actually need to draw, animate, or model the player's world, instead of just writing about it.

At some level, then, the options that IF offers can help players project identities into the game-playing world and to learn within its domain. For writing teachers, this observation, too, rings true. Providing students multiple options for writing and more freedom for expression often provides individuals the space they need to engage productively with assignments.

Gee's analysis of the tripartite identities he personally experienced when gaming hints at some additional complexity in connection with this issue. Gee observes that his role-playing game (RPG) character Bead-Bead allowed him greater interaction among the identities than did the Master Chief character he assumed in the first-person shooter *Halo* (p. 58). When Gee, as a real-world player took on the virtual identity of Master Chief, his projective identity was limited; in a game in which hordes of alien creatures try to kill you, if the real-world player wishes to be merciful and *not* annihilate every alien creature that materializes, it's going to be a terribly brief game. However, in the RPG character of Bead-Bead, Gee found a larger fictional space available for projecting his real-world desires and goals, and more choices available for determining his own actions, even though the programmed parameters of the virtual character were not infinite.

The importance of Gee's observations here is that the identities at play in gaming environments seem to be reflexive in their interaction:

> Once the player has made some choices about the virtual character, the virtual character is now developed in a way that sets certain parameters about what the player can do. The virtual character rebounds back on the player and affects his or her future actions. (p. 58)

Many of Gee's statements about identity and gaming environments find validation in the comments of the case-study participants. As Gee notes, these players sometimes "feel responsible to and for the character. They are projecting an identity as to who the character ought to be and what the trajectory of his or her acts in the virtual world ought, at the end of the day, to look like" (p. 58). Rachel, for example, notes:

> I find myself identifying with and subsuming into the PC. I want to care about their worries, understand their limitations, etc. In the best stories, what the player has to do to solve puzzles (push stuff around, put X in Y, and so on) all makes sense within the confines of the tale, and doesn't require me to dissociate from the PC in order to make progress as a puzzle-solver.

Some of the other case-study gamers, however, want their projective identity to be less dependent on the virtual character's programmed traits. Vivienne, for instance, prefers "the PC to be more of a blank slate for me to define . . . as neutral as possible, even in terms of gender." Brett concurs, stating that he will often try to ignore the PC's parameters set by the game's author:

> I usually feel as though the PC is my own character, almost regardless of how the author writes it. I do shape my own mental picture around what is presented, but my approach from game to game is extremely similar. I hate games where they force you to act out a character with no leeway.

Vivienne and Brett, then, prefer more choice and latitude in defining their projective identity and their actions as characters. As Paul puts it,

> The PC should have some characteristics that the author decides upon which give a sense of backstory, but should not overly impinge upon the play of the user unless they wish to force role playing upon them.

For Adam, his relation to the PC "depends very much on the game." Many IF games—especially the older games that were strings of puzzles—provide little detail to the identity of the virtual character. Adam finds that his sense of projective identity is at its largest "in games with the Ageless, Faceless, Gender-Neutral Protagonist, where, hey, it's *me* wandering through the Great Underground Empire [the setting of the classic *Zork* series]." However, Adam is also interested in games that provide a virtual identity with strong traits already determined:

> I adored playing the female servant in *Metamorphoses,* and I understood how being female and of the lower classes critically informed her perspective on her job and her life, which showed up, very subtly, as I dug through the game. Tracy Valencia [the PC in *Interstate Zero*] made me feel a little sleazy, because I felt like the game was very much intending for me to play her all slutty. The protagonist in *Anchorhead* needed to be female for the ending to have the force it did. . . . Sometimes it's neat to be forced into a very strange viewpoint: the robot in *Lash,* the one in *BadMachine,* someone hallucinating and dying of thirst in *Shad.*

Even though each player has his or her own preference for the play of tripartite identities, all of the players recognize, as Adam does above, that the degree of projection depends upon the game and the level of choice it allows. Put another way, in gaming environments, there are multiple levels of identity involvement, and the appropriate level of involvement is decided by both author and player. As Rachel explains,

> The author provides a framework for the PC, onto which the player is projected. There is room for variation, but the author should provide some direction. How much is needed depends on the story at hand—for example, in *Jigsaw,* it doesn't really matter [who the PC is]. But in *Anchorhead,* it's critical that you're the wife of this guy who has inherited a creepy old house, and that you love him, etc.

Gaming, Identity, and the Teaching of Composition

What can composition teachers learn from the literacy practices and values, from the life stories of these case-study subjects? Although generalizing from their experiences to the writing classroom is impossible, some tentative observations may be in order.

Observation #1

Students may enjoy reading and writing in gaming environments because these spaces succeed in providing each individual the degree of choice they require to invest productively and enjoyably in a projective identity.

Throughout the interviews with these case-study participants, each gamer expressed clear views on the relationship between identity and choice, factors crucial to their enjoyment of IF. In IF, identity and choice depend upon decisions made by both the game's author and player. When the author has programmed multiple options, the player has greater choice in how to shape the PC, the projective identity. Extending the author-player relationship to the teacher-student situation in the writing classroom can be illuminating.

> Brett: I hate games where they force you to act out a character with no leeway. It's like being an actor where you are forbidden to explore the role.
>
> Vivienne: [A] poor interactive experience [gives] the impression that the author is telling a story, a preset story, and the player is just playing it straight back, with little opportunity to influence it, or to discover it in new ways.
>
> Rachel: The author provides a framework for the PC, onto which the player is projected. There is room for variation, but the author should provide some direction.

Student writers similarly want some direction from teachers, but most do not want all of their decisions to be predetermined—to be given assignments "with no leeway." Teachers should provide the framework for students to form projective identities as writers, and this framework will shift according to the writing situation. In freewriting exercises, for instance, most teachers allow students to write with complete freedom; of course, such freedom is rarely "complete" because most students are aware that their writings might be shared with other students or the teacher. If teachers and students were to discuss the rhetorical constraints of such situations, they might then alter the projected identity in the freewriting—to write "freely" with a particular tone or with a particular audience in mind. Alternating between freewriting and these more directed freewriting exercises might help students practice with different projected identities in the classroom.

Playing with identity and choice could then continue in longer writing assignments. Instead of giving students assignments that are either specific or open in purpose, audience, and tone, teachers can give students a range of options not only in the topic itself but in the rhetorical choices. Writing instructors do not have to exhaust the possibilities (and themselves) in creating such assignments; they can devise a few examples of how students might adjust purpose, audience, and tone in a particular assignment, and then give students the option to devise their own.

Observation #2

Games provide low-risk environments and continuous assessment, reinforcing positive choices and encouraging players to take risks. Teachers should mirror these principles with low-stakes writing assignments and positive feedback.

From Infocom's *Borderzone*
The sounds of dogs barking madly and soldiers barking orders are close upon you. A muddled explosion—a signal flare lightens the sky with a red-orange glow. Before you can react, you are spotted! Brilliant white searchlights are aimed upon you, blinding you long enough for more soldiers and border guards to arrive. With no hope of escape, you surrender to the guards, and are led away, handcuffed, to the border station.
**** You have been arrested ****
Would you like to start over, restore a saved position, get a hint, or end this session of the game?
(Type RESTART, RESTORE, HINT, or QUIT)

In most video games, you are given a chance to restart the game or to restore to a saved position. Either way, you get to keep trying. In the composition classroom, the obvious counterpart is, of course, revision. Letting students try again and again without penalty to their grade is one way to create a low-risk environment. However, when students only have a few major assignments that count toward their grade, the writing situation seems much more fraught—even with revision. Providing only a few major assignments makes sense from a teacher's point of view: we have only so much time to plan for class, assign papers, and respond to them. Yet video game players are accustomed to different levels of risk and assessment in video games.

From Infocom's *Wishbringer*
Mr. Crisp reaches under the service counter and pulls out a mysterious envelope. "We just got this Special Delivery," he snarls, tossing it onto the service counter. "I want you to drop it off right away. That means NOW!"
>get envelope
Taken
(Your score just went up by 5 points! Your total score is 6 out of 100.)

Vivienne observes that IF games are similar to coursework that provides "smaller modular steps and continuous assessment." These smaller steps are assessed in IF when points are attributed to actions such as *get key, unlock door.* When players gain points, they are being rewarded for positive actions; the game is encouraging particular kinds of behavior that will serve the player well throughout the game. Vivienne notes that the learning that takes place throughout the game is often more important than the end point, a feeling she compares to coursework:

> Whenever I've got to the end of a course there's been a similar anticlimactic sense to finishing an IF game. Yes there may be a final mark, but I've been more conscious of the learning taking place while in the course itself and working on the smaller essays/projects/whatever that form the continuous assessment element. Remember that many IF games reward puzzle solving by increasing the player's score. IF players are aware of that, and it's a type of reward that isn't too dissimilar from getting a grade in continuous assessment.

Holistic grading and portfolio assessment are some ways in which the "anticlimactic sense" of the coursework is countered. These methods also stress the learning that has taken place over the term. As for the "smaller modular steps" described by Vivienne, teachers could provide more low-stakes writing assignments. Even though teachers may have to spend some time responding to these early in the semester, they could have students assess each other and themselves as the semester progresses (through rubrics and peer-review sheets/letters). Multiple smaller assignments and lots of positive feedback from the teacher and peers could help students to restart and revise—and not to quit.

Observation #3

The practices of affinity groups help players become insiders, critical users of the domain. In making the classroom into a community of writers, teachers could model some of these practices.

Playing and creating IF games may seem like isolated endeavors as they happen, but they actually involve a great community effort. IF affinity groups have set up numerous Internet sites and Usenet discussion groups to post games, game walkthroughs, opportunities for beta testing, FAQ lists, how-to manuals (for playing and creating games), and discussion threads for both theoretical and practical concerns. When Brett joined the community, he found a lot of people "just committed to making darn good games. There was a lot of help and seemingly few trolls. In short, it was a community, not a collection." He has written reviews of games, participated in beta testing, and runs a LiveJournal on IF. Brett participates within this affinity group and expects his efforts to be reciprocated: "I do all of these things because I love IF and the community, and I feel like I should give something back if I can. [In return], I request beta testing, programming info and feedback from the community. I think it's a fair trade."

Rachel went to the IF Usenet groups for help with writing her game. She knew how to become part of the group—she would have to participate before asking for help. As she states,

> I knew I would need help, and I also knew my questions would be more welcome (and more likely to get an answer) if I had a feel for the group and had perhaps contributed some answers myself. Mostly, I hoped to gain help learning [the programming language], *inform*, and help others out in return.

Their participation with an affinity group is part of what has made all five participants insiders. As writing teachers, we hope to instill our students with a sense of community so that they can learn from each other as writers. But what seems to happen more often is that they become a *collection,* and *not* a community. Studying the behaviors and practices of video game affinity groups may provide teachers with some methods for developing writing affinity groups.

For instance, having students create and add to an FAQ list from one semester to the next is one way of promoting the idea that writers are not born geniuses, scribbling brilliant, muse-inspired prose; instead, an FAQ list would be an excellent method of proving how knowledge is shared and distributed among writers. Starting an FAQ would be simple enough: students come up with questions about grammar, essay conventions, and research methods all the time. As the FAQ is passed from class to class, and as students revise and add material, they would credit themselves for the questions and answers they provide.

Online discussion groups (through e-mail listservs or online bulletin boards) would be another way to mirror the practices of video game affinity groups. Here, students can post writings and ask for feedback; ask and answer questions that might become an FAQ list; and post links to websites that help with grammar, development, research, and so on. Getting students to participate in such discussions is tricky. Making online participation a part of their grade is one way to encourage participation. But another, less coercive method might be to help them understand the purposes of and proper behaviors within an affinity group. To that end, assigning students to study online affinity groups—how they function, how people behave, how negative behavior is classified and treated, etcetera—may be one step in asking students to help develop the rules for their discussion group. Teachers could gather a few colleagues to make initial posts, modeling the kind of interaction that is expected. And, if possible, posts could be made available across semesters, so that the knowledge created and shared by one class benefits the next class, which would only help to encourage similar behaviors.

Conclusion

It is probably impossible to replicate in the classroom the exact level of engagement students have with games. The pleasure of playing IF, for instance, comes through encountering story, puzzle, identity alteration, interaction, fantasy, or mystery, etc—all in a low-risk environment. Given the necessary context of the classroom, with its grades and judgment of teachers and peers, removing risk entirely from writing situations is not feasible. However, such risks can be mitigated. Through producing assignments and exercises that offer identity choices, low-stakes situations, and possibilities for becoming insiders, we can create learning experiences that come closer to students' preferred ways of learning.

References

Gee, James Paul. (2003). *What video games have to teach us about learning and literacy*. New York: Palgrave Macmillan.

King, Brad, and John Borland. (2003). *Dungeons and dreamers: The rise of computer game culture from geek to chic*. New York: McGraw-Hill.

What Some Girls Say about Gaming

Brynn Carlson, Age 5 ½

My favorite game is called *Cory's Money Maze*. I like it because me and my sister play it together. It is fun because you get to move your fingers real fast as you are running around. Our score is ranked against all the other online players. Another game is called *Science Blaster Junior*. I play this at school a lot. It is about outer space. I get to do a "pound thing" where monsters come up. If they have the right gem, then you smash them with the hammer. You have to match the numbers of gems with the right colors to win. There are also other games in *Science Blaster*.

Anna Prior, Age 12

Some of my favorite games are *Harvest Moon* (gameboy), *Zoombinies* (computer), *Word Munchers* (computer), *Tetris* (video game and cell phones), and *Carmon's Math Adventures* (computer). *Harvest Moon* is just a fun game. I like the logic and thoughtfulness that *Zoombinies*, *Word Munchers*, and *Carmon's Math Adventures*. *Tetris* is just addictive!!

In *Harvest Moon* you actually have to do things that you normally do like sleep, eat, etc. There is one of your friends who owns a farm, and he left it to you to take care of while he is gone. Yet it is kind of your own because you get to buy horses, cattle, cats, dogs, etc. The Zoombinies are these weird little creatures whose homeland was taken over. So your job is to get the Zoombinies to their new home through various logic and matching puzzles. In *Word Munchers* you choose a category of words and have to pick the words from that category out of a group of words. You also have these monsters that eat up word munchers and you have to swerve. In *Carmon's Math Adventures* you are a secret agent who is trying to stop Carmon from shrinking big monuments that stand for special things in our world (Brooklyn Bridge, Eiffel Tower, etc.). So your job is to find and break the codes so you can get all of the things Carmon shrunk back to normal size. Ah Tetris!! This game is kind of hard to explain. Basically you have to put a puzzle together really fast with only one chance to put it in the right place. The music is what I think addicts you.

I have something you should take into account when you look at what I have answered. I do not play as many computer, gameboy, video, and cell-phone games as most kids my age. It is weird if at least one kid doesn't have and play a gameboy or cell phone in class. Whether he/she gets in trouble is another question. The point is I am not quite as into video games as other people are.

Kylie Carlson, Age 8

My first favorite game is *Jump Start 3rd Grade*. I enjoy playing this game because it is different from a lot of the other games. Polly, a girl, who is also the inventor's daughter, sends robots back in time using her father's time machine. What I have to do in this game is move around his mansion trying to find clues. A robot helps me find the clues. If I find all three and earn enough invention points I get to go to a place where I'm asked questions about the clues. I learn about the clues because of the questions. The clues are all items that have been invented in the past. Once I find out who, where, what, and why the clue was invented, I get to go in the time machine. I rescue the robot and put it back in its home.

I also like a lot of the games that are on disneychannel.com. One of them is called *Cory's Money Maze*. In this game you move around a house collecting money without running into various people running into you. I like the games because the games use the same characters of my favorite Disney shows. I like being able to put myself into a setting with the characters—I like being in place with them.

At school I play a game called *Rodeo West*. In this game you have to solve various math problems. There are other games as well, but they all involve solving math questions. Some are multiplication, some division, some just adding and subtracting. There are some questions about "place value" also. You can choose a level which is a name of a horse and you solve the problems until you miss one. The higher the level, the less time you have to answer the question. When you finally miss a question, the horse will do a trick according to how many questions you got right. I like trying to get the highest score.

References

Carlson, Brynn. (2004, May 27). Personal interview.
Carlson, Kylie. (2004, May 27). Personal interview.
Prior, Anna. (2004, May 11). Personal interview.

Part II

The Social Dimensions of Gaming

5

Narrative, Action, and Learning: The Stories of *Myst*

Debra Journet

Real learning is active and always a new way of experiencing the world.

(James Gee, What Video Games Have to Teach Us
about Learning and Literacy, p. 26)

The system by which people organize their experience in, knowledge about, and transactions with the social world . . . is narrative rather than conceptual.

(Jerome Bruner, Acts of Meaning, *p. 35)*

One of James Gee's (2003) most powerful arguments for learning in video games is the "situated meaning principle," or the claim that "the meanings of signs . . . are situated in embodied experience" (p. 58). Elaborating on Gee's analysis, I argue that video games make virtual experiences feel embodied or real to players through their narrative shape. Video games narrate an imagined world in which the purposive actions of players characters have consequences, and it is in relation to this story that learning becomes situated. Narrative thus provides a contextual framework through which actions come to have meaning. This sense of embodied meaning is created not only by the player's growing understanding of the game's unfolding story lines, but also by the developing narrative of game play generated by her own dramatic engagement with the game itself.

Embodiment is an important concept for Gee because it calls attention to the way "learning is not just a matter of what goes on inside people's heads but is fully embedded in (situated within) a material, social, and cultural world" (p. 8). This view of learning as contextual and situated has also been very important in composition studies, which has increasingly emphasized the material, social, and cultural dimensions of writing. Thus, many composition pedagogies focus not on discrete or isolated skills but on ways of enacting and communicating meaning within diverse worlds—a view of learning and teaching that resonates well with Gee's claim that "reading and thinking [and I would add composing] are social achievements connected to social groups" (p. 3). Learning to value and participate in the literate practices of particular groups thus means more than acquiring forms and conventions; it also requires learners to be able to recognize and participate in the ways those groups think, read, write, speak, and otherwise communicate in order to make meaning.[1]

Learning, then, according to Gee and to much composition scholarship, is connected to identity; as humans enter new semiotic domains, new ways of making meaning, they acquire new identities and connect those identities to other identities already formed (Gee, p. 51). But those identities do not come ready-made; they must be experienced and constructed within specific contextual frameworks. In other words, learning requires the learner to be able to tell new stories about herself or to find new ways of narrating her relation to the world—as, for example, a student, a scientist, or a gamer. Identity can thus be understood as a set of narrative practices by which people organize and interpret themselves and the world they live in.[2]

Storytelling is one of the most compelling activities humans engage in, evoking what Peter Brooks (1984) has called "narrative desire," or a relationship to narrative that "carries us forward, onward through the text" (p. 37). Narrative desire is both mimetic and performative, a way stories are shaped and a process by which stories are comprehended: "Narratives both tell of desire—typically present some story of desire—and arouse and make use of desire a dynamic of signification" (Brooks, p. 37). Many video games offer compelling stories of desire, such as the quest for lost treasures or the rescue of a civilization. But because games put players directly into the action, they are also very effective in allowing players to engage themselves in a narrative of signification: as players solve riddles or look for new locations, they are pushed forward by the unfolding and directional movement of game play. In this chapter, I argue that these two forms of narrative—the stories in the game and the stories about playing the game—contribute directly to the kinds of active learning Gee finds characteristic of good video games. Moreover, the kind of narrative engagement with new forms of knowledge that is so compelling and provocative in video games may also be a feature of other kinds of learning, including the forms of reading and composing valued in academic settings such as English classes.

Video games succeed, Gee claims, when "they situate meaning in multimodal space through embodied experiences to solve problems and reflect on the intricacies of the design of imagined worlds and the design of both real and imagined social relationships and identities in the modern world" (p. 48). These goals are familiar to English teachers, who also hope to offer students opportunities to create meaning as readers and writers. In particular, we often ask students to solve problems, such as interpreting, critiquing, arguing, analyzing, synthesizing; to recognize and attend to the intricacies of specific details; and to relate these experiences to other experiences in their lives. Additionally, we would probably like our students to feel that reading and composing alphabetic texts is as engaging and entertaining as playing video games—or, ideally, even more so. One way to do this, I suggest, is to look carefully at how successful video games employ and evoke narrative desire. In particular, games underscore the importance of situating knowledge and knowledge-making in narrative modes; of paying attention to contextual, storied character of learning; and of finding texts and tasks that evoke narrative desire in students and teachers.

My argument that narrative provides an important way to understand the experience of playing video games exists, however, within a dense and ongoing theoretical debate about the degree to which video games are or are not narrative.[3] Critics who argue that computer games are narrative generally point to the way recognizable stories are embedded into most computer games. Critics who argue that computer games are not narrative see these stories as peripheral to what they consider the essential qualities of game play, especially player agency or interactivity. Much of this debate focuses on how key concepts—such as "games" or "narrative"—are defined. But for the most part, definitions of narrative are drawn from structuralist or "narratological" theories that deal primarily with how narrative is organized and represented in literary texts. In particular, structuralist theories of narrative emphasize the distinction between "story" (the sequence of causally and chronologically related events enacted by characters in settings) and "discourse" (the manner of telling or modes of representation through which the underlying story is revealed).[4] Thus, arguments that computer games are narrative tend to focus on the way the "same story" can be told in different discourses or media, whereas arguments that games are not narrative tend to underline the ways game elements change story.

This debate has been remarkably vigorous. Henry Jenkins (2004) describes, for example, the "blood feud" that has "threatened to erupt" between "the self-proclaimed ludologists, who want to see the focus shift onto the mechanics of game play, and the narratologists, who were interested in studying games alongside other storytelling media" (p. 118). But the general debate, Jenkins argues, is often characterized as a "series of conceptual blind spots" that prevent a "full understanding of the interplay between narrative and games" (p. 120). Most important to my argument is Jenkins's claim that discussion about the relation of games and narrative generally "operates with too limited an understanding of narration, focusing more on the activities and aspirations of the storyteller and too little on the process of narrative comprehension" (p. 121). Jenkins thus invites us to reframe the argument so that it is concerned not so much with the structure of narrative "texts" or artifacts as it is with the processes by which readers (or hearers or players) comprehend and interpret them.[5]

There is within literary studies a "hermeneutic" strand of theory that focuses on interpretation and reader-response and on narrative as rhetoric, as well as a robust theoretical discussion, much of which has been located in the human sciences, that examines narrative as a form of action rather than as mode of discourse or representation.[6] These theoretical approaches share an interest in how culturally constituted narratives shape self and experience. Narrative, seen from these perspectives, offers what Kenneth Burke calls "symbolic action"—an intentional, goal-directed, and motivated way of making meaning. Drawing on Burkean assumptions, Donald Polkinghorne (1988) explains how such a "narrative approach" changes the way we understand human action:

> Human action is the physical texture of an embodied agent's meaningful statement, and bodily movement is "caused" by the meaning to be expressed. Human action, understood to be more than mere physical movement, but as the result of the human competence to comprehend particular movements as the acts of agents, can be refigured or represented symbolically in the acts of speaking or writing. The bodily movements of the hand when holding a pen and writing a note or of the tongue and larynx when speaking to someone make no sense when explained as mechanical movements of organic pulleys and bellows; they are aspects of an integrated person giving expression. In a similar way, one's movement across a room or the focusing of the eyes to see something small are expressive of a personal involvement with the world. (p. 142)

Thus, when a player manipulates a pulley or bellows while playing a video game, she is not simply initiating (or imitating on the screen) mechanical motion. Rather, she is enacting a narrative of embodied and expressive action.

Understanding narrative as human action as well as textual structure seems particularly relevant to the goal-oriented, directional experience of video game play, in which the player is involved "in a compelling world of action and interaction" (Gee, p. 68). This world of action is embodied both in the player's direct experience of the game, what Gee calls "embodied action," and in the story elements that make up the game's framework, what Gee calls "embodied stories." Though Gee distinguishes "embodied stories" from "embodied actions," in my own game playing they seemed inextricably linked—because it was in the context of these stories that my actions as a player made sense. (As Gee explains, "embodied" means "in the body" or "in the mind" [p. 82].) Thinking about narrative as a way to experience the activity of playing the game as well as a component of the game's structure may help explain how video games are able to provide the kind of situated learning Gee finds so compelling.

In this chapter, I reflect on the multiple ways in which narrative functions in the video games of *Myst* (chiefly the third game, *Exile*). In particular, I want to consider what narrative added to my experience when I play these games—how encountering and engaging with narrative affected my response and fostered learning. In the first section, I describe my background as a player and explore how the embedded narratives in *Myst* games supplied a context for my actions. My focus here is on the explicit narratives articulated in *Myst,* what Celia Pearce (2004) calls the game's "metastory." In the second section, I draw primarily on Janet Murray's (1997) taxonomy of aesthetics in computer narratives in order to describe how my own embodied actions as a player became themselves a narrative—a story of contest and efforts to achieve solutions—and how these narrative actions connect to goals fostered in many composition classes. My focus here is on what Pearce calls the "experiential narrative" that is created in the context of game play itself.[7] In the last section, I consider how these two ways of responding to and enacting stories in *Myst* enriched and intensified the experience of game play and enabled the kind of active learning, that Gee argues, video games promote.

Myst and Narrative: Stories into Action

The "Gamer" and the Game

Need to call this "Obsession." I spent four days doing nothing else but this. I have gone way past the need to do "research." Why is this compelling? What's going on?

(From my *Exile* journal)

I am the "gamer," though I am somewhat reluctant to adopt that title, since I have only really played three computer games: *Myst, Riven,* and *Myst III: Exile.* I first played *Myst* in the spring of 2002, when I was spending a semester in Sibiu Romania as a Fulbright scholar. Lacking access to English-language entertainment—such as television, radio, magazines, movies, or newspapers—I was starved for some kind of compelling narrative engagement. I remembered a computer game called *Myst* someone had once shown me, and I arranged to have copies of *Myst* and then *Riven* mailed to me. I spent a good three months playing them. Once back in the United States, I never thought of playing computer games again—despite the fact that my experience of playing *Myst* and *Riven* had been utterly entrancing.

I returned to playing video games in May 2004, when I played *Exile* in preparation for writing this chapter. I kidded myself that I was doing it as "research." But in fact, as in spring 2002, I became obsessed. I spent hours and hours playing it. And when I was not playing *Exile,* I thought about it. I fell asleep and woke up trying to piece together puzzles. I went over possibilities while I was walking and exercising or during trips to the movies or to the symphony. I kept elaborate (though disorganized) notes. I visited online sites where other *Myst*-obsessed people gathered to help novices through the game or to speculate on such topics as the construction of the D'Ni language or the psychological motivation of some of the *Myst* characters. After about four weeks, I finally finished the game, and did so through luck, some skill and problem solving, and a fairly judicious use of *Myst*-related websites to find "clues" and "walk-throughs" that helped me when I was stalled. (Had I not gone on the Internet, I would in all likelihood still be playing.)

I offer this history of my game playing to underscore that I have played only three computer games. Thus I recognize that much of what I say may (or may not) be relevant only to *Myst.* But I also want to emphasize how captivated I was by the worlds of *Myst* while I was living in them as a player. I was engrossed in these worlds in much the same way I have found myself enthralled by the experience of reading certain novels: unable to stop thinking about them; constantly gauging whether to rush through or go slowly and savor; feeling compelled to return to them (even when I knew there were other things I should be doing).

I am not the first person to be seduced by *Myst.* The first *Myst* game was released in 1993, and by 1994 it had become the most popular computer game in the world. The original *Myst* is generally considered to have been groundbreaking because of the beauty of its graphics, the complexity of its story, the ingenuity of its puzzles, and the ease of its interface (simple point-and-click). In 1997, *Riven,* the sequel appeared. *Myst* and *Riven* were created by Rand Miller and Robyn

Miller, two brothers who are often described as "geniuses." After the Millers sold the rights to *Myst*, Presto Studies produced two further games: *Myst III: Exile* in 2001 and *Myst IV: Revelation* in 2004. *Myst* and its successors have also spawned a series of novels (Miller, Wingrove, & Miller, 2004) and an extensive fan base who meet on websites and at the annual "convention," Mysterium. In this chapter, I will refer to each of the various *Myst* games, but I will focus my analysis on *Exile*—not because it is necessarily the most cognitively challenging or aesthetically satisfying game, but because it is the one I played most recently.[8]

As first-person games, the *Myst* series renders the action from the point of view of the player. Besides instantiating a perspective, the first three *Myst* games offer the player few ways to specify an identity within the game world. In these games, the player has very few identifiable attributes: age, gender, ethnicity, or class is never indicated. The player cannot name, dress, or otherwise identify her character. She is merely a benevolent "stranger" who has first stumbled upon and then come back to the world of the *Myst* games. Nor is the player's motivation developed, except in the general sense that it is assumed she is there to help.[9] Moreover, her interactions with the game world are very limited in kind and scope. Though the player can choose the order in which she solves some of (but not all) the puzzles, there is no choice about the solution itself. All the puzzles have one "correct" solution; and until this solution is found and enacted, there is no progress.

The player's interactions in *Myst* are characterized by what Marie-Laure Ryan (2001) (drawing on terminology developed by Espen Aarseth, 1997) calls "internal-exploratory interactivity,"

> in which the user takes a virtual body with her into the fictional world, but her role in this world is limited to actions that have no bearing on the narrative events. . . . The user has a seat on the stage; she may even play a cameo role, but she is not a protagonist in the action. This does not mean that her persona is limited to passive roles. Her character within the fictional world may be scripted as that of a traveler, a confidante, a historian, or a detective who tries to solve a mystery. The user exercises her agency by moving around the fictional world, picking up objects and looking at them, viewing the action from different points of view, investigating a case, and trying to reconstitute events that have taken place a long time ago.

Internal-exploratory interactivity lends itself to many types of plots, Ryan (July 2001) argues, including "the mystery story, in which two narrative levels are connected: one constituted by the actions of the detective, the other by the story to be reconstructed. In this case, one level is predetermined, while the other is created in real time by the actions of the user." An example of such games is *Myst*, "where the user explores an island and solves certain puzzles in order to crack the mystery of what happened in the past."

Myst Stories

I'm in the first age, J'aninin or something—the one age Atrus "forgot" to visit from earlier. Couldn't figure out what that was until I remembered to read the journal. Why is the journal so long and boring? I like the part about Saavedro, but I'm already bored with all the Dunny history. Figured out that there is a visual device that you can turn 3 times and can look at from 3 perspectives. Trying to figure out what's the best way to explore the island. I keep getting disoriented because of the mouse/transition thing, which I still haven't worked out.

(From my *Exile* journal)

Myst games are based on a complex and complicated metastory that is the source of much of the games' attraction and criticism. This metastory operates at two levels: the larger history of the *Myst* world that links each of the games, and the specific set of events with which each particular game deals. In its metastory, the *Myst* series offers some of the most conventionally structured narratives in video games, which is probably why players seem to either love or hate them. It is also at the level of metastory that *Myst* is most amenable to a narratological textual analysis.

Behind all the games is a history whose details are increasingly filled in as the games progress. This history focuses on a mage figure named Atrus who has acquired the ability to "write" into existence new worlds or, as the game calls them, "ages." The history of Atrus and his family is itself part of the larger story of a lost race of people called the D'Ni (pronounced "Dunny") who had produced a rich and complex civilization and whose history the player works to reconstruct. The extended history of the D'Ni has been compared to Tolkien's *Lord of the Rings* and is, to me (someone who has never been drawn to fantasy), the least-interesting level of narrative in the game. But to many players it seems amazingly compelling, as various websites related to such topics as the linguistic roots of the D'Ni or the details of the genealogy of Atrus and his family *attest.* (See, for example, *Guild of the Linguists Homepage,* or *Tales of the D'Ni.*)

Embedded in the history of the D'Ni, however, are what I found to be the more detailed and psychologically gripping stories that underlie each specific game. (Hence, it is possible to enjoy the *Myst* games without knowing—or caring—much about the larger history of the D'Ni.) Each of the game stories centers on Atrus and his complicated Oedipal relations with his sons and his own father. In the first *Myst* game, Atrus has been betrayed by his two evil sons, Sirrus and Achenar; in *Riven* the betrayal comes from Atrus's father, Gehn.[10] In each game, Atrus has somehow summoned the player to help him, and this nameless stranger takes on the task of solving puzzles in order to first discover what happened to Atrus or other members of his family, and then to find ways to save them.[11]

Exile opens with Atrus having summoned the player once again, this time to a place called Tomahna. The player is invited into Atrus's study, where, while waiting for Atrus, she is able to gain information by reading a letter left on the desk. Apparently, Atrus has been worried by signs that someone has been breaking into his study. Atrus appears and explains that he has created a new age for the D'Ni, this time called Releeshahn. He then offers the player the journal he kept while creating Releeshahn (this is important because the journal, which the player has with her throughout the game, provides important clues for puzzle solving), and invites the player to join him in a preliminary visit to this new age. However before Atrus and the player can leave, a rather wild-looking man (who the player later learns is named Saavedro) appears, throws a fire ball at Atrus, seizes the book to Releeshahn, and drops another linking book, this time an age called J'Nanin. The player is left to follow.

As the player makes her way through J'Nanin and various related worlds, she slowly uncovers Saavedro's story. She learns that many years ago when Sirrus and Achenar (Atrus's evil sons from *Myst*) were young, Atrus sent them to Saavedro's home in Narayan to learn the art of age writing. Unbeknownst to Atrus, Sirrus and Achenar later returned to Narayan to corrupt it and destroy its people. While there, they also tormented Saavedro, purportedly killing his wife and daughters, and then isolating him on a dead and frozen Narayan. Saavedro has spent the last several years suffering from a kind of posttraumatic-stress disorder, obsessing about revenge on Atrus (who he believes countenanced his sons' actions). The action of the game begins at a point in time when Saavedro has discovered a way to link to Atrus in Tomahna. He hopes to lure Atrus to Narayan, so that he can exact revenge on Atrus and use Atrus's magical powers to resurrect his lost family.

What I have just condensed in the preceding paragraph is what narratologists call the "story" of Saavedro's life: that is, the chronological sequence of events involving characters who engage in acts and the settings in which events occur. This story, which according to some narratologists exists separately from, or "pre-exists," its representation, is mediated through what narratologists call the narrative "discourse." In *Exile,* we learn Saavedro's story in nonsequential bits—from dropped pages of his journal, murals he has painted, and various "hologram" messages he leaves for Atrus. (And the order in which we receive these bits is, to some extent, dependent on the order in which we play the game.) *Exile* thus has the discourse structure of many detective-type novels. The discourse provides information about the past in a nonchronological and incoherent fashion; the player or reader must reconstruct this information in order to form a consistent and sequential "story" of past events. But unlike conventional mysteries, in which the reader mentally reconstructs a story she only observes, hears, or reads about, computer-game mysteries allow the player to actively engage in the disclosure of the narrative itself. That is, the player is not just responding to *Exile's* story; she is also a participant in its narrative world.

Playing Games in Narrative

Okay, I need to stop playing and reflect. Over the weekend, I got very frustrated, then yesterday a good day. I got myself back to where I was earlier—finding all the relevant places I had visited but forgotten where they were. Found the room where Saavedro talks about what the evil brothers did. And I solved the circuit puzzle all by myself. But I got bogged down in the lava room. The controls are manually frustrating. You have to keep toggling and pulling and pushing. Just sitting there fiddling with that knob, doing and redoing. I gave up in frustration and went online to find a hint. It didn't help. Looked for another and another. Finally a detailed walkthrough. And I did it, but I'm still not sure I understand what I did or why. But why did I go for a hint? Because life is too short to fiddle around when you know that the answer will be found hit-or-miss, and you may never hit. Grrh. (But looking for a hint on-line is another kind of problem-solving?) Now the damn steam valves. I know it's something to do with a spaceship, which I am supposed to be able to see.

Somehow the spaceship takes you back to Saavedro's past. But I can't figure out
where it is and how it works.

(From my *Exile* journal)

As a participant in *Exile*, the player is involved in two parallel quests: she must find
the visual and verbal texts scattered through the various worlds that tell the story
of Saavedro, and she must solve the puzzles of J'Nanin and its connected worlds
of Voltaic, Edana, and Amateria. These two quests are related because it is only by
solving the puzzles that the player is able to go to the various places in the game
where different parts of Saavedro's history are revealed. But, I would argue, it is in
the context of the narrative that the puzzles of *Exile* (like those of the other *Myst*
games) are rich, deep, and meaningful. The player, or at least this player, invests in
the *Myst* puzzles because they are part of a larger story in which something more
than simply solving the puzzle is at stake.[12]

More specifically, what is at stake is the imagined *Myst* world and the player's
place within it. As Gee (2003) suggests, good video games ask players to apply the
"probing principle," or to probe/hypothesize/reprobe and rethink—a cycle that
exactly describes the optimum strategy for puzzle solving in *Myst* games. And, as
Gee also argues, the player completes this strategy within the context of an appreciative system—a domain-specific set of values that helps her evaluate what constitutes a "good," deep solution. But the *Myst* player is driven forward—induced
to invest the time, effort, and concentration that the game requires—not just
because of the cleverness of the puzzle (and many puzzles in the *Myst* games are
extraordinarily clever) but also because of the visual beauty and narrative density
of the imagined world in which those puzzles are embedded.

Most theoretical discussion of *Myst* games has focused on the metastory, leading
to the criticism that *Myst* is "dramatically static" (Murray, 1997, p. 108). But while it
is true that *Myst* and its successors do not involve the degree of action and interaction that characterizes the games Gee describes, there is, nevertheless, forward
movement. In *Exile*, for example, the visits to the various ages allow the player to
learn more and more about Saavedro's story: his past experiences, present plans, and
future hopes. That is, the player responds to the game as she might to other kinds of
narratives: she is moved ahead directionally by the story's teleological "sense of an
ending" (Kermode, 1966). Puzzles, labyrinths, and other kinds of problem-solving
activities become purposive because they are situated within the unfolding mystery
the player is attempting to solve. And the clues and information the player uncovers
become important in resolving Saavedro's history. Metastory thus keeps the puzzles
from seeming abstract or decontextualized and provides a narrative context that
makes the sequence of finding new graphics meaningful. Even more important,
though, to my own experience of game play as situated, embodied learning was the
experiential narrative that arose out of my own actions as a player.

Myst and Narrative: Action into Stories

In *Hamlet on the Holodeck*, Janet Murray (1997) explores the properties and
pleasures of storytelling in a range of digital environments. In an ambitious

argument, Murray suggests that new storytelling formats—such as those of computer games, MUDs, or hypertext fiction—suggest the "promise of a new medium of expression . . . as varied as the printed book or the moving picture" (p. 28). But Murray also emphasizes that because such formats are still in their infancy, "it would be a mistake to compare the first fruits of a new medium too directly with the accustomed yield of older media" (p. 28). Rather, new digital narratives are analogous to "incunabula," or early books printed 50 years after the invention of the printing press. Like these early experiments in bookmaking, current cybertexts reveal ongoing evolution of the formal conventions necessary for coherent communication.

Based on current applications, Murray identifies three "aesthetic principles" that have the potential to provide "pleasure" in digital narratives: immersion, agency, and transformation. Immersion refers to "the experience of being transported to an elaborately simulated place," or the sense of being "surrounded by other reality." Agency is the ability to "take meaningful action and see the results of our decisions in our choices." Transformation suggests the power to "shift shapes or identity." While Murray concedes that these aesthetic principles exist mainly as potential—they "are not so much current pleasures as they are pleasures we are anticipating as our desires are aroused by the emergence of a new medium" (p. 181)—they nevertheless predict what may be the greater aesthetic reward of digital narratives in the future.

These pleasures were very much a part of my own experience with the narratives of *Myst*. Aesthetic pleasures made narrative desire deeper and more compelling—motivating me to begin the story, to move through the middle to the end, and to make sense of the narrative world that the character is a part of. These qualities, and the narrative desires they help stimulate, may explain why players find video games so gripping and why they are able to invest so deeply in what Gee calls the "practice principle," in which

> learners gets lots and lots of practice in a context where the practice is not boring (i.e., in a virtual world that is compelling to learners on their own terms and where learners experience ongoing success). They spend lots of time on task. (p. 71)

Thus, in this section, I want to use Murray's categories of pleasure to explore how narrative desire shaped my own experience with video games: making game play feel "compelling" or "not boring"; allowing me to configure my actions in ways that led to narrative and game "success"; and keeping me resolutely "on task."

Immersion: The Visit

> *Edana.* Nature. Lush rainforest. Strangler figs, weird plants. Very, very hard to remember where you've been. A maze in the jungle. Horribly frustrating. Can't remember one place from another. It started with a bare vertical tree. Nothing to see. Spare. But then as I moved from one level to another, it got more and more dense. Everything curving, sinuous. Green predominates. Just like Louisville this May— with the cicadas and all the steam from the rain. A continuous puzzle—moving

from one stage to another. The main fun was figuring out what all the plants did. But the visual concentration was very wearing in the end. Too much peering and trying to remember tiny landscapes. Lost forever in damn log tunnels. In the end the pay-off, the flying bird, wasn't as dramatic as the spaceship in Voltaic.

(From my *Exile* journal)

The *Myst* games are often (and I think justly) praised for their visual beauty and detail.[13] Commentary on *Myst* and its successors even suggests that the primary appeal of these games, as in many hypertext genres, may lie in the way they employ visual rhetoric—allowing players to negotiate space and explore new landscapes. In *Myst* games, players navigate through landscapes using visual qualities such as color, line, and shape to find connections and relations. Mood and tempo are evoked in large part through visual details. And the sites in which the game's stories are located gain much of their significance through the visual cues and suggestions they offer, for example, abandoned libraries, secret texts, or lonely mage figures living in secluded towers.[14]

There is, indeed, little action in *Myst* games. Instead, the player clicks her way through the landscape. As she moves (clicks) from one space to another, the game shifts from one (relatively) static, prerendered scene to another. The movement of the game, which has the effect of a kind of slide show, thus mimes the movement of the player in the Myst world. Similarly, there is little interaction with other characters or players in *Myst* games; *Myst* worlds are "weirdly depopulated" (Murray, 1997, p. 10). (*Riven* and *Exile* are a little different because you track various characters and hear them speak—though you cannot answer back—and your actions, to some extent, determine theirs.)

Adventure games, such as *Myst,* are often described using metaphors of a "visit" or a "quest." In such games, the player navigates space in order to solve puzzles; solving puzzles provides new space for the player to navigate. (This access to new space is usually quite dramatic—with the sudden appearance of doors, tunnels, towers, or even elaborate transportation devices.) All the *Myst* games offer various ages or worlds to visit or explore, and each age has its own distinctive visual (and in some cases aural) style. *Exile,* for example, includes five ages. J'Nanin, the anchor world, from which the player (through successful puzzle solving) enters the other worlds, features a Frank Lloyd Wright-style greenhouse and observatory that is situated in a volcanic lake and is ringed by rocky cliffs that house three odd-looking vertical "tusks." Edana resembles a rain-forested island, with strange vegetation, whose atmosphere becomes increasingly dark and entangled as you move downward to the forest floor. Voltaic follows a deep canyon through red rock. Amateria houses a series of Chinese-looking pagodas, linked by bridges and a rail system, and (as the one place in *Myst*-lands where the weather is not always sunny) takes place at sunset with occasional thunder and lightning signaling an incipient storm.

I cannot really describe in words the visual appeal of *Exile* or the other *Myst* games, and interested readers should look for themselves at screen shots (UbiSoft, n.d.). However, I can say that for me, one of the greatest and most intense pleasures in playing these games came from the gradual way they moved me from one wondrous place to another. I solved puzzles primarily to find new places to look at. And each new place, once explored, made me want to find another. Immersion in the *Myst* worlds was thus a significant inducement for me to spend time learning how to solve puzzles, negotiate mazes, or figure out complicated family histories. And while the learning associated with these activities was also fun, I do not believe I would have invested the time and effort they took, had there not been the ongoing reward of more varied and deeper immersion in the game's graphic detail.[15]

This heightened sense of visual interest is very unusual for me, as a reader or spectator of other media, because I am not generally drawn to texts that create what Jenkins (2004) calls "spatial stories"—narratives that offer "richly developed worlds" rather than the kind of "character psychology or plot development" that are a feature of the predominant tradition of literary narratives. Spatial stories, Jenkins argues, create narratives by using "evocative spaces," or sites that draw on "previously existing narrative competencies" to generate meaning (p. 123). Space becomes meaningful because it is the setting for narratives—read, viewed, or lived. Thus, when I progressed through *Myst* landscapes, I was not merely finding one beautiful set of graphics after another—an experience I can achieve at many sites on the Internet. Rather, I was discovering locales or settings that had meaning within the various levels of narrative offered by the game. These locales provided the clues necessary to construct a metastory about Saavedro and his history with Atrus. But even more importantly, spatial immersion contributed directly to the experiential narrative I was building about my own game play.[16]

In *Exile,* for example, I had to retrace my steps many times in order to orient myself in space. Over and over, I had to move back and forth between various locations in order to determine if an action I made in one place (such as adjusting a scale or raising a lever) had an effect on something somewhere else (such as how a ball moved on a track or whether steam was escaping from a vent). I often "found" places but could not find them again until I was able to locate specific cues about where to click. More experienced players report that they continue to explore the landscapes of these games even after all the puzzles have been solved, hoping to find hidden details or jokes (called Easter Eggs) that have been coded into the background. This repetition—particularly some of the endless back and forth to determine the effects of actions—was often frustrating (and very time-consuming), but it also contributed to my feeling of being anchored to a real, though paradoxically imagined, narrated world.

Repetition may seem, in one sense, to be opposed to narrative, as it suggests cycling back rather than moving forward. But repetition also helps create the impression of what Paul Ricoeur (1981) calls "temporality," or (following Heidegger) the feeling of being "within-time." Temporality, as Ricoeur explains it, refers to the human *experience* of time, a phenomenon quite different from the "ordinary" notion of time as a "linear series of 'nows'" (p. 166). That is, we experience time not as a "neutral series of abstract instants" (p. 169), but as a shaped story—as something "extended" between birth and death, or beginning and end (p. 177). This experiential sense of time—the "existential now" of our "preoccupations"—contributes to the feeling that we live "in" time. As Ricoeur's metaphors suggest, the lived experience of temporality has a concrete, almost tangible, quality: thus, our sense of "'having time to,' 'taking time to,' 'wasting time,' and so on" (p. 169). This existential sense of temporality was fundamental to the way I experienced computer games. My time of game playing (as opposed to the time of the story that the game was revealing) became an intense (often negative) preoccupation as I played: I "spent time," "wasted time," "used time." But the game's forward movement—puzzles to solve, spaces to negotiate, histories to discover, characters to learn more about—also made time into narrative. The temporality of gameplay itself became a story with beginning, middle, and end: a repetitive history of my false starts or successful conclusions.[17]

The experience of temporality as repetition and immersion is more insistent, Ricoeur suggests, in narratives (such as fairy tales) that represent "primitive" or even "regressive" versions of quest stories.[18] Computer games such as *Myst* are clearly still at this earlier, more "primitive" stage, involving players in repetitions that have little to do with—in fact, are often completely detached from—the psychological development of the characters or even the narrative structure of the game itself.[19] But even if the repetitions remain at the level of the fantastic, they are still important to the pleasure *Myst* games provide. For many players of course, "immersion and confinement in the midst of dark powers" (Ricoeur, p. 181) is itself pleasurable; they are drawn to the *Myst* world *because* it is a detailed, consistent, and constantly evolving fantasy. But even for someone like me who does not enjoy fantasy genres, the immersive repetitions of *Myst* contribute to my narrative pleasures. Repetitions anchor the player, temporally as well as spatially, to the reality of the imagined world in which the game exists. They give the puzzles weight and meaning. Indeed, without such repetitions and the narrative time they create, the puzzles would seem totally arbitrary (as witnessed by how dull it is to read a "walk-through" of a game one has never played). The game's visual and aural details thus provide not just abstract beauty or interest, but sites for embodied action.

Games thus help teach players how to employ visual conventions and use visual qualities to expand meaning—communicative tasks that are increasingly important in the multimodal compositions they will create now and in the future. But attention to concrete, sensory images is also important for readers and writers of alphabetic texts, and video games may help readers and writers learn to immerse themselves in such images. At their best, video games offer detail-rich environments in which players must recognize subtle distinctions, explore dramatic resonance, and engage in fine-grained analysis—skills that are important as they compose in a variety of texts and genres.

Agency: The Maze and the Puzzle

Amateria. There are 3 puzzles here—all connected with these crystal, charged balls. One puzzle has to do with placement; one with weights (that are somehow related to the toys I found in Saavedro's study); one with sounds. I solved the first puzzle (placement) by trial-and-error (in a strangely efficient manner). But I didn't know why it worked, so I went on-line to find out what I had done—what was the operating principle—and I could not understand the explanations. A good example of Gee's distinction between knowing and telling: if I had figured out the theory of the puzzle myself, the explanation might have made more sense. The second puzzle, I solved basically from hints. I had the theory (the relative weights, etc.) but I had the composition of the ball all wrong. (Purely a perspective problem.) I *should* have figured it out myself. That is probably the most frustrating experience: to have someone show you something you could have done yourself. The third puzzle I solved on my own (pretty much). And then at the end, to get out of Amateria, there was a maze negotiation that I completely cheated on. I worked out the theory myself, but it was just too complicated and too time-consuming to get myself through the maze.

(From my *Exile* journal)

While many traditional forms of narrative are described in terms of immersion and transformation (novel readers frequently speak of their sense of traveling to a new world or taking on a new identity), agency is more often characterized solely as a consequence of game play. Many theorists, in fact, who argue that video games are *not* narratives, do so because of the kind of player agency games offer. For Gee (2003), player agency is key to the embodied action that characterizes video games—but not other conventional narrative genres. Video games, Gee explains, allow the player to "find different things and discover information relevant to the story line in a different order," and to "engage in actions that are themselves part of the story line" (p. 81). Thus, Gee sees stories in video games as "embodied in the player's own choices and actions in a way they cannot be in books and movies" (p. 82). But while it may be true that readers (or viewers) of other genres are constrained in different ways than are players in a video game, they nevertheless enact agency as they construct meaning and interpret textual features. Indeed, our goal in English classes is to make students into active readers and writers who engage in forms of agency not unlike those employed by game players. In particular, games—like other texts—ask players to find patterns among details, to organize information in relevant ways, and to map relationships using a range of semiotic systems (e.g., verbal, visual, mathematical).

The primary forms of player agency in *Myst* games include solving puzzles and negotiating mazes. These activities are related in that solving a puzzle often reveals a new space to explore, and negotiating new space often provides the player with a new puzzle to solve. Negotiating the maze is a form of agency that connects to immersion: as the player progresses through the game, she comes to know more and more about the world that the game inhabits. This immersive agency provides opportunities to "experience pleasures specific to inventional navigation: orienting ourselves by landmarks, mapping a space mentally to match our experience, and admiring the juxtaposition and changes in perspective that derive from moving through an intricate environment" (Murray, 1997, p. 129). Puzzle solving is agency linked with transformation: as the player completes a puzzle, the game world and her relation to it change in some significant way. The transformative "pleasures of problem-solving" that are produced by completing puzzles "are most satisfying when the actions have a dramatic appropriateness, when they serve as a way of increasing our belief in the solidity and consistency of the illusory world" (Murray, p. 139).

When I played the *Myst* games, I solved puzzles in three ways: (inefficiently but sometimes with luck) using trial and error; (embarrassingly) going to "hints" or "cheats" from Internet sites; and (most satisfyingly) applying the "probe, hypothesize, reprobe, rethink cycle" that Gee argues is "the basis of expert reflective practice in any complex semiotic domain" (p. 91). In this last mode, I would perform an action, such as manipulating an object or trying to decipher a code, in order to determine what effect that action had either there or somewhere else. On the basis of my observations, I would make a guess about the logic or causal mechanism at work. I would then readjust levers or reenter codes, and after evaluating my new observations, I would revise my thinking. Eventually (if the puzzle or maze was within my "regime of competence," or my Vygotskian "zone of proximal development"), I would reach the solution. How did I know when I solved the puzzle? In *Myst* games this is always obvious (if one knows where to look): something happens. But the pleasures of puzzles do not just lie in attaining the solution—which is why it was never as much fun to get an answer by "hints" or "cheats" or luck as it was to figure it out for myself.

Solving puzzles in *Myst* advances the story line of the game, in that each puzzle allows the player to find out more about the background of the characters and to proceed further in her quest to right the wrong that initiated the game's dramatic action. But puzzle solving also exists within the narrative context of game play itself—a narrative that can exist independently of the game's story. Thus, as Jesper Juul (2004) (who is one of the most vocal advocates of the position that computer games are *not* narratives) explains, even a game like *Tetris* that lacks an explicit narrative component, elicits narrative-like, motivated action on the part of the player: "The player is motivated to perform a cognitive analysis of the game's situation because the game is a task that the player has undertaken as a real-world person."[20]

Myst games are (often fiendishly) compelling precisely because they exist within a context of motive and desire. As a player, my sense of motive and purpose was created in part, as Gee (2003) suggests, through my relation to various "appreciative systems": the "goals, desires, feelings and values that 'insiders' in that domain recognize as the sorts members of that domain (the affinity group associated with that domain) typically have" (Gee, p. 97). But I also believe puzzles and mazes were meaningful to me because of the narrative frameworks in which they were located, including my own experiential narrative of contest and solution. Thus, as Murray (1997) suggests, the game itself allows players "a chance to enact our most basic relationships to the world—our desire to prevail over adversity, to survive our inevitable defeats, to shape our environment, to master complexity, and to make our lives fit together like the pieces of a jigsaw puzzle" (p. 143). Through experiential narrative, players enact agency. Indeed, without narrative, agency would be impossible, and games would offer only purposeless, mechanical tasks.

The sense of agency, which is so central to video games, is a major goal of many other educational experiences that similarly hope to invoke in students the sense that they can solve problems and enact meaningful solutions. Composition classes, for instance, often try to inculcate agency in students by helping them become "strong" readers and writers who do not simply react passively to texts, but use information and ideas creatively and for their own needs and interests. Video games thus provide a powerful example of a text that requires strenuous observation, inference, logic, and extrapolation on the part of its readers/players—responses we hope to foster in students as they learn to read and compose the kinds of texts privileged in our classrooms. Games may thus model forms of readerly or writerly agency that can carry over into other aspects of the players' lives. And games may also show us the power of situating academic problems into compelling narrative contexts in order to help readers and writers feel they are making embodied choices.

Transformation: The Choice

Voltaic. I finally did the airship thing; pretty cool graphics. But I forgot to save the game, so I had to go back and do the steam again in order to see the airship again. From the airship, it's pretty straightforward. Onto the ship, over to the ruined tower. Then everything kind of falls into place, and you get the symbol. It was visually very striking. Someone has a lot of imagination. But I have to quit for a while. I went to sleep thinking Myst, and woke up thinking Myst. I need to get obsessed about something else for a change. I also need to remember that I am doing this as "research," and that eventually I have to think of something clever to say about it. So far, I have mainly figured out that there are some damn smart kids out there. Voltaic all about power and movement (lots of math). In the end all the visual elements click into place; it all makes "sense." What seemed extraneous was revealed to have function. Movement through the landscape. Movement of gadgets. Movement of space ship. Then the symbol revealed in movement (swirling papers underneath rising ruin).

(From my *Exile* journal)

Transformation, as Murray (1997) explains it, involves a range of shape-shifting phenomena: kaleidoscopic, nonlinear narratives characteristic of hypertext and other computer applications; morphing story environments in which interactors construct their own scenarios out of formulaic elements; personal transformations effected through mosaic, nonlinear structures; and the masquerade of changing identities. Michael Mateas (2004) has argued that transformation "is the most problematic of Murray's three categories" because it has three distinct meanings: "masquerade, variety, and transformation" (pp. 21–22). But these meanings seem to me not so much distinct as interrelated. Masquerades allow players to try out different personae; personae are enacted through multiple varieties of experience offered by the game; deep engagement with diverse points of view and morphing story lines can lead to personal transformation.

It is perhaps in this last attribute, their capacity for personal transformation, that computer games are most like other narratives and thus like the kinds of texts we ask students to read and write about in many English classes. As we read books, watch movies, listen to stories, we enter into the narrative in ways that have transformative potential. When stories are most arresting or most engaging, we forget the other "real" world—losing track of time and space. In its place, we enter into a narrated world that often feels real and immediate: thus our ability to directly experience emotions such as fear and sadness or to respond to fictional characters as we would to real people. But this sense of personal engagement is also different in computer games because we are *in* the game world, enacting narratives in ways that are different from our interactions with other media. These kinds of "enacted events," Murray suggests, "have a transformative power that exceeds narrated and conventionally dramatized events because we assimilate them as personal experience" (p. 170).

Players in *Myst* games are more detached from the action than they are in many other game genres: they lack the ability, for example, to construct an avatar or to directly influence the game's story line. But while these games do not offer the same degree of firsthand engagement in the narrative structure characteristic of the action games Gee played, they nevertheless seem to compel many people in deeply personal and immediate ways. As a player of *Exile*, I discovered at least two kinds of transformative experiences. The first, which was for me the most central, was connected to the way my own life became transformed during play: I simply lost track of my ordinary existence when I sat down at the computer—often captivated for hours, unaware of my surroundings or passing time. The second kind of transformation, which I discovered primarily through reports of other players' experience, concerned the ways the game encouraged players to reflect critically on and even change their own identities, both in the game and out of it.

The first kind of transformation seems connected to escapist pleasures for which video games are often criticized. This ability to draw players in—to induce them to invest increasing amounts of time, money, or other resources—is a consequence frequently noted and often bemoaned of such games. But for many players (including me), one of the most important transformative pleasures of video games lies in the ability to "lose oneself" in the experience of game play and to forget, for a while, the "real" world of responsibilities, assignments, and other day-to-day worries. The power of this kind of transformation seems connected to what Murray calls the "refused closure" that is a feature of adventure games such as *Myst:* the way such games pile on levels of complexity and complication, making resolution of the puzzles increasingly difficult and hard-won.[21] And as Gee (2003) notes, such games are constantly becoming longer and more challenging (p. 6). Video games then, when they are enthralling, seem to offer players the same kind of emotional release reported in other compelling experiences (such as running or meditation), in which participants are able to let go of the stresses and concerns of daily life.

But just as the pleasures of transformation seem connected for some (such as me) to "loss of self," for others transformation appears to be a way to reflect on or even restructure self and identity. As a parallel example of how prolonged imaginative play can reshape lived experience, Murray (1997) points to the way the Brontë children created elaborate fantasy worlds that allowed them to "assimilate" the formulaic conventions of gothic, magical and other fantasy genres and to "appropriate them to their own use" (p. 165).[22] Video games, of course, are even more formulaic and perhaps less adaptable to individual psychological use. But the ability to project oneself vicariously into the game world seems for many one of the most attractive features of these games.

This kind of transformation of self is connected to what Gee (2003) calls the "identity principle," or the ability to take on and play with identities and to meditate on the relation between new identities and old ones. Video games, Gee argues, enable players to enact three kinds of identity: "virtual identity," the character one plays in the game world; "real-world identity," the nonvirtual person playing the game; and "projective identity." This third identity is not only the most difficult to explain but also the most important for understanding the way video games promote learning. The term "projective identity," Gee explains, plays on "two senses of the word 'project,' meaning both 'to project one's values and desires onto the virtual character' . . . and 'seeing the virtual character as one's own project in the making, a creature whom I imbue with a certain trajectory through time defined by my aspirations for what I want that character to be and become (within the limitations of her capacities, of course)'" (p. 56). Thus, in *Exile*, I play with my virtual identity, the nameless stranger who has been summoned to help Atrus and who follows Saavedro; my real identity, "Debra Journet," the nonvirtual, real-world person who plays the game; and my projective identity, "Debra Journet as helpful, exploring stranger."

Exile does not allow the player to manipulate identities in the way Gee describes in his playing of the game *Arcanium*.[23] As a player of *Exile*, there were few places where I could directly affect the story told by the game, though I was always in charge (through the degree of my skills) of the tempo with which that story was revealed. There is, however, a moment at the end of *Exile* where I had a real choice deciding whether or not to save Saavedro. *Exile* has several obviously wrong endings: if the player doesn't control Saavedro before making her escape, Saavedro will (depending on how the player has configured things at the close), either maroon her on Narayan, attack her, or kill her with a hammer. If you are, as I was, confused enough to end the game any of these ways, your only other option is to go back to a saved game and play the end again. In this, *Exile* is like *Myst* and *Riven* in offering several obviously "losing endings." The difference, though, is that in *Exile* there are also two possible "winning" endings: one in which the player escapes to save Atrus and leaves Saavedro imprisoned once again on Narayan; the other in which the player also escapes, saves Atrus, but this time frees Saavedro to try to find his wife and children (who, as it turns out, may actually be alive). The two winning endings feature film clips (in which Saavedro is played by the actor Brad Dourif), and both are, in their own way, quite moving. In the ending where Saavedro is left imprisoned, he begs you over and over to give him a chance to search for his missing wife and children. In the alternative ending where Saavedro is freed, he offers you a wordless but gallant salute, before sailing away to search for his missing family.

The decision whether or not to free Saavedro came up several times on the *Exile* websites I monitored, and many players reflected on their choices. (This online reflection is a good example of what Pearson calls "descriptive narrative," or "the retelling of description of game to third parties, and the culture that emerges out of that" [p. 145].) The following excerpt, from a fan website for *Exile*, entitled, "Finished it—many possible endings and a moral dilemma (possible spoiler)," gives some sense of the ethical and moral dimensions of these discussions:

I finally finished Exile to my satisfaction. I believe I went through 5 possible endings, none of them agreeable—either I was killed in a fit of Saav's rage, or Saav took off after disposing of the book leaving me to go to Catherine and Atrus in defeat. But then I found a way to get the book and go back, but that meant leaving Saav stranded. That didn't settle too well with me either—my moral and ethical side did not sleep well (who would have thought that I would ever take a "game" so seriously. :-) I thought and thought about it all day until I hit on a solution that gave everyone what they needed, especially that poor, miserable sod Saavedro, and it worked out as I expected. It even surprised me that the post-ending ruminations of Atrus were different and fit the outcome had solved. It's a great game and I was wondering how many folks worked it out where everyone ended up happy or were just glad to get the book back. I read a post by someone who said he wondered what would happen if Saav got away in the gondola—so it makes me think that not everyone went for the complete solution.

Sorry for being so long winded, but the ending choices took me back to a time when I had to make those life altering choices for real and made me realize that they still aren't easy to make. (devildog201, 2004)

Devildog201's deliberations about how to end the game are not just a function of "winning"; saving or imprisoning Saavedro results in the same resolution of the game's primary story in which the player rescues Releeshahn and returns to Atrus. Rather, the two endings carry with them different sorts of emotional resonance, and the investment in one ending over another seems a consequence of the projective identities devildog201 was able to construct within the game's constraints.

Transformation is an overarching goal of most, if not all, educational experiences. Indeed, the very act of learning requires moving toward the not-yet-known. As the learner assimilates new knowledge or new practice, she is changed in some manner, though the nature and degree of her changes may differ according to situation. In composition classes, for example, transformative goals range from asking students to reflect on identities already forged to helping them perform new identities—such as members of academic disciplines or professions. The opportunity to "try on" a new self that is a feature of many video games may, in fact, be a powerful model for other kinds of rhetorical transformations. At their best, games—like the kinds of active learning experiences we hope to provide our students—do not ask players to adopt passively an identity already formed; rather they invite players to "morph" established identities into new and different versions of the self. Moreover, by foregrounding narrative, video games point to the importance of compelling stories in which individuals can situate and make sense of their own experiences. Helping students compose and critique such narratives of identity is a frequent goal of composition classes.

What Did I Learn and How Did I Learn It?

Gee's (2003) argument about the value of video games is based in part on the claim that "there is really no such thing as learning 'in general.' We always learn *something*" (p. 22). Thus, in assessing what and how we learn, we must ask ourselves questions such as, What semiotic domain are we entering when we learn something new? Is it valuable? Am I learning simply to understand or to participate?

In discussing learning in video games, Gee talks most closely about their relation to science education. Indeed, the very terms of formulating and refining hypotheses suggest thinking patterns often used in science. But while it seems very plausible to connect video games with the kind of active problem solving often promoted in science classrooms, English teachers (like me) may wonder how video games can encourage the kinds of literate activities that are the domain of the humanities. More specifically, how can video games promote the sorts of literacies valued in English classes, where the emphasis is on the production and reception of mostly verbal texts?

I believe there are connections between video games and the critical reading, writing, and thinking skills that are the objectives of many teachers in the humanities. This does not mean that I advocate turning our English composition or literature classes into places where we teach students to play or write video games. But I do agree with Gee that in attending to kinds of thinking and acting video games encourage, we may discover principles of teaching and learning that are valuable for our students and for us. In this concluding section, I want to speculate on what and how I learned as I played video games, and more particularly how that learning was enhanced by narrative.

Learning to play video games required me to participate in a new semiotic domain. But this domain was not entirely unfamiliar because it drew on competencies I had already developed. I was attracted to *Myst* games, I am sure, because they employ elaborate and conventional narrative frameworks and thus fit very well with semiotic domains in which I was already an expert. I have read narratives, taught narratives, and written about narratives virtually all my life. I have a critical vocabulary, a conceptual framework, and lots of examples to draw on. In many ways, my experience playing *Myst* games drew on very familiar conventions of storytelling. Heroes and villains are easily identifiable and strongly contrasted. Intergenerational conflict is a well-known theme. And probably most importantly, the mystery plot, in which a detective assembles clues in order to reconstruct what happened in the past, is a narrative genre I particularly enjoy. Moreover, I love narrative, and, as I have tried to demonstrate in the discussion above, the narrative desire *Myst* stories evoked was a significant inducement for me to start, continue, and finally end the game.

In playing *Myst*, I was able to use a powerful set of critical and interpretive tools that I knew how to employ but that are not yet as familiar to younger players. My experience suggests that computer games may increasingly become an important way in which players, particularly new readers, begin to learn conventions of storytelling that are important not only in video games but in many other narrative genres as well. That is, as players learn how to tell and read the stories of video games, they are learning how to compose and manipulate cultural narratives. These narratives are both enacted within the unfolding story of the game world and written in the many texts that exist in the context of the game. In *Myst,* for example, players read long and complicated journals in order to perform such narrative tasks as interpreting the psychological motivation of the characters, understanding how particular images work, or establishing family trees. Most players do this, in part, by keeping notebooks or records of what they have discovered. Others go further and compose coherent narratives or backstories that supply missing details or fill in connections between characters or events.[24] That is, games seem to be a powerful way of evoking in players intense "narrative desire." But while the narratives players encounter in computer games like *Myst* resemble stories already familiar to many readers, they also differ in important ways. Thus, in learning to play video games, players also learn how to respond to a different kind of story and a different way of telling stories.

Active learning, Gee (2003) argues, must fulfill three criteria: "*experiencing* the world in new ways, forming new *affiliations*, and *preparation* for future learning" (p. 21). Among the most difficult challenges for me in playing *Myst* was learning how to experience a narrative that developed primarily through visual images, particularly learning to interpret what Jenkins (2004) calls "spatial storytelling" (p. 123). Understanding the affordances or capabilities of visual narrative is important not just to playing games, but also to a range of digital applications, including many of the kinds of composing tasks our students will likely encounter. Thus, in learning to play *Myst*, I was also able to affiliate with new groups of people for whom visual narrative is more familiar. These groups include online players whose postings I read as well as, more indirectly, students in English composition and literature classes who increasingly learn about how narratives operate through their own game-play. Moreover, the experience of playing *Myst* provided resources for future learning. By playing *Myst*, I became more knowledgeable about how video games work and also gathered new technical skills—such as how to navigate a mouse in a three-dimensional environment or how to download the latest version of DirectX (not to mention learning what DirectX is). I also drew on and strengthened my abilities to recognize patterns and to solve problems using logic and mathematics. Perhaps most importantly, I learned something about how to move through digital texts, finding connections that depended on spatial juxtaposition and alignment as much as they did on character development or plot line. Moreover, in my ability to determine, to some degree, how I moved through the game, I experienced a different, more open-ended relationship to the narrative text than I do to print genres. *Myst* games thus introduced me to new narrative genres and helped teach me how to read and respond to those genres.

This kind of applied learning is certainly important to the experience of playing video games, but in trying to understand the value of the "something" that I learned while I played the *Myst* games, I also want to consider the quality of the experience and what made it so compelling. This is harder to describe, and I am reminded of Gee's story about telling someone at a party that playing *Time Machine* for eight straight hours was a "life-enhancing experience without even knowing what [he] meant by that" (p. 5). Similarly, I was astonished at how deep and even compulsive my game-playing was.

Playing *Myst* evoked great pleasure in me. And the source of this pleasure lay in the *act* of playing. I did not want the answer to the riddle; I wanted to solve the riddle. When I did this, when I finally figured something out, I experienced a great "aha!" This "aha!" moment took different forms. Sometimes, I realized that things I had earlier thought unrelated were, indeed, connected. Or I understood that I had been looking at objects in the wrong way. Or I noticed something I had been seeing but not attending to. When this happened, things clicked into place, and I felt clever and triumphant. When I did not wait long enough or put in sufficient effort to find the solution myself, I felt cheated and disappointed. There was limited pleasure in the answer itself; most of the joy lay in finding the answer.

In this chapter, I argue that this process of finding the answer is part of the game's narrative framework and is also itself a narrative action. That is, the game offers both a story in the game and a story about playing the game. Both these stories seem important to the kind of active learning video games promote. The more I invest in the narrative world of the game, the more deeply I feel and respond to the story I am constructing during my own play. While this may not be true for all players, it is for me (and clearly many others). Hence, I will spend hours and hours playing *Myst*, but I will not spend comparable amounts of time playing *Tetris*. Even though playing *Tetris* also evokes a narrative of contest and solution, it is not one I find meaningful or seductive. For me, narrative seems an essential component. The narrative density of the game's represented world provides a context that makes puzzles and other learning tasks deep and rich.

I agree with Jenkins (2004) that consideration of the role of narrative in video games has operated from an unnecessarily limited perspective—focusing on classical linear storytelling at the expense of other kinds of narrative, on the act of telling rather than comprehending stories, and on whole games rather than narrative elements within games (pp. 120–121). Jenkins thus advocates that we understand games "less as stories than as spaces ripe with narrative possibility" (p. 119)—a conclusion I also agree with. The narrative spaces Jenkins describes seem very important to the kind and degree of learning that effective video games promote: they are, in many ways, the reasons for playing the game in the first place. Thus, if games are, as Gee (2003) suggests, good places to learn, we need to think about how to build, evaluate, and encourage those games that really do provide deep, rich, and compelling narrative experiences. We need to identify and understand which games offer players the most intense and vivid opportunities to experience narrative pleasures such as immersion, agency, and transformation.

Paying attention to the quality of experience in game play, then, means that we need to pay attention to the quality of narrative. In particular, we need to augment debates about whether games are or are not fundamentally (or even primarily) narrative with consideration of the kinds of narrative experience games offer. We also need to develop tools that will help us evaluate those narrative experiences that are most conducive to learning. In this chapter, I suggest that we can begin to do this in at least two important ways. One step in this process is to construct a theoretical framework that moves beyond questions about narrative structure to emphasize instead questions about narrative action. Such a project would draw generally on work in the human sciences that has theorized narrative as a form of human action, as well as on work from scholars of video games and digital narrative—such as Murray, Jenkins, or Pearce—that has more specifically analyzed the role of narrative in the experience of game play. Secondly, we need to find ways to experience for ourselves what video games offer—either directly by playing these games or indirectly by listening to the reports of other players. When I told friends that I was playing *Myst*, I usually got one of two responses. Those who had not played video games themselves generally seemed surprised (though often interested) that I would spend my time this way. Those who had played a game, particularly *Myst*, almost unanimously described a response similar to my own. My point is simply that without some kind of experience with games, we cannot always know how they work or what they offer.

Just as we would not evaluate books written for children or adolescents without having read them or read about them or listened to what kids said about them, we need to be informed about particular games before making judgments. It is sometimes difficult to articulate the criteria by which we value the experience of reading a book or seeing a film. Different texts, different genres, different occasions lead us to different kinds of narrative engagements. But understanding narrative as a way to enact meaning in and through video games may help us better understand the claims for learning Gee makes—allowing us to recognize both the kinds of stories games teach and the way games use stories to make active learning into pleasure.

Notes

1. Gee (2003) makes a comparable point when he describes his own relation to an affinity group associated with the semiotic domain of theoretical linguistics. One becomes a theoretical linguist, Gee argues, not only by learning a particular body of "content," but also by learning how linguists "tend to think, interact, value, and believe when they are being linguists" (p. 28). Composition scholarship—particularly work in such areas as genre studies, situated cognition, and writing across the curriculum—works from similar premises, except that it adds reading and composing to the activities that define an affinity group or a disciplinary community. That is, affinity groups that make up academic disciplines are united by rhetorical as well as theoretical or methodological commitments. See, for example, Bazerman (1994), Berkenkotter and Huckin (1995), Haas (1994), Prior (1998), Russell (1997).
2. Bruner (1990) provides an extended and powerful instance of this argument.
3. See, for example, Montford (2003) or Ryan (2001) for arguments that computer games are narrative, and Aarseth (1997) or Juul (n.d.) for arguments that they are not.
4. See, for example, Chatman (1978), Martin (1986), and Abbott (2002) for overviews of narratological theory.
5. Jenkins (2004) has begun to outline the multiple ways in which narrative functions in video games; by focusing on what he calls their "narrative architecture," Jenkins identifies four ways in which "narrative possibilities might get mapped onto game space" (p. 128). The first possibility lies in the way games offer "evocative spaces," that "build upon stories or genre traditions already well known" to players. The second comes from the opportunities games offer for players to "enact stories," by either performing

or witnessing narrative events. The third narrative possibility comes from the way players respond to "embedded narratives." And the fourth arises from the "emergent narratives" provided by the "authoring environments within which players can define
their own goals and write their own stories."

6. See, for example, Polkinghorne (1988), Herman (2003), and Hinchman and
   Hinchman (2001) for overviews of narrative and the human sciences.

7. Pearce (2004) identifies six levels, what she calls "narrative operators," that can exist
   within a game: "*Experiential.* The emergent narrative that develops out of the inherent
   'conflict' of the game as it is played, as experienced by the players themselves.
   Performative. The emergent narrative as seen by spectators watching and/or interpreting the game underway. *Augmentary.* Layers of information, interpretation, back-story,
   and contextual frameworks around the game that enhance other narrative operators.
   Descriptive. The retelling of description of game events to third parties, and the culture
   that emerges out of that. *Metastory.* A specific narrative 'overlay' that creates a conflict
   or framework for the game conflict. *Story System.* A rule-based story system of kit of
   generic narrative parts that allows the player to create their own narrative content:
   story systems can exist independent of or in conjunction with metastory" (pp.
   144–145). Pearce explains that while the first operator is a "component of all games,"
   the rest can exist "in various combinations or not at all" (p. 145). Thus, in the discussion that follows, in which I reflect on my own game-playing history, I am able to differentiate several kinds of narrative engagement. The most immediate expression of
   narrative was experiential: the deep and compelling story I enacted while playing. This
   "experiential narrative" is conveyed through several layers of "descriptive narrative":
   first the play journal I kept and which I selectively quote from, and second this chapter itself. I also observed, via the Internet, other players' descriptive narratives.
   Additionally, I encountered the "metastory" that organizes the particular computer
   games I played, as well as the enhancing "augmentary story" that has subsequently
   arisen, primarily on the Internet. I have little to say about performative operators or
   story system because they are not a part of my playing history.

8. *Exile* was, in fact, the least satisfying of the three games I played. *Myst* offered the most
   challenges, possibly because as I was playing it, I was also learning the conventions and
   assumptions of adventure video games; *Riven* had the most compelling and complex
   narrative structure.

9. As one player put it, "The stranger, in my opinion, is the embodiment of everyone's
   dream to vicariously live through a superhuman. The stranger of the *Myst* trilogy can
   vault fences, solve dastardly puzzles, creep under gates, and go for days, nay, weeks without eating or using a rest facility. He has eyes of steel and a stomach which would put
   Nietzche's [*sic*] vision of the demigod to mortal shame. His legs never tire and he has the
   uncanny capacity to stare at exactly the same spot of land every time he hits the exact
   same spot of ground. His steps are traced perfectly—at no point does the stranger
   observe what he is not meant to observe. He can communicate with others merely by
   standing like a glob of jelly, and men and women of all ages are only too happy to bab-
   ble away at this mute mollusk. In short, he's what we all want to be—
   practically living in the spirit alone, and requiring only presence to get people either to
   open up or shut up" (ha nekira, 2003).

10. In *Myst,* the player wanders through the deserted Myst island and its associated worlds
    solving puzzles; each solved puzzle provides the player with further information about
    what happened to Atrus and his sons, Sirrus and Achenar, before the game began. At
    the end, the player must decide whom to save: Atrus (the correct answer) or one of his
    two sons. In *Riven,* the player again comes to Atrus's aid, this time to save Atrus's wife,

Catherine, who has been imprisoned by Atrus's own estranged father, Gehn. Gehn hopes to use Catherine to lure his son back to Riven (another world or age) so that he can destroy him, and once more the player wanders through a series of sites solving various puzzles in order to get the information needed (this time in the form of lengthy journals written by the various characters) to thwart Gehn's evil plan. Again, there are several possible endings, but the "right" one allows the player to rescue Catherine and to trap Gehn in the collapsing world of *Riven*.

11. The stranger (i.e., the player) spends a great deal of time helping Atrus out, and as several players note, Atrus does not seem particularly grateful for all the hard work you do.

12. Or as a fan wrote on an Internet forum: "Both [*Myst* and *Riven*] revolve around a mystery, a story. In Myst, it's, 'Good heavens! What happened here?' In Riven, it's, 'What is happening here?' In both cases, you must observe the details presented in the various worlds which gives you clues about the sinister past, the cultures of those inhabitants, and how members of Atrus's family *changed* the customs/art/lifestyles of the native inhabitants into something else. Even Catherine organizes and changes profoundly those she touches. The solution to the game hinges on piecing these clues together, working out what happened—the mystery—in order to determine who's trustworthy." The writer goes on to criticize *Exile* because it lacks this narrative context: "There's just puzzles to be solved. However pretty, they haven't any backstory" (Sepdet, 2002).

13. Such visual aesthetics were even more striking in 1993, when *Myst* appeared, because as many have suggested, there was nothing like it. But as the games have progressed, the visuals have become even more detailed and complexly rendered. When I first played *Myst* I was stunned by its visual appeal. But when I went back to it, after having played *Riven* and then *Exile*, I realized how limited it was.

14. Edana, for example, takes place in a complicated rain forest, an appropriate site for a world whose puzzles depend on principles of connectivity and interrelatedness and whose motto, as we learn at the game's end, is "Nature encourages mutual dependence." Similarly, Volatic's stark canyon is home to a series of puzzles that have to do with various forms of power (electricity, hydropower, etc.) and embodies the motto "Energy powers future motion." Amateria's unstable weather may also, if less overtly, connect to its movement-related puzzles and its motto that "Dynamic forces spur change."

15. Murray (1997) also emphasizes the game's auditory qualities. But my computer's speakers did not allow me to experience the game's sound subtleties.

16. And if I were to join *Myst* groups, on the computer or elsewhere, narrative would also operate for me within context of the "performative" (my play as watched and commented on by other players) or the "augmentary" (mainly novels and websites that provide further layers of history, interpretation, background, and context).

17. This experiential sense of being-in-time as a player contrasts with the rather static time offered by the game itself. Once in the *Myst* world, story-time almost stands still. The weather never changes; the clock never ticks. No one dies. Players who proceed slowly are treated no differently than players who speed through. In this way, these games are unlike those Gee (2003) played, as they are unlike novels or other fictional narratives that can either speed up time (recounting years in a few words) or slow it down (representing the minute-by-minute thoughts or actions of a character). In contrast, the pace of time within the game is a product of my actions, rather than (or as well as) those of the game's author. The game moved as quickly—or as slowly—as I was able to solve its puzzles. Nothing happens, except what the player makes happen as she moves from space to

space—manipulating devices, reading texts, or pushing buttons that allow holograms to speak. But there is a strange moment in *Exile,* in the rain forest world of Edana, where time feels different. Here, the player comes across a baby bird whose mother has become stuck in a strange plant and who is squawking pitifully for food. Until she can solve the puzzles of Edana, the player cannot free the mother bird. However, every time the player returns to the baby bird, she hears the same horrible cries. The baby bird's need for food seems to be operating in the real world, where the unfed become dehydrated or starved in a matter of hours. However, the game operates in a world where puzzle solving can take place over days. The emotional conflict that this generated for me (I got to the point that I almost never returned to any place that I knew I would hear the baby bird) became very distressing; I read postings by other players who report a similar response.

18. "Before projecting the hero forward for the sake of the quest, many tales send the hero or heroine into some dark forest where he or she goes astray or meets some devouring beast. . . . These initial episodes do more than merely introduce the mischief that is to be suppressed; they bring the hero or heroine *back* into a primordial space and time that is more akin to the realm of dreams than to the sphere of action. Thanks to this preliminary disorientation, the linear chain of time is broken and the tale assumes an oneiric dimension that is more or less preserved alongside the heroic dimension of the quest. Two qualities of time are thus intertwined: the circularity of the imaginary travel and the linearity of the quest as such. I agree that the kind of repetition involved in this travel toward the origin is rather primitive, even regressive, in the psychoanalytic sense of the word. It has the character of an immersion and confinement in the midst of dark powers. (Ricoeur, 1981, p. xxx). Eventually, in Ricoeur's account of the development of Western narrative, stories that enact a "mere fantasy of repetition" become superseded by more internal quests (e.g. Augustine, Rousseau, or Proust) in which the journey is the process by which the hero "becomes *who he is*" (Ricoeur, p. 182).

19. In *Exile,* for example, the rationale for sending the player to the three intermediate worlds of Edana, Voltaic, and Amateria—rather than straight to work saving Narayan—is very thin: Saavedro wants to "teach Atrus a lesson" and make him suffer, even though these lessons consequently delay the fulfillment of Saavedro's hopes.

20. The critic Jesper Juul (2004), who argues extensively that video games are *not* narratives, makes a persuasive argument when he calls attention to the contextual elements of game play, asking "How can computer games be abstract and without points of identification, and yet be interesting?—No matter how variable or even absent the protagonist in computer games, there is always one constant: The player. It is probably true that the reader/viewer needs an emotional motivation for investing energy in the movie or book; that we need a human actant to identify with. This is probably also true for the computer game, only this actant is always present—it is the player. The player is motivated to perform a cognitive analysis of the game's situation because the game is a task that the player has undertaken as a real-world person. And this is why a computer game can be much more abstract than a movie or a novel."

21. "Adventure games demand hundreds of hours of play, of mostly frustrating trial and error, to discover the way forward. Sometimes their secrets must be discovered outside the game, from magazines or by trading information with fellow players or perhaps by finding one's way over the Internet to the right Web site or news-group. In the solutionless rhizome or the solvable maze, we are confronted with a world that lures us in with the promise of treasures but that is chiefly designed to resist our efforts.

Perhaps this is a virtue. To be always in search of secret information, in pursuit of refused reward, can be emotionally riveting. Because we are aware that this is a created world, we can experience its resistance to our efforts as a dramatic contest with the programmer or writer over a gift that is purposely withheld. We may experience this withholding presence as a demanding parent, a challenging teacher, a coy lover, or a secretive boss. Or we may experience it as a sustained arousal, a prolonged lovemaking with the climax always a little out of reach." (Murray, 1997, p. 173).

22. Murray (1997) argues that "projection of highly personal (but universally felt) emotional content onto the figures of the formulaic story moves the content into a field where it is safe to think about it. It is putting your most dangerous fantasies in a dungeon to which you hold the keys. Because the fantasy has been externalized, it can be manipulated" (p. 169).

23. Gee (2003) explains how he reflected on his own identity as "Bead Bead," a character he played in *Arcanium:* why he chose to become this character (a female half-elf); what kind of pleasures he received in her actions (such as picking rich people's pockets); and what consequences flowed from decisions he made (at one point, he replays the game because he decided that certain behaviors "just seemed *wrong* for the creature I wanted Bead Bead to be" [p. 57]).

24. See, for example, the website fanfiction.net, in which players post stories about video games and other popular genres and offer each other detailed feedback and critique.

References

Aarseth, Espen. (1997). Cybertext: Perspectives on ergodic literature. Baltimore: Johns Hopkins University Press.

Abbott, H. Porter. (2002). The Cambridge introduction to narrative. New York: Cambridge University Press.

Bazerman, Charles. (1994). Constructing experience. Carbondale: Southern Illinois University Press.

Berkenkotter, Carol, & Huckin, Thomas N. (1995). Genre knowledge in disciplinary communication: Cognition/culture/power. Mahwah, NJ: Lawrence Erlbaum Associates.

Brooks, Peter. (1984). Reading for the plot: Design and intention in narrative. New York: Alfred A. Knopf.

Bruner, Jerome. (1990). Acts of meaning. Cambridge: Harvard University Press.

Chatman, Seymour. (1978). Story and discourse: Narrative structure in fiction and film. Ithaca: Cornell University Press.

Devildog201. (2004, 26 May). Finished it—many possible endings and a moral dilemma. (possible spoiler). *Myst Forums.* Retrieved on September 7, 2004, from http://ubbxforums. ubi.com/6/ubb.x?a=tpc&s=400102&f=153106941&m=790103334&r=625105534 #625105534

Fanfiction.net. Retrieved December 1, 2004, from http://www.fanfiction.net

Gee, James. (2003). What video games have to teach us about learning and literacy. New York: Palgrave Macmillan.

Guild of linguists homepage: The D'Nin language site for beginners and experts. Retrieved October 25, 2004, from http://linguists.riedl.org/old/main.htm

Hass, Christina. (1994, January). Learning to read biology: One student's rhetorical development in college. Written Communication, 11, 43–84.

ha nekira. (July 20, 2003). Response to stranger in exile. *Mystcommunity.com.* Retrieved on October 25, 2003, from http://www.*Myst*community.com/board/index.php? showtopic=7297&hl=atrus,and,stranger.

Herman, David, ed. (2003). Narrative theory and the cognitive sciences. Stanford: Center for the Study of Languages and Information.

Hinchman, Lewis P., & Hinchman, Sandra K. (Eds.) (2001). Memory, identity, community: The idea of narrative in the human sciences. Albany: State University of New York Press.

Jenkins, Henry. (2004). Game design as narrative architecture. In Noah Wardrip-Fruin, & Pat Harrigan, (Eds.) First person: New media as story, performance, and game (pp. 118–130). Cambridge: MIT Press.

Juul, Jesper. (2004). A clash between video games and narrative. Retrieved October 25, 2004, from http://www.jesperjuul.dk/thesis/

Kermode, Frank. (1966). The sense of an ending: Studies in the theory of fiction. New York: Oxford University Press.

Martin, Wallace. (1986). Recent theories of narrative. Ithaca, NY: Cornell University Press.

Mateas, Michael. (2004). A preliminary poetics for interactive drama and games. In Noah Wardrip-Fruin, & Pat Harrigan, (Eds.) First person: New media as story, performance, and game (pp. 19–33). Cambridge: MIT Press.

Miller, Rand, Wingrove, David, & Miller, Robyn. (2004). The Myst Reader. Basking Ridge, NJ: Hyperion. [Includes Myst: The Book of Ti'ana, Myst: The Book of Atrus, and Myst: The Book of D'ni.]

Montford, Nick. (2003). Twisty little passages: An approach to interactive fiction. Cambridge: MIT Press.

Murray, Janet. (1997). Hamlet on the holodeck: The future of narrative in cyberspace. New York: Free Press.

Pearce, Celia. (2004). Toward a game theory of game. In Noah Wardrip-Fruin, & Pat Harrigan, (Eds.) First person: New media as story, performance, and game (pp. 143–153). Cambridge: MIT Press.

Polkinghorne, Donald E. (1988). Narrative knowing and the human sciences. Albany: State University of New York Press.

Prior, Paul. (1998). Writing/Disciplinarity: A sociohistoric account of literate activity in the academy. Mahwah, NJ: Lawrence Erlbaum Associates.

Ricoeur, Paul. (1981). Narrative time. In W. J. T. Mitchell (Ed.), On narrative (pp. 165–186). Chicago: University of Chicago Press.

Russell, David. (1997). Rethinking genre in school and society: An activity theory analysis. Written Communication, 14, 504–554.

Ryan, Marie-Laure. (2001, July). Beyond myth and metaphor: The case for narrative in digital media. Game Studies 1. Retrieved October 25, 2004, from http://www.gamestudies.org/0101/ryan/

Ryan, Marie-Laure. (2001). Narrative as virtual reality: Immersion and interactivity in electronic media. Baltimore: Johns Hopkins University Press.

Sepdet. (2002, June 2). Response to "Anti-climactic?" Retrieved October 10, 2004, from http://www.Mystrealm.com/forums/topic.asp?TOPIC_ID=841

Tales of the D'Ni. Retrieved October 24, 2004, from http://www.geocities.com/kishlisandra/index.html

UbiSoft. Retrieved October 25, 2004, from http://www.ubi.com/US/

6

Gaming, Agency, and Imagination: Locating Gaming within a Larger Constellation of Literacies

Deanna McGaughey-Summers and Russell Summers

We fail to build on the literacies that students already have—and we fail to learn about these literacies or why they seem so important to so many students. We also fail, as we deny the value of these new literacies, to recognize ourselves as illiterate in some spheres. And in this intellectual arrogance, we neglect to open ourselves to learning new literacies that could teach us more about human discursive practices.

(Hawisher and Selfe, 2004, Becoming Literate in the Information Age: Cultural Ecologies and Literacies of Technology, p. 676)

Compositionists have increasingly devoted attention to how new technologies have informed our understanding of writing and literacy as well as the implications of new media, such as the Internet, for writing. Essentially, these new technologies have forced us to complicate "what it means to write" (Alfano & O'Brien, 2005); how we understand the concept of literacy (Faigley, George, Palchik, & Selfe, 2004); and how new technologies can be incorporated into the classroom environment to enhance the practice and outcomes of writing (Castellani & Jeffs, 2001). Considering that many students have new technologies available to them at home, and that writing is a central feature of these technologies (e.g., text messaging on cell phones, chat rooms, discussion boards, homepages on the Internet, video games) it is important to consider how they are engaging these technologies and how such engagement informs their understanding and practice of writing. Therefore, as Hawisher and Selfe (2004) argue, compositionists should examine what resources and literacies students in the information age are bringing to class.

The notion that students are not blank slates and that they bring literacies with them to class has begun to be addressed in recent scholarship on literacy and composition. In his recently published composition textbook, *Convergences: Message, Method, and Medium,* for example, Atwan (2002) explains that the impetus for writing the text "came from watching my children and my students connect ideas they discovered in their textbooks to ideas they saw in other kinds of texts. . . . All these things are compositions, even if they are not traditionally part of the syllabus for a composition course" (p. v). Atwan (2002) suggests that students are engaging texts and genres compositionally and rhetorically that are considered outside the domain of a traditional writing course. Not only are students engaging multiple genres through new technologies, they are also practicing techniques typically associated with "good" writing with existing popular technology. In *Tuned In,* for example, Williams (2002) found that although students did not recognize viewing techniques as similar to the type of critical thinking they are asked to do in the classroom, they nevertheless demonstrated that through their viewing, they were able to take a stance toward the argument constructed in the text and to take into account rhetorical features of the text, in this case, television. Although Atwan (2004) focused on genre, and Williams (2002) on transferability, both works encourage compositionists to consider what students already know about writing and how this knowledge can be incorporated into the writing classroom. An important point to keep in mind, however, is that "extracurricular" technologies are not valued the same and some, like television or video gaming, are considered base or dangerous. Consider, for example, television viewing, which has been seen as mind-numbing (Williams, 2002), or gaming, which has been seen as encouraging antisocial behavior in teens (Smith, Lachlan, & Tamborini, 2003). With these attitudes in mind, we should consider, as compositionists, how we are illiterate with respect to new technologies as well as how we might devalue certain kinds of literacies on the basis of our own involvement in larger cultural narratives and controversies. As Macintyre (2001) explains:

> In successfully identifying and understanding what someone else is doing, we always move toward placing a particular episode in the context of a set of narrative histories, histories both of the individual concerned and of the settings in which they act and suffer. It is now becoming clear that we render the actions of others intelligible in this way because action itself has a basically historical character. It is because we all live our narratives in our own lives, and because we understand our own lives in terms of the narratives that we live out, that the form of narrative is appropriate for understanding the actions of others. (p. 249)

In this chapter, we explore the experiences of a 37-year-old male, rural, gamer in order to understand the relationship between gaming, literacy, and imagination in an effort to move beyond dualistic thinking regarding the merits of gaming, particularly for compositionists interested in incorporating new technologies and students' existing mastery of these in the classroom. We seek to understand these issues by locating Martin McClave's personal narrative of gaming within the larger cultural and political narrative of video gaming.

The Video Gaming Controversy

In 2002, the video gaming industry received an "F" from the National Institute on Media and Family for objectionable violent and sexual content in video games

(Wright, 2002). The concerns of the National Institute on Media and Family are mirrored in both public and congressional debates regarding video games. In the current social climate, critical attention is being given to the *Grand Theft Auto: San Andreas* video game because players can now download and insert a modification into the game that includes explicit sex scenes. In light of this development, Senator Hillary Clinton has asked the Federal Trade Commission to consider changing the rating from a M (+17) to AO (Adults Only) and has begun calling for stricter fines for those who sell adult-rated games to children ("Clinton Seeks," 2005).

The concerns are predicated upon the belief that playing games that include what is considered antisocial behavior will encourage a culture of violence. For example, Senator Joseph Lieberman has been quoted as saying: "These games . . . are part of a toxic culture of violence that is enveloping our children, that is helping to desensitize them and blur the lines between right and wrong, and encouraging some of the most vulnerable of them to commit violence" (qtd. In Smith, Lachlan, & Tamborini, 2003, p. 58). In the face of such concerns, some major retailers have limited the sale of mature-rated games (e.g., Montgomery Ward and Sears, Roebuck, and Co.); have completely stopped selling all video games (e.g., Zany Brainy); or have begun instituting bar codes to ensure that mature games are not sold to people under age 17 (K-Mart and Wal-Mart) (LaMotte & Morris, 2000). Also reflecting the concern over video games is the current 246-million-dollar lawsuit against Sony, Take-Two Interactive Software, Rockstar Games, and Wal-Mart, for *Grand Theft Auto,* which was identified as a motivating factor by two teens standing trial for murder (Toobin, 2003). In general, the concern is with the divide between the distinction between "the real" and "the imagined."

While there has been much attention by researchers, public officials, and the public-at-large regarding some potentially insidious effects of video games, others have begun to highlight potential benefits of gaming. Din and Calao (2001) found in their research of kindergartners that those students who played educational video games showed marked improvement in their reading and spelling abilities. Demarest (2000) found that video games offered many therapeutic benefits for her autistic son, including language, math, reading, and social skills. And most recently, research has even suggested that doctors who spent three or more hours per week gaming made 37 percent fewer mistakes during complicated laparoscopic surgeries. The surgeons who participated in this study explained that the games involved the same eye-hand coordination as the surgery. Encouraged by these findings, the researchers recommended practicing surgical techniques through gaming, and one of the researchers, James Rosser, developed a course entitled *Top Gun* that was to serve as a kind of "warm up" before surgery ("Research Shows," 2004). Thus, some research demonstrates that gaming can improve various professional practices. Therefore, compositionists would do well to consider how such literacies can inform the writing practices of students and how such literacies inform our understanding of student writers' "abilities."

In general, what we are seeing in public discourse is simplistic either/or thinking regarding whether video games are "good" or "bad." In the discussion that follows, we will present the experiences of an adult gamer in the interest of moving beyond such simplistic approaches by focusing on how gaming is located within the gamer's larger constellation of literacy practices.

Martin McClave, Age 36

Martin is a 36-year-old white male employed in maintenance and security at a retirement community in Louisville, Kentucky. He earns an annual income of $29,000 ($17,000 income and $12,000 inheritance) and is married to a full-time college student. They have no children. He resides in a house with his wife in the suburbs of Louisville.

Martin is originally from a small town in western Kentucky, which he describes as like *The Dukes of Hazard:*

> It was just little. The whole county had three stop lights and our city [La Center] was fortunate enough to have one, but it just blinked. It didn't change colors. I think it actually changes colors now. The city was La Center. The center of the universe. That's what the sign in front of City Hall said.

According to the census, Ballard County is predominately white, with a total population of 8,286. In terms of education, about 40 percent of Ballard County residents earn high school diplomas, 20 percent attend some college, and 5 percent earn a bachelor's degree. These statistics have been relatively unchanged since 1970. In terms of occupation, 21 percent of the population is involved in management, professional, and related occupations; 14 percent in service occupations; 25 percent in sales; 17 percent in construction; and 20 percent in production, transportation, and material moving. The dominant industries in Ballard County are construction, manufacturing, and education. The median household income is $32,130. Median earnings for male, full-time, year-round workers is $32,345 compared with that of females, which is $20,902. In 1999, 10 percent of Ballard County families were living in poverty; 40 percent of which were female-headed households (US Census Bureau, 2005).

Martin comes from a fairly large family consisting of two older sisters and two older brothers (both now deceased). His mother was a full-time homemaker and his father was a nuclear physicist and bar owner.

Although his early family life was fairly normal—he lived with both parents and two brothers, played G.I. Joe, and ate at the supper table every day at 6:30—his family did move frequently: "We moved in the first grade, third grade, and again in the 5th grade. We moved because of Dad's work. He was transferred. He was a nuclear physicist." Nevertheless, Martin has always considered Ballard County to be his home because it was where he felt most comfortable, where "everything was familiar."

One factor that does make his home life notable and tragic is that his mother died unexpectedly from a brain aneurysm when he was eight: "I couldn't quite comprehend the meaning of forever. I knew I wouldn't see her again, but I didn't know how long that would actually be. It seemed like I felt worse for Dad than me because I never seen him cry. I never seen him cry until that day. Seen a lot of it after that day." After his mother died, Martin lived with his father, in Chicago, who had quit his job as a nuclear physicist to run a bar:

> It was different. I more or less played mother or wife and it wasn't right as young as I was. I would have dinner ready for him. I did the cleaning. More or less, I did anything to keep him from crying. I didn't want that to happen again. I lived with him until I was about nine or so. There was a party that got a little out of hand; 'bout burned the house down. And he said . . . he couldn't be there for me, then. . . . I was given the choice to live with my oldest sister, an aunt, or military school. I went with the aunt.

After moving in with his aunt, he says "the pace slowed down a lot. Aunt Mary cooked for me and *she* cleaned. That's when I started gaming. Dungeons and Dragons." Martin became involved with *Dungeons and Dragons (D&D)* through friends. During a sleepover, one of his friends showed him one of the *D&D* books. Martin liked it because it was different from other games he played, such as Monopoly or card games. As he explains, "You used your mind, your imagination, not just luck. With Monopoly, you either buy or don't buy. But in *D&D* you choose everything, just like in real life. You decide if you're going to go to a town or a dungeon or a cave instead of just rolling dice." In this sense, Martin's initiation into gaming allowed him to exercise agency and make choices. In the context of having things happen to him, through *D&D*, Martin was able to re-vision and re-write life experiences.

Martin remembers his middle and high school years best. He went to Ballard County Middle School, a small school (there were 80 students in his graduating class) that was actually part of the high school: same building, different wing. There was very little use of, and exposure to, "contemporary" forms of technology:

> It wasn't allowed (laughs). You were sent to detention if you had a calculator. I remember dad taught me how to add and subtract on a slide rule. They took that away from me. I couldn't even use it. It was considered cheating. Now you have to. It's on the list with pencils and papers. . . . A typewriter was as modern as we got. Our class had two electrics. I used it one day, when it was my turn. Everyone got a turn and after everyone went, the good students got to use them. We didn't have computers. Not even in the office. You have to remember, this was before 1986. They were amazed with the fax.

Martin was unaware of the importance of contemporary forms of technology: "When I was in school, I can remember Dad paying over six hundred dollars for a calculator. You got to realize, we didn't have technology like we have today. We didn't even have a push button phone at our house and it's hard to win a radio contest with a rotary phone." With respect to the electric typewriters: "I think the teacher bought those and brought them in. And that was because she was one of the richest people in the county."

The only recollection Martin has of computers in his early years involved his younger cousin: "My cousin was the only person I knew who had a PC and they paid I don't know how much for that thing. I think there was a couple of games he could play on it, but he didn't like it." Although given the chance, Martin opted out of trying the PC himself: "I was never one of those people that liked to do things if I didn't have a chance to get one. I wouldn't ride another person's motorcycle if I couldn't get one. I was never one for living beyond my means." At the time, Martin played with a three-wheeler/ATV and remote control cars and bicycles and in doing so, spent a lot of time outside: "Did a lot of fishing and camping, wasn't much of a hunter. I don't mind duck hunting as long as someone else deals with the dead duck. I don't like shooting deer. They're too pretty." He explains that he liked to be outside: "It's easier to find adventure and excitement outside. We used to have BB fights. Now they have paintball guns. We didn't have paintball guns. It's a wonder I'm not sitting here with a patch over my eye. We used squirt guns once, but they didn't shoot far enough and after one of my friends peed in his, no one would play with us anymore." When Martin was 15, he met with another tragedy: his father died of cirrhosis of the liver. While in Korea, in the army, his father was shot in the stomach and had to have a third of his stomach removed. When he worked at the nuclear plant, he developed stomach cancer and they had to remove more of his stomach. Martin is not sure if his father died from drinking or "from the plant where all those people were getting cancer." In response to his father's death, Martin noted: "I hate to say it, but it had no effect. I had already felt like he had given me up. Now I can understand why he gave me to Aunt Mary, but at the time, I just knew he didn't want me." As a coping mechanism, Martin spent a lot of time on his three-wheeler, listening to, and playing, music. Martin explains that the music he listened to became harder: "It was just one of those things most my friends seemed to be listening to. I don't think it had much to do with that [his father dying]." He was also playing music, in school, saxophone, bass guitar, and drums. He had been playing saxophone since the fourth grade, but his interest in guitars and drums coincided with his changing interest in music.

After High School

Throughout high school, Martin continued to live with his aunt and work at Sears in retail. After high school, he moved to Louisville to live with another aunt and continue working at Sears, though this time in shipping and receiving. After Sears, Martin went to work for the Glenview Condominiums, where he has been for the last 12 years. He started at the Glenview as a painter and was eventually hired on as a valet for second shift and is currently in maintenance and security on the third shift, his favorite: "Don't have to deal with all the people."

Martin has completed some college at two community colleges, one in Paducah, Kentucky, and one in Louisville, Kentucky. He attended college right after high school, but quit because he did not like it. In college, Martin had taken general education classes: algebra, composition, public speech, and art and music appreciation. He did not like getting up early and going to class. "It was just as interesting when I was at home reading it. Classes seemed like a waste of time. Some of the other classes, I didn't see the point of being there." The classes Martin took were based on the standard lecture. Martin felt that they were ineffective because the courses encouraged passivity. As he demonstrated through his

previous interests in gaming, music, and outdoor activities, Martin preferred literacy contexts that required agency. Eventually, however, he went back to school
because of "family encouragement" but has yet to finish a degree. Interestingly,
Martin attributes his lack of focus and commitment to school as an effect of *not*
gaming: "I was a wild one in my younger years. Externally [when I was playing
video games] I was more subdued. Internally, your mind is working when you're
playing video games." So for Martin, gaming allowed him to focus on a task while
being actively engaged. In contrast to today's critics of video games, gaming in
general improved his scholastic endeavors.

Gaming has long been central to Martin's life, though he did not use "technology" for gaming until recent years. His earliest gaming experiences were with
D&D, but he was also involved in the arcades, consoles, and computing gaming.
Currently, he is an avid gamer, playing at home and work about eight hours
a day.

As discussed earlier, Martin became involved in *D&D* when he was ten because
a friend had introduced him to the books upon which the game is based. Martin
was attracted to *D&D* because it allowed him the chance to be creative, to create
his own reality. "It's all role playing. You think up a character and go fight the evils
of the world unless you want to be evil. . . . I was a cleric. A healer." There were several types of characters available—fighters, paladin (ultra-good fighter), thief,
magic user, cleric, and bard (monk)—and these characters ranged from good to
bad. Martin, however, reports that he does not really know why he was interested
in being a healer. His experiences encourage us to ask *how* people are engaging
complicated literacies and to broaden assumptions about the "dangerousness" of
particular games. A "dangerous" game obviously provides the opportunity to play
the role of good characters. In this sense, to play these games, one is required to
recognize the importance of ethos in writing and that there are many different
ways of representing one's self as "author" in various texts.

When Martin was 13 or 14, he received a Sears console from his aunt. She had
purchased the Sears brand for him for Christmas, although he wanted an Atari.
She was unaware that there were different brands. He notes that he was not bothered by the mistake his aunt had made in choosing a console. "I could play Atari
at any of my friend's houses, but I was the only one with a Sears brand." Martin
never told his aunt of her mistake, but his sister did. He notes: "I didn't see no
need to tell them, to hurt their feelings. They tried. They wanted to show me that
I had a parental figure that loved me. It was good to know the effort was there." As
part of the *Pac-Man* craze of the 1980s, Martin began playing arcade games when
he was 16:

> Where I grew up, I didn't get to go to the arcades until I was 16. The closest one was
> 40 miles away. But the Jiffy Mart had a Pac Man machine. I played it a lot. Played
> everyday. I liked getting the high score. Beating the high score. There was always a
> crowd around when somebody good was playing.

For Martin, arcade games were appealing for the sociality they encouraged and
because they provided the opportunity for skill building. Rather than discouraging him from creating relations gaming facilitated social relations with others.

Currently, Martin is heavily involved in console (Playstation 2 and Xbox), computer, and fantasy games (football).

Martin became involved in console games in his twenties after his friends became involved and enjoyed these games for the same reasons he enjoyed arcade games: "On *Mario Brothers,* for the original Nintendo, I could run through the whole thing, the whole game, and the looks on people's faces when I would do it. It took me seven minutes or eight minutes to beat the game from start to finish." Martin is not sure what made him so good at it. He says, "It was just a natural kind of thing." He notes that eye-hand coordination, persistence, and deductive reasoning are necessary for being successful at these games.

Of computer games, he says:

> I got involved in computer games when I met my fiancé. About 15 years behind everybody else in the country. I never really had the money for a computer and I didn't think I had the knowledge. Looked like too much work to play a game. TV made me feel like I could mess them up.

Martin began to use the computer for gaming when he met his wife, a full-time college student. Computer technology was essential to his wife's literacy practices and provided him with a new opportunity and platform for his own interests. She would load the games and he would use the tutorials to learn how to operate the games. Although Martin does not see himself as "computer savvy," he does prefer computer games to console or platform games: "There seems to be more thinking games than on the platforms. When computers first came out, most of the people who had them were your smarter people." Again, Martin's interests illustrate his need to be actively involved in the literacy practices and the connection between this active involvement and intelligence.

Currently, his favorite platform and computer games include *ESPN Football* (Xbox) and *Civilization 3* (Computer).

> With *ESPN,* you take your favorite football team and play through the season. They have the real players and real schedule and you try and make it through the super-bowl. No matter who your favorite team is, if you play them in football, you can see them win the superbowl. It gives you more control than when you're a spectator. That "could have, should have, been." "If I would have been there." I like how realistic it gets each year. How it looks. What the announcers say. It's a fill in until football season. The new game comes out about a month before the season starts and it kind of shows you what they think of your team.

To be successful in football, you have to have knowledge of the game itself and know the players on the team. And you have to know which buttons to push to throw. Of Civilization 3, he says:

> You start out at the beginning of mankind. You pick a civilization like the Aztecs, the English and you try and survive and take over the world. You play up until modern day. It's neat because it's a micromanaged game because you determine what you produce, what your city will produce, how you train your army. It was a challenging

game. It took me a while to beat it. You rewrite history. You have to keep your people happy. If there's not enough temples or theatres or if you've drafted too many people into the army, you have to do something to make them happy all the while trying to gain more territory. You have to have management skills.

Civilization 3, in contrast to the fantasy game, involves trial and error. "It's a strategy game. You set goals. It's a turn-based game. You don't have to have quick reflexes. You think about your next move and think about the consequences of it are."

He also says,

I got involved [with fantasy football] through friends. You have a draft and everybody picks one player from real football teams and creates a team. Through the season, whatever that player does each game, you get so many points. You compete against the other people you drafted with. When you win, it makes you look knowledgeable about football. You have to know about the teams and how to play the game. Before I had satellite, it gave me a reason to watch games that weren't my favorite team. That's the main reason. You feel like you're pulling for yourself as much as the team. It seems to take a little more research than other forms of gaming. It could be my favorite if the season lasted longer. It's my most anticipated.

Fantasy football is similar to other gaming experiences he has had by "making your own little reality. But in fantasy football, you're taking reality and making it your reality. You're taking a real football player and using their stats for your game. So you can make better teams."

In general, Martin has always preferred games that allow him a creative role, the opportunity to rewrite the world. He enjoys games that emphasize thinking, creativity, and problem solving. These characteristics are reflected in how he chooses games: "I want something easy to learn but hard to master. Something that's easy to play but hard to beat."

Another interesting aspect of Martin's gaming is that he frequently chooses to assume the role of characters who allow him to create a better world, whether it is as a cleric/healer in his younger days playing *D&D* or as a Jedi in his current gaming:

I generally try to be the good guy. I don't know why. Generally after I beat [the game] with the good guy, I go back and play it with the bad guy. . . . In the last game I played, I was a Jedi [who are] masters of the force. I was a good Jedi. He was ultra-good. I tried not to do anything remotely bad with him, which was a challenge. . . . It's like real life. Everyone has choices to make. I try to model the character after how I live.

Even though Martin did not mention violent games as among his favorites, he has regularly played some of the most controversial games, such as Doom, the Grand Theft Auto series, Mortal Kombat, and Twisted Metal I and II. Martin believes that these games are controversial because "the people that say its bad see that it gives kids a chance to act out what they see on TV. Generally, in most video games, the way to work things out is through violence and a lot of people apparently think that's going to be how kids are going to resolve their differences when they grow up." How does Martin feel about the controversy? "I think it's the individual parent's responsibility to teach their kids morals and good values." Martin believes the violent games should have ratings. "I don't think an 8-or 9-year-old kid should play the games I listed. But it's my right as an adult to pay for, and play, those games."

Martin fits the description of a "troubled" kid who would be geared toward games. But ironically, he does not believe that the tragedies he faced in his youth led him to gaming in general, or violent games in particular. In fact, he suggests that the opposite may have occurred: "Because of the tragedy I've gone through, I feel I have a higher value of life. The Columbine killers, both of them come from upper-middle-class, two-parent homes. And the boy that shot up Heath High School was from an upper-middle-class, two-parent home. It's about the parenting. I all the time see my friends cussing their mom, yelling at their parents, or totally ignoring them, and I think if I had parents I would never yell at them. I'd be over there every Sunday for dinner. And the thought of killing someone, that makes me think that's somebody's parent or somebody's child."

Gaming and "Real" Life

Although Martin has yet to complete a college degree, like his experiences with gaming, he prefers to live in the "real" world in a creative and engaged way and finds that lived experiences provide the best education:

> I like seeing new stuff. Not new, different. Plus, overseas, things have a real history. In America, once it's "outdated" it gets torn down and replaced with something else. I have seen the trench lines from WWI. I have been to where they signed Versailles. I've seen the Reichstag. People hear about concentration camp cars, but I've been in one and that had more of an impact on me than the black and white pictures I've seen.

Ironically, Martin defines himself as only "semi" intelligent and defines literacy in a simplistic way: "Being able to read and write. I feel I can play games because I am literate." Although he has traveled far and wide, and has survived family tragedy, and has become absorbed in various forms of gaming (even in light of a lack of technological resources) to create "better" worlds, he does not consider himself to have any kind of specialized knowledge or literacy: "I hate to say it, but the only thing I can do is probably hook up a console quicker than anybody else" (laughs).

Emerging Thoughts

Although Martin experienced much tragedy in his youth and may fit the stereotype of a "vulnerable" child attracted to violent games, his actual experiences may suggest the opposite. Martin appears to have an aversion to violence in general and in gaming as well. What Martin's experience suggests to us is that we should focus on how people actually engage gaming rather than considering gaming as violent or not.

Among other interesting and important insights from Martin is the significance of agency and imagination in his life. In most areas of his life, he prefers activities, which include gaming, that allow him to envision and work to change the world. We have seen this in his aversion to college courses that encourage passivity, his taking on the role of a healer when he was involved in *D&D*, and his construction of his characters as "ultra good," as he did with his Jedi in the Star Wars games. It can also be seen in his preference to travel to learn about the world and his preference for outdoor activities and for playing, rather than simply listening to music.

Martin's experiences with gaming do not necessarily suggest that gaming is good, but his experiences with gaming do point to the necessity of actually finding out how gaming relates to other activities and literacies with which someone is involved.

For compositionists, Martin's narrative can encourage us to consider contexts in which students are already practicing principles of "good writing": revision, audience awareness, ethos, et cetera. Acknowledging such skills and transferring them into the classroom requires that we acknowledge what little we know about particular technologies as well as how what we know is tempered through existing cultural and historical narratives that render these literacies in negative terms.

References

Alfano, Christine, & O'Brien, Alyssa. (2005) *Envision: Persuasive writing in a visual world.* New York: Longman.

Atwan, Robert. (2002) *Convergences: Message, method, and medium.* New York: Bedford / St. Martins.

Castellani, John, & Jeffs, Tara. (2001). Emerging reading and writing strategies using technology. *Exceptional Children, 35*(5), 30–67.

Clinton seeks video game sex scene probe. (2005, July 15). Retrieved July 15, 2005, from http://www.cnn.com/2005/POLITICS/07/15/senate. videogame.reut/

Demarest, Kandie. (2000). Video games—What are they good for? *Lesson Tutor.* Retrieved February 3, 2006, from http://www.lessontutor.com/ kd3.html

Din, Feng, & Calao, Josephine. (2001). The effects of playing educational videos on kindergarten achievement. *Child Study Journal, 31*(2), 95–123.

Faigley, Lester, George, Diana, Palchik, Anna, & Selfe, Cynthia. (2004). *Picturing Texts.* New York: W. W. Norton.

Hawisher, Gail E., & Selfe, Cynthia L. (2004). Becoming literate in the information age: Cultural ecologies and literacies of technology. *College Composition and Communication, 55*(4), 642–692.

LaMotte, Greg, & Morris, Jim. (2000, September 11). Feds: Violent entertainment industry intentionally aimed at young, but regulators say industry itself, not government, is the remedy. *CNN.* Retrieved February 3, 2006, from http://www.cnn.com/2000/US/09/11/ entertain.report.02/index.html

MacIntyre, Alasdair. (2001). The virtues, the unity of a human life, and the concept of tradition. In Lewis Hinchman, & Sandra Hinchman (Eds.), *Memory, identity, community: The idea of narrative in the human sciences* (pp. 241–263). New York: State University of New York Press.

Research shows video game playing may help surgeons. (2004). *CNN*. Retrieved July 15, 2005, from http://www.cnn.com/2004/HEALTH/04/07/video.surgeons.ap/index.html

Smith, Stacy, Lachlan, Ken, & Tamborini, Ron. (2003). Popular video games: Quantifying the presentation of violence in popular video games. *Journal of Broadcasting and Electronic Media, 47,* 58–72.

Toobin, Jeffrey. (2003). It's hard to prove video game caused shootings. *CNN*. Retrieved February 3, 2006, from http://www.cnn.com/2003/LAW/10/23/otsc.toobin/index.html

United States Census Bureau. (2005). Kentucky quickfacts: Ballard county. Retrieved February 1, 2005, from http://quickfacts.census.gov/qfd/states/21/21007.html

Williams, Bronwyn. (2002). *Tuned in: Television and the teaching of writing.* New York: Cook.

Wright, B. (2002). Sounding the alarm on video game ratings. *CNN*. Retrieved July 15, 2005, from http://www.cnn.com/2002/TECH/fun.games/12/19/games.ratings/

7

Relationship Gaming and Identity: Stephanie and Josh

JoAnn Griffin

Video games recruit identities and encourage identity work and reflection on identities in clear and powerful ways.

(James Paul Gee, 2003)

Composition teachers spend a lot of time reflecting on their students' identities and the ways in which those identities are or are not expressed, stifled, encouraged, or developed in and around the composition classroom. It is unlikely, however, that many of us think much about whether our students play video games or not and even less likely that we wonder why, or how, or to what ends. Nonetheless, as James Paul Gee (2003) observes in his study of video gaming as a learning environment, the semiotic domains of video games "encourage people new to them to take on and play with new identities" (p. 51). Games require both "taking on a new identity and forming bridges from one's old identities to the new one" (p. 51). As reflective practitioners in the mode of Hillocks (1995), striving to meet students at Vygotsky's "zone of proximal development," composition teachers may find student gaming interests and practices useful in the construction of "environments for active learning" (pp. 54–55), spaces where students can share their experiences of gaming to develop insights that they might not reach on their own.

This case study of a gaming couple, Stephanie and Josh, explores one instance of identity experimentation within game play. Stephanie and Josh are graduate students who play *Tiger Woods Golf 2004* (*TWG*) together as a couple. Josh plays other games as well, but *TWG* is the only game that Stephanie plays. Her motivations for and experiences with the game suggest that identity formation is the primary focus of her gaming activity. At the time of this study, Stephanie and Josh had been dating for just under a year and were planning to marry in the following calendar year. Both identify time together as an important feature of their gaming activity, and this study suggests that, for Stephanie, game playing with

Josh may be enabling the formation of an important new identity—her role as a simultaneous member of two family groups and a member of a socially acknowledged couple. Examined in light of narrative theories of identity, Stephanie and Josh's gaming experience suggests possibilities for furthering students' explorations of identities in composition classrooms.

Gaming and Literacy

Born in a computer-saturated age, Stephanie and Josh inhabit a world shaped by technology. The IBM PC was introduced in 1981, exactly between their birth years. Before Stephanie and Josh were six years old, the compact disc (CD) appeared (1983), the Internet took its first step toward today's World Wide Web (1983), and the first computer mouse was introduced by Apple (1984), all events that forever changed the daily interactions between middle-class America and computer technology (*American History Timeline*). Before Stephanie and Josh were driving, the World Wide Web became available to anyone with the equipment to access it (1991); HTML was introduced, making the language of Web page creation available to the general public (1992); and Mosaic, the first Web browser, appeared, making the Web accessible to an even larger audience (1993). Stephanie and Josh also came of computer gaming age during a period of market expansion for video games. As a consequence of that watershed, Nintendo Entertainment Systems would become the highest-selling system in history, outselling its competitors 10 to 1 in 1986 (Rutter, 2004).

Today, Stephanie and Josh are both students pursuing graduate degrees. Both write creatively, Stephanie in text and Josh as a videographer. They operate fluently in multiple literacies. Both grew up in semirural households that they describe as transitioning from lower middle to upper middle class during their growing-up years, and both describe their fathers as the technology-savvy members of their families. Stephanie's father introduced her to video games when she was "10 or 11." Josh recalls learning about computers from a teacher in the second or third grade. Both Stephanie and Josh read alphabetic text before they entered kindergarten. Both identify their mothers as the chief sponsors of alphabetic literacy in their lives. Josh's mother is a teacher who "put a lot of emphasis on reading well."

Stephanie's mother often talks about reading as a child, and Stephanie suspects that her father perceives reading as a "feminine" activity because his mother always read, but his father never did. Both parents, however, "pushed college" as a way for Stephanie to achieve greater career satisfaction than their own two-year college associate degrees afforded. According to Stephanie, although her parents "have very good jobs from a financial perspective, they have both always relayed a certain unhappiness in their positions because they weren't fulfilled emotionally." Stephanie's experiences of her family's literacies illustrate Brandt's (2001) claim that the changes "of earlier generations become the deep infrastructures for literacy encounters by later generations" (p. 103). Partly as a result of her parents' experiences and partly due to the cultural ecology of her time, Stephanie's understanding of literacies includes early engagement with alphabetic text and four-year college degrees, as well as digital literacy through computers and gaming.

Gaming and Identity

In spite of their position in a technology-rich generation, Josh and Stephanie both engage in thoughtful use of the technologies in their lives. Computers, says Stephanie, "make me nervous. Not P.C.s so much but rather the self-check-out aisle in Kroger. I'm thinking Stanley Kubrick was onto something in *2001*." Josh echoes Stephanie's sentiment by suggesting that "people are becoming too dependent on computers." Both Stephanie and Josh, however, differentiate their gaming experiences from their cultural apprehensions about computer technology in general. According to Josh, "It's not the same. People aren't dependent on video games. They choose to enjoy them by playing them. Whereas computers—people are needing them to carry out everyday tasks such as groceries, ebay, cars." Josh and Stephanie's discrimination about the value of various technologies extends to their gaming experiences. Stephanie, for example, remembers growing up in an age when computer games were the gift of choice at holidays, yet they weren't important to her life. Though she and her younger sister lobbied for Nintendo as a holiday gift, they "never played it that much. . . . It most certainly was not an intricate part of my childhood like reading or writing or music or tennis. . . . I think I probably just wanted one because everybody had one, played it for a while, and got tired of it."

In contrast with Stephanie's lack of interest in an earlier generation of games, both she and Josh, when asked, identify character development and social interaction as key to their involvement in *TWG*. Both give attention to their gaming avatars and the sculpting of their identities within the game. Josh plays other games but finds that he enjoys sports games such as *TWG* "more than any other because of my ability to make characters and put them through the sports challenges." Josh also enjoys the interaction between gaming identities and real-life identities. He handles character creation in his *TWG* circle. Josh created his, Stephanie's, and his father's characters:

> I try to make the characters look exactly like their real counterparts. I also didn't stray from their style of clothing or hair style or jewelry. I even picked the same clubs on the game that my dad and I use in real life. And I gave Stephanie the same clubs as me because those are the ones she thinks she wants to use when she starts playing real golf. I sort of try to make it as much like reality as possible but the great thing is, it's not reality. And when you mix fantasy with partial reality it seems more real.

Also important to Stephanie is the role Josh is playing in the formation of an identity for her game character:

> Josh did it all by himself. He loves doing that. I joke with him that he would buy any game that lets you create your own characters. But, I did help pick out my girl's outfit, and sometimes I'll change her hair. But it's usually me telling Josh to do it. I

don't like to fool with that stuff. I just like to play and have my girl look cute at the same time.

Stephanie and Josh play *TWG* with each other, with the male members of Josh's family, and with Josh's friends. *TWG* appears to enable the formation of an identity important to Stephanie's new role as a simultaneous member of two family groups. It is important to her that by playing *TWG* she is fitting in with Josh's family in a recreational way. She notes,

> Josh and his dad both think it's really cool that I do that with them. I guess I feel like one of the boys. But at the same time, I have my cute little girl on the game that Josh created for me. She wears a little skirt and looks just like me. So, that feminizes it a lot for me. Golf is such a uni-sexual game. It's not like I'm playing with a man character or shooting anyone in the street. I'm a girly-girl. This game fully supports that.

So, to be a "girly-girl" and a functioning member of her spouse-to-be's cohort, Stephanie is making use of *TWG* to construct, in concert with others, an identity consistent with other self-relevant events and with the current identity she seeks to form ("girly-girl," one of the boys, fiancé, daughter-in-law, spouse).

The narrative theorists Gergen and Gergen (1997) base their understanding of self-narrative on the premise that we strive as individuals "to understand life events as systematically related [because] . . . narrative order may be essential in giving one's life a sense of meaning and direction" (p. 162). From this perspective, Stephanie's experience with *TWG* assists her in making meaning from a significant change in life circumstances. As Gergen and Gergen explain, we actively negotiate our sense of self through our interactions with others. Such interaction is more than necessary; it is the stuff out of which our self, or selves, is constituted. Our ability to maintain any specific conception of our place in the world depends on "others' willingness to play out certain parts in relationship " to us (Gergen & Gergen, 1997, p. 178). Incorporating others' narratives into one's own insulates these stabilizing forces of reciprocity that maintain relationships (p. 179). Individuals come to view their mutual relationship as a "new entity." "Objectification" of the relationship shifts "to the simpler task of negotiating one narrative rather than two" (p. 179), a narrative construction of identity of which Stephanie and Josh, in their *TWG* interactions, provide a vivid example.

Stephanie and Josh also demonstrate another important process of identity formation via their joint participation in *TWG*. The "implicit social act" (Gergen & Gergen, p. 176) of narrating a self demonstrates an inherent social and individual value in the "self-stability" narrative, the notion of a consistent identity (p. 173). At the same time, however, an identity cannot be perceived as stagnant. As Gergen and Gergen note, "One must be reliable but demonstrate progress; one must be changing but maintain a stable character. Achieving such diverse ends is primarily a matter of negotiating the meaning of events in relationship to each other. Thus, with sufficient skill, one and the same event may figure in both a stability and a progressive narrative" (p. 174). In this way, Stephanie can maintain her identity as "girly-girl" while joining the boys' club.

For Stephanie, her character's interaction with Josh's character and those of his family and friends is intimately related to her real-life character identity in interaction with the players themselves:

> I feel like I fit in with Josh and his dad (who plays with us a lot). They play real golf together all the time, and I often go with them out to the country club just to sit in the cart and watch. But I'm just now starting to learn to play real golf, and I'm too embarrassed to play with them for real. So, I get to play *TWG* with them and keep up.

Stephanie's *TWG* character works, in this way, as a stand-in for her real-life self in her developing relationships with Josh and his family and the identity(ies) that are forming within those relationships. Gee explains such interactions by naming three identities at work within and between a player and her character. The real-world player, Stephanie, negotiates identity with the obviously virtual character (avatar) and the less obvious but richly textured "projective identity" (p. 55). This "projective identity" represents the relationship between Stephanie and her *TWG* avatar. Players both project their "values and desires onto the virtual character" and view that character as a "project in the making" (Gee, p. 56). The capacity of the projective identity to assist in real-world identity formation lies in its representation of overlap between the real-world player and the player's gaming avatar. The projective identity allows a player to move beyond her limitations and those of her avatar. The simplest way to understand the role of the projective identity is to consider its interaction with the other two. As Gee points out, it is possible for the real-world player (Stephanie) to fail the game player (Stephanie's avatar) by making choices that cause the projective identity to appear less than ideal (pp. 56–58). Stephanie experiences this interaction when she feels "nervous" for her "computer self" while guiding her avatar through *TWG*.

As an example, one of the features important to Stephanie is the serenity of *TWG*, but she also rises to the competitive challenge: "We're a competitive couple, so it's a challenge to see if I can beat him [Josh]. Which I have, one time, and I am very proud of that." *TWG* is not without competitive features; it is billed, in fact, as the most comprehensive and most competitive golf game available ("Tiger Woods Golf," 2004). In her relationship with her projective identity, Stephanie experiences the tripartite interaction that Gee describes:

> I get very nervous for my computer self. You win money by playing in tournaments. That money, in turn, can be used to buy skills like ball striking, luck, putting, etc. Josh has won every tournament and has bought every skill possible. I'm still trying to build my girl up. So, when I'm playing I'm nervous. I want the money so I can compete with Josh. I don't like to lose. If I get nervous that I'm going to lose the tournament I always make Josh finish it for me because he's so good at it.

The story of Stephanie and Josh playing *TWG* can be viewed as the joint construction of an evolving identity for an evolving couple relationship, an "objectification," to use Gergen and Gergen's term, that simplifies the maintenance of the relationship as an entity in both Josh's and Stephanie's identities and

strengthens the reciprocity of their mutually reinforcing identity constructions. For Stephanie, the experience is also clearly a project of identity in the
making, of bridging both the virtual and real worlds as well as her pre- and
post-relationship identities. Although many will perceive Stephanie as taking
on a very female role as a "girly-girl," this is the identity she has chosen in her
relationship with Josh.

Gaming and Identity in Composition

Composition teachers might draw on students' existing gaming experience to help
student writers explore their own relationships between the three identities Gee
articulates. How do they feel, for example, about their virtual identities? What
similarities or differences can they identify between those identities? What do they
think of Gee's theory? As Curtis and Herrington (2003) point out in their exploration of development in student writing, students often "use our assignments for
their own ends" in ways that foster their developing personas or identities (p. 85).
By tapping into the identity-developing characteristics of game play in the
composition classroom, we may be able to assist our students in the work they are
already doing and further their academic achievements.

  MacIntyre's (1997) narrative theory offers another tool for examining game
play in and through the composition classroom. MacIntyre, like Gergen and
Gergen, understands the existence of a sense of self, an identity, as necessarily part
of a larger whole, a lifelong narrative that transcends "a sequence of individual
actions and episodes" (p. 241). Our concept of self depends upon "the unity of a
narrative which links birth to life to death as narrative beginning to middle to
end" (p. 243). It is, therefore, natural that we envision "self in a narrative mode."
In addition, each behavior can rightfully belong to and be interpreted within any
number of competing narrative segments depending upon the agent's (player's)
intentions. The narrative frame is essential to intelligibility. We can't make sense
of ourselves or others without it. Therefore, the stories that we tell, that we
construct in our relationships and activities with other people, become part of
who we are, part of our identities. Understanding how we view them is part of the
process of developing a self.

  In MacIntyre's illustration of his point, a man digging in a garden might be
"'Digging'; 'Gardening'; 'Taking exercise'; 'Preparing for winter'; or 'Pleasing his
wife'" (p. 243). Some of these interpretations reveal the man's intentions. Others
represent unintended consequences. Each belongs to a separate setting that has its
own history. The behavior, digging, belongs to all settings and generates all of the
named consequences, either intended or unintended. For MacIntyre, the agent's
intentions are key. Stephanie, while playing *TWG*, intends to spend time with
Josh, to be part of the boys' club, and to maintain her "girly" persona. We might
ascribe other consequences based on our understandings of other settings with
other histories. We might, for example, perceive Josh as authoring Stephanie's
identity at the expense of her agency, but, according to MacIntyre's theory,
Stephanie's own intentions must be considered: "There is no such thing as behavior, to be identified prior to and independently of intentions, beliefs, and settings"

(p. 245). As much as composition teachers might wish to urge students toward consideration of other possible explanations, the narrative of self is only useful to its author within the context of her intentions and her interactions with others. MacIntyre asserts that meaning happens in concert with actions. Everything fits within a narrative frame at the time of its occurrence. We are, according to MacIntyre, looking for "a conception of *the* good" (p. 256) that will give meaning to our lives. We construct our narratives and our shared identities in social interaction with others. This is part of the work being done by Stephanie in her *TWG* games.

Along with these narrative theorists and against those who argue that cultural critique is the only valid position from which to express a self, Newkirk (1997) suggests the utility and power of commonplaces of individual agency that are disparaged by postmodern critical thinking. While the notion that "life is what you make it" may represent a myth in academic discourse, it can also be "empowering" and "self-verifying" (pp. 43–45) just as Stephanie's projective identity in *TWG* has meaning and utility for her. In considering identity as evoked in the composition classroom, Newkirk (2004) takes a historical look at student writing and observes that today's pedagogies, in both the expressivist and cultural studies "camps" (p. 263), are similarly motivated by "a sense of developmental urgency" (p. 263) absent in early twentieth-century instructors. He traces that sense of urgency to a general understanding among composition instructors of all stripes that our students, immersed in "a global media culture," are subject to powerful messages from "corporations, government spokespersons and popular culture outlets," messages that "seek to construct them . . . [and] to define the 'normal'" (p. 263). Many of our pedagogical interventions, therefore, seek to "immunize the student" (p. 264) against the onslaught of corporate America in order to help the student maintain his or her identity(ies) (however we define the term).

In particular, Newkirk notes the "dogma of transformation" (from which he draws the title of the piece) or the turn demanded of student writers as they produce texts in composition courses, a requisite reflective stance that is intended to make meaning out of observation. It is a turn, Newkirk notes, that by virtue of their age and life experience, beginning college students are ill prepared to make. Newkirk, instead, urges consideration of Macrorie's admonition to "put the student in direct touch with the observed world" (p. 269) and to appreciate the observer's stance. Contemporary composition instructors seek to forge connections with "the observed world" through service-learning curricula, ethnographic writing, and other assignments and strategies, and through the publication of student writing. As an addition to the list of possibilities, video gaming is, today, a significant feature of many student worlds. We can serve students and our pedagogical goals if we assist student writers to get in touch with their gaming activities through self-observation, sharing their experiences with each other, and documenting those experiences as they engage in what appears to be important identity construction.

Brandt offers a cautionary note on the use of these technologies and assumed experiences in classrooms. To the extent that schools mirror market interests, they "may disadvantage the already economically disadvantaged" (p. 186). She notes, clearly, that video gaming is a classed activity. Game equipment and games as well as PCs and Internet connections require substantial capital investments. Not all students have experienced equal access to these tools. Those who already possess gaming experiences may feel more comfortable writing about them than those who do not, even if the classroom can provide those experiences as potential texts.

Proceed with Caution: Gaming's Multiple Contexts

Observers of and designers within the gaming world have noted for some time the distinctiveness of women's interaction with games. As Lanza, a game designer, puts it, "Girls are looking for experiences, and boys are looking for bragging rights" (quoted in Herz, 1997, p. 173). Thomas and Walkerdine (2004) articulate the same observation more circumspectly when they note a marked difference in "style" between young boy gamers and young girl gamers.

In academia, Cassell (1998), among others, responds to concerns about a gendered gaming environment by producing computer games and scenarios that allow players to "engage in the serious business of learning about themselves, constructing a social identity, and collaborating with others in the process of understanding that identity" (p. 299). Cassell began her development project as a way to interest girls in computers and video games. What she finds, however, is that both girls and boys like the games she and her students build.

Hence, out of a rapidly receding world of commonplaces about girls, computers, and video games—girls don't like computers (American Association of University Women, 2000), girls don't play video games (Cassell & Jenkins, 1998), girls can't play (Thomas & Walkerdine, 2004)[1]—a new generation of games and gaming has emerged, driven by an uneasy marriage of market forces and feminist scholarship. The gaming industry has taken up Cassell's project in earnest during the last decade, and according to industry studies, women constitute a rapidly growing market segment (Carlton, 1994; Cloutier, 2004; Gaudiosi, 2005; Xiong, 2003). Indeed, the 2005 Women's Game Conference program includes "A Discussion with Professional Female Gamers." While explanations for women's attraction to certain video games varies from a craving for domestic order (Carlton) to character development (Xiong), the power of narrative potential appears consistently in both industry and scholarly publications on the subject. *TWG* and Stephanie's and Josh's experiences with it are part of this world. It is a gaming world that can interest girls and boys, men and women, and intersects with the concerns of composition instructors at the point where players (many of our composition students) experience a process of meaning-making as they experiment with and construct identities for themselves through games and gaming.

As composition instructors we should be aware of the differences between the construction of meaning when students engage each other over written texts and the construction of meaning in a social gaming environment. Gee describes the navigation of a tripartite gaming identity as transcendent when compared with identification with characters from movies or novels. He points out that the "play of identities" in gaming is both "*active* (the player actively does things) and *reflexive,* in the sense that once the player has made some choices about the virtual character. . . . The virtual character rebounds back on the player and affects his or her future actions" (p. 58). In a similar way, players gaming together really do construct meaning concurrently. When a class reads a text and then shares individual experiences of it, they construct a shared meaning, but they do so after the initial engagement has ended. The immediacy of the gaming experience can be challenging in its fluidity and pace. However, the same features that complicate an understanding of its power to influence identities make gaming a potentially rewarding tool for asking questions about how one sees oneself in relationship to other identities and why.

Clearly, agency and control figure prominently in Stephanie's assessments of gaming and technology as they must also for our students. Cassell's research suggests that the construction of power often occurs within manipulations of "who speaks and who says what . . . in fantasy play and storytelling" (p. 310). Stephanie is "nervous" for her "computer self" and is actively constructing, in conjunction with her fellow golfers, an identity of belonging to the boys' club, a potentially powerful and creative engagement with the affordances of the technology and culture made available by *TWG.* She is actively negotiating and claiming a number of new identities in her evolution as an individual and as a member of a partnership that includes Josh and his family. She is a self-described "girly-girl" who uses computers daily in her life as a graduate student, who was afforded the opportunity to engage with games and technology from a young age, but who found them insignificant until very recently. At this point, she recognizes the opportunity afforded by at least one game; she selectively chooses the affordances of the particular technology and social situation to help her construct a "self-narrative" composed of "self-relevant events" (Gergen & Gergen, p. 162) from her experience both before Josh and after Josh.

Notes

Thomas and Walkerdine (2004) observe that "Girls cannot play the games in the same way that boys do," noting a difference in "style" of playing. They go on to thoughtfully explore the possible ramifications of this stylistic difference.

References

American Association of University Women Educational Foundation Commission on Technology, Gender, and Teacher Education. (2000). *Tech-savvy: Educating girls in the new computer age.* Washington, D.C.: AAUW Educational Foundation.

American History Timeline. Retrieved April 14, 2004, from http://www.historytimeline.com/Norm/1990-1999.htm

Brandt, Deborah. (2001). *Literacy in American lives.* Cambridge: Cambridge University Press.

Carlton, Jim. (1994, May 10). Computers: Game makers study how Tetris hooks women. *Wall Street Journal,* p. B1.

Cassell, Justine. (1998). Storytelling as a nexus of change in the relationship between gender and technology: A feminist approach to software design. In Justine Cassell & Henry

Jenkins (Eds.), *From Barbie to Mortal Kombat: Gender and computer games* (pp. 298–326). Cambridge: MIT Press.

Cassell, Justine, & Jenkins, Henry. (1998). Chess for girls? Feminism and computer games. In Justine Cassell & Henry Jenkins (Eds.), *From Barbie to Mortal Kombat: Gender and computer games* (pp. 2–45). Cambridge: MIT Press.

Cloutier, Rhoda. (2004, September 20). Online gaming: The new social circle? *Mass High Tech, 22*(38), 16.

Curtis, Marcia, & Herrington, Anne. (2003). Writing development in the college years: By whose definition? *College Composition and Communication, 55,* 69–90.

Gaudiosi, John. (2005, April 17–23). Games growing beyond male demo. *Video Store Magazine,* 19.

Gee, James Paul. (2003). *What video games have to teach us about learning and literacy.* New York: Palgrave Macmillan.

Gergen, Kenneth, & Gergen, Mary. (1997). Narratives of the self. In Lewis Hinchman & Sandra Hinchman (Eds.), *Memory, identity, community* (pp. 161–184). Albany: SUNY Press.

Herz, J. C. (1997). *Joystick nation: How videogames ate our quarters, won our hearts, and rewired our minds.* Boston: Little, Brown.

Hillocks, George. (1995). *Teaching writing as reflective practice.* New York: Teachers College Press.

MacIntyre, Alasdair. (1997). The virtues, the unity of a human life, and the concept of a tradition. In Lewis Hinchman & Sandra Hinchman (Eds.), *Memory, identity, community* (pp. 241–263). Albany: SUNY Press.

Newkirk, Thomas. (1997). *The performance of self in student writing.* Boston: Boynton/Cook.

Newkirk, Thomas. (2004). The dogma of transformation. *College Composition and Communication, 56,* 251–271.

Rutter, Jason. (2004). Computer gaming timeline: 1889-2002. In *Digiplay initiative: Research into computer gamers and the industry they are a part of.* Retrieved April 29, 2004, from http://digiplay.org.uk/timeline.php

Thomas, Angela, & Walkerdine, Valerie. (2004). *Girls and computer games.* Retrieved July 18, 2005, from http://www.women.it/quarta/workshops/laracroft5/angelathomas.htm

Tiger Woods Golf 2004. (2004). In *Xbox365.com.* Retrieved July 19, 2005, from http://www.xbox365.com/games.cgi?id=EpVpFulyAABzEUycma

Women's Game Conference Program 2005. (2005). Retrieved July 18, 2005, from http://www.womensgameconference.com/program.html

Xiong, Chao. (2003, October 28). Where the girls are; they're online, solving puzzles and making up characters in narrative-driven games. *Wall Street Journal,* B1.

8

Dungeons, Dragons, and Discretion: A Gateway to Gaming, Technology, and Literacy

Stephanie Owen Fleischer, Susan A. Wright, and Matthew L. Barnes

I just don't think video games are bad just because they're video games. I think they're better than TV because they force you to think and interact.

(Hayden Daniel Kessler)

What kinds of experiences form the cultural ecology of literacy? What role does gaming (computer, console, or otherwise) play in this cultural ecology? During the preliminary interviews we conducted in the spring of 2004, we discovered trends that suggested a connection between gaming, digital, and print literacies in two members of Generation X, the generation born in the United States and Canada from the early 1960s through the late 1970s. These case-study participants, now in their early 30s and 40s, did not have the exposure and access to technology for which Generation Y, the group representing the majority of current college students, is famous. However, gaming still had an impact on how these case-study participants learned to be digitally literate in ways that can be informative for teachers of Generation Y and beyond.

Matthew Lee Barnes and Hayden Daniel Kessler[1] were both born in the American Southeast in the early 1970s. While Matt attended rural public schools in Kentucky, Hayden attended relatively affluent public schools in suburban Tennessee. Yet each was encouraged by his parents to excel academically and achieve at least a middle-class lifestyle. Both men currently work with technology in their jobs and cite similar influences—specifically gaming—on their technological interests and in their literacy development. Both individuals were inspired by gaming to develop their digital and print literacies in various ways.

Our goal in this chapter is to trace the results of the "conditions of access" to computer and other video-gaming technologies and the influence of particular factors of access on the development of digital literacies (Selfe & Hawisher, 2004, p. 111).

In addition, we investigate the ways in which gaming has affected how these two case-study participants developed particular types of digital literacies—not only conventional literacies—language learning and problem-solving skills—but also a sense of agency (a sense of self and control over one's self and the world) and sense of community ethics (care and respect for the other).

The practices involved in gaming appear to have inspired Matt and Hayden not only to learn more about the technological intricacies of digital environments, but also, through their active participation in these environments, to enhance their linguistic and mathematical abilities, as well as their own senses of self and community. As James Gee states in *What Video Games Have to Teach Us,* "The learner must be enticed to try" (2003, p. 65). We believe that gaming in digital contexts is one gateway through which this enticement occurs for some individuals. After all, gaming allows people to assume virtual identities and to merge some of the characteristics of these identities with their real-world experiences. According to Gee, a similar kind of identity work needs to happen in the classroom for optimal learning. Students "also must come to see [their academic] virtual identity as their own project in the making, an identity they take on that entails a certain trajectory through time defined by their own values, desires, choices, goals, and actions" (Gee, 2003, p. 65). Understanding the role of gaming in the identity formation and literacy development of young people, then, appears not only important but also vital to teaching students those literacies that will enable them to attain a greater degree of participation in and power over their lives, learning, and community in an increasingly complex technological world.

The Case Study of Matthew Barnes

Matthew Lee Barnes, born in Elizabethtown, Kentucky, in 1974, was working as a graphic artist at the time of our interview. He grew up in the countryside just beyond the city limits of a town that, at the time, owed its livelihood to its factories, its location at the intersection of several major interstates, and its nearness to Fort Knox. Currently, he remains in Elizabethtown, which has expanded commercially over the last decade, and he designs ad layouts for the local newspaper. His job requires him to use programs such as Illustrator, Photoshop, and Pagemaker. Basically, he says his job requires him to "design clean, visually-pleasing ads that incorporate all the pictures and text a customer requests."

Matt was born the same year the "first commercial role-playing game ever," *Dungeons & Dragons (D&D),* was first released (Park & Chin, 2004) and during the administration of Gerald Ford, a time when OPEC increased oil prices, "stagflation" began, and Ford pardoned Nixon (Brinkley, 1995, p. 894). He grew up in a working-class home; his father was first an auto mechanic and later an insurance salesman, and his mother mostly stayed at home, although she also cleaned houses or babysat. Matt's parents, who both graduated from high school, always encouraged him to pursue his studies, requiring him to do his homework before playing as a child and urging him to attend college as an adult. Matt was encouraged to read regularly, and he made many trips to the church and local library to check out choose-your-own-adventure books or fantasy novels such as the *Chronicles of Narnia.*

Like most parents of the late 1970s and early 1980s, Matt's mother and father saw computers and gaming as having little consequence for his literacy. Thus, computers played a small role in Matt's early education. In 1986, however, he first encountered computers at school as a sixth grader at Hardin Central Middle School. There, he used the computers to learn typing and basic programming skills. Matt's family bought a computer in 1989, when he was 15. Matt remembers that "the main purpose of my computer . . . was as a mode of entertainment, allowing me to play the SSI [*D&D*] computer games. I had no knowledge that word-processing software could be purchased at that time. But in high school and college I played several computer games, including *Pool of Radiance, Hillsfar, Icewind Dale,* and *Eye of the Beholder.* These were all games I found out about through my friends or from gaming magazines."

Matt's digital literacy didn't develop solely with computer games, however. "As a kid, I also played console games, starting with *Pong.* Later, we got an Atari, then a Nintendo, then a Super Nintendo, and now I have a Game Cube, an Xbox, and a Play Station 2. I've played a few driving games, like *Super Mario Kart,* and a few 'hack and slash' games like *Dynasty Warriors,* but I have always mostly played RPG [role-playing games] like *The Legend of Zelda.*"

Predictably, during his high school years, Matt's teachers and parents sometimes objected to the amount of time he spent playing computer and console games: "My teachers thought my gaming was a waste of time. My parents went back and forth. My mom thought it was more of a waste than my dad." However, Matt performed well at school, staying on the honor roll even as he participated on the wrestling team, and his grades in the classes which focused on traditional literacies were no exception: Matt got As and Bs in English, where he wrote personal narratives and book reports and read classics such as *Hamlet.* Despite these good grades, however, Matt's teachers would have never imagined that a personal narrative or a report could in any way be informed by his gaming. "It's simply not true," Matt reflects. "*D&D* caused me to do a lot of reading, writing, and research on my own time."

Indeed, Matt believes that gaming and technology had a profound effect on his traditional literacy. To explain why, Matt relates an experience he had as a ten-year-old, learning to play the *D&D,* "pen and paper," RPG.

> At the age of 10 I was introduced to the fantasy world of *Dungeons & Dragons,* a world rich with imagination and detail, a world epitomizing the struggle between good and evil. It's no surprise that this world appealed to me. After familiarizing myself with the rules, I introduced the world to my friends and began to write stories, simplistic at first but they grew in complexity over the years.

Matt's experiences at the micro level coincided with the rise of both gaming and personal computing in the United States. In 1984, the same year Matt first began playing *D&D,* the game's publisher, TSR, Inc. celebrated the second anniversary of both its education department, which successfully created "curriculum programs for reading, math, history, and problem-solving," and the publication of its materials in over ten different languages ("The History of TSR," 2003). Two years later, in 1986, as Microsoft released *Windows* internationally, the Reagan era ended, and the Berlin Wall fell—ushering in the end of the Cold War—Matt worked on his first computer at school. During this same year, TSR, Inc. launched *Dungeon* magazine, which Matt still reads to this day. In 1989, when Matt's family purchased their first computer, TSR, Inc. released the second edition of *Advanced Dungeons and Dragons,* and the Role Playing Game Association network expanded to include Norway, Sweden, Denmark, the UK, Israel, and Australia ("The History of TSR," 2003).

During this time, Matt continued to attend school in Hardin County. The district had one old computer in most every classroom and began planning a new high school, to be opened in the fall of 1990, which would support two computer labs. During his attendance at the new Central Hardin High School from 1990–1992, Matt was allowed to use these computers only for learning keyboarding skills.

Despite relatively little use of computers in school, Matt believes that his experiences as a Dungeon Master (DM)—the story-crafter of *D&D*—and his later experiences playing computer and console games based on *D&D*, strengthened his conventional literacy skills in discernible ways.

> I believe that playing video games had a profound beneficial effect upon my reading and writing abilities. Role-playing games, the type of game I prefer, consist of equal amounts of dialogue as it does "hack and slash." In fact, one particular game I used to play called Zork consisted primarily of descriptive text with a picture and dialogue options. There was no "hack and slash" or action; the entire game consisted of interaction through dialogue and complicated riddles. Due to games like this coupled with my growing interest in *D&D*, my writing and reading skills advanced at an early age. Reading and DM-ing also gave me an extensive and descriptive vocabulary. I remember learning words such as *reconnoiter* and learning how to describe a room so the other players could "see" it. It's not just a tavern, there's the smell of ale, sweat, and freshly baked bread in the air, or there is a pudgy, balding barkeep who has a patch over one eye. . . . Many games also develop depth perception, logic, deductive thinking and problem solving. If it's a role-playing game there is a chance it could even extend your vocabulary through dialogue options.

Matt's role as DM, or storyteller, in *D&D* has, perhaps, had the greatest influence on his conventional literacy practices. Not only does Matt cite the game as influencing his vocabulary and descriptive language, but he also sees a direct link between DM-ing and the writing of fiction:

> Like a novelist, a DM has to take everything into account. Unless you buy a module that has a ready-made adventure in it, you have to create the entire story yourself. Let's say you're using Forgotten Realms [a specific world in *D&D*]. You have to choose a location. Are you going to start your adventure in the Underdark with the drow [an evil subrace of elves]? If so, which city? Menzoberranzan? That city has its own history, power structure, and NPCs [nonplayer characters] that you have to

take into account. Or are you going to start in Waterdeep, a city on the Sword Coast? Where do you want your characters to end up? What kind of monsters and villains do you want them to face? And what kind of characters have the other players chosen to play? A paladin? A wizard? A rogue? Do they have good, neutral, or evil alignments? What kind of history has each player written up for his character?

You have to take all of that into consideration as you create the plot for your adventure. Then once you have written about the skeleton of your adventure, you have to adjust your story based on what choices the players make. This means sometimes you have to make spur of the moment changes. Well, a novelist doesn't have to deal with that, but a good DM will describe the setting and the NPCs like a novelist would describe settings and characters. A good DM wants to describe things well enough to make the players feel like they're really there, and I want my adventures that I write to be engaging and believable. And I think that is what most novelists want, too. It's not so different.

In fact, because I've written out my own adventures, when I've been assigned to write short stories for classes, I've found I didn't have any trouble at all, like one I wrote in college for my Greek and Roman History class. My teacher loved it. But I guess these connections are not surprising. When you think about it, some of the people who write adventure modules or resource books for *D&D* also write novels set in one of the *D&D* worlds or even write original fantasy fiction.

Likewise, Matt sees a connection between *D&D* and both research and communication in general:

> I'm all the time buying resource books or magazines or looking up things online so I can get even more information about some particular setting I want to start an adventure in. I also buy a lot of *D&D* maps—you definitely have to be able to read maps to really do a good job with this game. And sometimes I do research about the "real world" in order to flesh out an adventure. If I wanted to set an adventure in Calimshan [a nation from the Forgotten Realms campaign setting] then I might do some research on ancient Arabia or read some stories set in ancient Arabia, since Calimshan is similar to ancient Arabia. . . . As for other forms of communication, I do a lot of emailing or private messaging with my group members when I'm playing an online game, and I also spend time on message boards, reading and writing messages.

Today, in a culture characterized by rapidly changing technology, Matt continues not only the conventional literacies he's practiced through the pen-and-paper version of *D&D*, but also the use of computers for both entertainment and work and to play *D&D* and other RPGs in both the computer and console versions. Among the games he has played are *Everquest, Champions of Norrath, Baldur's Gate: Dark Alliance,* and *Baldur's Gate: Dark Alliance II.*

Matt cites stress relief and his desire for a sense of effective agency—the ability to have control over some aspect of the world—as his major reasons for gaming:

> When I was young, I played video games both as a form of entertainment and escapism. . . . Now, video games serve as a medium for relieving the stress of everyday life. I usually play a game for an hour or two each day if there is time. Immersing myself in a virtual world allows me to "veg" out, letting my mind recover from a difficult day of dealing with people and events out of my control. I suppose a measure of

this stress relief comes not only from displacing my frustration on pixels, but also from the structure of the game. Like most movies, video games follow a formula plot, and there is a measure of comfort in following a preset plot. Often life is full of numerous tangents and unplanned setbacks out of your control, many of which contribute to undue stress. In video games this structured environment is dependent upon the actions I choose to take, empowering me with control over the outcome. The last thing I want to do is play a video game resembling the chaos of life.

Matt contrasts the sense of agency he gets from gaming—an environment in which he can control many factors—with the stresses he encounters in his real life, and over which he feels he has no control. These stresses range from events that happen at work during the day to the current scarcity of jobs in the Elizabethtown area to worldwide events such as global terrorism. As he explains, no matter how disturbing terrorism becomes in his real life, Matt cannot personally rid the world of terrorists. Similarly, there are many much simpler stresses over which Matt has no control—the driver who cuts him off and nearly causes a wreck on the way home, his small frustrations at work. Matt can temporarily relieve or escape the effects of these factors by punishing the "bad guys" in a game.

Deeply connected to stress relief is Matt's tendency to play heroic roles in games. Playing games not only provides Matt some simple stress relief, but also helps him to develop a sense of identity and agency as he helps others in the world of the game.

> Nightly [as a child] I assumed the role of a hero in one of the myriad virtual worlds available. Filled with a desire to do good, I would traverse the many levels dispensing justice to those who would oppose me in an attempt to reach the goal. . . . I've almost always chosen [the role] of a hero. There have been a handful of times that I've actually chosen the role of a villain and even then I found myself migrating towards the morally responsible choices presented.

Matt cites as an example a character he played in the online game *Everquest.*

> My second character was a Dark Elf, a cruel and twisted race who generally worships the god of hate, Innoruuk. Luckily your deity choice is dependent upon not only your race, but your class or profession, as well. After very little deliberation I settled upon a role for my new character; he would be a rogue. However, instead of choosing Innoruuk as his deity I opted for the light-hearted god of trickery, Bristlebane. This significantly improved my traveling portfolio in the world of Norrath since your choice of deity has a direct impact upon your faction, how other racial groups and organizations perceive your character. Once again I found myself resuming the role of the stalwart hero, working hard to improve my faction with the forces of good so that I could travel openly in their cities with my friends.

This heroism is also reflected in Matt's sense of ethics, as he rented and then rejected controversial games such as *Grand Theft Auto: Vice City* and feels only *mature* adults (meaning not *all* adults) should play such games. Such heroism both does and does not transfer into the real world. Matt's choice to play the hero likely springs from early experiences at home and church and early literature choices such as C. S. Lewis fantasy series and Jerry Siegel's *Superman*. Even as an adult, Matt often chooses authors such as R. A. Salvatore, who writes fantasy-hero novels, which means that the influence flows from real life to the world of the game. But as for the game influencing real life, being such a hero in the real world is impossible. Matt explains:

> I maintain a sense of morality and ethics from playing the part of a hero, but I am not that kind of hero in real life and would not attempt any such act of vigilantism because the consequences would be very real and dire. Still, I try to assume the role of the hero in the game, and I will help my friends or sometimes complete strangers in the game as I can. This means I save them from being killed, tell them about a quest they may be unaware of, or give them items I've picked up and don't need [e.g., magical swords, armor]. Actually, I'm usually a pretty nice guy, in both the game and in real life. Just like I tend to tip well when I go to a restaurant, I tend to help others in the game by giving them items or healing them if I'm playing a cleric. I guess there's a connection there between the me in the game and the me in real life.

In fact, in addition to digital and traditional literacies, Matt's social literacy has also been developed by gaming.

> At first I played the pen-and-paper version of *D&D* with my friends, and I also played console games with friends and family members, like my nephews. I also game with my fiancé. But later I actually made friends through the online computer games I've played. I've made friends in both other states and other countries through Everquest. Of course, I also play online games with friends that I've known for years. For example, if my friends and I all have Saturday afternoon off, we'll call each other up and agree to all play Everquest that afternoon. Of course, we also randomly meet each other in the game and will team up. But, yeah, past just making friends, being able to get along with people is a big deal in an online game like Everquest. I might be a member of a guild [a group] that has, say, one person from California, a husband and wife from Germany, a guy from Britain, a girl from France, and two guys from Taiwan. Not only do you have to get along as a group in order to play the game, you have to sometimes deal with language barriers. I've taught some English words to a few people, and I've learned some language too, like a few French words and some British slang

For Matt, then, digital literacies have been inspired by as well as an inspiration for both print literacies and social literacies, particularly as a result of his participation in gaming.

The Case Study of Hayden Kessler

Hayden Daniel Kessler, born to a middle-class family in early 1973, in Kingsport, Tennessee——a town based primarily around the Eastman chemical plant and thus having a range of inhabitants from Tennessee-born working-class laborers to scientists from around the world——was working as a network control technician at the time of our interview. In Hayden's words, his job entails "maintaining, supporting, installing, etc. of: cabling infrastructure, connectivity devices (routers, switches, etc.), public switched connections, Internet access, firewalls, web content filtering, remote access, network design, DNS and DHCP administration, wireless implementation, etc." However, in layman's terms this means that he is responsible for the communication of all of the computers within a statewide hospital system, that is, he controls what comes into, goes out of, and travels among this network of computers.

Hayden was born in the midst of the Watergate investigation of President Nixon and his staff and in the last days of U.S. involvement in the Vietnam War, and one year after "Magnavox introduce[d] *Odyssey,* the first video game machine, featuring a primitive form of paddle ball" ("History of Toys," 2004) and "*Pong,* one of the first mass-produced video games, ha[d] become the rage" ("Technology Timeline," 2000).

Hayden's father, a research chemist with a B.A. degree from the University of Louisville, and his mother, a preschool teacher who attended one year of college at the University of Kentucky, always encouraged Hayden's literacy. According to Hayden he was "always encouraged to read" as his mother was an "avid reader" while his father was "more musical." He says that neither parent "ever really had a problem buying books for me if I wanted them." According to Hayden, his mother would "cave on those before she'd cave on anything else" and would often take him to "book fairs and stuff like that, because all of her friends were educators and a couple were librarians."

Unlike many parents, Hayden's mother in particular viewed his participation in the *D&D* as beneficial to his learning and literacy:

> I know she thought that dice were a good way to learn mathematical skills, and [she felt that] basically . . . anything that encouraged reading wasn't all bad. I owe a lot of vocabulary learning at an early age to it, and it encouraged me to read historical accounts [such as] King Arthur, what the Roman military was like, stuff like that. I remember specifically in *Dragon* [a *D&D*-related magazine] a module about the Aztecs and then going to look stuff up about the Aztecs.

As his mother predicted, Hayden claims that his introduction to *D&D* also led to his interest in various print texts, such as the works of J. R. R. Tolkien on which the *D&D* games are based.

However, Hayden's mother seems to have regarded his video gaming as somewhat less educational than his participation in RPGs, occasionally encouraging him to "go outside and play instead of sitting inside and playing [on the television] so much." But, through his mother's encouragement and his brother's and peers' involvement with role-playing, Hayden's interest in *D&D* influenced his print literacies early on and eventually inspired his digital literacies as well.

Computers played a very small role in Hayden's early education. According to Hayden, his first experience with a computer in the classroom was in 1983 when he was in the fourth grade,

> when I switched from county schools to city schools which generally had a much bigger budget and were better schools, and I started in an advanced studies program.

We had an Apple IIC computer, and we got to work on it. I think we mostly wrote programs ourselves. I think they were very simple kinds of programs in BASIC. I enjoyed that. In fifth grade we did more complicated ones—I remember making a graphic.

However, Hayden's experience with computer *gaming* only occurred outside of the classroom. Unlike console-based video games, computer-based games appear to have been encouraged in Hayden's life:

I don't remember playing games on our computers at school, but one of my neighbors also had an Apple and his mother was a teacher and we played several games. There was one called *Lode Runner,* one called *Aztec,* and a couple of educational ones like *Oregon Trail* where you traveled out West and tried not to starve; and there was one where you were a fish in a lake and tried to survive. I remember that one because the best one to be was the rainbow trout.

Hayden's family, however, did not actually purchase a computer until 1990 or 1991 when he was 16 or 17 years old because, for them, it seemed cost-prohibitive: "My parents bought me one when I was in high school—eleventh or twelfth grade. It wasn't an insignificant expense and my dad sure bitched about the cost of it." However, such access to computer technology did not automatically result in Hayden's enthusiasm for the medium:

That particular computer was a pain and I didn't know much about it, so I was constantly getting help from people. . . . My parents didn't know anything about it nor have any real desire to know anything about it. I went to friends at school that knew more about computers than I did. . . . Back then it was very specialized and so if you had WordPerfect and someone was using WordStar, there were absolutely no commonalities between them, so that didn't help. My computer had one of the first versions of Windows on it, and the people I asked were used to using DOS-based programs and didn't know anything about it.

Hayden says of this experience:

I hated [computers]. Kinda funny that I started out early with them then I kinda got out of them. It was somewhat frustrating because I think my parents saw all this money they spent on this tool and yet there was no easy way to know how to use it. It wasn't like it was a weedeater with operating instructions. So I felt there was pressure on me to make use of it, but it wasn't easy to pick up.

Because of this lack of a support system for his technology learning, Hayden's primary use of his computer was for games. "I could play Solitaire on it . . . oh, and Tetris." Unlike Matt, Hayden did not play *D&D* computer games in high school, primarily because of cost. He says that not only did his parents view such games as cost-prohibitive, particularly in addition to the purchase of a computer, but also at the time that he got the computer he was at an age at which he would rather spend his money on other things, such as dating, driving, and hanging out with friends. Thus, Hayden's computer gaming did not intensify until after high school.

In 1991, at the same time that Hayden was graduating from high school and beginning his college career at Butler University in Indianapolis, Indiana, U.S. Senator Al Gore "held hearings that led to the passage of the National High-Performance Computer Technology Act" that "boosted federal support of the Internet by about $1 billion a year" ("1990–1999," 2002). In addition to this governmental endorsement of technology, many important events were taking place on the computer gaming stage. *Pool of Radiance*, a *D&D*-based computer game, had been released in 1988 ("Pool of Radiance," 2004). In 1993, the gaming software company id "released its much-anticipated *DOOM*," which is "recognized as the catalyst and inspiration of what we know now as 3-D action gaming" ("id History," 2003). At the same time, "The computer game 'Myst' swept the US with its eerie puzzle plot" ("1990–1999," 2002). During this period, there was a deluge of role-playing, 3-D, and puzzle-type computer games were released on the market. And it was during college, Hayden claims, that his faith in computers was restored. Hayden explains his reacquaintance with computers: "I got more into computers [in college] just because you had to use them to get your papers ready and for other things, class-specific programs. . . . As far as gaming, probably because other people were into it and there were also some *D&D*-based games that came around at that time that I was interested in playing." This period was an important one in Hayden's computer literacy development. He explains: "In fact, after my sophomore year was the first time I did any hardware work on my computer when I upgraded my PC from 1 megabyte of RAM to 4 megabytes of RAM in order to play *Pools of Radiance*, a *D&D* game. I was more or less a consistent gamer of the PC kind from then on." As Hayden's major in college was in psychology, such experiences with computer enhancement were solely responsible for Hayden's obtaining a job providing computer support in the computer center at Butler University, and, most likely, his eventual career in computer support and, eventually, network engineering.

Hayden's gaming experiences should not be underestimated in contributing to his digital literacy in other ways as well. He agrees with his mother that games such as *D&D* can be highly educational, regardless of the medium:

> They tend to have sci-fi things and I liked the challenge of it; I liked how some of them progressed as a story that you get to act in; it's probably why I like role-playing games. You got to use your imagination; I think that's what I liked about it; you played with people more than against them usually; it was cooperative. I think it kind of teaches people a level of resourcefulness. I think role-playing games have played a bigger role, but computer games have definitely played into that. Math skills, map-reading skills, vocabulary, knowing things about history, mythology.
>
> If you're on a CRPG (Computer Role-Playing Game) or MMORPG (Massively Multiplayer Online Role-Playing Game), what you're doing is reading a story, so it's very similar to fiction.

Additionally, Hayden's gaming encourages various forms of related print literacy practices. For instance, in addition to reading *D&D*-based magazines like *Dragon*,

Hayden reads "reviews or articles online, web comics about gaming" and message boards regarding role-play gaming of all varieties. He also does a great deal of writing in the course of his participation in gaming, including character backstories, and

> segue adventures like things between two published adventures—like if you buy an adventure that you're supposed to play and you buy another that's supposed to be played by higher level characters, and you're at the end of one and you need to get to the other, you write something to bridge that gap.

Like Matt, Hayden occasionally serves as DM, a position in which he is responsible for making up the story on the spur of the moment and adding in details like dialogue. Additionally, even as a mere player in the game, Hayden claims that there is writing involved. The following excerpt, for instance, is an example of one of his character backstories.

Background:

Silvhidaris Harkosaa was the youngest of fifteen children. His parents owned a mill in the grain district. They died when Silvhidaris was 11, and leadership of the mill and the family business fell to his brother Thandharis. Thandharis was an authoritative sort and he and Silvhidaris were constantly at odds.

Silvhidaris left home at 13 and began his life on the street. Ever charismatic, he made his way by his charm and his wits——resorting to actual thievery when those failed. As a grifter and a pickpocket, he moved around from port to port, looking for new marks. He was careful to stay one step ahead of the watch and the local crimelords. He always targeted the wealthy for any score larger than a meal and would not prey heavily on the working classes, with whom he felt an affinity. In fact, there were many legitimate shopkeepers and tavern owners who welcomed Silvhidaris into their establishments, sometimes sharing in his profits. He was likeable and good-natured, and, while he could charm a troll into an oven, he was a kind man at heart.

Everything changed when Silvhidaris was about 17. A local gang was about to teach him a lesson about grifting in their territory, when Silvhidaris said strange words and made odd gestures similar to those he had observed the mages in the Mage District to make. He had used this bluff to great effect before, but this time, the ruffians were not buying it. Then, the oddest thing happened, as a bolt of energy flew from his hand, striking the lead goon in the chest. The thugs gaped in horror and tended to their leader. Silvhidaris did not linger to see if they would still press their attack and disappeared in to the midday shadows.

From that day forward, he worked to develop his gift. He relocated to the Mage District and found out what he could by stealthily observing private magical tutorings, sneaking into mage symposiums, and "borrowing" the occasional tome on magic. He learned much this way, but practice was the real key that allowed him to hone his art.

When he felt that he had learned all that his back-alley practice could teach him, Silvhidaris began hanging out in the taverns where adventurers were rumored to go. He sold his services as both a sneak and an adept, and went on several adventures that let him test his abilities in the field. He always came away with a generous share of the treasure, but never worked with the same group more than once. He is presently looking for another group with whom he could go adventuring.

Description:

> Silvhidaris Harkosaa is a man in his early twenties. He has jet black hair that falls to his shoulders and a forked goatee to match. His green eyes have a piercing quality to them that makes his gaze border on hypnotic. At 5'10" and 170 lbs, Silvhidaris is only of average strength, but his frame is lithe and his movements feline. He has a sword at his hip, bow on his back, and a bandolier of various useful vials crossing his chest. He owns only what he can carry and appears just as one would expect an adventurer to appear——well-armed, dressed for harsh climates, and prepared for nearly anything.

Such writing reveals not only a deftness but also an immense creativity with language, all marshaled in the endeavor of gaming. Hayden claims to have even learned words such as *necromancer, melee,* and *vicissitude* from RPGs. Hayden also attests that there is a type of literacy specific to gaming: "They've got their own jargon, . . . there's a literacy to each individual game to some degree . . . their own guidelines for interaction, guidelines for play. Rules and language, syntax and vocabulary." A computer-based RPG such as *Diablo II* has a specific vocabulary, one that can enhance the general vocabulary of the player. For example, one must acquire "manna," a small blue orb that fuels the character's magical power within the game. How much magical energy, or manna, a character possesses will also determine whether she should go on particular quests or spend a certain amount of money that the character has earned in the course of the game in order to enhance the character's ability to accomplish certain tasks within the game. Such choices, however, must be made by the player and require a good amount of strategizing in order for the player to succeed at the game.

Today, in a world increasingly reliant upon technology, Hayden now uses computers for work as a network control technician *as well as* for various types of gaming, including *D&D* in its various computer-based incarnations. He, like Matt, claims that it is not only challenging and fun, but it can also serve as a stress-reliever:

> It's relaxing most of the time if it's not ridiculously frustrating. It's challenging for one. I find if it's a little bit challenging not to the point of frustration, I find that relaxing, you know you feel, you figure out a puzzle and you have a sense of accomplishment, which I think is relaxing, particularly compared to work if you've had a really crappy day with a lot harder problems. At least most of the problems in the game are meant to be solved, whereas problems at work—

he says sarcastically, "well, who knows!"

Also, like Matt, Hayden's choice of characters in game play tends toward "the good":

> A lot of the games you don't have any real choice so choosing a game means you're choosing a default character. Like in the RPG's (role-playing games) you have an alignment, and I usually stick with the good. . . . I don't know I guess it's more fun that way. In ones where there's conversation options I usually try to be benevolent. Sometimes there's options for being rude or aggressive, and I'm usually along the lines of what people would really actually do. I lean toward the way people usually

act toward each other. . . . My favorite is a Druid which is a nature guy with an affinity for animals and elemental magic. I guess . . . because I've always kind of aligned that way toward the natural—that's kind of who I am . . . a pro-wildlife plant and animal person.

Unlike Matt, however, Hayden has no problem playing violent games like *Grand Theft Auto: Vice City.* He explains:

> You're playing a hood so you beat people up and take their money. It's like acting, you're playing a role. You know, if you were playing Hitler [in a play], you wouldn't be all sunshine and puppies.

Hayden also claims it is possible that his willingness to play violent characters in certain games may have to do with the lack of agency in choosing that character and his or her traits in those games. That is, the more agency he is allowed over a character, the more he is able to create and thus identify with that character, the less violent his portrayal of that character is in game play. And, conversely, the less agency he has in terms of a character's creation, the more willing he is to portray that character violently in game play.

Unlike Matt, though, there are no games that Hayden excludes from his repertoire because of their content, violent or otherwise. In terms of calls for censorship of games due to violent or graphic content, Hayden claims:

> If you find people with compulsive or fantasy prone personalities to a dangerous level, video games are not for them, but I don't think [video games are] going to be that much worse than anything else. If people are going to be obsessive, they're going to be obsessive—it's a personality type that's really obsession-independent.

In fact, when asked about widespread claims about the dangers of gaming, Hayden responded: "I wouldn't advocate gaming to the exclusion of other things, [but] I just don't think video games are bad just because they're video games. I think they're better than TV because they force you to think and interact." For Hayden, then, not only do games promote active thinking, but they also offer opportunities for social interaction as well:

> I think you can have fun with video games even if the video game isn't fun or interesting [if you are playing with someone else]. I mean it's a social interaction like anything else. Like a sports game, I don't play by myself, but I'd play *with* somebody. . . . When you're playing by yourself, it's more about the content, but if you're playing with someone, much less so.

As a matter of fact, Hayden feels that, in general, games are a "hobby, just like anything else" and can even aid one in social relationships: "Doing anything fun gets you in a better mood . . . occasionally you can take out your aggressive tendencies on a bunch of computer-generated enemies which is a lot healthier than taking them out on real human beings." And additionally, for Hayden, gaming, whether with someone on a console or with a variety of people in an online setting, can create community and the need for social interaction and cooperation. For these reasons, Hayden prefers to know or even to get to know the people with whom he games. He explains this preference by quoting Monte Cook, game designer and publisher, and one of the designers of the third edition of *D&D:* "Don't game with someone you wouldn't spend an evening doing something else with." However, Hayden has several people with whom he games and has even formed friendships through his interest in gaming:

> I play video games with my brother and my nephew when I see them. I play video games with my friend in Frankfort [who he met on a gaming message board]. I have a friend who comes to visit sometimes and we spend 90% of the time he's here playing video games. And sometimes I play with my wife.

For Hayden, like Matt, gaming has inspired a plethora of digital and print literacies, literacies that in turn promote a strong sense of self and community.

Concluding Thoughts

For both Matt and Hayden, issues of access influenced their technological literacy. Matt had limited access to computers in middle school—primarily learning how to type—while Hayden first used computers at school in fourth grade, learning basic programming. Here, class—at the community, or medial level, instead of the individual, or microlevel—becomes an issue. As Selfe and Hawisher (2004) note:

> For more than twenty years, U.S. educators have known that *access* to computers plays a key role in when, how, if, and to what extent students acquire and develop those skills and values associated with digital, or electronic, literacy. Educators have also been aware that access to computers in this nation has remained aligned, in persistent and embarrassing ways, along the related axes of race and class. (p. 110)

Matt's school, located in a rural country, had limited funding for computer labs; on the other hand, Hayden's school, located in a comparatively affluent community, received a great deal of community financial support for the provision of computers, enabling the school to offer various types of computer classes and even after-school lab time during which students could write their papers. However, at the microlevel, neither participant had computers at home until their mid-teens. In both cases, due to the dearth of a technological support system, the boys utilized their computers only for gaming. And gaming became the route through which they chose to pursue greater knowledge of computer software and hardware and, eventually, developed their digital literacies.

D&D proved to be a vital factor of access for both participants to digital environments. Playing the pen-and-paper version of *D&D* provided Matt and Hayden the stepping-stone for avid computer gaming, as both became increasingly involved in gaming upon discovering *D&D*-esque computer games such as *Pool of Radiance*. In addition, *D&D* furthered traditional print literacies such as story writing, vocabulary building, mathematics, map reading, and the learning of mythology, and reinforced enthusiasm for reading both fiction and nonfiction texts. The result is an intersection between gaming, digital, and print literacies as computer gaming stems from and inspires print literacies and digital literacies through reading and writing supplemental to gaming and the rules for acting in the gaming world.

Other useful proficiencies, or nontraditional "real world" literacies, namely individual agency and a sense of community ethics, are also developed through gaming. The typical classroom deals only with academics, causing a separation between school learning and real-world learning. "In school, many times children are expected to read texts with little or no knowledge about any social practices within which those texts are used. They are rarely allowed to engage in an actual social practice in ways that are recognizable to 'insiders' . . . as meaningful and acceptable before and as they read texts relevant to the practice" (Gee, 2003, 16). In contrast, gaming—both in the pen-and-paper and computer/console versions—develops social skills such as sharing and diplomacy among gamers. For example, Hayden and Matt have gained and maintained friends through gaming and its surrounding literacies, and both prefer cooperative, multiplayer games, a fact that opposes the common notion that gaming and technology result in isolation or antisocial behaviors.

Likewise, gaming promotes a sense of agency through what James Gee (2003) calls "projective identities." Gee explains the multiple identities a gamer assumes during game play and explores the effect these identities have on agency and self-hood:

> I, the real-world person, James Paul Gee, a creature with multiple identities, face the fact that I am fixed in certain ways. Though I am, like all beings, ever-changing, at the moment, I am who I am. . . . The kind of person I want Bead Bead [a character Gee created for the fantasy game *Arcanum*] to be, the kind of history I want her to have, the kind of person in history I am trying to build in and through her is what I mean by a projective identity. Since these aspirations are *my* desires for Bead Bead, the projective identity is both mine and hers, and it is a space in which I can transcend both her limitations and my own. (p. 56)

By projecting themselves and their own personalities—or perhaps an idealized version of themselves—into the game, Matt and Hayden are able to assume power they cannot have in reality. Both men report playing games allows them to relieve stress by taking control of the environment of the game by either pounding out their frustration on the "bad guys" or relaxing in the comfortable game world with its formulaic plot. The formulaic plot, though, Hayden says, only exists "on the grand scale. The thinking comes with puzzle-solving in the details. It's kinda a big picture vs. small picture thing. You know the character is going to defeat the big evil thing at the end but how you get there is unknown." Above all, then, teachers should note that it is through language and literacy practices in digital environments—knowledge of the "rules and language, syntax and vocabulary" of the games—that these men acquire additional control over their virtual actions.

This agency over the characters also promotes a sense of ethics concerning the actions of those characters. Gee explains:

> They feel responsible to and for the character. They are projecting an identity as to who the character ought to be and what the trajectory of his or her acts in the virtual world ought, at the end of the day, to look like.
>
> Likewise, while some young people will let a superhero first-person shooter character kill "civilians" and not just enemies, a good many others will not, since they feel that it just isn't fitting for such a superperson—that is, the person they are projecting into the world—to do such a thing. (p. 58)

In fact, the less agency that Hayden has over the creation of a character, the less responsibility he seems to take for that character's actions. However, both Matt and Hayden tend to play good-aligned characters and to take on the role of hero in the game. Perhaps this tendency, for some, reinforces or promotes ethics through the making of moral choices in order to succeed in the game. If this is so, then despite popular belief, pen-and-paper and computer RPGs do not necessarily result in immorality or homicidal rampages. It would seem that such games, provided that they allow for a good deal of character agency and control, may accomplish just the opposite—a greater sense of individual responsibility and respect for human cooperation. In fact, such games may help some individuals cope with everyday stresses that would otherwise simply accumulate. Matt notes, "[Games] have never affected my ethics detrimentally; if anything the games I play tend to reinforce a strong set of morals and ethics."

The development of all of these literacies is vital to our students in the context of the global society in which we live. Born in a United States just pulling out of the Vietnam War, a disastrous war to say the least, and a United States in which the president and his staff were in the process of being impeached for corruption, Hayden and Matt have been living in a rapidly changing and increasingly uncertain world, socially and technologically. In addition to great social and political upheaval, they have lived through the U.S. transition from an industrialized to a technologically-driven information society. They experienced the hope of the Internet boom and the disappointment of the dot-com bust, not to mention the widespread fears of technological failure on the eve of Y2K. To ignore the digital literacies of our students, then, is not only to be unmindful but also blatantly negligent, for they are and will be developing these literacies with or without our help. As to how they develop these literacies and what these literacies look like, however, we do have some control. And one of the ways that we might take such control is through our students' gaming practices. Furthermore, for students who are resistant to school or who have little faith in their capacity to learn, teachers can call attention to digital literacies they've pursued and succeeded with—possibly with little help—and enable these students to draw connections between these digital literacies and traditional ones. For example, a student who claims to be incapable of writing or too uninspired to write might have a gaming literacy like Hayden's and Matt's upon which teachers may build: we might say, "Consider the plotline of a typical role-playing game you play, such as Baldur's Gate"; or "For an exercise in description, I want you to describe a dungeon or a town in Champions of Norrath." For teachers, it would simply be a matter of asking students what kinds of console or computer games they play and then asking them to consider how the game's story progresses or what the environment of the game (e.g., dungeons, rooms, streets) looks like. The story lines or environments may be clichéd, but by accessing students' traditional literacy through digital literacy, teachers might enable them to see just how much knowledge or learning capacity they possess.

Although the various worlds of gaming may, unlike the real world, be comfortable and formulaic, they seem, on the other hand, to teach some valuable real-world literacies, literacies such as linguistic proficiency, problem-solving abilities, self-confidence, and a proclivity for cooperation, skills that may help them not only to cope with the uncertainty of the real world but also to remedy the ills of such a world in which these skills are scarce even among our leaders. As scholars such as Gee (2003) and Selfe and Hawisher (2004) have pointed out, literacy far exceeds the mere skills of math and reading—it involves countless abilities ranging from language use to technological proficiency to social relations. Our students' acquisition of these literacies derives not just from schools but also from their various communities such as those in which they game. Matt's and Hayden's experiences with the classroom, computers, and gaming support the notion that the best learning often occurs in nonacademic contexts. Thus, it is the job of teachers to begin to incorporate some of the conditions of these contexts into their classrooms. Teachers must become active leaders and participants in their students' digital literacies, through such routes as gaming, if we are to be at all effectual *as* teachers in the rapidly changing technological world in which we and our students live and work. As Gee reveals, "The theory of learning in good video games fits better with the modern, high-tech, global world today's children and teenagers live in than do the theories (and practices) of learning that they see in school" (2003, p. 7). Matt and Hayden would agree.

Notes

1. Some of the names have been changed to protect the anonymity of the study participants.

References

Brinkley, Alan. (1995). *American history: A survey.* New York: McGraw-Hill.

Gee, James P. (2003). *What video games have to teach us about learning and literacy.* New York: Palgrave Macmillan.

History of Toys and Games Timeline: 1965–1977. (2004). Retrieved March 13, 2004, from http://www.historychannel.com/exhibits/toys/gijoe.html

The History of TSR. (2003). Retrieved March 24, 2004, from http://www.wizards.com/dnd/DnDArchives_history.asp

id History. (2003, December 9). Retrieved March 24, 2004, from http://www.doomworld.com/pageofdoom/idhistory.html *Decades.com 1990–1999.* (2002). Retrieved March 13, 2004, from http://www.decades.com/ByDecade/1990-1999/1.htm

Park, Andrew, & Chin, Elliott. (2004). History of *Advanced Dungeons and Dragons*. Retrieved March 24, 2004, from http://www.gamespot.com/features/history_add/

Pool of Radiance: Ruins of Myth Drannor. (2004). Retrieved March 29, 2004, from http://archive.gamespy.com/articles/september03/25overrated/index16.shtml

Selfe, Cynthia, & Hawisher, Gail. (2004). *Literate lives in the information age: Stories from the United States*. Mahwah, NJ: Lawrence Erlbaum.

Technology Timeline: 1752–1990. (2000). Retrieved March 13, 2004, from http://www.pbs.org/wgbh/amex/telephone/timeline/timeline_text.html

Interchapter II

What Some 20-Something Players Say about Gaming

Derek Van Ittersum

The game I've probably spent the most time playing is *Mario Kart 64* for the Nintendo 64 system (one generation old). In this game, you control a character driving a go kart and race other characters, or do battle with them. I was never much into the involved games that require you to figure out puzzles and play for days before moving to the next level. With *Mario Kart*, a race lasts a couple of minutes, and a battle session lasts just a bit longer. Both races and battles can be played with up to four players, and playing with other people was the main attraction for me.

I started playing the game with both my high school friends and my younger brother at home. While I did play alone sometimes, it was usually just to get better so that I would win more races or battles. What I also liked about the game was how different it was from "real" racing games, which I found boring. In *Mario Kart* you collect items, such as turtle shells that you can shoot at other players to knock them off the track, banana peels to slow them down, mushrooms to give your character a speed boost. If you played enough, you could memorize where these items are in the track and develop a strategy to collect them and use them against your opponents at the most opportune moments. During the battle sessions, instead of racing, you use these items to hit other players, and the last player standing wins. I still continue to play the game against my brother when I go home to visit, but we've both become so good at it it's a different experience for me now. I can sink into a pretty deep connection with the game, trying to hit every corner just right and pop every jump—it's very relaxing (although my brother might tell a different story—I tend to get frustrated if I can't get into the rhythm and he likes to laugh when I try to relax but end up grumpy because I couldn't get first place). We try to beat our top finishing times; it's much less about beating the other person and more about just totally mastering the game.

I'm afraid my taste in games seems to have become outdated, most games now are just too complicated for me—even the racing games have moved away from the easy and silly (like *Mario Kart*) to the hyper realistic that require one to learn to shift the car and not turn too sharply since the game follows real physics.

Samantha Looker

I'm giving you two favorite games. I play both of them on the Nintendo Game Cube, which is my favorite platform. It has better titles than the other video game consoles, and I prefer it to computer games because, with how much of my work is done on the computer, it's hard for me to associate sitting in front of the computer with relaxing. :-) Sitting in the recliner playing Nintendo, on the other hand, really feels like getting away from my work. And it has great graphics. So, the games.

Smash Brothers: This is a game involving Mario Bros. characters as well as some other familiar Nintendo characters such as Samus and Link. It's a fighting game, but different from the more arcade-style one-on-one fighting games, which I'm terrible at because they tend to require a lot more finger dexterity than I have. (I'm a little disadvantaged, having not grown up with video games like many of my peers; my parents wouldn't let me get a Nintendo when I was younger. My 15-year-old sister has—and loves—her own Game Cube now, though. How times have changed!) This one has a fairly simple set of button combinations for different attacks, and usually the fight involves four characters on a fairly large stage, so you can run around between opponents. I like this game in that it takes a genre that could be pretty repetitive—the fighting game—and makes it fun by putting in characters that you know and love and giving them all sorts of interesting items to beat up on each other with! :-) Also, I like that it's not terribly realistic—no blood, half the characters aren't even human, etc.—so you can use it to vent frustrations in a semi-nonviolent way. Also, it's a fun one to play with my husband—the four-player fighting means we can beat up computer characters and avoid beating each other up . . . most of the time. :-)

Metroid: This is a more adventure-style game, a genre that I really credit Brian (my husband) for getting me into (my sister was more responsible for the previous game). It features Samus Aran, quite possibly the most nonsexualized female video-game character ever—she spends the whole game in a really high-tech space suit, and you only occasionally even catch a glimpse of her eyes. And she's really powerful, with all kinds of weapons and gadgets. It's a first-person game, meaning you see most things through her eyes, which adds to the realism of making you feel like you're there. As Samus (she isn't from earth), you explore an alien planet, hunting the space pirates who have taken over it and looking for artifacts from an ancient race that used to inhabit the planet. One of the things I love most about this game is all the mysteries and problems that you solve along the way— Samus's helmet lets her scan buildings, objects, and enemies for descriptive clues, and her abilities grow as you progress through the game, so you can find more secrets once she has heat vision and x-ray abilities. And the graphics are absolutely gorgeous, from big things like detailed creatures right down to the tiny details like the raindrops that fall on Samus's visor when she goes outside. And the soundtrack! This game easily has the best video-game music I've ever heard. It's well composed, sets the mood well, and is complex and varied, unlike a lot of video-game music that can get really repetitive.

Jessica Bannon

As you can see, there are points in this game [*Super Mario Bros.*] and you get points for just about everything you do—busting blocks, killing creatures, retrieving mushrooms or fire power, etc. The amount of points you get varies for each task. As with most games I play, I don't pay much attention to points. Well, sometimes I do, but it's more because I want to complete every possible task that would give me points (except busting blocks because there are too many and it would take forever) than it is to get the highest amount of points, if that makes sense. As with other games, I'm interested in completing tasks successfully—that in itself is the reward. The points don't really mean much. After all, it's a game ;)

The main reason I like this game, as simple as it might sound, is because it's fun. Why is it fun? For some of the same reasons as *Zelda,* but it's not so much a riddle as that game. In other words, while in *Zelda* you need to complete certain tasks or talk to certain characters in order to get information that will help you figure out what to do next, in *Super Mario Bros.* you just learn by doing. And once you've made it past the first world, you're pretty much doing the same things over and over, just with a little more difficulty. But there's no riddle to figure out—you know where the princess is and you just have to get through the last castle. (Although, the last castle is sort of like a maze, but it's not that difficult ;) So, given that the plot is pretty clear and you know what needs to be done, you can concentrate on all of the intricacies of each level. There's just so much to find, get, or do, that each time I play, it's a little different. Or maybe what changes is my focus. In other words, when I sit down to play *Zelda,* I do so with the intention of getting a little closer to the final goal. When I sit down to play *Super Mario Bros.,* I don't really care about getting to the end of the game or finding the princess, etc. I might decide to try and get every single coin in every level I play. Or I might try to get every single prize, or kill every single creature, or just get through each level as fast as possible, without stopping for any coins or prizes or creatures. So, I might have a different goal every time I play. I suppose that's why I like it—I'm familiar enough with it that I know basically what will happen in each level, so there's not a huge challenge. Therefore, I can just play for fun—whatever fun might mean for me on a given occasion.

What made playing *Zelda* even more enjoyable is the fact that my boyfriend, Nick, and I would play together. It was a sort of bonding experience for us, not too different from watching a certain television show together every week, or going to the woods on Sundays. However, in playing this game together, we were problem-solving together, figuring out how to get through each task. We played almost every night, for about an hour at a time, until we finished it—beat Agahnim and found Zelda. We haven't played it since. I suppose we both felt that once all of the puzzles were solved, there was no reason to play anymore.

References

Bannon, Jessica. (2004, May 17). Personal interview.
Looker, Samantha. (2004, May 18). Personal interview.
Van Ittersum, Derek. (2004, May 11). Personal interview.

Part III

Gaming and Difference

9

"A Real Effect on the Gameplay": Computer Gaming, Sexuality, and Literacy

Jonathan Alexander with Mack McCoy and Carlos Velez

During the summer of 2004, two of my former students, Mike and Michael, insisted that I play *Final Fantasy XI (FF11)* with them. *FF11* is a massively multiple online role-playing game (MMORPG) that's fairly typical of its genre: players select a character, join "parties" of other online players, kill various creatures, amass experience points to "level up," and chat, often voraciously, with their fellow online warriors and gamers. Part of my gaming experience with my two students involved periodically setting up a "LAN party," in which our various computers and Play Station 2 game consoles (PS2s) were all in the same room. We would play for hours, sometimes all night, conversing both with each other and with online friends from around the country and sometimes from around the world.

During one heated moment of game play, around 3 a.m. of a hot summer morning, Mike chastised Michael for making a bad move in the game. His comment was quick and simple, nearly a knee-jerk reaction: "Don't be such a fag." Almost immediately, he shot me a glance and said, "Oh god, I'm sorry." "That's OK," I said. "We'll talk about it later." And we all continued to play.

Being the only "fag" in the room, I understood Mike's need to apologize, and I honestly did not think much of his comment. I had grown up hearing such remarks, and now, as an adult, I even hear the word "gay" used derogatorily, as in "That's so gay" or "You're so gay," when a (generally) young person wants to verbally admonish another. In fact, as I played *FF11* throughout the summer, I noticed how frequently "fag," "gay," "homo," and other such markers were used to punish other players or to express displeasure during the heated chat sessions that accompanied and were often vital to game play, as parties formed and battled fantasy creatures. At times, players would also flirt with one another or make lewd (but generally playful) comments; and, when things were not going well for a party, they might suggest that the party as a whole was "taking it up the rear."

Certainly, I was pleased that Mike wanted to acknowledge that such comments might be offensive to me, and I saw him, during various chats, admonish other players that such language was not particularly sensitive or mature. But the ease with which he and others communicated their feelings about the game using such sexually loaded and often homophobic comments struck me as speaking directly to the literacy practices of gamers as they intersect knowledges, beliefs, and ideologies about sex and sexuality. I began asking myself what such experiences might suggest about the intersections among gaming, sexuality, and literacy.

But more than this, my own response—"That's OK. We'll talk about it later"—struck me as odd. I have seldom given up the opportunity to educate others, particularly students, about the power of language to shape ideas and to be used in deploying ideologies that can harm and separate us, particularly along lines of gender and sexuality. In this case, though, I was "caught up in the game" and wanted to play. On other occasions, during various chat sessions, I began to comment a little snidely or pointedly about some homophobic comments, and, in a very different vein, I must admit that I even flirted a bit with other characters/players, generally male, from my player perspective as a female Mithra named Tephenson, whom both Mike and Michael assured me was a "hottie." (I thought she was pretty sexy too.) All of this began to make me think that my own experience as a gay man playing an MMORPG with such complex components—visuals, chat, required group play—was suggesting some rich things about the experience of gay gamers and how they interact with other players, understand the use of sexually loaded and often homophobic comments during game play, and participate in and resist such usages. In general, I began wondering what the literacy practices of gay gamers are, particularly since gay gamers who enjoy MMORPGs would most likely be playing in comparable environments—where the use of sexually loaded and homophobic language seems not uncommon. I became particularly interested in how *younger* gay gamers might be approaching and interacting within such environments. Why younger gamers? As this volume in general demonstrates, it is "digital youth" who are often most engaged with computer and online games, and their literacies are, at least in part, being shaped by their interactions on and participation in such games. Furthermore, in a climate of greater gay visibility and increased tolerance for alternative sexualities, I was curious about how younger gay gamers might be dealing with homophobic comments in particular and sexuality in general as encountered in these online environments, where they may not seem central to game play but may nonetheless be a significant component of player interaction.

To explore such issues, I turned to my domestic partner, Mack, a long-time gamer, and we began discussing his experiences as a gay gamer. Our initial discussions led to an exploration of websites and message boards aimed at gay gamers, and I asked my two student friends, Mike and Michael if they knew of any college-aged gay gamers with whom we could talk. When the opportunity arose to contribute to this volume, we began processing our reflections in earnest, and this chapter has come together collaboratively as an exploration and examination of how some gay gamers encounter and consider issues of sex and sexuality while playing computer games. Our research is based on both analyses of message boards that serve the interests of gay gamers and an in-depth interview with a gay gamer, as well as our own experiences as gamers playing with younger people. In particular, we look at what literacy practices of gay gamers might reveal about sexuality, about ideologies of sex and sexuality, and about the intersections among gaming, gayness, and literacy. For ease of reading, I (Jonathan) narrate and discuss our research, while interweaving throughout Mack's commentary, the discussion I had with Carlos, the gay gamer whom I interviewed, and material found on gay gamer websites. References to scholarly work on gaming and literacy attempt to link this material to larger considerations of how gaming, literacy, and sexuality intersect. We conclude with some possible implications of this initial research for the teaching of literacy and writing.

Ultimately, examining some gay gamers and their interactions with computer games show us how players' literacy experience of the games is often intimately, if not always overtly, tied to issues of sexuality. More specifically, some sexual norms, particularly heterosexual norms, are reproduced in many games as part of their basic narrative structure, and gay gamers show us the possibilities and strategies of resisting such norms and opening up a space for thinking differently and more diversely about sexual expression and intimacy. As such, computer games offer us the opportunity to learn not just about literacy practices, but also about the reproduction in our culture of *sexual literacies,* a concept that we will describe in the following section.

Before we begin, a necessary caveat: we acknowledge that this research is *exploratory* at this stage; it is only an initial attempt to understand the literacy practices of gay gamers. It is limited in its focus on gay men, primarily because it was far easier to find gay male gamers than lesbian, bisexual, or transgendered gamers. Still, as an exploratory study, we feel that this chapter opens up a space for considering the literacy practices of gay gamers—*in light of what practices might contribute to our understanding of the intersections among gaming, sexuality, and literacy.* Indeed, we begin this chapter with a consideration of the scholarly literature on gaming and how our research contributes to and expands that critical undertaking.

Gay Gamers and Scholarly Invisibility

While online and computer gaming has attracted increasing scholarly attention in the last few years, as this book itself attests, the scholarly literature on issues of gaming, gender, and sexuality (broadly defined) has tended to focus on women's access to, use of, and experience with computer games. In *Growing Up Digital,* Don Tapscott (1998) noted early on that the central concerns about the impact of computer games on youth with Internet access seem to focus on the violent content of many games and the differences in how boys and girls approach and play such games (pp. 162–168). In 1995, Helen Cunningham could argue convincingly in "Moral Kombat and Computer Game Girls" that, while "[c]omputer games as a medium have a great potential for involving girls in new technology," still, "the continuing portrayal of computer games as an activity only of boys is very worrying. As in so many accounts of previous youth cultures, female participants have been rendered invisible" (pp. 198, 199). In more recent work, however, there has been nearly an explosion of interest in women and gaming, particularly in acknowledging the growing presence of women gamers. Thurlow, Lengel, and Tomic (2004) summarize research about women and gaming and argue that, while computer games are largely played by men, there is a growing minority of women players in the United States; further, they suggest that "[w]omen are more likely to participate in online chat and emailing than men." They also note, however, that "[f]eminist scholars argue that a majority of female stereotypes in gaming are also associated with violence—and these characters are created for men to play"(p. 131).

Other works such as Karen Orr Vered's (1998) "Blue Group Boys Play *Incredible Machine,* Girls Play Hopscotch: Social Discourse and Gendered Play at the Computer" and Justine Cassell and Henry Jenkins's (1998) edited collection, *From Barbie to Mortal Kombat: Gender and Computer Games,* pick up on such themes and examine access to and quality of games for girls. In particular, the use of sexist stereotypes for female characters has come under much scrutiny. Sheri Graner Ray's (2004) *Gender Inclusive Game Design: Expanding the Market* describes the often highly sexualized representation of women in computer games such as *Anarchy Online.* At the same time, some scholars are hopeful that increased participation by girls and women will foster productive and even progressive change. Cassell and Jenkins suggest that "[t]he girls' games movement is brand new. . . . With time we expect that, by pushing at both ends of the spectrum of what games for girls look like, a gender neutral space may open up in the middle, a space that allows multiple definitions of both girlhood and boyhood, and multiple types of interaction with computer games of all sorts" (p. 36).[1] Some scholars have even begun looking at issues of masculinity as constructed and deployed in computer games. Lori Kendall's *Hanging Out in the Virtual Pub: Masculinities and Relationships Online* (2002) examines hegemonic masculinities as they are performed, maintained, and challenged in some online spaces, including some game spaces.

While such scholars note both the growing market for "girls' games" and the possibility of questioning and challenging gender stereotypes, it is surprising that little attention has been paid to issues of sexual orientation, especially since gender, sexuality, sexism, and homophobia are so inextricably linked in our society. Fortunately, there is a growing body of academic work that examines lesbian, gay, bisexual, and transgender (LGBT) use of the Internet and the World Wide Web. Summarizing much of the work of LGBT use of the Internet and computers in general, John Edward Campbell (2004) notes in *Getting It on Online: Cyberspace, Gay Male Sexuality, and Embodied Identity,* for many LGBT people, "Computer-mediated communication offers possibilities for the exploration and expression of identity, for affiliation and solidarity among otherwise isolated and even stigmatized individuals" (p. xi).[2] Given this, gays' participation in online gaming, which seems a forum rife with "possibilities for the exploration and expression of identity, for affiliation and solidarity," needs examination, particularly since gaming is a forum through which many young people are exploring and developing a variety of potentially powerful literacy practices.

Along such lines, some popular press writing, primarily targeting gamers and the gaming community, has considered both the potential presence of gay gamers and the paucity of images of gay characters in most online games. For instance, in *GameSpotting Jump Around,* an online gaming zine, Avery Score (n.d.) notes the following in "Rainbow Road":

> In a country where television shows like *Queer Eye for the Straight Guy, Boy Meets Boy,* and *Will and Grace* are pulling in top ratings, week after week, it is reasonable to suggest that—regardless of whether the Constitution is one day amended to prohibit homosexual unions—gay culture is growing a greater acceptance. You might say that it, like video gaming, is becoming part of the mainstream American experience. So, is there any overlap? Video games have oft been criticized for their violent or sexual content, but rarely for their inclusion of homosexual innuendo.

In contrast, Score suggests the following:

> [W]hile homosexual content is a relatively new frontier for games created on American soil, it's quite old hat for the Japanese market. Big-name publishers, such as Squaresoft, often place their leading men in homoerotic settings, or in relationships that could be construed, by bevies of giddy, female gamers, as homosexual. There is even a convention—employed in anime and manga, as well as in games—as to how these homosexual pairings should play out. Male characters are relegated to the status of either "seme" or "uke," words that imply a series of distinct differences in personality and physiognomy. Seme tend to be tall, steely-eyed, and full of manly vigor. Uke are shorter, more boyish, and submissive. The seme is typically demonstrative or abusive toward the uke, and this provides the major source of tension between the two.

Such content, according to Score, exists as a "way to entice the female youth demographic." On the American front, though, Score seems skeptical that such a strategy would work. He quips at the end of his article that "with the growing acceptance of 'gay-themed' TV shows and movies joining mainstream media, how long is it until a *Queer Eye* video game is released, in which you must help a hapless straight male adopt a fashion-forward lifestyle [?]" The attitude here seems to be that sexuality could only be treated fairly blandly in a computer or video game, and that a "gay-themed" computer game would not be particularly compelling. At the very least, Score suggests that games with gay characters might not move beyond the representations, often fairly stereotypical, in the mass market media.

Other online commentary follows in a similar, if much less biting, vein. Matthew D. Barton (2004), in "Gay Characters in Videogames" for *Armchair Arcade,* another online gaming zine, maintains that "we should admit that classic computer role-playing games (and the majority of modern games) are sexist, if by that term we mean that they exclude females and gays as potential players." Interestingly, though, he argues hopefully along the lines of Cassell and Jenkins (1998) and suggests that some gaming software developers might consider experimenting with gay characters:

> [They might] create either very abstract avatars which anyone can identify with, or an abundance of avatars that cover most particularities. It is not true that a gay gamer would always want to choose a stereotypically "gay" avatar; the idea here is that enough choices would be present to *include* possibilities like playing black, female, gay, young, old, or even non-human avatars. So far, we have yet to see games where these choices have a real effect on the gameplay.

Such comments are suggestive in at least two ways. On the one hand, they propose that game play should be open and accessible to a potentially diverse number—and kind—of people. On the other hand, the comments assert that such diversity is relatively inconsequential to the experience of gaming, so "include[ing] possibilities like playing black, female, gay, young, old, or even non-human avatars" is important only as a "politically correct" kind of thing to do.

One of the very few *scholarly* essays to explore issues of sexuality in gaming in general is Mia Consalvo's (2003) "Hot Dates and Fairy-Tale Romances," which offers an introductory and exploratory mapping of gaming, and sexuality may be discussed from academic and theoretical perspectives. Consalvo's essay "focuses on the construction and continuing refinement of sexuality as a part of characterization and storyline in games" and also examines the "underlying presumption . . . that the player of the game desires a gaming experience where heterosexuality is seen as a social norm" (p. 172). Along those lines, Consalvo suggests that the normative heterosexuality structured into much game play can be "made visible and problematized" when considering how gay players might approach and engage such play (p. 179). She notes in particular that the *The Sims*, a computer game in which players create characters and monitor their day-to-day lives, offers possibilities of exploring "radical sexuality," since, for instance, creating gay characters is not forbidden; such characters can even be offered children to raise as part of the game. Specifically, according to Consalvo, "Sexuality for Sims is coded as an activity rather than a core aspect of identity, making almost any Sim potentially bisexual, homosexual, heterosexual, or even nonsexual" (pp. 181, 191). Such assertions about these games come from a useful analysis of the possibilities allowed—or foreclosed upon—within the games themselves.

This limited amount of writing—the online articles and Consalvo's piece—suggest two contradictory movements in thinking about gaming and sexuality. The popular press articles seem to assert that gaming and sexuality, particularly gayness, do not really intersect in substantive ways, at least not in ways that affect game play (in the United States). Consalvo, in contrast, sees some computer games as opening up a space for exploring "radical sexuality," for experimenting with and deploying alternate and nonnormative constructions of intimacy, relationship, sex, sexuality, and sexual practice. What is missing in Consalvo's discussion is a consideration of how gay gamers themselves approach such issues and what a reflection on their experiences might tell us. For instance, while Consalvo usefully explores some of the parameters and possibilities of exploring sexuality within games, such as *The Sims* themselves, she does not explore the specific literacy experiences, strategies, and reflections of *gay* gamers—who may have their own particular understanding of and insights into the intersections among gaming, sexuality, and literacy.

Indeed, the concept of *sexual literacy* may be useful in helping us unpack the connections among sexuality, discourse, and their construction in language. Specifically, sexual literacy encompasses the communication, interpretation, and reading of sexual orientations, identities, and knowledges about sexuality. For instance, how we present ourselves sexually and as beings with sexual interests is subject to our own fashioning *and* the interpretation of others—both modes that are shaped within the matrix of cultural codes that inform our understanding of what the "sexual" is. Michel Foucault (1978) has argued famously that "sexuality must not be thought of as a kind of natural given . . . [Rather, it] is the name that can be given to a historical construct: not a furtive reality that is difficult to grasp, but a great surface network in which the stimulation of bodies, the intensification of pleasures, the incitement to discourse, the formation of special knowledges, the strengthening of controls and resistances, are linked to one another" (pp. 105–106). Learning to "read" that "great surface network" and become acquainted with the discourses of sexuality—what one can and cannot say about the sexual, how one can speak about it, what knowledges about sexuality are pre-scribed, proscribed, or held as taboo—is a significant component of becoming *sexually literate* in our culture.

Some scholars are increasingly turning their attention to the study of lan-guage, sexuality, and the production of sexual literacies. In *Language and Sexuality,* Deborah Cameron and Don Kulick (2003) reflect on the slowly grow-ing body of research that attempts to think critically about how language and sexuality are intertwined, and convincingly argue that studies of sexuality *must* take into account language practices: "What we know or believe *about* sex is part of the baggage we bring *to* sex; and our knowledge does not come exclusively from firsthand experience; it is mediated by the discourse that circulates in our societies" (pp. 15–16). Even more to the point, "language *produces* the categories through which we organize our sexual desires, identities and practices" (p. 19). Language also functions to discipline sexual subject positions and knowledge about sexuality within the social matrix. Specifically, Cameron and Kulick argue the following:

> Although we may experience our sexual desires as uniquely personal and intensely private, their form is shaped by social and verbal interaction—including . . . the silences, the explicit and tacit prohibitions that are part of that interaction. It is in the social world that we learn what is desirable, which desires are appropriate for which kinds of people, and which desires are forbidden. (p. 131)

Inevitably, variations exist subculturally, and the contexts in which language and discourse are used to construct sexualities and knowledges about sexuality must be factored into consideration in any examination of sexual literacy.

To learn more about how gay gamers experience and participate in game play through their literacy practices, we need to turn our attention to their own commentary and reflection on gaming. What we find is that both modes of thinking about gaming and gayness are present among gay gamers them-selves: in some ways, many gay gamers do not see their gayness as impacting their game play in any significant way; in many other ways, however, the expe-riences of some gay gamers reveal that sexuality, particularly homophobic and hetero-normative sexualities, intimately and nearly inextricably inform many gaming narratives and interactions. The gay gamers' responses to such narra-tives and interactions take a variety of forms, and they reveal how some such gamers use specific online literacy practices in dealing with homophobia, problematizing heterosexism, and creating gaming experiences that acknowledge, support, and respect gay identities. Such literacy practices, as we shall see, include questioning the narrative structures and assumptions of games played, using role-playing to question (hetero)sexist assumptions about characters and players, and negotiating with other players appropriate and respectful discourse about gender and sexuality during real-time game play. Indeed, what I want to argue in the remaining pages of this chapter is that a more careful examination of the specific literacy practices of gay gamers, and straight gamers for that matter, might uncover for us how a variety of gamers use discourse to express, shape, and construct sexualities, sexual identities, and norms for discussing sexuality. In this way, gaming venues may offer a rich resource for understanding how literacy practices are used to discuss, debate, and construct sexuality.

Online Groups and Boards for Gay Gamers: Creating a Safe Space

One powerful way in which gay gamers explore issues of sexuality and gaming is through online forums, which offer a rich venue for seeing how such gamers write about, narrate, and discuss their gaming experiences. In our research, we discovered a few websites specifically for gay gamers, including Gamers Experimentations: The Gaymers Community (http://gamers.experimentations.org/) and ALLOUTGAMES.COM: The Gay Gamer/Straight Gamer Alliance (http://www.alloutgames.com/). The purpose of both sites is very similar: to provide a forum for gay gamers to chat, exchange information about games, discuss issues of importance and concern, and, simply, to meet other gay gamers. For instance, the Gamers Experimentations' FAQ list offers the following welcoming comments:

What is Gamers' Experimentations?

This is a community based site for gay gamers of all types. A place for people with similar interests to get together and have fun. People can come to talk about the games they enjoy or the issues that concern them without worrying about harassment.

Can I be a member?

Sure, anyone is welcome to join. Just be a civilized individual when you do, harassment isn't tolerated.

But I'm not gay?

Yeah so? Join up anyways if you think you'll enjoy chatting with us. (http://gamers.experimentations.org/boards/faq-aboutsite.php)

ALLOUTGAMES' self-description in the site's "Mission" section is more explicit in purpose and pointed in the desire to create an online "safe" space for gays who happen to game:

What the heck is going on here?

This site is intended as a community site for people that share a common bond. That is, a disgust with the way that some people treat those that are in some way different. What we provide here is a place that you can meet others that share a view that there is no place for hate speech in gaming or society in general. We have several goals:

- To allow gamers to connect with each other in order to better enjoy the gaming experience in a more positive environment.
- To create a "safe haven" for members of social minorities (including those of racial, gender, and sexual preference) where they will be respected and can be honest about their feelings and relationships.
- To educate visitors on how to deal with hatred, intolerance, and discrimination in society.
- To provide news, entertainment, and information of interest to gamers of different genres and platforms.

This site intends to combat hatred by encouraging people to band together to support each other and denounce hate speech whenever possible. (http://www.alloutgames.com/mission.php)

For the site designers of ALLOUTGAMES, these principles have some specific ramifications for the literacy practices of the participants:

> To that end, we allow users to express their feelings as honestly as possible as long as the discussion does not demean entire social groups such as those of race, sex, national origin, or sexual-orientation. All statements should be qualified to avoid casting all members of a group in a negative way. For instance, it's okay to criticize those that spout hate, but it's not okay to criticize an entire gender. Those making statements that overly generalize or stereotype people may find them edited or deleted. Those that persist in "trolling", "flaming", or causing disruption to the community will be sanctioned.
> Visitors must keep in mind that this website is private property and there is no right to free-speech here. We will always allow mature (or even vulgar) discussions about virtually any subject, but hate speech will never be tolerated here. (http://www.alloutgames.com/mission.php)

Based on my own experience with online gaming, it seems as though this site, and perhaps Gamers Experimentations, exists as a refuge for gay gamers, who very likely encounter homophobic comments during online game play. Indeed, another comment in ALLOUTGAMES' "Mission" section speaks directly to the notion of creating a "safe space" on the Web for gay gamers: "We seek to give support to this community of fair-minded and tolerant people. We want to give people better self-esteem and a feeling that there is at least this one little place on the net where they truly belong to a community that accepts them completely be they a person of color, gay or lesbian, or any other social minority" (http://www.alloutgames.com/mission.php). If anything, such comments suggest that, for many gay gamers, online game play may *not* be particularly safe.

We see similar themes in the more participatory forums on both sites.[3] The message boards on Gamers Experimentations offer visitors a chance to read and contribute postings on a variety of topics, including reviews of games, tips on video games and online gaming, and "general forums," which offer participants a chance to talk about themselves, post profiles, arrange to meet other gamers, and debate issues such as "marriage, politics, sex, relationships." ALLOUTGAMES has similar message boards about gaming, including a few extra sections entitled "Serious Topics," "Pride for Gay Gamers," and "Pride Politics (gay politics)." Such forums are certainly not common to other, "straight" gaming boards, and their presence speaks again of the attempt to create a "safe space" on the web for gay gamers. The discussion on such boards is often varied, sometimes heated. Participants share information not just about gaming but about the experience and process of "coming out" and discovering their sexuality. There is also a bit of discussion about political topics, such as the need for gay rights legislation, the possible national legalization of gay marriage, and the impact of presidential politics on the experience of gays across the country.

These forums are telling, then, along two important lines. First, they offer gay gamers, mostly young people it seems, an opportunity to explore issues of mutual concern with those who share common interests, not just a common identity. As such, these gamers can chat and explore topics in a "safe space" *and* help build a particular community at the same time. Second, the discussion reveals an interesting split between what we might call gaming issues and sexuality issues. There are forums for discussing and reviewing games, and there are forums for discussing issues related to gay life, experiences, and politics. Overlap is relatively infrequent, unless participants relate experiences of homophobia during game play. Given this, it seems that the literacy practices of these gay gamers regarding gaming and sexuality, at least as it is represented on the participatory forums on these websites, largely do *not* intersect. Gay gamers readily share information, debate issues, and challenge one another on issues related to gaming and sexuality—but often separately. It seems as though, to borrow from Barton's (2004) comment earlier, issues of sexuality do not have "a real effect on the game play" beyond encountering and dealing with homophobic comments from other gamers. At the same time, discussion of homophobic comments encountered during game play, as well as the necessity of creating "safe spaces" online for gay gamers, strongly suggests that sexuality *is* an important component of game play and that gay gamers are creating literacy spaces to process homophobic encounters and explore their identities as gay gamers. Again, such a difference actually seems contradictory: on the one hand, the assertion that sexuality does not have "a real effect on the gameplay" suggests that the material body of the players is not particularly important in the virtual worlds of gaming; on the other hand, the desire of some gay gamers (and some straight gamers as well) to explore and challenge homophobic discourse suggests that homophobia experienced during game play has a material effect on the gamers, which in turn impacts and shapes their experience of gaming and their own game play.

We can see this contradiction at play in our discussion with Carlos, a gay gamer we profile in depth in the next section. While Carlos sees his gayness and his gaming as generally separate, his comments and reflections suggest how his approach to computer gaming, as well as the literacy practices he deploys in gaming, is often intimately shaped by issues and considerations of sexuality. He also shows us particular ways in which a young gay man uses a variety of literacy practices, specifically around character building and questioning the narrative structures of games, to query, problematize, and respond to heteronormativity in the narratives of some computer games. What Carlos ultimately shows, I believe, is that some gaming literacy practices actually underscore the preexisting, if unacknowledged, connections between gaming and sexuality *and* also allow gay gamers a chance to intervene in games to construct gay-affirmative identities that challenge hetero-normative assumptions.

Considering the Intersections among Gaming, Sexuality, and Literacy: An Interview with Carlos

Carlos, a 24-year-old gay college student and gamer, has been involved in computer games for over five years and played role-playing "board" games such as *Dungeons and Dragons (D&D)* for several years before playing computer games. Carlos studies musical composition and wants to be a college professor and composer. He is articulate and thoughtful, and his comments reveal that he has thought much about how gaming plays a part in his life.

Carlos describes a congenial family background, tolerant and supportive of both reading and his sexuality:

> My parents are natives of Puerto Rico, both raised Christian (dad, Catholic; mom, Protestant) and came from poor/middle class families respectively. Now they are quite successful, both holding Master's degrees and would be financially considered middle class. They are politically liberal-minded, tending to vote democratic and while they encouraged Christian values in the house while I was growing up, they are socially liberal and warmly accepting of my being gay. Mom is an avid reader, absorbing books on global historical topics, mysteries, biographies etc. Dad reads political thrillers and science fiction.

The parents' interest in reading translated into Carlos's own literary interests, and we can see his father's interest in science fiction reflected in some of Carlos's reading choices: "Growing up, I enjoyed reading primarily comic books (anything from Calvin and Hobbes to X-Men) and fantasy novels (Tolkien, *Dungeons & Dragons* adventures, Ursula K. LeGuin, J. K. Rowling etc). I did not read often, but read quickly when I did."

Carlos is very articulate about how his reading interests tie directly into his gaming activities. For him, a rich "imaginary life" as a child manifested itself not just in reading, but also in television viewing and some initial role-playing gaming:

> My natural interest in fantasy was augmented by the kind of imaginary life I lived when I was young. I read numerous comic books and watched absurd cartoons such as She-Ra, Thundercats, Silverhawks etc., excited by the idea of people who had extraordinary abilities and the kind of conflicts they would have to deal with. My best friend and I would often pretend to be these characters (or characters of our own conception). Naturally, this led to an interest in fantasy gaming with a group of people whom we could more realistically interact with rather than just having two of us jumping around and fighting each other in capes emitting ridiculous sound effects. So in high school, I was asked by my friend Todd if I wanted to play D&D as an NPC Psionicist (whatever that meant, I didn't know back then) so I agreed, but we never played that campaign. Instead, since so many people in our mutual group of friends showed an interest, we decided to start as 1st level characters. I was a wizard, and I remember it well! We played with relative consistency, but stopped playing after a year and I didn't meet any other gamers until I was a graduate student. Of course I'd continued to play fantasy RPGs [role-playing games] on Playstation, and the *Final Fantasy* series was of course my favorite. My interest in fantasy gaming was far from quelled. Now I play regularly with a group of six and continue to play video games and computer RPGs as I find them.

Carlos now actively participates in reading, role-play gaming, and computer gaming, and it is clear from discussions with him that the three are connected by how they stimulate and enrich his imagination. Reading allows him to experience the creative worlds constructed by others, and the various games he plays, both with and without the computer, allow him the opportunity to participate in his own world construction. But what are the potential connections between his gaming and his sexuality? Carlos is clearly proud to be a gay man, and he presents as a confident, secure, and congenial person. He reports that he has not "had direct contact with gay rights activity, but it is an interest of mine and affects us all on the most basic human level." He initially reported no direct connection between sexuality and gaming, but after pursuing and examining our conversation with him further, we will see that Carlos's interest in gaming is tied in some complex ways to issues of sexuality and the literacy practices he deploys while gaming.

The computer game Carlos spends most of his time playing is *Neverwinter Nights,* which he describes as follows:

> Well, you make up your own character and you're kind of sent to investigate a plague that's been, you know, attacking the city of Neverwinter and there are four agents that you are sent to look for and they're actually creatures and so you go in four large districts of the city and you fight and you unravel more and more of the plot and you report back to your superior, Lady Arabeth. There are four chapters and as the chapters progress you get deeper and deeper into the plot of really what was going on because it's more than just a plague. So, it's just, you know, run-of-the-mill, by-the-book hack-and-slash kind of fun, you know, beating people up and getting plot and getting magical items and treasure and that sort of thing.

Carlos relates his experience of computer gaming in *textual* terms, referring to plots and chapters. Clearly, in his mind, gaming is a *literate* activity, one that is metaphorically comparable to reading and interacting with fiction.

In terms of sexuality, Carlos's comments initially reveal the same themes we encounter on Gamers Experimentations and ALLOUTGAMES. His emphasis is on playing games, developing his character, and enjoying the "plots" of the games he plays. I asked Carlos what kinds of characters he plays, as well as the possibilities for choosing genders and sexual orientations in the games he plays. He responded by saying that, generally, gender choice is limited to male and female and that he had not encountered games in which he could choose a sexual orientation. These limits did not seem to bother him. For him, gaming is primarily an expression and exploration of imagination:

> It's a land of make believe. It's just something, you know, you have your life and you do your things and, you know, it's fun, and then you can escape and do something that is totally different and totally impossible and totally, you know, magical and I really enjoy that. I need to. I just have a vast imagination and I think it can't go totally to waste. That would be kind of a shame.

On the surface, then, it seems as though issues of sexuality are not crucial to Carlos's understanding of his own game play. In fact, when I asked him more about the potential interaction between sexuality and game play, Carlos reiterated that he did not see much connection:

> [U]sually, since there are so many people playing, you've got to kind of go with the flow and do what everyone else wants to do and everyone else wants to go out and hack up orcs or cast spells or do fun things and get treasure. There's little time to really delve into any personal experiences and, you know, sometimes you can try and you can make something out of it and the dungeon master will roll with the punches or whatever. . . . So, yeah, but it rarely comes into play, sexuality of any kind.

If anything, such comments seem to mimic Barton's (2004) position: "So far, we have yet to see games where these choices [e.g., sexual preference] have a real effect on the gameplay."

Upon further discussion, however, Carlos's comments reveal an interaction between his own literacy practices in playing these games and his understanding of and reflection on issues of sexuality—an interaction that I contend, shows that gaming and sexuality intersect in some complex and even fundamental ways.

For instance, Carlos admits that he *does* flirt with other characters during game play. He revealed this when I probed his assertion that sexuality does not play a part in his gaming.

> This is kind of silly but every now and then I just kind of, you know, hit on the stable boy [the nonplayer character] or whatever and, you know, *simply*. Seriously. It's only partly a joke. I mean, everyone in the room [that I'm playing with] is well aware that I'm fully embracing my sexuality. . . . And it's just one of those things that I don't think anybody would really care if, you know, my character shacked up with the stable boy

but I, you know, I don't know, it's just . . . The other players rarely interact with each other although I have on occasion. I flirt with the male characters, oh sure . . . I ask them, you know, what their charisma is and if it'd be worth my time hitting on them. . . . It's partly a joke but we all do it in good fun, you know. . . . There's really no need or any desire to take it further than that. It's just a game and, you know, we just, the real fun part of the game is just going out there and, like I said, just getting out your sword and, you know, really getting into your character and just having fun, you know.

Of course, such flirtations do not always elicit positive or receptive responses, and Carlos acknowledges that homophobic encounters have also been a part of his experience of game play, an aspect of gaming that he attempts to address by encouraging toleration of diverse gaming styles and strategies:

Maybe simply a comment in the air by one of the straight male players that would be something kind of like a laugh like, that's gross Carlos, or something like that. . . . I say that you play your character your way and I'll play mine my way.

With such a strategy, Carlos hopes others will acknowledge that not all gamers are either straight or tolerant of homophobic comments, and he is encouraging fellow gamers to consider the diversity of those who play and enjoy such games.

Similarly, in thinking about gaming and cultural difference, Gonzalo Frasca (2004), in "Videogames of the Oppressed," argues the following about game play and fostering tolerance for diversity:

Neither art nor games can change reality, but I do believe that they can encourage people to question it and to envision possible changes. . . . Unlike narrative, simulations are a kaleidoscopic form of representation that can provide us with multiple and alternative points of view. By accepting this paradigm, players can realize that there are many possible ways to deal with their personal and social reality. Hopefully, this might lead to the development of a tolerant attitude that accepts multiplicity as the rule and not the exception. (p. 93)

I wonder if this is true, even as I hope it is. Let me return briefly to the story that opens this chapter. When I remember Mike's use of the word "fag" during game play, as well as his abashed response, then it seems as though Frasca might have a point. Indeed, when another player used the word "fag" during the online chat a few minutes later, Mike glanced at me for a second and wrote to the player that we all should "watch" our language. Certainly, Mike's response, and his disciplining of the chat, arose out of his unwillingness to offend me and his desire for me, as a gay man, to enjoy the game and not be offended by the homophobic comments of others. But I wonder if he would have done so if he did not know that I am gay. Moreover, would he have "corrected" another player had I not been *present* in the room? Was my *embodied* presence the necessary catalyst for prompting him to promote tolerance and an awareness that some players, unseen except virtually, might in fact be queer? Like Frasca, I hope that playing computer games with people from "multiple and alternative points of view" might "lead to the development of a tolerant attitude," but I suspect that more is at play in promoting such attitudes than just the game play itself. We need to consider a wider array of interactions as potentially contributing to tolerant—or even intolerant—attitudes with respect to diversity, sexual and otherwise.

Specifically, we can understand the relationship between game-play interaction and attitudes about sexuality by examining how characters are created and played in such games, as well as what literacy practices are important in the crafting and playing of game characters or avatars. In *Visual Digital Culture: Surface Play and Spectacle in New Media Genres*, Andrew Darley (2000) analyzes the computer game *Quake*, and asserts that "there are no discernible characters [in *Quake* and comparable games]—psychological depth does not enter into it—the motives both of players and their enemies are basic in the extreme" (p. 152). For Darley, what compels players to drive their characters through these games' narratives is a combination of the visual spectacle of the game and its narrative rules. Writing about the computer game *Blade Runner*, Darley notes that "narrative is subordinated to the more obvious fascination of being able to take an active part or role in a fictional world, to mingle with the exotic denizens of this future megalopolis exploring their spectacular environment" (p. 155). Carlos's comments corroborate this view to some extent:

> I play all sorts of characters. I tend to prefer spell casters because I think it's like a fantasy/imaginative thing, you know, it's one thing to swing a sword at every turn and that being the only thing you can do. . . . It's another thing to have an array of magical things that can never be done that you are capable of, you know, I don't care, priest, wizard, it doesn't matter. It's just interesting to have many things to choose from. . . . And you wave your hands and you say something and POOF, there's a fireball. I think that's the neatest thing.

Spectacle is clearly a key ingredient of game play, and Carlos obviously delights in the visual dimensions of the games he plays.

I would argue, though, that "psychological depth" is hardly missing in game play, even if it is not foregrounded in the narrative structure of the game. Rather, such depth is produced out of the relationship between player and character and *then also* between character and character (and even player and player) in a variety of interactions. James Paul Gee (2003), in his influential book *What Video Games Have to Teach Us about Learning and Literacy*, notes that three interconnected, interlocking, and interactive identities—virtual, real, and projective—are important to consider when analyzing game play. The "projective identity" involves both "project[ing] one's values and desires onto the virtual character" and "seeing the virtual character as one's own project in the making, a creature whom I imbue with a certain trajectory through time defined by my aspirations for what I want that character to be and become (within the limitations of her capacities, of course)" (Gee, p. 55). I believe that it is in such interactions—in the player's relationship to his/her character and the characters'/players' interactions with one another—that we see additional ways in which sexuality and gaming intersect and manifest themselves in gaming literacy practices.

For example, Carlos's work on his characters reveals how sexuality can inflect such character building and sense of the "virtual character as one's own project in the making." He almost exclusively plays female characters, a preference he explained at some length:

> You know, it goes along with the spell caster thing. There's this allure, this kind of secret mysticism about playing a female. . . . What, of course this is my opinion, but what's more interesting, you know, this kind of hooded female sorceress and she's got this really cool thing or just playing a male wizard. I don't know, I think the sorceress has so much more, you know, secrecy and just mystery about her. It's exotic. It's very interesting. . . . And I think from that perspective. It comes very naturally for me to play female characters and for me it's kind of odd to play a male. . . . [But] I don't necessarily think of gayness having anything to do with being feminine or masculine. . . . I just, I personally find it very, very easy to relate to a feminine perspective. I think it's easier for me to play a female character.

Such playing with identity is a popular concept in thinking about computer games. Brad King and John Borland (2003), in *The Rise of Computer Game Culture,* assert that "Children and adults alike take the raw materials of media stories and transform them to fit their own purposes" (p. 188). I believe that Carlos is engaging in such transforming by playing a female character. And, even though he suggests such gender play is not related to his gayness, he acknowledges that his penchant for playing female characters makes flirting with male characters easier, though he believes he is comfortable and confident enough to flirt with male characters from a male character's perspective, if he ever played from that perspective: "I could do that and I actually could do that very comfortably."

Dennis Waskul's (2003) research into online interactions and experiences of virtual embodiment has led him to assert that "to interact with others in online chat environments is to translate oneself into the conventions of the medium, and these conventions are like rules to a game that participants often 'play' with" (pp. 49–50). Carlos is clearly "playing with" the structural delimitations placed by many games on gender and that play allows him to express his sexuality. More specifically, since a player can usually only choose between male and female avatars, and next to no game prompts characters to choose a sexual orientation identity, Carlos can create a "homosexual" situation by acknowledging—to himself and to others—that he is a man playing a woman hitting on another male character. In such ways he torques the gender-delimiting parameters of the game and creates momentary queer spaces for him (and others) to enjoy. Still, he stresses that such play is not usually central to game play: "It's usually just a momentary thing. . . . It only comes up as a comment." The gender switching seems secondary, more of a sideline gimmick than a key element of game play.

In other ways, though, sexuality and game play intersect even more powerfully around the *prescribed choices and limitations* imposed on *creating* characters or avatars through which players interact with one another and the game's narrative or "plot." In "Cyber-utopias: The Politics and Ideology of Computer Games," Tom Henthorne (2003) examines computer games from the perspective of their potential utopian qualities: their ability to shape and participate in the shaping of realities that are very different from, and potentially more open and fulfilling than, the realities we inhabit in real life:

> Unlike literary utopias . . . cyber-utopias are interactive texts to the extent that they respond directly to user input; players feel as if they are constructing their own worlds, or "personal utopias," even though these utopias are largely computer generated. Rather than simply provide escape, cyber-utopias induce players to rethink the nature of their social lives as they play out alternative social realities. (p. 64)

At the same time, Henthorne notes the limitations of thinking about computer games in utopian terms: "Cyber-utopias do not allow free play, however. The parameters of the personal utopias player[s] can create . . . are limited by the games' structures, structures that reflect the beliefs and values of the games' designers just as much as *The Republic* reflects Plato's" (p. 64). One of the areas of computer game play that offers the most latitude for personal intervention and expression is character building. Specifically, players are often invited to create characters (usually involving choices of race and job class), but most games delimit player choice in terms of gender and sexuality, usually emphasizing a bigender model and a heterosexual default.

Indeed, one way in which players are "limited by the games' structures" is in the *representation* of gender—a representation that, in many cases, reinforces a hetero-normative sense of sexuality. Sheri Graner Ray (2004), in *Gender Inclusive Game Design: Expanding the Market,* describes the often highly sexualized representation of women in computer games, such as *Anarchy Online.* I myself saw such portrayals in the character I played in *FF11,* a catlike female named Tephenson, who was lithe, breasty, and very scantly clad. Male characters, by comparison, were generally fully clothed, rugged, and often hulking—more mass than anything. This corroborates Ray's analysis of the representation of male characters in many computer games:

> Male avatars are very often presented with exaggerated signals of youth and virility, such as broad shoulders, slim hips, and well-muscled arms. They are not, however, presented as hypersexualized. They do not display anything that indicates sexual receptiveness, such as an erection, red lips, or heavily lidded eyes, and their sexual organs are not enlarged to unrealistic proportions. The clothing they are clad in might often emphasize large shoulders and slim hips, but is certainly not designed to draw attention to the fact they are sexually receptive. (p. 104)

The visual dimension of game play suggests a visual *sexual* literacy: men and women look different, and those "looks" are suggestive of particular sexual roles and stances. Given the strict demarcation between male and female avatars, such gendered and sexualized characterizations are not only sexist but also *hetero*-sexist in that the couplings or pairings insinuated by the visuals reiterate a heterosexual norm: aggressive males and passive females make for obvious binary pairings.

In other ways, the limiting parameters that Henthorne describes are part of the experience of the computer game not just as a visual experience but also as a literacy event, and they impact the kinds of literacy practices in which players engage and the choices they make about their characters. In *Cybertext: Perspectives on Ergodic Literature,* Espen Aarseth (1997) uses Wolfgang Iser's reader-response theories to discuss how games invite—and change—players' interaction with games as "texts." Specifically, using "Iser's theory of literary *leerstellen,* the semantic gaps in the text that the reader must fill" in order to cocreate, as it were, a text and literary experience, Aarseth notes that the "adventure game has a . . . gap, a narrative vacancy, which must be filled by the reader for the 'text' to continue." (p. 110). At the same time, "[t]he 'openings' of determinative cybertexts are not gaps, in Iser's sense, since they are not used to complement the written parts in a game of imagination; rather, they are used as a filter, in which only the 'correct' response lets the user proceed through the text. To use another metaphor, they are keyholes, fitted by the text for very specific keys" (p. 111). Curiously, the "keyholes" in many computer games require that characters choose from a fixed and delimited set of gender and sexuality choices: players can be either male or female, and any possible sexual interactions with one another are predetermined as straight. Carlos describes such a delimited set of choices in the computer game he frequently plays, *Neverwinter Nights:*

> I will say that . . . in Neverwinter Nights, there's a brothel . . . It's in the first city area and I play a female character. However, [the game] only permits you to have relations with the male character or the male brothel person or whatever. . . . You know, and there are two other females, and I've walked into the female room like it'd be a little bit of a lesbian, wouldn't it? And [the game] won't let you do it. They say, you need to go see Tanith [a male computer character] in the room next door. Okay, fine, I'll go see Tanith. . . . You know, you can converse with the females [computer players] but they won't have anything to do with you in a sexual way. . . . You have to interact with the guy in that way.

Henthorne suggests that "ideological biases are not as evident [in many computer games] since what happens in the games results at least in part from decisions made by the player" (p. 64). I think that, in the case that Carlos describes, the *hetero-normative* ideological biases are clearly evident.

However, such biases and parameters do not preclude the possibility that "decisions made by the player" can offer points of resistance to such biases. Despite the hetero-normative defaults in *Neverwinter Nights,* Carlos acknowledges that he "queers up" the game in a variety of ways. At first, he suggests such queering is not related specifically to game play; upon further consideration, though, he asserts that it sometimes arises directly in response to the hetero-normative limitations of the game's narrative:

> [Y]ou notice by the fact that I'm a male playing a female character, I still slept with Tanith and had absolutely no problem with that. . . . I thought it was kind of fun. . . . And if I were playing a male character I still would have *tried* to sleep with Tanith. I don't know. . . . And that actually is the only part of the game where that sort of thing comes up. Everything else is you just follow a direct line of plot. . . . You know, I retract that statement because there is another male character as well as the female Arabeth, your superior, and the other males also eventually becomes your superior.

You can intensify your relationship with them based upon what gender you are. As a female character you can't really chat up Lady Arabeth and have a lesbian affair. . . . You can chat up Aaron Gin, the male superior, and you can, he'll give you items and, you know, you'll reveal more to him and he'll reveal more to you and you become very, very close. . . . And then you start falling in love with each other. . . . If you play a male character you could have that relationship with Arabeth. So, yes, that was actually something that I'd forgotten about that I think is a very valid point.

Gee argues that many games allow "learners" to "take risks in a space where real-world consequences are lowered" (p. 67). Such learning has several potential benefits. First, such learning "involves taking on and playing with identities in such a way that the learner has real choices and ample opportunity to mediate on the relationship between new identities and old ones" (p. 67). Second, for Gee, the "virtual world is constructed in such a way that learners learn not only about the domain but about themselves and their current and potential capacities" (p. 67). Part of what Carlos is potentially learning in playing games with hetero-normative constraints is how to resist and question hetero-normative structures—structures that are built into the narratives of many games, just as they are built into the social narratives that our culture tells about itself.

Indeed, Carlos's interactions with *Neverwinter Nights* allows us—and him—to see how these norms are often interwoven into the very narratives that drive such games. Barry Atkins (2003), in *More Than a Game: The Computer Game as Fictional Form,* asserts that "the player plays the game in the full knowledge that it is a game, and that life is not so conveniently organized according to the principles of narrative telling" (p. 139). Atkins is right—but only in part. Certainly, players such as Carlos realize that games such as *Neverwinter Nights* are only games, good for an afternoon's or evening's enjoyment. But his interaction with such a game suggests that the "principles of narrative telling" in terms of sexuality and the hetero-normative sexualities reiterated in the games seem "conveniently organized" to reflect those that many gays and lesbians encounter in life—the presumption of heterosexuality as a default. Moreover, such games offer a startling opportunity for players to think about literacy in specifically sexual terms, or to consider the importance of *sexual literacy;* that is, the games reinforce the dominant heterosexual story or narrative our culture tells itself about sex, sexuality, and intimacy: there are only a few allowed choices.

At the same time, while gay gamers such as Carlos have the opportunity to critique the hetero-normative assumptions and *presumptions* of many games, it is not clear that gay gamers will *necessarily* see such assumptions as part of the sexual literacy established, normalized, and reiterated by the games they play. In fact, they are such dominant and pervasive narrative defaults in the games that an astute gamer such as Carlos did not even recognize them as sexual at first, or as part of the story of sexuality our culture tells itself over and over again. In some ways, I am not surprised that Carlos, or others who have commented upon sexuality and its insignificance for game play, do not often realize the extent to which sexuality is a component of gaming. *Hetero*sexuality, as the "default" and normalized sexuality, is "unmarked" in our sociocultural matrix, and we tend only to "mark" sexuality when it deviates from the norm. Since the overtly gay or queer content of the games is generally so low, even nonexistent, it only makes sense that most would not see the games as addressing "sexuality." In their reiteration of the hetero-normative, the games only show us what we have become used to seeing; and that seeing is, as such, unremarkable. Over the course of our conversation, Carlos pinpointed many instances in which hetero-normative and gender-normative configurations were not only suggested by the game but also, in some senses, *required* for successful game play, at least in *Neverwinter Nights*. As such, Carlos's reflection on the game and his own game play prompted his awareness of how sexuality—*hetero*sexuality—is a significant part of gaming. Carlos's willingness to pay attention to his game play offers him—and others—the opportunity to see such hetero-normative paradigms and structures at work and in reiteration throughout many games.

Nonetheless, Carlos's playing of female characters, his flirtations, and his willingness to call into question homophobic discourse all underscore the various modes of agency that he utilizes to compose his online identities and collaboratively establish a respectful, or at least tolerant, ethos with regard to alternative sexualities in game play. In this way, some gay gamers use the various literacy practices of gaming not only to question hetero-normative assumptions but also actually to suggest changes in their virtual worlds—changes initiated *through* an interaction with the narratives they read and act out in their games.

Implications for Literacy Instruction: Recognizing the Connections

As we have seen in this chapter, for some young gay gamers, the virtual worlds of online gaming offer opportunities not only to meet other gay people but also to play with constructions and representations of self that question or challenge hetero-normative notions of subjectivity. Put another way, gay gamers' literacy practices in virtual worlds sometimes explore *critically* the impact of sexuality, gender conformity (and nonconformity), and heteronormativity on the shaping of identity in game play.

What are the possible implications of this for literacy scholars and educators? Certainly, if James Paul Gee (2003) is correct in asserting in *What Video Games Have to Teach Us about Learning and Literacy* that teachers should move to include computer games in literacy instruction, it is important to keep in mind the heterosexual defaults at work in many such games. These defaults preclude consideration of the experiences and interests of gay students, and they may, unintentionally, set up situations that might condone homophobic comments by not actively representing or even allowing for the consideration of alternative sexualities, intimacies, and ways of being in the world. As we saw through a consideration of sites such as Gamers Experimentations and ALLOUTGAMES, as well as Carlos's own commentary, many gay gamers encounter homophobic comments as a regular part of game play; instructors using such games in class need to be aware of both the frequency of such comments and their potential impact on the learning experiences of gay students.

More importantly, the experiences of gay gamers prompts us to consider the deep connections between sexuality and literacy in our culture. The hetero-normative and heterosexist narratives that drive many games, such as *Neverwinter*

Nights, simply reflect the dominant defaults about sexuality that still pervade our culture. The stories we tell about our lives and that we encounter in many games do not always allow for or encourage the consideration of alternative intimate arrangements, or of lives that do not fit easily into prevailing gender norms. The roles we play online and in real life exist as complex negotiations between the stories the culture tells about itself and its members and the stories we want to tell about ourselves. Gay gamers who reflect upon their experiences offer us the opportunity to consider how all of those stories intersect one another. At the same time, it is important to note that *reflection* is crucial: heterosexual defaults are so normative in our culture that, without reflection, we may fail to note what kinds of stories are being reiterated—both in real life and in computer games. Mia Consalvo may be right, to an extent: some games *may* open up the possibility of exploring "radical sexualities," but such exploration may only gain heft and depth with a metaconsideration of game play and may not be evident or explicit in the virtual worlds of gaming.

Beyond issues of narrative and literacy, we should think in larger terms of the impact of networked and computer technologies on our conception of ourselves as human, as creatures with identities. In her "Cyborg Manifesto," Donna Haraway (2003) argues famously that the "cyborg is a creature in a post-gender world: it has no truck with bisexuality, pre-oedipal symbiosis, unalienated labor, or other seductions to organic wholeness through a final appropriation of all the powers of the parts into a higher unity" (p. 517). In some ways, the gay gamer is a peculiar kind of cyborg gamer. He or she, like Carlos, need not pretend to occupy a position of "organic wholeness"; Carlos can play, as a gay man, a female character flirting with nonhuman male-presenting avatars and find the situation delightful and stimulating without having to identify it as anything beyond flirting, as sending signals along a current and prompting responses. At the same time, the sending of signals, the prompting, the flirting—none of this occurs in a vacuum. The gaming network, while not necessarily suggesting an "organic wholeness," nonetheless seduces players to think along set lines, within particular parameters. There is a "unity" even as gay players such as Carlos suggest how some players are moving into, or at least flirting with, a "post-gender world."

Furthermore, beyond gaming, it is worth keeping in mind the connection between gaming and other mass media, such as film and television. Some games have inspired filmmakers—and vice versa—and we should be attentive to how such connections reiterate norms of sexuality, or potentially open up spaces for thinking differently about gender and sexual-orientation norms. Film, as the less-interactive medium, might appear more iconic in its representation of identities, while game play may excite players with the potential to explore alternative stories, and alternative *sexual* stories for characters, much as fans of *Star Trek* or other television shows and movies have created complex fan fictions detailing involved sex lives for characters whose sexuality appears static on the screen.

Ultimately, we have only touched briefly here on how gay gamers might critically reflect upon the intersections among gaming, literacy, and sexuality. A larger sampling or polling of gay gamers would very likely reveal more complex and perhaps even divergent views than those offered by Carlos and us, and we should also be attentive to the specific insights to be offered by gamers who identify as lesbian, bisexual, and transgendered. As such, we offer our thoughts here as both a cursory exploration and a call to further research.

Notes

1. Mia Consalvo and Susanna Paasonen (2002) point out in their introduction to *Women and Everyday Uses of the Internet: Agency and Identity* that "the game industry . . . has tended to cater mainly to boys, while girls' games, such as Mattel's Barbie Fashion Designer and Purple Moon's Rockett series, have been accused of stereotyping" (p. 13). An article in Consalvo and Passonen's collection that addresses how young women game online, Virpi Oksman's (2002) "'So I got It Into My Head Hat I Should Set Up My Own Stable . . . ': Creating Virtual Stables on the Internet as Girls' Own Computer Culture," argues that some online games offer "opportunities for bringing out the voices of girls and young women in matters related to technology and for supporting their positive engagement with new technologies through the case of virtual stables," in which participants raise "virtual horses" (p. 192). Oksman warns that while "the virtual world affords possibilities for fantasy, trying out different roles and experimenting with identity," some online gamers discover that "the rules and regulations of the 'real world' were also present in the virtual world" (p. 203).
2. See also Alexander (2004) for another recent summary of this work.
3. To protect the privacy of participants on these forums, I am not citing any specific messages or postings; however, visitors to the forums can "get a taste" of the postings themselves.

References

Aarseth, Espen J. (1997). *Cybertext: Perspectives on ergodic literature.* Baltimore, MD: Johns Hopkins University Press.

Alexander, Jonathan. (2004, February). In their own words: How LGBT youth represent themselves on the Web." *Gay and Lesbian Alliance Against Defamation (GLAAD).* Retrieved February 4, 2006, from http://www.glaad.org/programs/csms/papers.php?

Atkins, Barry. (2003). *More than a game: The computer game as fictional form.* Manchester, UK: Manchester University Press.

Barton, Matthew D. (2004, March). Gay characters in videogames. *Armchair Arcade.* Retrieved October 7, 2004, from http://www.armchairarcade.com/aamain/content.php?article.27

Cameron, Deborah, & Kulick, Don. (2003). *Language and sexuality.* Cambridge: Cambridge University Press.

Campbell, John Edward. (2004). *Getting it on online: Cyberspace, gay male sexuality, and embodied identity.* New York: Harrington Park Press.

Cassell, Justine, & Jenkins, Henry. (Eds.). (1998). *From Barbie to Mortal Kombat: Gender and computer games.* Cambridge, MA: MIT Press.

Consalvo, Mia. (2003). Hot dates and fairy-tale romances. In Mark J. P. Wolf & Bernard Perron (Eds.), *The video game theory reader* (pp. 171–194). New York: Routledge.

Consalvo, Mia, & Paasonen, Susanna. (Eds.) (2002). *Women and everyday uses of the Internet: Agency and identity.* New York: Peter Lang.

Cunningham, Helen. (1995). Moral Kombat and computer game girls. In Cary Bazalgette & David Buckingham (Eds.), *In front of the children: Screen entertainment and young audiences* (pp. 188–200). London: British Film Institute.

Darley, Andrew. (2000). *Visual digital culture: Surface play and spectacle in new media genres*. London: Routledge.

Foucault, Michel. (1978/1990). *The history of sexuality: An introduction*, volume 1 (Robert Hurley, Trans.). Vintage Books: New York.

Frasca, Gonzalo. (2004). Videogames of the oppressed: Critical thinking, education, tolerance, and other trivial issues. In Noah Wardrip-Fruin & Pat Harrigan (Eds.), *First person: New media as story, performance, and game* (pp. 85–94). Cambridge: MIT Press.

Gee, James Paul. (2003). *What video games have to teach us about learning and literacy*. New York: Palgrave Macmillan.

Haraway, Donna. (2003). A cyborg manifesto: Science, technology, and socialist-feminism in the late twentieth century. In Noah Wardrip-Fruin & Nick Montfort (Eds.), *The new media reader*. Cambridge: MIT Press.

Henthorne, Tom. (2003, April). Cyber-utopias: The politics and ideology of computer games. *Studies in Popular Culture, 25*(3), 63–76.

Kendall, Lori. (2002). *Hanging out in the virtual pub: Masculinities and relationships online*. Berkeley: University of California Press.

King, Brad, & Borland, John. (2003). *The rise of computer game culture: From geek to chic*. New York: McGraw-Hill.

Oksman, Virpi. (2002). 'So I got it into my head hat I should set up my own stable . . .': Creating virtual stables on the Internet as girls' own computer culture. In Mia Consalvo & Susanna Paasonen (Eds.), *Women and everyday uses of the Internet: Agency and identity* (pp. 191–210). New York: Peter Lang.

Ray, Sheri Graner. (2004). *Gender inclusive game design: Expanding the market*. Hingham, MA: Charles River Media.

Score, Avery. (n.d.). Rainbow road. *GameSpotting Jump Around*. Retrieved October 7, 2004, from http://www.gamespot.com/features/6102243/p-3.html

Tapscott, Don. (1998). *Growing up digital*. New York: McGraw-Hill.

Thurlow, Crispin, Lengel, Laura, & Tomic, Alice. (2004). *Computer mediated communication: Social interactions and the Internet*. London: Sage.

Vered, Karen Orr. (1998). Blue group boys play *Incredible Machine*, girls play hopscotch: Social discourse and gendered play at the computer. In Julian Sefton-Green (Ed.), *Digital diversions: Youth culture in the age of multimedia* (pp. 43–61). London: UCL Press.

Waskul, Dennis. (2003). *Self-games and body-play: Personhood in online chat and cybersex*. New York: Peter Lang.

10

Taking Flight: Learning Differences Meet Gaming Literacies

Matthew Bunce, Marjorie Hebert, and J. Christopher Collins

Introduction (Matthew Bunce)

In April of 1993, I began attending Eagle Hill School in Hardwick, Massachusetts. Eagle Hill is a private, coed boarding school for high school students with learning differences (LD)—then called learning disabilities. This school was my home for four years. The curriculum at Eagle Hill included developmental reading, writing, math, geography, government, and rudimentary sciences, and students were placed in classes based on results of a battery of standardized assessment exams. The classes were small, and it was not uncommon to share a classroom with students from all four grade levels. I graduated from Eagle Hill in 1997, along with 24 other students.

In 1997, I moved to Amarillo, Texas, to attend Amarillo College. In the state of Texas, all incoming first-year students have to take the Texas Academic Skills Program (TASP) test, now called the Texas Higher Education Assessment (THEA) test. According to this standardized test designed to measure my reading, writing, and math skills, I was, at that time, underprepared to enter college or the workforce. If the state of Texas had its way, I would be bagging groceries today. I am grateful to Eagle Hill for the education that I received, but even now—as a graduate student in Michigan Tech's Rhetoric and Technical Communication program—I remain concerned that my schooling provided me, and the majority of LD students, with too few of the strategies for knowledge acquisition and production that we needed.

Like many students in my situation—who cannot depend solely on their formal educational preparation—I devised my own set of survival skills. In my case, academic and professional success has been tightly linked to technology. Long before I considered graduate school, I knew that learning about technology was important, especially as an LD student. I would go to bookstores and buy computer magazines such as *Wired* and *Yahoo!* I learned about applications such as Microsoft Office, discovered Internet search engines, and signed up for a Hotmail account with the help of the articles that I read. With access to the Internet, I also gained access to LD bulletin boards, which actually encouraged me to try harder in school by relating devastating stories about being stuck in dead-end jobs. I developed a strategy of trial and error, working with a new piece of technology or software, and exploring its uses. Today, as a composition instructor, I firmly believe I have an obligation to help students develop their own survival skills, a set of literacy practices that will help them evolve into key participants in today's world.

The authors of this chapter share a belief in the importance of helping LD students develop their own individually useful set of literacy practices. We believe that all LD students need to develop sustainable strategies for academic and personal success. Marjorie Hebert, for instance, has served for several years as associate director of Michigan Technological University's Electronic Communication Across the Curriculum summer institute, working closely with both LD students and their teachers at the elementary and secondary levels. Together, we write about one important strategy for LD survival—the use of multimodal information gathering and its implications for composition. Specifically, we examine the ways that the multimodal universe of video gaming can help students realize their composition potential. We are joined in this exploration by Christopher Collins, an LD college student and gamer. Throughout his interviews, Chris demonstrates the ways that the literacies practiced in gaming environments can help LD students become more confident composers and increasingly effective as citizens.

Pens, Pixels, and Pedagogies: LD Scholarship in Our Disciplines

In the last 20 years, the field of composition studies has paid relatively little attention to LD students. Patricia Dunn (1995), in her book *Learning Re-abled: The Learning Disability Controversy and Composition Studies,* discussed this gap in our scholarship, noting "there are controversies surrounding the field of LD, one of which is the controversies of teaching methods—whether [LD students] learn better in a whole language class, or in one based on explicit, multisensory, structured phonics instruction" (p. 10). The problem, wrote Dunn, was that composition scholars are not exposed to scholarship focused on LD. In fact, the majority of the scholarship in composition studies continues to ignore, for the most part, LD students. Indeed, many of the scholars interested in nonmainstream students and their approaches to instruction avoid "learning-disabilities" altogether, preferring instead to focus on "basic writers." The lack of work in this area has become increasingly problematic, as we begin to realize the sheer number of students who are dealing with some type of LD. Daniel P. Hallahan and Devery Mock (2003) cited the U.S. Department of Education as indicating that there are almost 3 million students in the United States who learn differently. With nearly

3 million students coping with LD, teachers, parents, and government officials need to reevaluate the learning styles of LD students and the teaching practices of their instructors. Until recently, student writers with LD were thought to be individuals primarily from poorer socioeconomic backgrounds; it is becoming increasingly clear, however, that such writers hail from all socioeconomic backgrounds (See Peck, Flower, & Higgins, 2001; Delpit, 2001).

In the mid-1990s, given increased attention to learning disabilities, two important forums for LD students and their teachers were established: LD Resources (ldresources.com) and the Learning Disabilities Association of America (LDA). LD Resources hosts several articles written by LD teacher Richard Wanderman. Wanderman (1990), in his article *Tips on Writing for People with Learning Disabilities*, argues that "focus needs to be taken off deficiencies (low points) and put on strengths (high points) to build self esteem." The deficiencies Wanderman identifies include students' performance on the mechanics of writing—often grammar and spelling. The strengths include their creativity and understanding of content. Wanderman, along with Patricia Dunn and other scholars (see Bartoli & Botel, 1988), was the first to argue that "verbal literacy is only one expression of intelligence and that students use other types of literacy to express their intelligence daily" (Wanderman, 1990). For that time—not too many years ago—such ideas were revolutionary in the LD community, and were frequently dismissed by LD professionals.

Linda Feldmeier White (2002), in her *College Composition and Communication* article "Learning Disability, Pedagogies, and Public Discourse," suggests that professional discourse (the discourses of psychologists and medical doctors) largely ignores scholarship on learning disabilities because of a "lot of uncertainty" (p. 709). Those ideas and beliefs about which professionals are certain are dispersed to the public in the context of the positivist discourses characterizing the medical model for learning. This discourse "dominates LD research and pedagogy" (p. 707). White notes that one dominating professional theory of LD, for example, has been offered by William Cruickshank: "Neurological dysfunctions lead to perceptual processing deficits which, in turn, result in a variety and complexity of learning disabilities" (p. 716).

Fortunately, there are exceptions to this discourse. White, for example, notes that if LD specialists "looked at research in other fields," they would "find a richer and more useful picture of language and learners" (p. 718). Instead of having teachers focus on remediation, White argues that educators need to help LD students find pleasure in writing. White's argument is not only relevant for LD students, but also for non-LD students, especially as schools are presently coping with No Child Left Behind (NCLB). This U.S. Department of Education program bases itself on the type of positivist discourse that White opposes. Under the NCLB legislation, rather than moving closer to thoughtful, open pedagogies, schools are being asked to prescribe pedagogy symptomatically based on clinical trials, as a doctor would prescribe medication to a sick patient.

Jesus-Nicasio Garcia and Ana Maria de Caso (2002), in their article "Effects of Motivational Intervention for Improving the Writing of Children with Learning Disabilities," point out that a lack of pleasure in writing, along with other factors, can contribute to a lack of a motivation to write. Citing Linnenbrink and Pintrich (2002), Garcia and de Caso (2002) argue that one reason LD students have difficulties in writing is that they lack the motivation to do so:

> Motivation is not exclusively a stable characteristic of a person, but also depends on situation, domain, and context (Mayer, 2001). This provides some hope for teachers and school psychologists, since it suggests that if we modify and design curricula, lessons and schools in a different way, we can enhance students' motivation to improve their academic achievement (Linnenbrink & Pintrich, 2002).

In response to this situation, Garcia and de Caso discuss modifying curricula to address the issue of motivation, suggesting process-oriented assignments that involve drafting, translating, and revising printed texts. Although process-oriented pedagogies are important, many composition theories have moved away from using them exclusively (See Cope and Kalantzis, 2000). The fact is that LD students not only compose in different ways, but also learn differently.

To the credit of the composition studies, in the last three years, valuable articles have appeared in *College Composition and Communication* and *College English* (See Brueggemann et al., 2001). At the same time, however, in 2000–2004, a total of only five presentations focused on students with LD at both the *College Composition and Communication* and the Computers and Writing conferences. Within this context, the teaching of LD students remains difficult. Our hope is that this chapter can help narrow the gap between teachers and students and parents and professionals and their understanding of literacy practices for those who learn differently.

A Gamer's Composition Transition: J. Christopher Collins

John Christopher Collins was born in McKinney, Texas, a suburb of Dallas, in 1980, and the Collins family has lived in and around Dallas since his birth. According to a 1999 survey by scholars at Texas A & M University, 8.1 percent of Dallas County households made less than $10,000, while only 3.2 percent of households earned over $200,000. The majority of Dallas County households earned between $20,000 and $30,000 a year ("Texas Data Center," 2000). According to the Center for Public Policy Priorities (2000, p. 4) the poverty level for a family of four was $17,050 in 2000. In other words, the gap between wealth and poverty in Dallas, for Chris's family and others'—is evident. Although Chris's mother, Susan, describes the family as "upper middle class"—noting that this means "we live in a nice house and a nice neighborhood"—she adds, "We are not wealthy by any stretch of the imagination." The Collins family, however, clearly comes from a wealthier socioeconomic background than the majority of Dallas County residents.

As Chris grew up, his family valued both education and knowledge of technology, although the two were generally considered separate factors until Chris's experiences suggested their intimate relationship. Chris's father graduated from Texas Tech University in the 1960s, and his mother completed two years of an undergraduate degree at the University of North Texas before leaving college.

Although the Collins family did not consider themselves wealthy during Chris's youth, they did have the resources needed to send both Chris and his sister Lindsay to Good Shepherd Episcopalian School in Dallas, a private, church-affiliated school that both children stopped attending after second grade because of a rise in tuition. Mrs. Collins recalls vividly the reasons for sending her children to private school:

> We were in the Dallas Independent School District, and they did not have a good reputation. The tuition [for Good Shepherd] was 2800 dollars a year. It was afford-able. [Sending our children to private school] was just sort of the thing to do. Most of our friends and neighbors did it. A lot of kids went to Catholic school or the Good Shepherd. I believe that parents were sending their children to private school when White Flight started—that's where you had good schools and the majority of schools were white. People then started moving out to go to schools where they are all white. It had nothing to do with racism for us. It's just that Dallas had a poor reputation.

It was understood, by Chris as well as his parents, that he would attend college, and that he would do well. What Chris's parents were not counting on was his LD, and the effect it would have on his educational success. From very early on, his LD impeded his learning in formal educational situations:

> When I did go to Private school, I was put into a class called primer, which was a class in between kindergarten and first grade . . . cause I didn't know how to read and needed some extra time for that, and it was at that time that I learned to read.

As Chris grew older, he found learning in school, and especially reading courses, to be increasingly difficult. He recalled, for example, material in English classes that he did not read owing to a lack of enjoyment and a lack of interest:

> I knew what I wanted to learn in life and it didn't involve Charles Dickens. I liked non-fiction in politics or anything that would teach me something about aviation.

Developing traditional literacy skills in formal educational settings remained largely an uphill battle for Chris. When he would try to read and write for school, his communicative skills often completely broke down. Mrs. Collins explained Chris's early literacy experiences to us:

> When he would write an essay, I could pick out the idea, but the sentences didn't make sense. They wouldn't be complete sentences, and they didn't follow a train of thought. You were able to see what he was trying to do and say, but they were not real thoughtful. Whatever popped into his mind he would write. He was writing the way he was thinking. He was a terrible speller! His spelling improved in spell check. Also, he was very creative. He had good ideas if you could figure out what he was saying. Age appropriately, his essays were interesting.
>
> He was a very poor reader, and only recently became a reader. I tried to instill reading in my children early. Comparing him to my daughter: she would read for hours. He would start talking and flipping pages. He ate more books than I read to him. He would tear out the pages and chew on them.

> When you diagnose a child with ADD, you put a label on them. It is really hard to explain to a younger child that is "okay" and there is "nothing" wrong with you. Perhaps in class they're treated differently. I wish the schools had better programs for students.

As Chris grew up, his family began to think more seriously about the value of computer technology, leading the national trend (See Selfe, 1999, p. 15–21). As Chris's mother notes, "We bought our first computer around 1991, and it came with a DOS operating system. It cost us about one thousand dollars." This amount, she acknowledges, represented a minimal investment for the family—in her words, "a drop in the bucket."

To the surprise of Chris's parents, the purchase of this computer had immediate effects on their son's school work. Chris's mother was very clear in describing the changes she observed when Chris began using the computer and playing video games:

> Writing and reading became easier for him on the computer. He was thinking faster than he could write, so being able to type it out was beneficial. . . . Chris' gaming became almost a type of liberation.

Chris's first forays into computer-based video gaming took the shape of "a civil war game," and *Oregon Trail*, a video game that became popular as a reward for good students in school districts with access to computers. The point of *Oregon Trail*, Chris recalls, was "to keep your family from dying on a long commute out west."

Chris's video game tastes matured as he did. About the same time, for instance, that the teenager Jessica Dubroff was making her well-publicized, and eventually fatal, attempt to be the youngest pilot to fly across the country, Chris began playing *Microsoft Flight Simulator for Windows 95* (MFS). Chris remembers his early motivations for playing this "reality" game:

> After I dropped off my sister [at the Dallas/Fort Worth airport] . . . all I could think about was *Flight Simulator*. It was the first experience I had with aviation and it put aviation into a realistic context. Back then, you could go into the airport and watch people board the plane . . . you know, get past security. It was the first time I saw an airliner up close. I remember my dad telling me that it was a Delta DC-10 heading for London and for a 9 or 10 year old kid that's a pretty fascinating sight.

Chris's interest in flying, however, did not stop at the edge of the monitor. As Chris remembers, "My dad and I would hang out at a small airport by my house and watch the airplanes take off and land." Chris relates this time in the hangar to both his video-gaming experience and his desire to fly: "I could go home [from the airport] and day dream of being a pilot while actually playing a video game in which I was flying a plane." At the same time, however, he notes, "I'd say that the flight simulator had a partial relationship to me wanting to become a pilot." Chris's dreams of becoming a pilot have since become a reality.

Once Chris was flying a real plane at age 14, his interest in the flight simulator diminished. This accomplishment, however, did not prove to be the end of his video-gaming career, however. At the turn of the decade, Chris moved on to another reality-based game, *SimCity 2000*—the second version of this popular game. In this game, Chris assumed the role of mayor.

The goal of *SimCity 2000* is to create a thriving city with a starting budget of $50,000. Of course, $50,000 does not go very far when a player is considering fundamental elements such as a power plant, power lines, water towers, and pipes, as well as the most important part of the city—zones: residential, commercial, and industrial. After the initial setup of his city, Chris remembers,

> I got the cheapest power plant . . . it was coal, which is horrible for the environment and doesn't produce a lot of power. Then you've got to make sure you start small in every sense of the word. Also, create a small economy that can stabilize and produce tax revenue . . . if you over-expand, then your budget is going to bust, no doubt.

And, just as real politicians receive feedback from their constituents, Chris received responses from his virtual constituents:

> All the city commissioners were happy when I'd check in with them. They would all have positive comments. However, if you ever cut anything out of their budgets, then they would be furious at you.

The effects of Chris's gaming experiences, however, were not limited solely to an interest in flying or politics. Rather, there was also a clear connection between his *MFS* and *SimCity* experiences and his developing literacy practices. Mrs. Collins speaks about how this connection played out in her son's early composition courses:

> I think when you're playing a video game, you are focusing. You can only do one thing at a time. You can't be doing two things at once—like reading and playing. Sentence structure improved.
>
> Before [using the computer], his [Chris's] writing was rambling. When he mastered writing, or got better at it, his sentences made sense. There was a main idea. He followed through with his ideas. When he was playing computer games, he focused. That was the first time he was able to do something for an extended period of time without losing his train of thought.
>
> You have to think when you're playing video games. You have to use some logic. I think that his playing video games transferred his focus to school. His grades improved. He was able to focus on his reading and writing more.

In addition to gaming's effect on his writing practices, Chris notes that his early gaming and the later experiences that these games led to helped him to develop other literacies well:

> My father purchased a small Cessna 150 for about the price of a used car in 1996. Since then, we have traded it in, and now are on our third, and nicest aircraft. It is a 1974 Piper Archer. It's a 4 seater, 180hp that cruises about 125 mph. It can get up to 12k feet, but above that you need oxygen tanks, which I do not own . . . but I don't need to go that high anyway. The technology I have learned about from

flying is the mechanics of an engine. I've got to know what a well-running engine sounds like . . . I've got to know what's going wrong if the engine begins to over-heat . . . and more importantly, I've got to know how to bring the heat down with-out ever leaving my pilot's chair . . . you can't pull over to the side of the road in an airplane . . . you've got to think fast. I can navigate [the airplane] by finding out where I am in relation to the radio signals I'm picking up. About four years ago I learned how to use a GPS [Global Positioning System]. This had revolu-tionized aviation and made me a safer pilot. I've got to be comfortable using this technology because again, if I don't know how to use it, I just can't pull over on the side of the road.

These literacy practices—although Chris describes them here as relating directly to his real-world flying experience—were also embodied in the environment of the flight simulator. As Chris notes:

[In *MFS*,] I did learn how not to crash the plane. I learned how to have smoother take offs and landings. Later, I learned how to navigate myself to other airports in the nation. I usually played the game until it made sense. Maybe a couple of weeks later, I would look at the manual to see if I could find any way that I could get better. For example, that is when I would find out that in MFS, I could raise my landing gear by pressing "g."

A similar connection between gaming and literacy is evident when he talks about the literacy practices of politics in conjunction with *SimCity*. Currently, for exam-ple, Chris holds a position as legislative aide to Texas state representative Eddie Rodriguez. Although Chris's communication with virtual constituents in *SimCity* came in the form of newspaper headlines and consultations with virtual advisors, his real-world constituents require a more active role. His successful practice of responding to these real-life constituents, as he acknowledges, may well have had their roots in those early *SimCity* exchanges. Chris, for instance, "regularly email[s] over 400 [of Eddie Rodriguez's] constituents, maintain[s] a database of the email addresses, and use[s] the web to research previous legislation. I also write press releases." Rather than reading fictional press releases and receiving information from virtual advisors, Chris now writes real press releases after researching, compiling, and interpreting the information that Representative Rodriguez needs in digital-communication environments.

Gee's Identity Principle Takes Flight

Chris's case represents one example of how video games shape literacy practices—especially composition. For Chris, the organization, focus, and audience aware-ness that he practiced in *MFS* transferred into the composition classroom as an awareness of organization, focus, and audience in composing texts. These skills, most teachers would further acknowledge, are the three primary traits that often characterize the writing of successful composition students.

This case, we believe, also demonstrates the way that James Gee's (2003) identity principle (p. 54) plays out in actual practice. When Chris relates stories of flying in *MFS* with us, as literacy interviewers, he is also relating stories of his emerging and developing identity as a pilot. The virtual context of *MFS* and *SimCity* are basic in comparison to the gaming environment that Gee writes about; however, these worlds may be of similar importance.

The virtual world of *MFS*, for instance, involved Chris in seeing the world through a pilot's eyes. As a player, he sat in the pilot's seat with all the controls familiar to a real pilot, including oxygen masks, a steering wheel, cabin pressure gauges, and several dials and buttons. In this world, Chris Collins—the "non-virtual person playing a computer game," in Gee's words (p. 55), the LD student who commonly failed in educational environments—assumed the virtual identity of Chris Collins—capable pilot, an individual responsible for successfully taking off and landing and, of course, for not losing cabin pressure and crashing the plane. If and when the plane crashed in this game, Chris Collins, as the virtual pilot, was also responsible for the virtual failure. As Chris became a more frequent gamer with *MFS* and an actual licensed pilot, for example, he projected values of determination and confidence, as well as the value of learning about the world of flying, including subjects like aerodynamics and GPS.

Chris's real-world identities, at least the ones we are familiar with—student, son, and a boy living in the suburbs of Dallas—were shaped by the virtual identity traits he assumed in games such as *MFS* and *SimCity*. As Chris's mother, for instance, recalls,

> [Video games, for Chris,] were a real eye opener. Video games and flying together gave him confidence. He assumed leadership roles; they had a comedy show in the mornings. He became very popular.

James Gee might explain this transformation by noting that the identity attributes that Chris took on in a virtual environment—a skilled and capable pilot, a responsible and responsive city manager—influenced his identity in the real, nongaming world as a problematic student incapable of succeeding in formal educational settings. In Gee's words, Chris was able to formulate a *projective identity* (p. 55): Chris-capable-both-as-a-real-word-student-and-real-world-pilot.

This projective identity did not mean that Chris—the real-world boy and the real-world pilot—was entirely freed from his personal limitations, as Gee points out. In the real world, he continued to face such limitations, even though he was also armed with the virtual experiences of a skilled pilot and a responsible mayor in the gaming world.

In the virtual world of *MFS*, for instance, Chris could only fly so far. In fact, given that there is no particular destination in the game, success is not based on whether or not Chris arrived at a particular airport location, but on whether or not Chris could fly through the air without crashing. In effect, therefore, Chris succeeded as a virtual-world pilot when he felt satisfied with his own personal achievements. The very fact that Chris *as* a pilot has no specific end goal makes dealing with his projective identity even more painstaking than if he were playing a more sophisticated role-playing game (RPG) such as the *Arcanum*, the game Gee focuses on at several points in his book. Instead of feeling responsible for a character, as Gee does while playing *Arcanum*, Chris feels responsible for his own flying and will "redo" it until he flies flawlessly.

Chris's identity-shaping experiences in *SimCity* were both like and unlike those he had with *MFS*. On the one hand, for instance, the objectives of the two games are different. In *SimCity*, for instance, gamers hope to build a city that thrives. In the virtual world of *SimCity*, Chris assumed the identity of mayor, an individual responsible for making several fundamental decisions: which type of power plant will generate the most power and which is the cleanest (coal, gas, oil, nuclear, microwave, wind, solar, or fusion). Chris, as the mayor in this virtual environment, had to lay power lines such that did not interfere with residential areas and schools, make sure that taxes were maintained at a comfortable percentage, and that people had opportunities to both work and play. Within this virtual environment—just as in the real world—high crime rates, towering infernos, alien invasions, dirty water, and smog can get out of control, and the occasional riot can occur. On the other hand, however, Chris's experiences as a capable and responsible mayor in *SimCity* were similar to those he had as a skilled pilot in *MFS*. For instance, while Chris could successfully address many of the social problems he encountered (and caused) as a virtual mayor, Chris, the real-world student and son, lived outside of Dallas—a huge city with many problems and social issues that were far beyond his scope. Dallas is an epicenter of wealth and power in the Southwest. A large city, in an even larger state that contains many miles of the U.S. border with Mexico, Dallas is flavored not only by historical relations with Mexico, but also by its own particularly complex blend of contemporary politics, social issues, and the ranching and cattle industries. In this real-world context, some citizens of Dallas are extremely wealthy and some are extremely poor as indicated earlier; Chris's actions as a virtual mayor, of course, had no impact on this situation. Informed by his knowledge of the city of Dallas, however, Chris constantly started his virtual cities over again, hoping each time for a better, more workable city. As in *MFS*, there was no definite end goal to Chris's experiences in *SimCity*. Informed by his successes and failures as a virtual mayor, Chris developed a projective identity characterized by an awareness of the role in these situations, a sense of personal responsibility and civic involvement, and an understanding of his own responsive capabilities. All of these characteristics were to influence his later political actions in the real world.

Gee's concept of "repair" work, or "a more intense version of good teaching, including enticing the learner to try, encouraging the learner to put in lots of effort, and making sure the student achieves meaningful success" (p. 62), we believe, can shed some light on how Chris's virtual identities and activities productively shaped his real-world identities and literacy practices, how his experiences as a gamer affected his experiences as a pilot, a politician, and a literate citizen. Before Chris played computer games, before he became a pilot and political figure, he struggled a great deal with traditional literacy practices in formal educational settings. To a great extent—at least as far as Chris and his mother believe—his difficulties stemmed from a learning difference, which, in turn, resulted in a discernible lack of confidence and a lack of strategies when he was confronted with formal literacy tasks in school. In gaming environments, however, Chris developed virtual identities that provided him with strategies and traits that he found useful in the real world. As he notes:

> Well, I think it's interesting that the two games I played the most have turned out to be major parts of my life . . . I think the flight simulator experience helped to put aviation within a realm of possibility, within my reach. I would say that I might not be a pilot now if it wasn't for the flight simulator.

Examining Practice: Gaming and Composition

We began this paper with a call for instructors to help students develop a set of personal and academic survival strategies, a set of literacy practices that they can take with them when they leave the composition classroom. Chris's case suggests one valuable tool that educators may be able to exploit in helping some students accomplish this goal. In Chris's case, his virtual gaming identity and experiences productively influenced his real identity and literacy practices. We do not mean to imply that gaming will work consistently for all teachers or all students, or even that it will work consistently for *some* students and *some* teachers. Instead, we note that in Chris's case, gaming provided another, more productive, approach to learning and the complex instruction problems faced by LD students.

So, how might composition teachers explore the benefits of games as environments for practicing literacy and developing the strategies needed for literate activities? Teachers and students could, for instance, enter into classroom-inquiry projects centered around gaming as a social practice and as a literacy environment. Taking this kind of approach, we could incorporate video games as objects of cultural and literacy study in our classrooms—and we could ask students to tell us what they learn from their gaming experiences. We could also ask students to help us explore the influences of their virtual identities on their real-world literacy actions, and help us learn to encourage values that are likely to improve composition skills. In a simple example, for instance, we might learn that games promoting self-confidence and collaborative interactions with others—those that may make receiving criticism more tolerable—may prove to be a better choice than games endorsing self-centeredness, which may have an adverse affect on a student's willingness to adapt her composition to a particular audience.

In classrooms where incorporating video games is not possible or preferable, designing a pedagogy informed by the principles of gaming may still be feasible. Gee (2003) points out that what makes video games successful is their ability to allow players to simultaneously practice increasingly difficult skills at their own pace; inhabit enjoyable, engaging environments for learning that are both richly challenging and low-risk; and assess their own skill levels as frequently as they desire. In writing classrooms (pp. 113–123), this means designing activities that perform these three functions, and sponsoring a classroom environment that is both instructive and pleasurable.

Such pedagogical approaches, it is possible, may benefit students. The virtual identities students assume in games, for instance, may well allow LD learners to step out from behind the "LD" label and may help these students experience new kinds of confidence and motivation, thus making course materials more accessible to them. Non-LD learners might also benefit from such pedagogical approaches. Being a member of a gaming team, or a member of a team studying gaming as a cultural artifact, may well help some students, both LD and non-LD, learn to tolerate and use criticism in more productive ways. For both students and teachers, pedagogies focused on gaming or built around gaming principles may also help restore some of the pleasure of creativity—the joys of composing in, and about, environments that are both appealing and important in the lives of young people like Chris.

References

Bartoli, Jill, & Botel, Morton. (1988). *Reading/learning disability: An ecological approach.* New York: Teacher's College Press.

Brueggemann, Brenda, Cheu, Johnson, Dunn, Patricia, & Heifferon, Barbara. (2001). Becoming visible: Lessons in disability. *College Composition and Communication, 52,* 368–398.

Center for Public Policy Priorities. (2000). Texas poverty: An overview. (n.d.). Retrieved September 27, 2004, from http://www.cppp.org/products/policypages/91-110/91-110pdf/pp107.pdf

Cope, Bill, & Kalantzis, Mary. (2000). *Multiliteracies: Literacy learning and the design of social futures.* London: Routledge.

Delpit, Lisa. (2001). The politics of teaching literate discourse. In Ellen Cushman, Eugene Kintgen, Barry Kroll, & Mike Rose (Eds.), *Literacy: A critical sourcebook* (pp. 545–554). Boston, MA: Bedford.

Dunn, Patricia A. (1995). *Learning re-abled: The learning disability controversy and composition studies.* Portsmouth, NH: Boynton/Cook.

Garcia, Jesus-Nicasio, & de Caso, Ana Maria. (2002). The effects of motivational intervention for improving the writing of children with learning disabilities. *Learning Disability Quarterly, 27*(3), 141–159.

Gee, James P. (2003). *What video games have to teach us about learning and literacy.* New York: Palgrave Macmillan.

Hallahan, Daniel P., & Mock, Devery R. (2003). A brief history of the field of learning disabilities. In H. Lee Swanson; Karen Harris, & Steve Graham (Eds.), *Handbook of learning disabilities* (pp. 16–29). New York: Guilford Press.

Linnenbrink, Elizabeth A., & Pintrich, Paul R. (2002). Motivation as an enabler for academic success. *School Psychology Review, 31*(3), 313–328.

Peck, Wayne C., Flower, Linda, & Higgins, Lorraine. (2001). Community literacy. In Ellen Cushman, Eugene Kintgen, Barry Kroll, & Mike Rose (Eds.), *Literacy: A critical sourcebook* (pp. 572–587). Boston, MA: Bedford.

Selfe, Cynthia. (1999). *Technology and literacy in the twenty-first century: The importance of paying attention.* Carbondale: Southern Illinois University Press.

Texas Data Center. (2000). Table 24: Number and percent of households by income category for the state of Texas and counties in Texas, 1999. (n.d.). Retrieved September 27, 2004, from http://txsdc.tamu.edu/data/census/2000/dp2_4/county/tab-016.txt

Wanderman, Richard. (1990). In Tips on writing for people with learning disabilities. (n.d.). Retrieved December 21, 2004, from http://www.ldresources.com/articles/writing_tips. html

White, Linda F. (2002). Learning disability, pedagogies, and public discourse. *College Composition and Communication, 53*(4), 705–735.

11

Racing toward Representation: An Understanding of Racial Representation in Video Games

Samantha Blackmon with Daniel J. Terrell

The meanings of signs (words, actions, objects, artifacts, symbols, texts, etc.) are situated in embodied experience. Meanings are not general or decontextualized. Whatever generality meanings come to have is discovered bottom up via embodied experiences.

(James Paul Gee, *What Video Games Have to Teach Us About Learning and Literacy*)

You see those images so much. I don't even know, you see 'em so much. I don't like 'em, but they show black people like that, like with the guns and . . . I guess like I said before it's just what the . . . I don't even know how they came up . . . I guess it's just like I think they get all the information from like music video and stuff like they see on there and what they hear in music and stuff like that. That's what I think.

(Daniel Terrell)

I have been a gamer for approximately 20 years; for me gaming started when my mother brought home our first PC. I soon discovered that there was something called *King's Quest* on this machine. I started the program and was delighted to see that this was an honest-to-goodness computer game. Back then my little knight was neither black nor white . . . he just *was*. This was nothing new to me. For years I had been playing *Pong*, football, and baseball on video-game consoles and handheld machines. There were no little avatars that needed racing. The players on the screen were tiny dashes that moved when I told them to (most of the time) and entertained me for hours. When video games evolved to include avatars and allowed "real" color, I remember being excited by the fact that I could choose an African American boxer when I was beating up on my cousin's little Caucasian boxer. That was my first memory of race in video games. Ten years later when I turned back to video games with a vengeance in order to relieve some graduate school stress, I played mostly fantasy games done in Japanese anime style. I explained away the lack of racial diversity based on the games' origins. Then one day I branched out and decided to return to one of my favorite genres of old, the boxing game. We bought a Sega Dreamcast and the new and popular game *Ready to Rumble.* I noticed that on the cover of the game there is as an African American man with a large afro. Stereotypical, yes, but nothing too disturbing . . . yet. We popped in the disc and started to play the game. I pushed the buttons and my fighter (the African American boxer just like the old days) fought, but between the action I watched my fighter "pimp" around, talk "smack," and head roll all over the ring. This was not my little brown boxer from the good old days. This was something different, something disturbing. I wondered if I was just getting old and overreacting.

I called in the experts. I called my aunts' four preteen and teenaged sons to see what they thought about the game.[1] What disturbed me even more than the "Stepnfetchit" show going on in the game was the fact that the boys did not seem to notice it. I put the game away swearing to myself that I would one day write a paper about it, when time allowed. People had to know that this kind of thing existed and that I found it offensive! Now it seems that time allows, and the connection between video games and gamer identity has become a viable topic for discussion.

In his 2003 text, *What Video Games Have to Teach Us about Learning and Literacy,* James Paul Gee makes it clear that he does not focus on issues of violence and gender representation. I argue that Gee summarily dismisses racial representation —while he sees problems with racialized character creation, he as well claims that "wider choices will, I am sure, be available as time goes on" (Gee, p. 11). What experience has told me is that time has gone on and that rather than things improving they seem to be getting progressively worse. Since the invention of raster graphics in video games in the early 1980s, representations of race have relied heavily upon the use of stereotypes to remove all doubt of race from the gamers' minds. Scholars such as Nina Huntemann (2000), in her documentary *Game Over: Gender, Race & Violence in Video Games,* have argued that racial stereotypes are evoked in video games in order to show nonwhiteness and that games that do have African American characters usually have a white protagonist whose purpose is to beat things back into a state of "normalcy."

In this chapter I interrogate how race in Rockstar Games' 2002 blockbuster hit *Grand Theft Auto: Vice City (GTA:VC)* gets read by gamers who embody the experiences in the game. I am coauthoring this chapter with a 16-year-old special-needs student, Daniel Terrell ("Danny"), who has spent most of his life in an urban area with a large minority population. The purpose of my interview with Danny, is to ascertain whether or not Gee's learning principles can be extended to critical thought about the game environment itself and whether or not these principles can be applied to those who fall outside the spectrum of "normal" cognitive abilities and practices (Gee, 2003). While Danny and I do talk specifically about race, we decided that it would be helpful (and interesting) to also talk about how he responds to gaming environments and what literacy abilities he brings to and learns from these environments. As a young man who knows the workings of life in the real and virtual inner cities firsthand, Danny has some interesting contributions to make to the discussion of the ways that race and class get read through games such as *GTA: VC.*

Danny was born in Detroit, Michigan, in 1988 and was a student at the Detroit Technology High School at the time of our first conversation.[2] Both of Daniel's parents have some college education, but place a high value on conventional literacy and little on digital literacy. Daniel feels that his parents see conventional literacy as being the key to success. According to him his mother places "a high [value], I would say, [on literacy] because that's what she always tells us to work on or do. We can't get nowhere without that. That's what she always says." He says that his parents read "books, novels, and newspapers. Mainly for my mom, I don't know what my dad reads. I think just newspapers."

Daniel's educational history is not the usual one. His first reaction to questions about where he lived and went to school was, "Whoa, you're talking about a lot of places here!" In his words:

> I lived in Detroit mainly, but I lived in Lafayette, Indiana . . . and that's like the only place out of Detroit I lived, but in Detroit I lived like all around the city like east side, west side, everywhere basically. I can't even begin to start. And in Pontiac, which is a neighboring city to Detroit.

Questions about his schooling history brought a similar response: "Oh God! Ok, I think I might be able to do a little better at this one." Of elementary school, he remembers the way that the schools look, but can not remember the names of any of them. He went to four different schools between sixth and eighth grades and has forgotten the name of one of the schools.

Danny remembers learning to read not at school, but by picking up comic books and then moving on to the Goosebumps series, things that were "interesting," "easy," and "felt good." Oddly, absent from the picture that he draws is the teacher. This went on throughout our conversations. The only time that he actually mentions a teacher is when he speaks of the teacher at his high school who sometimes holds *Halo* gaming matches for the students. When Danny talks about writing, a teacher does come into play. He learned to write because

> [t]eachers had us write essays, that's about it, or write paragraphs or whatever. I still remember when I had to use my finger to space between each word. I guess that's how I learned . . . I wrote a few stories with friends, and that's about it . . . mainly essays in school, that's where I had to learn to write the most, in school. Notes.

When Danny moves from talking about learning to read to learning to write, there is an absence of the mention of doing something that "felt good" and mostly the feeling of necessity.

Danny's first memories of computers consisted of the realization that there was a computer in his house when he was somewhere between the ages of seven and nine. This machine was used primarily by his mother to facilitate her real estate sales business. He also realizes that he did not actually learn to "use" a computer until he got to high school. Interestingly enough, using a computer for Danny, in this context, meant learning to use commercial software applications such as Flash rather than surfing the Web and playing video games. His mother used the computer to "talk to people on the Internet" and he used it to find video game hints and cheats and to download games on peer-to-peer networks. In his words:

> She was the one who would buy a computer book and learn how to do something that she wanted to do. We never talked about learning how to use computers. I guess you could say she had to think highly of it, she sent us to a computer school or a technology school, but I think that was just because it was a clean school you could say like all the rest of the schools were dirty . . . I still remember the first day we walked into the school . . . they had all the laptops up and like playing a video about the school, it was sweet, but that's about it.

Danny mentions *one* teacher who he said cared about educational computing. This was the teacher who gave him applications such as Flash and Maya and hardware to keep his computer working (but Danny never used them because he did not know how to install it).[3]

Danny's stories of computer use in the Detroit Public School system, sadly, seem to be pretty much the norm for school systems where computers are seen as being technology that you plug into the current curricula and play and where even if there is enough money available to purchase computers, there is not enough money (or motivation) to train teachers to use the computers in a pedagogically sound way. In Danny's middle school, computers were used to "teach" basic skills to special education students. There was no real monitoring of what students were doing with the computers. Students were given *edutainment* software that neither *educated* nor *entertained*. According to Danny:

> They wanted us to get familiar with the computers or something . . . Oh yeah, those whack games. What was the name of those? . . . DC something I still remember him saying that . . . It was like games that you were supposed to learn like what's two times two then like to make your guy jump or something . . . It was those kind of games. That's when I first started playing them . . . The game taught you . . . tedious stuff . . . I think I was in the seventh grade. I really didn't get any help, but I knew how to like use the mouse . . . so he just said like "run a program" like "click on the desktop" . . . You could go on the Internet and look up stuff . . . If you do what they say you don't have no access, you just have to run a program . . . Some stupid kind of tooty games . . . I can't even remember the name of them, they were really dumb. That's why you got bored with them after ten minutes . . . We got used to being next to [a computer] . . . If it was more exciting it could teach you a lot, but no it doesn't teach you anything.

Of these classes in general Danny tells us that "I was actually having fun [doing other things] but I was supposed to be learning."

This lack of pedagogical continuity seems to have continued in Danny's technology-rich classes in high school. In Danny's words, most of his class time is spent on "the Internet looking up stuff or doing stuff for other classes" because in his words "the teacher just stopped walking around, I guess he got bored with it too . . . it was that same thing every day." The typical day was spent "playing little dumb games like Yahoo checkers and stuff like that." There were no books about computers, applications, or video games available to him at school. He recalls the teacher teaching from the books but never having access to any of those books himself. He supposes that this was because teachers thought that the books were too difficult for the students. It was these things that Danny had to figure out for himself. He learned to navigate software applications and games and to figure out gaming grammar (a set of gaming rules that seemed present in most, if not all, games). For Danny, learning technology has always been about teaching himself based on the information he had readily available to him: his own experience as a special-needs, inner-city, African American boy.

In *What Video Games Have to Teach Us*, Gee (2003) lays out 36 learning principles that he believes are embedded in good video games (p. 7). These principles range in concentration from semiotics to critical thinking to intertextuality and beyond. The four principles that will be my primary focus in this chapter are the *identity, self-knowledge, situated meaning,* and *cultural models about the world* principles. These four principles focus specifically on the role that identity and identity-creation plays in and out of the game for the gamer, how the meanings of signs get situated in embodied experience, and how gamers come to think about world cultural models through the game (Gee, 2003). Looking at how these learning principles apply to Daniel may help us to determine whether or not and to what degree his experiences with and reactions to games in general and *GTA: VC* in particular can be applied to the more traditional learners that Gee specifically targets.

When I initially approached Danny about talking with me about video games and race in a professional context, he told me that he would be glad to talk to me about video games, but that he was not sure that he had too much to say about race in games because it was something that he had not thought much about. Because I had always seen Danny as a an insightful young man, I found this surprising and was more determined than ever to go forward with this project. After speaking with him for several hours, he and I both discovered that he had a lot to say about race in video games. The things that he said were poignant and shockingly apparent to both of us. We found ourselves in the midst of a simultaneous epiphany.

Gee (2003) defines the identity principle in terms of

> [l]earning [which] involves taking on and playing with identities in such a way that the learner has real choices (in developing the virtual identity) and ample opportunity to meditate on the relationship between new identities and old ones. There is a tripartite play of identities as learners relate, and reflect on, their multiple real-world identities, a virtual identity, and a projective identity. (p. 67)

He then discusses the principle's relation to gaming in terms of games that create the identity of the character based upon the players' actions. I argue, however, that for some gamers this identity development happens outside the game as well as or instead of, inside the game environment. Danny tells us that free will within *GTA:VC* allows a player the opportunity to be a good guy, or a bad guy, and for him this is something of a persona that he takes on as a player rather than/in addition to having it forced upon him by the game. Of *GTA:VC* Danny says:

> [W]ith Grand Theft Auto ... it's like a regular place, if you kill somebody in front of the police you're gonna go to jail ... if they catch you ... I just think of it as another city ... I just remember (the first time he played the game) it being better than what real life is, that's what I remember. You can do anything. It was real life, but it wasn't. I don't know how I can explain that, but it was like you can do anything you could do anything that you wanted to do, cuz it was so new the graphics looked better to me than they look to me now. So it looked like real life, so you can do anything you wanna do in real life. That's how it felt.

This notion is supported by Huntemann (2000), who argues that "you don't just interact with the game physically ... but you are asked to interact with the game psychologically and emotionally as well. You're not just watching the characters on the screen, you're becoming these characters." Danny's views on the objectives of game developers seem to support Huntemann's claims. Danny tells us that:

> I think their intentions were to just, um, suck you into it and make you feel like you're in a ... city. I think that was a main goal. To make you feel like you're in a city you're not playing a game. You're actually in a city, you're actually doing the things and that's how you felt when you first play it, you felt like you're inside the city and you can just do anything, you feel like, almost like you got powers, basically.

I argue that in addition to the player becoming the character, to some extent these characters become the player. As a gamer who is put into dicey situations, a player tends to make decisions that are very much affected by who the player is as a person as well as how the player is feeling emotionally and psychologically at that moment.

Gee's self-knowledge principle argues that

> The virtual world is constructed in such a way that learners learn not only about the domain but about themselves and their current and potential capacities. (p. 67)

It is this construction of the game environment that also contributes to players discovering important things about themselves and, in the case of individuals who are differently abled, discovering things about themselves that may seem to be deficiencies in the real world but can be understood as strengths in the virtual world. When discussing movement in unfamiliar game environs, Danny, who has an attention deficit disorder that sometimes prevents him from remembering directions and the order of things, finds that the way he has learned to deal with situations in the real world, such as finding his way home from a new place, is advantageous in the gaming world. Danny tells me that for him, studying or reading a game comes naturally, that it is "straight instinct," and links it to walking around an unfamiliar place but still being able to find one's way back to home base. For gamers such as Danny, the games facilitate the instinct:

> After you play them for so long it's natural . . . I don't even know if I can break it down anymore . . . Oh man. Straight instinct. That's how people, instinct. You just gotta, seem like . . . I was thinking about it yesterday when I was walking, it's like you know how like when you walk around for a long time like in a place that you don't know but you still know how to get back to like home? You still know how to get back home. It's kinda like that like you're doing all this stuff, but you still know what's going on over here while it's happening, it's like, it's like truly hard to explain. It's like you know it, but again you don't know. It's like instinct, that's all I can say. It's instinct.

For Danny the game (and the game developers) targets innate abilities in order to draw him further into the game itself.

Another interesting thing that Danny and I noticed while thinking and talking about *GTA:VC* was that his experience with the game not only made him aware his own capabilities, but also made him pay special attention to the notion of ethics. During our discussion Danny makes note of the fact that while the game does allow free will and mayhem, there are repercussions for negative behavior and positive reinforcement for good behavior. Danny tells me that while beating a hooker on the street may be entertaining, a player will be arrested if caught by the police. On governmental reactions to violent video games, he says:

> I know like the government was saying like the president said that they don't like the game or something like that, they don't want it to . . . they didn't want it to come out cuz it was too violent. It seem like it would teach people the difference between right and wrong if they had no police like you can even be a police officer and chase bad people like if you see a police officer chasing somebody down the street if you went up to the guy and hit him they'd be like, um civilian practices or something something'll pop on the screen and you get money for helping the police or you can go and jump in a police car and cut the sirens on and it'll be like a vigilante, you can chase somebody and catch him . . . I guess it'll teach the difference between right and wrong instead of making you do bad stuff . . . That's if you look at it that way. If you look at it the other way you can get a street sweeper and jump on somebody's car and just go down the street killing everybody or get in a tank and just run over everybody. It's the way you look at it.

Danny also makes note of the fact that it is a fairly common practice for him and his friends to stand at the bus stop and talk about how cool it would be if life were like *GTA: VC* and that they could carjack someone and get to school without having to wait for the bus, but it ends just there . . . with the talk. The interesting thing, as scholars such as Michael Morgan argue, is that there is no "switch" between fiction and reality and that over time things become blurred and the world of the game becomes another "stored experience" (qtd. in Huntemann, 2000). This lack of a switch manifests itself in that Danny finds himself applying the rules of the game to real life and vice versa. I don't think that the game is encouraging carjacking among this group of kids, but rather that it has made them aware of the fact that committing a crime does carry penalties (and critical-thinking skills help them realize that painting that stolen car won't necessarily help them elude police). This behavior corresponds to Gee's *"psychosocial* moratorium" principle, which states that "[l]earners can take risks in a space where real world consequences are lowered" (p. 67). This does seem to be the case with Danny and his friends, who freely carjack people to get around Vice City, but only ponder the possibilities in the real city.

It is this process of making meaning of the signs in the game based upon lived experience that Gee focuses on with the situated meaning principle. As noted in the epigraph, Gee defines this principle as follows:

> [T]he meanings of signs (words, actions, objects, artifacts, symbols, texts, etc.) are situated in embodied experience. Meanings are not general or decontextualized. Whatever generality meanings come to have is discovered bottom up via embodied experiences. (p. 209)

This principle relates to both Danny's discussion of ethics and interpreting right and wrong and to his discussion of racial representation in *GTA: VC*. While my experience with the game left me fuming not only about the depiction of African Americans, women, and Hispanics, but also about the portrayal of the Jewish attorney as an effeminate, cowardly poseur with the stereotypical intonation of the "New York Jew," this perception fell under Danny's radar most likely because of his lack of interaction with people of Jewish descent. What did stand out for him, however, was the portrayal of African Americans, Hispanics, and women, groups with which he has had significant interaction because of the demographic makeup of the areas in which he has lived.

Danny had very specific ideas about racial and gender representation in video games and why minorities are represented in the way that they are. This seems to come from lived experience. When asked about the African American characters in *GTA: VC*, Danny tells me that there is an African American character, Lance, in the game that would have been his choice of protagonist. He says that he finds Lance interesting because he wears "black clothes" and listens to "black music." When asked to explain what black clothes and black music are in this game Danny replied that "black clothes is all the flashy stuff he wears the white suit he drives the Corvette, you know stuff like that." He also says that he believes that Lance's house is probably messy because that's "just the way it is . . . cuz he spends his money on clothes and the car . . . Stereotype." When talking about the soon-to-be-released *Grand Theft Auto: San Andreas (GTA: SA)*, the next chapter in the GTA video games series that focuses on African American gangs in the early 1990s,[4] Danny says that he sees those images so much and that he does not like them. The Rockstar Games web site describes the plot of *GTA: SA* in this way:

> Five years ago Carl Johnson escaped from the pressures of life in Los Santos, San Andreas . . . a city tearing itself apart with gang trouble, drugs and corruption. Where filmstars and millionaires do their best to avoid the dealers and gangbangers.

Now, it's the early 90s. Carl's got to go home. His mother has been murdered, his family has fallen apart and his childhood friends are all heading towards disaster.

On his return to the neighborhood, a couple of corrupt cops frame him for homicide. CJ is forced on a journey that takes him across the entire state of San Andreas, to save his family and to take control of the streets. (http://www. rockstargames.com/sanandreas)

Of these images Danny says:

> You see those images so much. I don't even know, you see 'em so much. I don't like 'em, but they show black people like that, like with the guns and . . . I guess like I said before it's just what the . . . I don't even know how they came up . . . I guess it's just like I think they get all the information from like music video and stuff like they see on there and what they hear in music and stuff like that. That's what I think . . . What if we had a white person up there having sex with his mom or something? You know, how is that like? It's just the same to me. It's like one of them country people saying there go my daddy, my uncle, my cousin, one person. It's like, I don't know . . . It's so much of it I don't even know what to do now . . . At first when I was little I used to see movies like *Roots* or just see any of the other black movies where they be hanging black people or doing stuff like that it get you mad, but now we got movies coming out like *Undercover Brother* that like make you feel better about it like "so what?" . . . Because they glorify and they talk about the other (white) people like "Look at you, you eating mayonnaise." Like how are you better and stuff like that. Only thing I don't like is how they act about the white girls, ain't no good thing about no white girls . . . That's the only thing that made me mad about that.

He also says that this is a depiction of "what every white man thinks about every black man who wasn't raised in a white neighborhood. That's just what the game is." He finds the African American stereotypes that are prevalent elsewhere are simply being perpetuated in video games, and I tend to agree with him. Video games are not the problem here; it is the way that the games are being written, drawn, and marketed that is the problem. Perhaps it is that research and development for video games begins and ends with BET and MTV. Perhaps this is the reason we get best-selling basketball games that require you not only to exhibit your prowess on the court but also to collect enough "bling" off court in order to win the game. This speaks to what Danny says about the flashiness of the African American characters in *GTA: VC*. These are issues that cannot be ignored. As Steven Poole (2000), author of *Trigger Happy: Videogames and the Entertainment Revolution*, argues:

> Video games are not going to go away. You can't hide under the stairs. Resistance is futile. Any industry with such a vast amount of money sloshing around in it is by that token alone worthy of investigation. (p. 11)

Not only will the industry not simply dry up and go away, but also some video games can teach and reinforce many positive things for gamers, as Gee suggests. I argue, however, that we may need to take these games more seriously. Many will argue, "But, they're just kids playing!" This may or may not be the case. Poole points out that Plato defined play as:

> That which has neither utility nor truth nor likeness, nor yet in its effects, is harmful, can best be judged by the criterion of the charm that is in it, and by the pleasure it affords. Such pleasure, entailing as it does no appreciable good or ill, is play. (pp. 13–14)

For Plato, a game is just a game as long as it's not "harmful" and has no utility or likeness. This is something that is definitely not true of video games. Gee points to the utilitarian aspect of gaming with his learning principles, and I argue that some games can also be racist and harmful. Huntemann (2000) points out that video games depend on realism in order to improve the interactivity of games and that this realism is the "holy grail" of the video game industry. Eugene F. Provenzo, Jr., of the University of Miami adds that video games reflect what is going on in culture and society and that the way gender, race, and ethnicity are portrayed in video games is very telling (qtd. in Huntemann). This is not to say that depending on music videos and rap music for accurate portrayals of gender, race, and ethnicity is the way to go, but rather that the representations that populate video games are telling of the ways that game developers see women and minorities. Video games can be the game developers' way of (intentionally or unintentionally) perpetuating the stereotypes that they hold on to. All video games come complete with a set of embedded biases and assumptions. In *Joystick Nation: How Videogames Ate Our Quarters, Won Our Hearts, and Rewired Our Minds*, J. C. Herz (1997) points out that

> *SimCity* favors public transportation because Will Wright is a proponent of public transportation . . . And of course, there are always factors that are significantly absent. You can build something that looks like Detroit without building in the racial tension. And so, really, it boils down to a kind of social contract . . . You have accepted the designer's values and assumptions, at *least* for the duration of the game (emphasis mine). And that's fine, as long as you realize what you're doing. But often, especially if the sim is lavishly produced, people don't twig.[5] That's what makes sim so effective at convincing people that certain types of political behavior are appropriate. Once you are in the game, you've agreed to let someone else define the parameters. And so the question is who defines the parameters. Who has created this environment, and what do they want you to believe? . . . [I]f you're going to play these games—it's a good idea to know who's making the rules. (p. 223)

If it is indeed true that gamers accept designers' values, assumptions, and biases while playing a game and that games can influence what gamers believe in the real world, then it is imperative that we know who is making the rules and that we interrogate what these (re)constructed rules say about our society and how these rules may be helping or harming gamers (especially young ones) while entertaining them.

It has been argued for years that video games, music, movies, and other forms of media affect the way children see the world and that authors should be held responsible for what children learn from these things. Rather than attempting to censor and ban media that a random committee thinks are inappropriate for children (the technological equivalent to book burning), perhaps the answer is to better monitor what children see, hear, and play not only on the basis of rating systems but also as parents and guardians. Young gamers will find a way to see, hear, and play what they want, especially if it is splashed across every television screen, magazine cover, and billboard. For this reason it is necessary for scholars across disciplines to interrogate what and how video games are teaching children and to make others aware and a part of their studies. This is the point at which we can begin to address a larger social issue, the perception and representation of those deemed Other. According to Gee, good video games can teach gamers about cultural models of the world. Of these good games, Gee writes:

> Learning is set up in such a way that learners come to think consciously and reflectively about some of their cultural models regarding the world, without denigration of their identities, abilities, or social afflictions, and juxtapose them to new models that may conflict with or otherwise relate to them in various ways. (p. 211)

For him, this falls under the cultural models about the world principle. Despite the inherent biases in video games, we can use them as tools for critical thinking. Many gamers are like Danny, who claimed that he had never thought about racial representation in video games, but who, upon discussing it, had lots of very insightful things to say and at times found that he was angry at what he had seen and experienced in video games. These sorts of discussions should become a part of classroom discourse.

Discussions in this chapter have only begun to touch upon Gee's learning principles, Danny's gaming experiences, and the issue of racial representation in video games. What I have discovered is that Gee's principles, at least those examined specifically in this chapter, do seem to apply to Danny as a student and gamer who falls outside the definition of "traditional learner" despite his perceived need to have specific instruction in games and his need to learn through repetition in a hands-on environment. Gee's concept of multiple routes of progress and differing learning styles are especially apt for describing Daniel as a gamer and as a learner of and within games.

What Daniel and I discovered together is that while Gee chooses to ignore issues of race in his text, the learning principles that he applies to more benign topics relate specifically to issues of race representation and gamer identity. What I have learned in this process is that the connection between gamer identity and the way the gamer sees himself or herself portrayed in the game has a very real emotional effect on the gamer. The burden of stereotypes and racial oppression that exists in the real world makes its way into the game world as well. When race and problematic racial representations enter the equation, the Platonic notion of "play" exits. As long as gamers grow angry at the representation and liken it to visual representations of lynching, further connecting it to overt racism and societal ills, there is nothing playful about it. This phenomenon must be studied so that there is the hope of one day striking a happy medium and of connecting "play" with video games more predictably.

What have we learned about video games, rhetoric, and literacy education that teach us in composition studies? If we agree that one of our goals/tasks/obligations as teachers of composition is to teach students to think and write critically, video games offer a good vehicle for them to explore the rhetorical elements that are at work in everyday things. They also have the chance to read what the "writers" are trying to say and to consider how others (and Others) respond to what is "said" in video games. Video games are a form of richly embedded rhetoric and, as is the case with most other texts, are never truly objective or interpreted by all of its readers as being so.

In a recent interview with the Onion A.V. Club, the game developer Will Wright, of Sims fame, talked about the fact that while game developers do not control the worlds that we experience "in game," they do determine how game players control it (Phipps, 2005). Working with video games in composition classrooms gives educators the opportunity to ask students to think about video games as texts that are rhetorical already and the students are free to write them (through game play) in any way that they please. This is something that Danny realizes when he talks about character creation in video games. We are limited in the skin tones, hair styles, and body shapes that we can choose for "ourselves" and the limited choices regarding what we can do and how we can do it continue throughout the games. Students can be asked to interrogate anything from why having sex with prostitutes in *GTA: VC* is part of the game to why only certain hair styles are available for certain skin tones in *The Sims 2* and what this says about the way that women and minorities are being rhetorically constructed and what it says about game developers and to game players.

In short, video games give us the opportunity to look at different kinds of texts and to work with the notion that things that seem to be the most benign (at least in the mind of the student) are rhetorically charged and that it is important to pay close attention to both what they are saying as rhetors and how they are saying it. This analysis also gives student readers/writers the opportunity to think critically about the texts that they are reading and simultaneously gives them material about which to write critically. These are the texts that many students regularly interact with. This is where they "live." Video games give us an idea of what those who are not of the worlds represented in video games think of these worlds, even those gamers such as Danny, who may experience in video games their first and only interaction with folks of these underrepresented groups. This is our teachable moment. This is the place at which we can meet our students to talk about race, rhetoric, and representation.

Notes

1. This was nothing out of the ordinary, as we had shared games, hints, and threats over video games for some time.
2. At the time of the writing of the article, Danny is not regularly attending school and is considering joining the Job Corps program, where he can learn a trade and complete high school at the same time.

3. One thing that seemed a constant in Danny's discussion about education was the fact that he never admitted to any of his teachers, parents, or fellow students that he did not know how to do something. It was an issue of pride for him; he would try to learn it himself and give up if he found it to be too difficult.

4. The advertisements for this game, which were released on October 26, 2004, comprised a collage of images that included an African American in a tank top sitting on the hood of a car holding a gun; a blond-haired woman who was light complexioned but of undetermined race, bending over and revealing lots of cleavage, wearing gold jewelry and sunglasses, and licking her lips in a provocative way; and the African American protagonist squatting in a standard prison pose, with a handgun dangling between his legs. The commercials airing about this game included a sound track with a heavily based version of "Welcome to the Jungle" and a supposedly Hispanic woman moaning heavily and uttering what seem to be endearments in "Spanish," while animated drive-bys occurred on the screen. The trailers and screenshots for the game can be found online at http://www.rockstargames.com/sanandreas.

5. Consider the earlier discussion of the necessity of realism in the video-gaming industry.

References

Gee, James Paul. (2003). What video games have to teach us about learning and literacy. New York: Palgrave Macmillan.

Herz, J. C. (1997). Joystick nation: How videogames ate our quarters, won our hearts, and rewired our minds. Boston: Little, Brown.

Huntemann, Nina B., & Media Education Foundation. (2000). Game over: Gender, race & violence in video games [Video]. Northhampton, MA: Media Education Foundation.

Phipps, Keith. (2005, February 2). Will Wright. The Onion. Retrieved February 6, 2006, from http://www.avclub.com/content/node/24900/1/1

Poole, Steven. (2000). Trigger happy: Videogames and the entertainment revolution. New York: Arcade Pub.

12

Portrait of a Gray Gamer: A Macro-Self Reading the Big Picture

John E. Branscum with Frank Quickert

Different people can read the world differently just as they can read different types of texts differently.

(James Paul Gee, 2003)

I like to think about issues and events in terms of the big picture.

(Frank Quickert, Gamer)

While considerable critical attention has been directed toward digital literacy in recent years, most of the research has focused on young people. There are few articles on elderly gamers and not one of these specifically addresses digital literacy. Partially, this void is due to the historically limited usage of the term, "literacy." Only recently has this usage begun to be replaced in professional conversations by the concept of multiple literacies[1] in order to foreground the fact that literacy can be talked about in ways other than the alphabetical. Another reason for the dearth of research on digital literacy and the elderly is the fact that, within our contemporary cultural ecology, a rhetoric of rehabilitation has predominated conversations about the elderly's use of computers. While the first article on the elderly and computing, "Computers and Technology: Aiding Tomorrow's Aged," appeared in 1973, actually a few years *before* the advent of personal computers, it was more interested in how the elderly could shore up existing cognitive skills than in how they acquire new literacies. The lion's share of elderly/gaming articles over the next two decades continued to focus solely on the concept of rehabilitation.[2] Then, in the 1990s, the baby boomers, entering their twilight years, began to champion a portrayal of the elderly as both physically and intellectually vibrant, as in effect active learners, not only capable of but eager to conquer new cognitive domains.

A 2003 article that expresses this shift in sentiment claims that counter to the much-vaunted technophobia of the elderly, "increasing numbers of over 60s are picking up joysticks to play video games" ("Pensioners Catch," p. 1). In and of itself, this claim is interesting since video games are generally portrayed as the sole province of adolescents and young adults. But even more significant for this chapter is the article's observation that there are crucial differences between the games routinely sought out by young gamers and those preferred by their older counterparts,[3] with the elderly tending to prefer strategic and historical titles, such as the *Civilization*[4] games, which "require lateral thinking and problem-solving," versus first-person shooters.

Reading "Pensioners Catch the Gaming Bug" piqued my curiosity. Was there in fact such a difference? If so, what was the reason for it? What kind of semiotic work were the elderly doing with these games? Did it relate to differences between their sense of self and the more-hesitant (some would say less-calcified) sense of self of the young? And finally, would the answers to these questions offer insights for our work as instructors of composition and rhetoric?

Of course, such questions are based on a number of assumptions. The first is the very idea that video games might have any relationship to learning at all. Interestingly, such a relationship is actually implied by the fact that computers were so early on in their history seen as having a rehabilitative function—that they, in other words, were seen as having the ability to reinforce cognitive skills which then could be transferred from the digital domain to the real world. However, it took a few more decades for this connection to be seriously explored. One of the more impressive recent efforts in this direction is James Paul Gee's *What Video Games Have to Teach Us about Learning and Literacy* (2003). Working from the insight that literacy and thinking are not solely mental but are, in fact, developed by and shaped through social practices, Gee explores the multimodality of video games and ultimately claims that various game genres belong to distinct "semiotic domains," each in effect constituting a different type of literacy as people learn to recognize and produce different semiotic configurations of sound, music, taxonomies, and movements. Essential to understanding the link between video games and learning is a reformulation of the definition of literacy from the individual manipulation of alphabetic elements to the socially located manipulation (and understanding) of semiotic elements in general.

The second assumption implied by the above set of questions is that literacy, whether digital or alphabetic, is related to identity. Key to understanding the connection here is the reformulation of the self from a static, internal entity to a construction that is the product of a variety of social transactions—in other words, a continually composed or narrated self. As Donald Polkingham (1988) explains:

> We achieve our personal identities and self-concept through the use of the narrative configuration, and make our existence into a whole by understanding it as an expression of a single unfolding and developing story. We are in the middle of our stories and cannot be sure how they will end; we are constantly having to revise the plot as new events are added to our lives. Self, then, is not a static thing or a substance, but a configuring of personal events into an historical unity which includes not only what one has been but also anticipations of what one will be. (p. 89)

Working from a similar theoretical position, Gee (2003) argues specifically that video-game environments give players the chance to try out multiple identities and encourage them to see differences between various individual and group interests. Pivotal to this claim is his concept of "projective identity," a hybrid of a player's real-world self and her "virtual identity" (the characters she chooses from the world of a game who act as her avatars). As Gee explains it, a player projects her values and desires on to her virtual character who, while shaped by the player in a virtual world and drawing upon her various fields of expertise, is also seen as her real-world "project in the making," as an extension of who she is, her agent in a digital world (p. 55). Thus video-gaming experiences exhibit what Anthony Giddens (1984) refers to as *the duality of structuration,* the dynamic wherein individuals simultaneously shape and are shaped by the social structures in which they live and act. Whom we envision ourselves to be affects the visions we wish to learn and construct and, indeed, are even capable of perceiving and interpreting.

With these issues in mind, I will be using the case study of Frank Quickert, a 65-year-old semiretired financial analyst from the midsized southeastern city of Louisville, Kentucky, as a means of exploring the link between gaming preferences as they relate to identity and the mastery of semiotic domains. I shall also be discussing the possible implications of my findings for the twenty-first-century composition classroom.

Frank's interview shows that he is drawn to the historical and strategic gaming genres because, within them, he can use language—and other semiotic systems—to read and explore macrolevel historical, cultural, and economic texts and learn macrolevel strategies for interacting with these texts. Relatedly, Frank is also attracted to the fact that he can author his identity in terms that are familiar, attractive, and useful to him. This identity work relates to Gee's (2003) notion of projective identity (in that it requires Frank to use various kinds of expertise) and shows that in taking part in (and shaping) stories in digital spaces, Frank explores/practices his own sense of productive *agency* vis-à-vis the cultures/societies with which he interacts. Furthermore, through the enactment of these stories, Frank authors his identity as a social agent able to affect positive changes in his environment.

Learning to See the "Big Picture"

In contrast to the gamers Gee (2003) examines, primarily young people intensely involved in social networks centered around their gaming, Frank is a relatively isolated gamer. He does not read gaming magazines, visit online gaming sites, or talk about his game playing with anyone other than his sister, Diane, who is not herself a gamer. Diane, also in her 60s, in fact, confesses to being amused by Frank's pastime. "Frankie loves his games," she says, then shakes her head and half chuckles. "He'll stay up half the night with those things. It's the same way he was with books."

While Diane's comment is brief, it underscores something important via the connection she draws between Frank's reading habits and his gaming. That is, it suggests that while we may talk about separate literacies or semiotic domains, this does not mean our multiple domains bear no connection to one another. Rather, they may overlap such that they comprise significant existential orientations toward the world. Indeed, a cursory examination of Frank's cultural ecology, especially his early literacy experiences in other domains, seems to predict his willingness to acquire digital literacy later in life and also what forms this digital literacy will take (the video game genres he will be attracted to and that he will use to interpret these experiences).

Frank's Home-centered Education

When asked about the education in his home, Frank reports that while both his parents, a working-class couple of German-Dutch descent, valued education, he was especially influenced by his mother's habits. Frank reports:

> My father wasn't much of a reader outside of the newspaper . . . and the Bible. . . . My mother though loved to read. Momma Quickert read everything: novels, magazines, nonfiction.

Influenced by his mother, and following his own inner promptings, Frank saw mastery of alphabetic literacy as essential to his construction of self. "I saw myself as *the reader* in the family. Of course, my sister read too, everyone did, but me . . . I ate books up. I was that little twerp people call *the brain*." Frank's reading habits were driven not so much by escapism as they were by a need to create a meaningful narrative (or group of narratives) about the world that would later function as a sort of map for what he did in life. Franks explains that for him, "books held clues to the world, a way of understanding it. And I wanted to understand how things worked, what made them work."

Because of the type of valuation Frank put on reading, as an activity that helped him in his enterprise of world construction, his interest in this semiotic domain soon led him to explore others—especially those that touched upon his increasingly preferred method of world construction, what he dubs a "big picture" approach to both the world and the self. Asked what he means by the "big picture," Frank explains, "Seeing the world in terms of the big picture means you're on the lookout for how events are connected, for the larger pattern. . . . It means you look for keys to the present and the future in the past, that you understand the effect that political, legal, and economic events have on one another and how these are related to past relationships."

What Frank means by a "big picture" approach is more clearly seen when he discusses his early training in economic analysis. As Frank describes it:

> My mother studied the market. She's the one who got me interested in the market as a matter of fact. Every weekend, she would pour over *Barron's*[5] and *Value Line*[6] and decide what stocks to invest in. She invented a stock-picking system which I use to this day—the Momma Quickert system.

Frank was immediately fascinated by his mother's interest in the market. "I would sit by her and do crossword puzzles or draw and ask her questions as she went through the *Value Line*," recalls Frank. These question-and-answer sessions proved pivotal in how he later understood the multiple senses of the act of reading. To this day, he puts great emphasis on what can be "read" through an understanding of economic data. Frank reports:

> To me, numbers tell a story. . . . Take the Department of Labor's recent employment figures. They're fudging them. The same is true with the way they figure inflation. You wouldn't know this unless you knew how they calculate their findings. If you want to understand what's really going on in the world, you have to understand the numbers. If you pay attention to the data, which really must reflect relationships in the world, you can ignore the spin and cut through the bullshit.

Obviously, a "big picture" way of reading the world, as Frank understands it, entails the adoption of a meta or top-down view of social and economic structures. In other words, mastery of this domain involves an ability to adjust one's perceptual lens to "see" individual events and data as part of larger-scale phenomena, whether those phenomena are viewed as cycles, movements, or trends. In terms of identity work, it also necessitates an awareness of oneself not simply as an individual, but as part of a macro-self, that is, as part of a social body such as "the Democrats," "the Americans," or "the Corlione family." Such big-picture thinking might, in fact, be said to constitute a distinct group of semiotic domains. One might even talk about levels of abstraction as analogous to the different points of view one may adopt when constructing a narrative. Self is, to an extent, a matter of perspective, and to speak from the stance of this self versus that self is to see the world differently, in the same way that the visual appearance of topography changes depending on whether one is in the cockpit of an airplane or standing on the ground. Narratology, in fact, offers us a term for this—*focalization*.

While sometimes equated with point of view, focalization has a somewhat different meaning. Rhetorically, the framing of cause and effect—indeed, what constitutes a cause and what constitutes an effect—and what determines major versus minor characters are matters that are heavily dependent on the presented origin and termination points of a given narrative. A course of action within one time frame, such as the elimination of capital gains taxes, may be narrated in a much more positive manner in another time frame. As Mieke Bal (1985) puts it, "Whenever events are presented, they are always presented from within a certain 'vision.' A point of view is chosen, a certain way of seeing things, a certain angle, whether 'real' historical facts are concerned or fictitious events" (p. 142). Bal prefers the term focalization to such words as "perception" or "point of view" for this dynamic because it looks technical. She writes: "As any 'vision' presented can have a strong manipulative effect, and is, consequently, very difficult to extract from the emotions, not only those attributed to the focalizer and the character but also from those of the reader, a technical term will help us keep our attention on the technical side of such a means of manipulation" (p. 144).

With the concept of focalization in mind, we see how Frank's "big picture" approach actually constitutes a literacy act, for it colors the data he perceives and favors the understanding and generation of some types of arguments over others.

It also casts him as a particular type of agent engaged with and obligated to master certain types of acts. His "big picture" approach to the world in fact affected his conception of the possible roles he could play in his lifetime and indeed those he was *obligated* to play as a political subject. In turn, such conceptions affected how Frank chose to move through the world, thus explicitly linking the composition of the self and the range of possibilities that one is able to envision oneself occupying. One of the earliest examples of this from his life is his startlingly precocious interest in politics. As Frank remembers it:

> When I first got interested in politics, I was oh, about nine or so. Happy Chandler was governor then and I just didn't like the man. One week, we went downtown to see him speak and after he finished, and they were taking questions, I raised my hand and told him point-blank that he was a bad man. I didn't like where he stood on race.

In his teens, Frank went on to work on behalf of particular candidates in certain elections. Later, his early development of "big picture" literacy guided the subjects he found worthy of academic study. Frank articulates this connection well. "I wanted a career where I was actively involved with the big things: guiding the spiritual health of a diocese or improving our legal system. I suppose you could say I was on an ego trip but I don't see it that way. It wasn't about me . . . it was about doing my bit."

Frank's Formal Academic Pursuits

At first glance, Frank's education seems quite varied. He was educated in a series of Catholic schools until what would have been his sophomore year, when he entered St. Thomas's seminary to train as a priest. In the seminary, Frank's ability to think in terms of the macro-self was highly prized. From the ages of 13 to 23, he led an existence that centered on abstract, historical, and spiritual knowledge as opposed to concrete, temporal, and carnal knowledge. He was taught to look at church doctrine not as a matter of rules but as underlying principles that generate different instantiations of themselves in different times and places. He was also urged to see himself not as a fragmented individual but rather as a sort of archetype, a proxy for Christ's love for his people. One might say, making use of a popular religious phrase, that he was "in the world but not of it." Yet this is not entirely accurate, for it implies Frank was cut off from the world in some fundamental way. It is more true to say that he was taught to prize a particular way of viewing the world, one that operates at a level of abstraction higher than the individual person or event.

Eventually, when Frank decided that a priestly vocation was not the best way for him to serve God, he left the seminary to study philosophy and theology at Bellarmine College (a private Catholic college located in his hometown) and then law at the University of Louisville Law School. It was as a lawyer that Frank began his professional years.

Though they seem quite distinct at first glance, all of Frank's study areas are connected in that their concentration upon semiotic domains that center on a macro or "big picture" view of human affairs. Not surprisingly, these educational experiences later dictated the professional activities Frank involved himself in. In fact, a review of Frank's professional years reveals how our early experiences with particular semiotic domains shape how we see ourselves and affect our ability to envision certain life paths as possible.

Frank's Professional Years

In 1971, Nutting Associates released *Computer Space,* the first arcade video game. Frank, along with most of society, proved resistant to the game's charms, and it quietly disappeared from the cultural landscape. It was not as if Frank had ample time to play games at this point anyway. He had just spent several years working as a lawyer for Greenbaum and Associates and was now drumming up support for his run as Kentucky state representative. But by the time he became director of law for the city of Louisville in 1982, computing technology had caught his and most of America's attention.

In 1980, Namco released *Pac Man,* and Atari's famous games were rolling off the assembly line. Frank sensed a new world dawning. He felt that computers would usher in a new era, a not-uncommon claim when personal computers first hit the market. With this in mind, the director of law became what he calls "the technology guy" and updated the department so that it had its first computers, Commodores. Later, he was instrumental in the development of a new city department, "Data Processing."

However, despite his efforts to equip his department for the computer age, Frank relates he had no interest in computer gaming at this time because he was "too busy running a city." His apathy toward gaming would remain the case for the next 13 years.

In 1990, fearing an economic crisis in the United States, Frank left his position as director of law and set up shop as an investment advisor. The clamor of techno-utopianism during this period dwarfed that of the 1980s. In the field of composition studies, speculation was rife that a whole new kind of liberatory pedagogy was made possible by electronic spaces that might help even the playing ground in terms of gender, sexuality, and race. But the excitement in composition studies was just a subset of a larger cultural enthusiasm. More relevant to Frank's case, this was when Internet stocks took off in an unrivalled speculative frenzy. As an investment advisor, Frank noted the huge amount of capital pouring into this sector, and he understood that this money was being invested not because of present company earnings but because of the widespread assumption that the fundamental nature of society would change thanks to computing technology. In some respects, it did indeed seem like a "new world." There were such phenomena as online shopping, message boards, e-mail, and a whole slough of video games. Frank wanted to explore this new world more but the task seemed overwhelming . . . that is until, in 1995, Frank's life took a drastic turn.

Into the Myst and Going Tropico

In 1995, a collapsed colon and an impaired right lung caused Frank to dramatically cut his working hours and begin semiretirement. What was he to do with all this free time? Throughout his life, Frank had read voraciously, but now he was burned out on reading and, what is more, found it taxing, given his physical impairments. Searching for a new way to occupy his leisure hours, he decided to at last give video games a try, thanks to the market savvy of Circuit City, where he went to buy a new computer. Frank recalls:

> I was buying some new computers for my office at Circuit City. They had a video game sale and I thought why not try one of the fancy ones, to see if I was missing something.

Frank's awakened interest in gaming could not have been more serendipitously timed. In 1995, Microsoft released its user-friendly operating system, Windows 95. This year also marked two years since Cyan has released *Myst*, an adventure-puzzle game, and word has now gotten around that this was a game like no other.

The story behind *Myst* is simple. You have found a book with a description of an enchanted island. The next thing you know you have been magically transported to this island and are faced with the task of figuring out its past and its mystery. From this point on, *Myst* is essentially a free-form role-playing game (RPG) sans dice or weapons, where the object is to solve a series of puzzles. In this environment, the player's most important tool is his analytical prowess.

Frank, who avoids violent movies, had been turned off by the violent reputation of video games up to this point. He was also not interested in the individual character adventures of most RPGs. In his words, "The characters are not as important to me as a game with a big picture." Although *Myst*[7] employed a first-person perspective, unlike the ubiquitous shoot-em-ups, the game allowed Frank to employ the skills he valued most highly: strategy and big-picture thinking and which were essential aspects of his sense of self—what he was, what he could do, and what kind of story his life constituted. *Myst* depended on piecing together hints to construct the "Big Picture"—in Frank's words, "the mystery and history of an entire world." He recalls, "I was always fascinated by historical mysteries such as what happened to the library of Alexandria, or the discovery of Troy. I was one of those kids who wanted to discover the gold of Cortez. And it wasn't finding the gold at the rainbow that drew me to these sorts of fantasies either. What I liked was looking at the available historical evidence putting together the facts to solve the mysteries."

Frank's next "big picture" game, one he vastly preferred to *Myst* and that set him on a path devoted to god games,[8] was *Tropico*. *Tropico* requires long-term planning and a macro-sense of both self and society. The player acts as a newly installed leader of a banana republic. While, like first-person shooters, the gamer occupies the identity position of one particular player, the emphasis is not on your own physical survival but rather the survival and flowering of an entire civilization. The object of this game is to guide the island to social and economic prosperity, and

Tropico centers on ordering the economy, handling political snafus, setting wages and rents, and quelling civil unrest. It is not a game of immediate gratification like shoot-em-ups. Game years (and real-time weeks) may pass between the time you build a factory, acquire the necessary raw materials for production, and release a finished product on the market. All the time, short-term goals must serve longer-range planning.

Macro-Social Selves

Frank's affinity for such games as *Myst* and *Tropico* and the type of identity work they foster is what makes his gaming history especially relevant to those scholars and teachers interested in alternative literacies and the educational possibilities of computer gaming. It also shows how focalization is an essential consideration in rhetorical analysis. As Gee (2003) notes, "Any specific way of reading and thinking is, in fact, a way of being, a certain 'kind of person,' a way of taking on a certain sort of identity" (pp. 3-4). While Gee explores some of the possible identity positions of games and associated semiotic domains, Frank's case elucidates further possible identity positions and underscores the fact that apart from an individual having an identity such as "father," "engineer," and "writer," we also move through the world and make meaning as part of larger social gestalts such as "the church," depending on the type of lens we are using to read the world. This lens is both shaped by the way we choose to read and shapes the way we read. In the semiotic domains Frank has occupied in both his real and gaming lives, he has stressed a macro-social sense of self where he is both a player in and an avatar of larger social forces: as God's shepherd in his role as priest, as the people's voice in his role as state representative, as an incarnation of the law in his role as director of law, and as part of a larger, transhistorical, economic leviathan in his role as investment advisor. Graphically, Frank's games even represent this mode of seeing, for they frequently offer magnified views of cities and access to maps, charts, and databases that display information in various large-scale manners. I will now close this exploratory chapter by looking closely at two distinct identity positions that are visible in Frank's reported life and gaming experiences and touch upon their import for teachers of the "new" composition classroom.

The Leadership Self

Throughout his life, Frank has chosen to occupy leadership positions. His choice to do so is distinctly tied to his macro-world view and his valuing of the "big picture." One can speculate this might be true to varying degrees of other elderly gamers as well. By the time one enters one's golden years, one has often climbed various career ladders. While leadership is sometimes cast simply as dominance over others, it also, as teachers well know, urges us to think not so much of ourselves as of the collective, to widen our lens of self.

Games such as *Tropico* and *Civilization* mimic this manner of thinking. In such games, Frank acts as a leader who navigates macrocosmic social and economic terrains, using particular cognitive skills to manipulate economics and politics, quell public unrest, and balance the competing interests of different groups, often in the context of a time line that exceeds the average human life expectancy.

As discussed previously, perspective and identity are connected. Leadership affords a unique vantage point from which to view the world. A leader simultaneously feels responsible for others and is called upon to think of the practical problems of parceling out finite resources (financial, temporal, environmental, or human). In short, a leadership position forces one to look at the world in a "big picture" manner, beyond one's individual and immediate interests, and as such is a valuable form of literacy. One is not simply a finite and fragmented self but the proxy for a complex group of people and interests. Such an identity position is rarely available to most students owing either to their impoverished backgrounds or their dearth of years. But such an identity position and the habits of thought that result from occupying such a position would be extremely valuable not only to students interested in business or law but also to those involved in the humanities and the social sciences. While group-work initiatives in the classroom can also afford students the opportunity to explore this subjectivity, video games offer the possibility of allowing one to rhetorically foreground the particular points of view and cognitive models associated with a leadership perspective and how arguments depend as much on the focalization presented as their formal logics (indeed, one could argue that focalization is the presentation of a certain logic).

The Historical Self

Another type of macro-identity and hence macro-perspective, afforded by certain video games is a historical self, a self that embraces an extended time line from which to view human affairs. By this, I do not mean that one thinks of the present simply in terms of the past but rather that one sees contemporary events as either an extension of the past or a cycle of events similar to past cycles.

A historical approach to economic and social issues is qualitatively different from a short-term approach. Decisions regarding whether or not to go to war, or whether or not to adopt particular economic policies are strongly affected by the time horizon in which these phenomena and their consequences are viewed. Our present actions must be based on lessons from the past and predictions of future consequences. In Frank's life, he has occupied such an identity position when he has made long-term investment decisions, introduced legislation in the House of Representatives, or changed particular policies as director of law. God games offer a unique "literacy" experience in terms of historical selves. It is no surprise then that many of Frank's favored games are of the historical variety. In *Tropico*, one must contend with a time line that is 70 years long, and in *Civilization*, where one's goal is to build and defend a society from the ground up, the game time can span centuries.

Once again, this is a type of self rarely available to students. A sense of history is often something that simply accompanies age. But an appreciation for historical complexity, and the consequences of today's actions for tomorrow, can enrich our understanding of the present and the actions we take within the present. More to the point, when critically evaluating any number of essays or theories (especially political ones), one needs to address the often-ignored dimension of time (For example, is time seen as progressive and linear or as cyclical and recursive?). In the same manner that interpretations of line charts will vary according to where one draws the origin point, so do a number of arguments stand or fall depending on their assumed time scales.

Final Thoughts

Frank's case suggests that specific ways of reading and thinking are reinforced by certain types of life experiences, and these experiences and the semiotic domains they call upon may be simulated in gaming environments. It also suggests that gaming experiences may reinforce or awaken students to certain identity positions and the rhetorical and narrative nature of these positions. As such scholars as Facer et al. (2003) argue that computer games seem to be a medium for allowing players to explore and model different ways of being, to "examine what it would be like if they were able to take responsibility for cities, empires, soldiers, creatures," and "to imaginatively inhabit alternative realities in which they were able to test out what it was like to 'take control'" (p. 74). Hopefully, if nothing else, Frank's case also reveals a potential future direction for gaming and literacy studies as well as the rhetorical analysis of mainstream texts.

Notes

1. Howard Gardner's concept of multiple intelligences has had a huge impact on the elaboration of the theory of multiple literacies.
2. A further example includes McGuire (1986).
3. This statement can be further complicated by taking account of the links between gender and gaming preferences noted by some researchers. It has been widely claimed that adolescent females tend to opt for simulation-type games while males tend to gravitate toward more violent and fantasy-oriented games. Examples of this research include Bennett, Bruner, and Honey (1998) and Dill and Dill (1998).
   But one should keep in mind that all such categorical distinctions run the danger of ignoring other important sociocultural factors such as sexual orientation, religion, class, and birth chart.
4. In *Civilization*, the player's goal is to build a powerful civilization and to expand into unknown territory. A player can select what time periods and geographical areas he or she wishes to play in, from the time of the Carthaginians to the beginnings of Chinese civilization. Planning and strategy are key in this game. The player needs to perform such actions as moving large numbers of forces, coordinating attacks, and exercising deft diplomacy. The player must make a number of trade-offs such as choosing between city improvements and expanding military forces.
5. *Barron's* is a national business and financial weekly.
6. *Value Line Investment Survey* is a weekly publication that provides the performance and safety rankings of both individual stocks and investment sectors.

7. Frank was not the only person to fall under *Myst*'s sway. In fact, *Myst* became the best-selling computer game of all time, and effectively changed the way computer games were made. Much of *Myst*'s success was due to its graphics, the best ever seen on a PC. Its rendered scenery quickly became the industry standard for computer games. But it was *Myst*'s game play that truly made it special. *Myst* was quite probably the most challenging video game invented up to this point. Players disappeared into its puzzles and false paths for months.

8. What Gee (2003) classifies as "god games" are games where the player controls the construction of a civilization and relies on a wide variety of computer simulations to structure this civilization.

References

Bal, Mieke. (1985). *Narratology: Introduction to the theory of narrative.* Buffalo: University of Toronto Press.

Bennett, Dorothy, Bruner, Cornelia, & Honey, Margaret. (1998). Girl games and technological desire. In Justine Casell and Henry Jenkins (Eds.), *From Barbie to Mortal Kombat: Gender and computer games* (pp. 72–89). Boston: MIT Press.

Dill, Jody C., & Dill, Karen. (1998). Video game violence: A review of the empirical literature. *Aggression and Violent Behavior, 3*(4), 407–428.

Facer, Keri, Furlong, John, Furlong, Ruth, & Sutherland Rosamund. (2003). *Screen play: Children and computing in the home.* London: Routledge Falmer.

Gee, James Paul. (2003). *What video games have to teach us about learning and literacy.* New York: Palgrave Macmillan.

Gianturco, Daniel T., & Ramm, Dietolf. (1973). Computers and technology: Aiding tomorrow's aged. *Gerontologist, 13,* 322–326.

Giddens, Anthony. (1984). *The construction of society: Outline of the theory of structuration.* Berkeley: University of California Press.

McGuire, Francis A. (Ed.). (1986). *Computer technology and the aged: Implications and applications for activity programs.* New York: Haworth Press.

Pensioners catch the gaming bug. (2003, December 3). *BBC Online.* Retrieved March 12, 2004, from http://news.bbc.co.uk

Polkingham, Donald. (1988). *Narrative knowing and the human sciences.* Albany, NY: SUNY Press.

13

Gender Matters: Literacy, Learning, and Gaming in One American Family

Pamela Takayoshi

Learning involves mastering, at some level, semiotic domains, and being able to participate, at some level, in the affinity group or groups connected to them.

(*Gee, 2003, p. 207*)[1]

I asked some of the girls if they play video games and why they were not participating. Every girl I asked said they did play video games at home and that they did not participate in electronics day mostly because the boys were too competitive and said things to them like, "You don't know how to play," "Let me do that hard part for you," "This is a boy thing," "Only boys can play."

(*Meghan Huot*)

Some guys just assume the girls don't want to play—i experienced that last year when i was at a guy's house with 2 guys and they played some of the old old games on the first nintendo system and didn't even invite me to play, when those are some of my favorite games.

(*Emily Huot*)

In his book *What Video Games Teach Us about Literacy,* James Paul Gee (2003) focuses on video games as a semiotic domain, which he defines as "any set of practices that recruits one or more modalities (e.g., oral or written language, images, equations, symbols, sounds, gestures, graphs, artifacts, etc.) to communicate distinctive types of meaning" (p. 18). By thinking about video games as a semiotic domain, Gee (2003) focuses our attention on a practice that is of increasing importance and centrality to many literacy learners' lives, arguing that "people need to be able to learn to be literate in new semiotic domains throughout their lives. If our modern, global, high-tech, and science-driven world does anything, it certainly gives rise to new semiotic domains and transforms old ones at an ever faster rate" (p. 19). As a parent of video game–playing children as well as a writing researcher and teacher, I believe Gee (2003) is right when he argues that good video games "operate with—that is, they build into their designs and encourage—good principles of learning, principles that are better than those in many of our skill-and-drill, back-to-basics, test-them-until-they-drop schools" (p. 205) (which is not to say that all video games do this—Gee carefully points out that his claims are about *good* video games). Gee offers a validation for what children know and experience outside formal educational settings, evidence of the need for thinking about the relationship between nonacademic and academic lives, and a strong articulation of how media shape literacy experiences now.[2] But as a parent of female video gamers, I found myself thinking about the meaningful and significant ways gender is intimately tied to learning (Gilligan, 1983), literacy (Finders, 1997), and video games (see below). Gee (2003) acknowledges this connection: "Two issues have taken up the vast majority of writing about video games: violence (i.e., shooting and killing in games, depictions of violence) and gender (i.e., whether and how much girls play, whether and how video games depict women poorly). I have nothing whatsoever to say about these issues in this book. They are well discussed elsewhere" (p. 10). While gender is not an explicit focus for Gee, however, gender informs many experiences with video games, learning, and literacy. In fact, Gee (2003) himself describes the ways gender might inform claims about video games when he offers the example of how Chomsky based his theories of language on his own first language:

> Noam Chomsky and his early students spoke English as their native language and, thus, tended to use this language as their initial database for forming their theories. These were, in fact, theories not about English but about what is universal in language or common to the design of all languages. This early emphasis on English (treating English as the "typical" language) gave the theory a certain sort of initial shape that helped lead to certain developments and not others. Later the theory changed as more languages—ones quite different from English—received more careful consideration. Nonetheless, no matter how good the theory is now (assuming for the moment the theory is good), if Chomsky and others had been speakers of Navajo, it might be equally good now but somewhat different. (p. 29)

In this chapter, I am interested in exploring the ways gender influences what video games teach us about literacy and learning. In their study of adolescent girls' construction of sexual identity on the Web, Ashley Grisso and David Weiss (2005) point out that "until the last two decades of the twentieth century, the vast majority of the research purporting to study 'adolescence' actually focused almost exclusively on adolescent *boys* and their development" (p. 30). However, they continue, "girls negotiate their own gender-specific transitions. In order to investigate the issues of greatest importance to girls in this transitional age group, it is important to hear them speak using their own words" (2005, p. 30). Justine Cassell and Henry Jenkins (1998) argue that this has been the case particularly with computer games: "Too often, the study of computer games has meant the study of *boys* playing computer games" (p. 5, original italics). In recognition that gender does matter, feminist scholars have, as Gee acknowledges, built a well-developed body of scholarship not only investigating whether and when girls play and (mis)representations of gender in video games but also demonstrating that

- the majority of video games do not offer female protagonists; when they do, the female characters are overly sexualized and eroticized (Cassell & Jenkins, 1998; Children Now, 2000; Provenzo, 1991), "designed to please male urges" (Herbst, 2004);
- male and female gamers play different kinds of games; whereas males play more role-playing, battle games, women play traditional card games, board games, and trivia games (Jenkins, 2001; Subrahmanyam & Greenfield, 1998);
- girls' experiences playing video games differ in significant ways from boys' experiences (McNamee, 1998);
- the majority of video games do not appeal to girls nor are they marketed to girls (Provenzo, 1991; Cassell & Jenkins, 1998);
- girls end up playing the games which their brothers have and are available to them rather than games of their own choice (Haddon, 1992);
- white characters are the majority of the video-game population (Children Now, 2000);
- video games can contribute to players' beliefs in gendered stereotypes (Subrahmanyam et al. 2000); and
- some studies suggest that boys play video and computer games more than girls do (Kubey & Larson, 1990), although recent figures suggest otherwise: according to PC Data (as reported by Children Now, 2000), 45 percent of computer and video game players in 2000 were female.

Taking Gee's claims about video games, learning, and literacy as a departure point and accepting Grisso and Weiss's challenge to "hear [girls] speak using their own words" (2005, p. 30), I investigate in this chapter four young women's experiences with literacy, learning, and video gaming[3] to foreground that gender matters, especially when we are thinking about the always- and already-gendered activities of video gaming and literacy. Game playing represents a domain that demands specialized semiotic knowledge, and games are gendered environments within which people practice literacy. By examining the gaming experiences of the girls in one white, American, middle-class family, I articulate some of the ways gender matters in video gaming and literacy activities. Specifically, I focus on four female game players: my sister, Allison (30 at the time of this writing); my stepdaughters, Meghan (21) and Emily (19); and my niece, Jordan (15). These young women have been constant and active game players who have regularly played with one another, occasionally checking web-sites for walkthroughs (which take players step-by-step through the difficult parts of particular video games) and cheats (which reveal secrets about different functions in the games), and sometimes sharing games with friends. Each of these women began playing at different ages in their lives: Allison when she was 26; Meghan at the age of 10; Emily when she was 8; and Jordan at the early age of 5. In popular parlance, the label "gamer" conjures a particular image: the stereotype of a teenaged, geeky, white (indeed, probably pasty white from spending too much time inside) male who spends every waking minute of his life thinking about video games—poring over video game magazines and websites, hanging out in video game stores, trading up used video games, and keeping up with the release dates of new versions of old games and new games. This chapter suggests the many ways this stereotypical understanding of "gamer" is incomplete.[4] Against this stereotypical male player, I present a picture of active, engaged, and interested female video game players. For these reasons, I refer to them here as "gamers," at the same time recognizing that the "gamer" identity in popular culture does not typically include these individuals (casual, but regular, female players).

The four gamers discussed their video gaming experiences with me through a tape-recorded group interview; an initial e-mail questionnaire; several follow-up e-mail questions that built on responses to the initial questionnaire; and numerous follow-up e-mail, telephone, and face-to-face conversations focusing more specifically on issues that arose in their responses to my questionnaire. Additionally, the four gamers read a draft of this chapter and gave their feedback and suggestions for development and revision. Because of my relationship to the participants, I was able to contextualize their answers against the ecology of our shared experiences as a family.[5] So while my knowledge of their experiences with literacy, video gaming, schooling, and gender created a context for listening to what they told me in response to my specific questions about video gaming, as a nongame player, I could only arrive at conclusions about video gaming and gender through their contributions. Given that these four game players come from the same family and that the four played influential roles in each others' gaming lives, their stories are not easily extricable from one another.

In this chapter, I do not make claims for representativeness; four case studies can never be representative of a general human experience. There is obviously a lot more to be learned about the complicated and multilayered relationship between gender, video gaming, literacy, and learning. These women's experiences, however, are suggestive of the multiple ways that gender might always be present in learning, literacy, and gaming for people of both genders. Indeed, their experiences contribute to our understanding of what we do not know and where we might head in our future attempts to understand the learning practices involved in gaming and their relationship with literacy, literate practices, and literacy learning. At the end of each section of this chapter, I articulate questions important to developing a fuller understanding of what we can learn about literacy and learning from video games.

Becoming Gaming Women

Allison, Meghan, Emily, and Jordan belong to the same family through marriage. My younger sister, Allison, is Jordan's mother and aunt to my stepdaughters, Meghan and Emily. When Meghan and Emily were six and four, they first met Allison, and Jordan had just been born. Although from different generations, the four shared a common bond in video gaming, with Allison often serving as expert video-game adviser for the three younger girls. These four young women have built a relationship over the years through the medium of video-gaming. Getting together for Thanksgiving dinner, for example, has almost always begun with the girls asking Allison to "get us to the next level" or to help them solve some difficult passage in a game. Early on in their young lives, the girls recognized Allison as an authority they could turn to for help when they had gone as far as they could on their own; it was only after they had tried by themselves to solve the problem, and not succeeded, that they turned to an outside source. But it was more than learning how and when to turn to experts for help; Allison was one of them. When Meghan and Emily were only ten and eight, they described Allison as "like us" because she could play video games. Being a gamer made her young and fun for the girls. Allison knew about video-gaming *as a gamer*. As I discuss in the following section, Allison's being "like us" played an important role in the girls' video-gaming experiences.

In fact, though, Allison was more "like them" as an adult than she was as a child. Unlike the girls, who began playing games at a young age, Allison was born at and into a different historical moment and familial structure than Meghan, Emily, and Jordan. Allison was born in Indianapolis in 1969, three years before the first home video-gaming console (Magnavox's *Odyssey*) was showcased in California and three years before *Pong*, the first Atari game, was created.[6] Although she grew up in a literate household where books and trips to the library were a regular feature (in part because our mother was an avid reader), as for many bright and curious young people, school did not engage Allison, and she ended up dropping out of high school before graduation. As an adult she developed into a reader who often gets hooked on an author or a theme and reads everything by that author or about that theme (after reading Truman Capote's *Breakfast at Tiffany's*, for example, she read "nothing but Capote for months"). It was not until Allison was in high school that video-gaming platforms (personal computers and consoles) entered the homes of most Americans. In our working-class neighborhood during the 1970s, both computers and video games were a luxury few could afford. Allison did not become familiar with computers, in fact, until fairly recently, long after she was already an experienced gamer: "The first time I was really interested in computers was about five years ago [1999] when David and I received a computer from Mom for Christmas. David pretty much taught himself but he really couldn't explain it to me. The computer itself was discouraging so all I did was check email and play around."

Allison entered high school in 1983, three years before Nintendo's NES (Nintendo Entertainment System) was released in the United States. Within the economic realities of her single parent-headed household and her friends' working-class and working-poor families, Allison had little opportunity as a young girl to experience video gaming; even when video-gaming systems and personal computers became more affordable for many in this country, our family had limited disposable income and did not invest in computers or game-playing systems. Instead, Allison learned video gaming as an adult, through her relationships with her children and her husband. She first learned about video games from Meghan and Emily, who had a Nintendo 64 gaming console Allison would play when she visited (and Meghan and Emily would take the gaming console with them when they went to visit her). Allison's daughter, Jordan, received her first Nintendo 64 from her grandmother when she was about five years old, and Allison remembers playing that with all three of the girls, adding that she was so interested even then that "J and I would play even after they went to bed!" Jordan's Nintendo 64 introduced Allison and Jordan to Donkey Kong, the main character in the game that came with the system. Allison and her husband bought a Nintendo gaming system shortly after Jordan got hers, and Allison then played regularly with her husband, by herself, or with Jordan.

The younger girls, on the other hand, had access to video-gaming systems at much earlier ages, being born into families with more disposable income to support their involvement in the gaming platforms and the games themselves. Born in Tennessee in 1983 and 1985, respectively, Meghan and Emily grew up in a culture that was much more saturated with video gaming than did Allison. By the time Meghan was ten and Emily was eight in 1993, for example, video games had become such a prominent part of the cultural landscape that Senators Joseph Lieberman and Herbert Kohl launched a Senate investigation into violence in video games. The following year, 1994, saw the initiation of the Entertainment Software Rating Board (ESRB), which "independently applies and enforces ratings, advertising guidelines, and online privacy principles adopted by the computer and video game industry" ("About ESRB," n.d.). Clearly, video games were more prevalent and also part of the cultural landscape in ways that Allison did not experience.

Video games were more accessible in Meghan and Emily's households, as well. Meghan and Emily grew up in a comfortable middle-class rural Kentucky neighborhood with their mother and stepfather, and they regularly spent time with their father in Louisville. Both girls grew up in very literate surroundings, with an English professor father and stepmother whom they watched go through graduate school in English. Both girls did well in school, although they were frequently frustrated by what their teachers asked of them. For example, although both Meghan and Emily had authored their own Web pages in 1997, when they were 14 and 12, their school experiences with technology were limited to worksheets and other activities structured more around technology consumption rather than production. From this frustration and their experiences as Web authors grew an article we coauthored about girls' experiences on the Web (Takayoshi, Huot, & Huot, 1999). As authors of a published article about girls and technology, their experiences with technology in school were particularly poignant, with teachers monitoring students' movements through the Web, for example, and not allowing computer-savvy students to navigate on their own. About the limits of educational uses of technologies in their lives, we wrote, "Surrounded as we are by the myth that girls and children are in danger every time they log onto the Web, it is understandable that schools should be cautious. Still, this concern often overlooks the sophisticated skills students may already have" (1999, p. 105).

Similarly, the skills Emily and Meghan (and Jordan following them) acquired from video gaming were disconnected from their experiences with technology in school. Meghan does not remember playing any games at school, noting that "you weren't really allowed to in the computer labs," although Emily remembers "having a typing unit in 4th grade and there was a computer program to help us learn. it was a Mario game and we had to type the letters as we saw them to help Mario go through the level. that was right up my alley, i loved that game." Around the time Emily was playing the Mario typing game, the girls received their first videogame console (a Super Nintendo) bundled with Super Mario Brothers 3 as a Christmas gift from their father and me. They left the gaming system at our house because their stepfather had expressed negative opinions about video games and they did not believe their mother and stepfather would allow them to have it (several years later, at the girls' request, we also got them Nintendo Game Boys). So weekends and summers were spent catching up on the video-game playing they missed at their mother and stepfather's home. During summers, too, Meghan and Emily read numerous books, often working toward a reward they negotiated with their father for a certain number of books read. The rewards were often related to new media—among the rewards they worked toward were an external CD burner and video games.

In the five to seven years that separate Jordan, born in Indianapolis in 1990, from Emily and Meghan, video games became an even more common feature of the American childhood landscape. Jordan's birth coincides with the birth of Sonic the Hedgehog, the Sega gaming character designed to compete with the widespread popularity of Nintendo's Mario Brothers (by this time widely recognized cultural figures), and by the time she was 10, she had multiple gaming consoles—Nintendo, Sega, PlayStation, and Game Boy—from which to choose. Notably, when Jordan was six, *Barbie: Fashion Designer* was released and became a huge success as the first piece of leisure software to be aimed at the girl gaming market. With this game (and particularly with its previously unwitnessed success with a female gaming audience), gender and video gaming demanded the attention of cultural critics, feminists, and concerned parents. One year after Jordan's birth, Eugene Provenzo (1991) studied the cover art of 47 contemporary video games and discovered that representations of men outnumbered representations of women by a ratio of thirteen to one. In a study of 100 arcade games, he reported, 92 percent contained no female roles at all. In 1994, the first video game targeted specifically at girls, "Hawaii High: The Mystery of the Tiki," was released, which feminist cultural critics and concerned parents hoped was the beginning of more positive video-game characters and role models. Justine Cassell and Henry Jenkins (1998) characterize "Hawaii High" as a model for this movement: "It did introduce some of the features that would dominate the girls' game movement: more character-driven plots, issues of friendship and social relationships, and bright colorful graphics" (p. 10). The girls' game movement never really took off, though, in part because "unlike *Barbie Fashion Designer,* none of the games targeted to girls sold significant numbers of copies. In fact, until very recently, for both console and PC games, girls made up no more than 25 percent of the market" (Cassell & Jenkins, 1998, p. 10). Indeed, Jordan as a young gamer (she began playing at five, remember) did not have the financial resources to purchase games on her own and relied on her parents and grandmother to support her gaming. Without very much knowledge of video games themselves, her parents and grandmother tended to purchase the most popular games on the market; the first game she played with her first gaming console was *Donkey Kong Country,* selected by her grandmother because the salesclerk told her it was currently the best-selling game.

Jordan, like her mother before her, was a disengaged student although she was an "A" student when she had some incentive (either an interest in the work, or the teacher, or the promise of a reward from her parents for a job well done). Too often, though, school did not engage her in the ways videogaming did. James Gee's rumination on video games—"Wouldn't it be great if kids were willing to put in this much time on task on such challenging material in school and enjoy it so much?" (p. 5)—speaks especially well to Jordan's relationship to the learning she experiences as a videogamer versus the learning she experiences as a student in school. Although Jordan reads several levels above her reading level and reads regularly (oftentimes beginning a book and reading well into the morning hours to finish it), she describes her English class as "boring" and "not really about reading the way I like to read." The disconnect between "the way I like to read" and the way reading is taught in her school is similar to the disconnect between the engaged learning processes Jordan experiences with video games and the role video games occupy in her schooling experience, as she notes: "Our teachers never talk to us about it. One time, my history teacher was asking us about video games before class, but I don't remember why. It didn't have anything to do with what we were talking about in class."

While these four gamers' experiences with schooling, literacy, and learning vary across a spectrum of engagement and disconnection, their engagement with video games and their attendant learning and literacy processes has brought them together as a learning community and given them an experience as learners that their school experiences too often did not give them. In a political culture of increasingly high stakes and state-mandated assessment, theories of learning based on the ways people actually learn best are squeezed out in favor of more direct routes to successful test scores. These four young women are evidence of the gap created by this gulf between what learners do in their nonacademic lives and what schools ask of them as learners. What is striking is that their experiences remain so constant across generations—all four are highly literate women who have varying degrees of success with school and whose engagement with video gaming stands in contrast to their disengagement from school. Additionally, while video gaming has become more affordable, accessible, and visible in the cultural landscape of American life, the gendering of the games has not made such visible strides. Adopting the personas of characters such as Mario, his brother, Luigi, and Donkey Kong, these four female gamers navigated game spaces imbued with gendered meaning—while all the time, those gendered meanings and messages were implicit and quietly worked into the background of the video gaming and learning. Unpacking the ways this gendering functioned in these four female gamers' learning, literacy, and video gaming experiences reveals much about the ways culture implicitly works through literacy and video gaming and provides some beginning points for thinking about the meaning of video games, literacy, and learning in everyday lives.

Barbie, Velma, and Princess Peach: Gender Identification and Resistance in Learning to Game

As actively as the girls engaged in playing video games, as female players, they were aware of the ways the learning environment (including especially the way the semiotic domain was designed and presented) was gendered. As Meghan notes, video games are stereotyped as appropriate for boys: "I can remember being bothered at a very young age about the way boys and girls are stereotyped. Boys wear blue. Girls wear pink. Boys play with cars and video games. Girls play with Barbies and dolls." Jordan too, recognizes the ways video games are coded, commenting that "I find video games to be designed for boys," but she imagines a different kind of video game, where gender matters in a different way:

> It would be nice to have more girl video games (not Barbie or makeup video games). Mario Carts does have girls but it's like Princess Peach and her sister Princess something. It would be good to have games where you had like a Mario girl or a Luigi girl who would go through the different worlds and fight the bad guys. And maybe save Mario or Luigi, because it's always been Mario and Luigi saving the princess.

Jordan's mother, Allison, also recognizes the limitations of the "rescuing the princess" theme: "I have seen the games where you 'rescue' the princess and that seems silly and outdated!" On the other hand, she notes that in the Scooby Doo video game, a female character does enjoy some measure of power: "You have Velma, who is certainly smarter than Fred and Shaggy; hell, without her there wouldn't be a Mystery, Inc.!"

These comments, especially Jordan's desire for a game where a female character or female player could save the guys, suggest that for these female game players, actively engaging in video-game worlds means crossing genders, at least part of the time. With few video games featuring female protagonists, female game players have to "be" the male character. With an almost wistful desire for an alternative world, these female gamers often played as Mario, Luigi, PacMan, James Bond, and Crash Bandicoot. Cassell & Jenkins (1998) note that girls have traditionally had fewer choices—there are more toys, games, and activities that feature boys or cater to their play styles. Thus, they wonder, "In playing with computer games that are not explicitly targeted for girls, are girls simply showing their increased flexibility—their ability to engage in both girls' and boys' play—or are they making of computer games a real girls' space?" (1998, p. 35). For Allison, Meghan, Emily, and Jordan, the answer to that question, rather than being increased flexibility or the creation of a real girls' space, seems to be a bit of both. All four gamers agree that there are too few female video-game characters with whom they can identify:

> There arent enough female characters. i used to like super mario 2 because in that game you could be the princess. i've never played a game where females are treated badly, nor have i played any where their bodies are highly sexualized, but i have seen them. i never understood that either. i never understood why sexualizing animation is well sexy. i just think it's weird. *Emily*

In a lot of video games I have seen the women characters play minor roles and are dressed pretty seductively. However there also games in which women are the main characters, like Lara Croft Tomb Raider and the game Emily and I used to play that was like james bond, i can't remember the name of it. The female character was pretty much just a sexy/female version of James Bond, but it was kind of cool to have a female playing for you instead of a man. I did like playing James Bond, it was fun, there were different kinds of guns and you got to hunt for bad guys in different settings. I believe there were female counterparts but I don't remember much about them, except that they were sexy. I don't remember if they had names or not. *Meghan*

There have been either few females or they have been very built up to reflect what a guy might think the "perfect" girl should look like. You know, with big boobs, tiny waist. It would be nice to have more video games with real girls or women in them. *Jordan*

And yet, they do identify with the games at some level, which overrides the lack of identity with the female character, as they indicate when they describe why they keep playing:

I like beating games the best, although it's disappointing when it's all over. i also like getting really good. i am a champ at super mario world for super nintendo. i have beaten that game so many times. i played it this year with matt and a couple of the guys in his fraternity and i was ten times better than all of them, which was pretty exciting since they are the ones who play video games all the time. *Emily*

I just like to play because I could just focus on one thing and get out of my head. It also felt good to get past a really hard level. Emily and I used to kind of compete with each other. It felt good to get past a hard level because it was like we had accomplished something, and we had worked hard to accomplish it. Emily and I would compete to see who could beat the hard levels first, but we would be working together, however who ever did beat it would get the title of beating it. *Meghan*

i enjoy it a lot when i get a new game. i always want to keep playing games until i get past the parts that are hard, the parts that frustrate me. i have been known to play video games for at least 4 hours straight. *Jordan*

i like playing games, getting better at them, beating them. Except when you do reach the end where else is there to go?? The game is dead in the water! It is pretty gratifying figuring it out and beating it, though. *Allison*

For these gamers, the reasons for playing the games seem to be related to their sense of identity as gamers and thinkers, if not as women. Gee (2003) suggests that "learning involves taking on and playing with identities in such a way that the learner has real choices (in developing the virtual identity) and ample opportunity to meditate on the relationship between new identities and old one" (p. 208). In these gamers' experiences, though, the choices of identities offered continue to be limited by gender—there are either no female protagonists to identify with or the female protagonists who are offered have such a tangential connection to average women that these gamers do not identify with them. How, then, might these complications interfere with these women's potential learning and the development of learning strategies they might carry into other semiotic domains? How does gender complicate women's development of learning strategies in gendered spaces? At the least, these women's experiences suggest that a lack of female characters with which to identify does affect female gamers' ability to take on new identities and limits their choices in developing their virtual identity. Constrained by the dominant gender represented in video games, the ability to learn through playing with identities is limited. However, these gamers do get from their play a stronger sense of themselves—as being "a champ," as having accomplished something, as overcoming difficult problems, and as getting better and beating the games. Meghan's description of the process of play is about beating the game, not the other player—she and Emily compete to see who can beat the hard levels first, but they are really working together to get to the end. In their game playing, the "title" of beating the level or the game is honorary. This cooperative competition, where the two compete against each other so they both can profit in the game, is a strategy that works well for them as gamers and one that can be productive for them as learners in other semiotic domains (for example, as writers, as students, as workers, as civic participants).

Indeed, these women's abilities to critically read and understand gender as a feature of these multimedia environments—for example, reading against such leitmotifs as the princess needing rescue and such visual iconography as the large-breasted, skinny woman—might also be productive for them in various learning and participation arenas of their lives. In particular, these gamers' experiences demonstrate once again that students often enter literacy classrooms with an understanding (although oftentimes an implicit) that the linguistic is not the only—or even necessarily the primary—semiotic register through which communication takes place. Indeed, students often enter literacy classrooms with an understanding (again, oftentimes implicit) that there are many communicative modalities through which one reads and writes, although schools (and literacy classrooms) continue to privilege the written as the only mode that counts. These women's responses to the leitmotifs and iconography of their video game experiences also reflect an ability students have, often unacknowledged in schools and literacy classrooms, to understand the limits of "texts" and to be able to read critically—knowledge and strategies which serve thinkers, students, citizens, and workers well in numerous arenas. But like all learning, without active, critical reflection and a metacognitive awareness of what is being learned, these lessons and their potential for influencing participation in other semiotic domains risk being lost in an educational landscape that devalues or fails to recognize the learning strategies people are developing in their nonacademic practices.

These female gamers' negotiations with what they understood to be the gendered terrain of gaming intersect with questions being asked by literacy scholars, researchers, and teachers, and raise related new questions:

- What practices, strategies, experiences have learners developed in their nonacademic lives that might be beneficial to build on in academic settings?
- What is the relationship between academic and nonacademic learning and literacy practices? What might a productive relationship between the two look like?

- Are female learners and their learning experiences affected by a lack of female role models and female protagonists/identity positions to occupy? Or, ironically, are they given necessary life experience (in a patriarchal society) in how to adopt the male perspective?
- How does the negotiation of meaning in multimodal compositions (i.e., texts that employ numerous semiotic channels—linguistic, aural, visual, video—to communicate meaning) affect learning? Which semiotic channels are primary for readers of the compositions? How is that determined? How does it affect learning and the acquisition of meaning?
- How is learning affected when one's gender identity is ignored?
- What are the difficulties and possibilities afforded learners when they occupy subject positions coded in the gender opposite to their own?

Getting in the Game: The Importance of Affinity Groups for Learning

The persistence of these female gamers despite the gendered terrain was supported in large part through their relationship with one another. Although some of their friends played video games, for the most part, these four gamers relied on one another for assistance and support in learning how to play and in progressing past points where they went as far as they could on their own. As I discuss later in this section, Jordan was the only gamer who could rely on her parents for help in gaming. As Emily notes, "My mom is not good at computer games i dont know why, but she has never been able to grasp how to do it well, plus she has no interest in it." And although their father played with them, Meghan remembers that he wasn't an expert: "Dad uses the computer a lot for work, email, surfing the net and stuff, and he used to play our videogames with us, but he was not very good, he used to make us laugh. I can just remember playing with him on the floor in front of the television and he was on this one round on yoshi eating these cactuses and it made him laugh and his face got all red so then we all started laughing."

Jordan's parents are both much more involved with video gaming. She describes her father's expertise as "ok. he is good at playing video games." Her mother, Allison, though, is

> really good on the computer. she is also good at playing games. she helped me a lot when i was little. I never really learned gaming from my friends i mostly learned it from my mom. From what i remember i mostly watched my moms hands and the screen and sort of figured it out. I think it would be difficult for someone to try to help you do it because its a small controller."

Indeed, Allison played a central and influential role in all three girls' learning and playing experiences. Unlike the other parents in the girls' lives, Allison was an active video gamer the girls saw as an expert who could be relied on to help them when they were stuck. Meghan recalls that "when Allison would come visit she would help us pass castles that we couldn't pass. She always knew how to. It was always really fun to play with Allison because we would be silly and it also helped us get to know her." Allison, too, remembers the role she played in the girls' learning processes: "I absolutely remember playing not only with J but with Meghan and Emily as well. I remember that I would come over to your house, and the Nintendo would be set up and ready to go when I walked in the front door!"

The girls' experiences with Allison suggest at least two issues important to thinking about learning. Primarily, she provided the girls with a female role model (as a female expert game player) that counterbalanced the dominant gendering of the gaming experience for the girls. Although these female gamers could not identify with a single female video game protagonist, they could identify with an older, "cool" female video game player. Through their relationship with Allison, the girls identified themselves with a female expert (she was the one they knew had the answers), associated her with learning and the acquisition of difficult strategies (she was their teacher and guide), and modeled her behavior (watching how her hands moved and trying the same). Vygotsky (1978) maintained that with appropriate adult assistance, children can often perform tasks they are incapable of performing on their own. By following the example of adults, children gradually develop the ability to do the task without assistance. The girls' identification of Allison as the expert is a clear example of what Vygotsky (1978) called the "zone of proximal development," the difference between what a child can do alone and what she can do with assistance. Through their play with Allison, the girls recognized that they had reached a point where they needed help to go further, understood who the expert was to rely upon, and learned from that expert how to accomplish the task on their own. In other words, the girls displayed a metacognitive awareness of learning from which they might benefit in other semiotic domains where learning, literacy, and communication were central.

Secondarily, through their learning and playing experiences with Allison, video gaming became a site for developing and maintaining an emotional and familial bond between the players.

> Mom and i have played internet backgammon together numerous times. We would call each other and tell each other to get on and we would go to zone.com and to a certain room and play against each other. We have also gotten each other addicted to spider solitaire and freecell. My mom and i haven't always been in touch and when we were playing this game we connected and while we played we would chat too. In some ways it was like playing a game in the same room with her. *Jordan*

Playing video games was a medium through which these gamers connected and maintained relationships:

> I learned a lot about gaming from emily, she plays games on the computer more than I do. *Meghan*

> I usually learn by listening to some of my friends. i learned a lot from matt, mainly about rpg's because i have had to sit and watch him play a decent amount of times. Most of what i learned was through my own experience, back when i used to play with my sister. *Emily*

Through video gaming, these four young women maintained emotional and familial bonds across time and geographic distance. Meghan and Emily identify each other as their main teachers. For Jordan and Allison, video gaming supported their connection as though they were "in the same room." In other comments, these gamers suggest additional ways that, for girls, video gaming might be a connective medium:

> After being around both George and Jordan and George's girl cousins I see that they do differ in their style of playing and by the choice of game they play as well. I think boys play more games and that girls use the computer more for social reasons, like communicating by chatting online with people. My two children play games differently. Jordan is not nearly as bossy as George is. George will ask for my help and then tell me that I am doing it wrong! I enjoyed playing with J way more! George is also competitive with me. I think that boys lean more towards strategy and violent games and girls go more for the mild gaming style. I actually prefer both types. I like to play the war games but I also like the Scooby Doo type games. I don't discriminate (haha). *Allison*

> guys are more competitive and girls just do it for fun. when my friends and I play it's more of a thing to do and try to get past a certain level. *Jordan*

> i recently learned to play a game called halo on xbox. halo is one of those first person shooter games. it is pretty fun, but it is frustrating to play games like that with guys—usually guys are the ones who take the time to master those types of games—because sometimes they wont even give you a chance to figure out what you're doing, and they just keep killing you. *Emily*

The relational aspect of video gaming these gamers suggest is based on their anecdotal observations and is suggestive of how gender factors into video-gaming experience—either through perceptions or actions. Emily suggests that male gamers not only play differently than female players but that the male players she has played with do not even allow for other ways of playing: "They wont even give you a chance to figure out what youre doing, and they just keep killing you." Allison, too, gets more pleasure from playing with her daughter than her son, who at half his sister's age is more bossy and competitive with his mother. "Competitive" is the word Jordan also uses to capture her perception of male game players.

The emotional connection these gamers experienced through video games and that they suggest through their own observations stands in contrast to research conducted by Robert Kubey and Reed Larson (1990). In a study of 483 young people between the ages of 9 and 15, Kubey and Larson discovered that young boys feel better emotionally than girls do when playing video games, in part because boys and girls are socialized differently and because much of the content in video media is deliberately targeted toward boys. The emotional connection Allison, Meghan, Emily, and Jordan felt stands in contrast to the majority of girls in Kubey and Larson's study, although Kubey's comment on the study offers a possible explanation: "Certainly in the United States, boys are socialized [toward electronics, computers, and technology in general] more than girls, who are still socialized toward more nurturing roles and oriented to social network maintenance, or 'kin-keeping'" ("Researchers find gender differences," n.d.). For Allison, Meghan, Emily, and Jordan, social network maintenance (or kin-keeping) was enacted through the platform of the video games.

Indeed, for the most part, these four gamers had very limited interactions with video games beyond the familial. In this way, they serve as a specific example and a complication of what Gee (2003) refers to as "affinity groups" which, he empha-sizes, are central to developing active and critical learning practices: "If learning is to be active, it must involve experiencing the world in new ways. I have spelled this out in terms of learning new ways to situate the meanings of words, images, sym-bols, artifacts, and so forth when operating within specific situations in new semi-otic domains. Active learning must also involve forming new affiliations. I have explained this in terms of learners joining new affinity groups associated with new semiotic domains" (p. 39). The girls' experiences with video gaming do follow this pattern of experiencing the world in new ways and forming new affiliations that support and encourage their discovery of new ways to situate meaning within spe-cific situations in new semiotic domains. But for these gamers, there was little connection, either through physical contact with actual gamers or through asso-ciation with gaming culture, with a larger affinity group of gamers envisioned by Gee (2003):

> People in an affinity group can recognize others as more or less "insiders" to the group. They may not see many people in the group face-to-face, but when they inter-act with someone on the Internet or read something about the domain, they can rec-ognize certain ways of thinking, acting, interacting, valuing, and believing as more or less typical of people who are "into" the semiotic domain. Thus we can talk about the typical ways of thinking, acting, interacting, valuing, and believing as well as the typ-ical sorts of social practices associated with a given semiotic domain. (p. 27).

Outside of their small, four member affinity group, Allison, Meghan, Emily, and Jordan found very little affinity with other gamers they knew, instead often feel-ing at odds with other gamers' "certain ways of thinking, acting, interacting, valu-ing, and believing." Although they knew and sometimes played video games with others outside the family, each of the four gamers reported that they knew very few female gamers. When they did play with male gamers, they tended to play with boyfriends, husbands, or brothers—males they had relationships with dis-tinct from gaming:

> i think generally it is mostly boys that play computer games. i have one or two girl-friends that regularly play video games and who are really good at them; most oth-ers have no interest. i used to be a lot more interested than i am now—i mainly just like the mario games. however, almost every guy i know plays video games regularly, and is able to sit and play a game for hours on end. that is beyond me. my boyfriend, who is one of the people who can sit and play a video game for hours, always wants me to play with him. he always wants to teach me games so i can play with him, and he wants me to go in with him and buy a new mario game that is coming out for gamecube so that we can play it together. *Emily*

It is way more common for boys to play games than girls. I don't really have any friends who play. I hear guy friends talking about gaming all the time. Guys my age will actually get together and hang out and play games, and talk about them. I don't really know any girls that do that. Dave [a former boyfriend] would play for ever, he had magazines he would use to help him figure out levels. We never played games together, he always played one person games. *Meghan*

my dad plays with my little brother when he goes over to my dads and he and I play video games when i go to visit him. *Jordan*

I learned to play video games from David [ex-husband] and George [four–year-old son]. David got George involved in playing. George would sit and watch David and want to play himself. . . . It was hard to decide what games to buy George because David would let him play war games and at that time I was not interested in the computer so I was unaware that he was playing those types of games so when we go to purchase games it is almost a battle of wits. *Allison*

These four female gamers did not encounter the kind of support, interaction, and exchange of knowledge with others that they did with each other in their small, female affinity group. Instead, Emily does not understand her male friends' ways with video gaming, Meghan's boyfriend plays while he is with her but does not involve her in the games, Jordan plays with her dad if he is playing with her brother, and Allison is an outsider when it comes to decisions about which games her son plays. In other words when they encounter others in the larger gaming community, there is very little true interaction. Without ongoing social interactions about gaming outside their small affinity group, these gamers existed outside a larger gaming community, constantly reminded of boundaries around the semiotic domain of gamers that establish who is rightfully a member of the affinity group. Gender boundaries in an affinity group serve to limit what can be learned by those accepted by the affinity group and those denied access. In other words, gender matters when we realize that "learning involves mastering, at some level, semiotic domains, and being able to participate, at some level, in the affinity group or groups connected to them" (Gee, 2003, p. 207). Noting that "I don't think it is as socially acceptable for girls to play video games as it is for boys," Meghan witnessed the way gender operates in affinity groups in her work at an after-school center on "Electronics Day":

I have just started a new job working at an after school program with kids ages 5-12. One day out of the week, they have electronics day. I became very curious about why I only saw boys playing the video games. So the next day I asked some of the girls if they play video games and why they were not participating. Every girl I asked said they did play video games at home and that they did not participate in electronics day mostly because the boys were too competitive and said things to them like, "You don't know how to play," "Let me do that hard part for you," "This is a boy thing," "Only boys can play." This outraged me! Is our society still this narrow minded? I think that video games are as much a girl thing as they are a boy thing, being a girl who has played her fair share. . . . However, it does [appear], especially after electronics day, that society associates video games with boys.

Emily, too, has experienced the same gendered response to game playing firsthand: "Some guys just assume the girls don't want to play—i experienced that last year when i was at a guy's house with 2 guys and they played some of the old old games on the first nintendo system and didn't even invite me to play, when those are some of my favorite games." These gamers' experiences suggest that being a girl gamer around male gamers means regularly facing the assumption that you are not interested in playing, that you do not know how to play, or that you will be interested in merely watching as the guys play, in other words, regularly facing the assumption that you are not a member of the affinity group.

Outside of their small female affinity group, these four gamers' connections to other gamers were always accidental and often gendered. They did not and do not have connections with other video gamers as video gamers—instead, their access to video gamers rested on who in their family played games and the males with whom they had relationships not grounded in video games. This accidental and gendered connection to video-gaming culture (and video gamers) also prevailed in terms of which games the girls experienced and played. Meghan, Emily, and Jordan all "try out" video games that cross their paths through friends or family. While the girls actively and regularly played video games, they were not players who read gaming magazines, kept up with the latest game releases, or hung out in gaming stores. Instead, these girls played games that were available to them (either through family members who bought them games or friends who shared their games) rather than games of their own active choosing.

> When i was younger and played super nintendo, we didnt have many games, but the ones we did have were bought for us. that's how i learned about them. today there are gaming magazines and there are things all over the internet about different games. there are walkthroughs that tell you exactly how to beat each level that you play. i dont go out of my way to learn about games like some others do though. i usually learn by listening to some of my friends. *Emily*

> I got games I played off the computer or from you and my dad. Emily and I learned about different games from cousins. *Meghan*

> Got them from my grandma, mom, dad, aunts, uncles i learned about them by getting them. I got my first Nintendo because all my friends had one and when i did play one it was really cool. My grandma bought me my first one for a christmas present. i did ask for it. *Jordan*

While all three of these girls accessed and learned about video games from the adults and peers in their lives, Allison, on the other hand, learned about video games from the girls, who were a generation behind her: "Actually, I first learned about video games from the girls. Jordan got a Nintendo 64 I think from Sherry [Allison's mother; Jordan's grandmother] when she was about George's age." Decisions about which games the girls played, then, were largely determined by others who knew them and were interested in supporting their growth as learners, but being cut off from the decisionmaking process limited what they might have learned going through that process themselves. As females, these gamers experienced limited access to a larger video-gaming affinity group. As outsiders to that community, these gamers did not have access to information (what games existed, what was new, what connected with their interests, where to purchase inexpensive ones, what print or electronic sources to consult), to others' games (they shared only with one another), or to strategies (outside their small affinity group and some online cheat sites, they did not have others to turn to for guidance through games). While these gamers might have implicitly learned a valuable lesson about being female in a male-dominated culture, without access to a larger affinity group, the strategies for learning and the actual learning these gamers experienced might have been limited.

These gamers' experiences with one another provide one example of how affinity groups are central to active learning. What might have happened to them as learners if they had had more meaningful and deeper interactions with others, if their affinity group had included more than four female family members? As with the formation of any human group, gender is always present in the formation and maintenance of affinity groups, as it is in our interactions with technologies which too often are culturally defined and understood in highly gendered terms. If we are to better understand and take advantage of affinity groups as a learning principle, then, it is crucial that we understand how gender matters in the formation and maintenance of affinity groups and how it affects the learning one experiences within and through the support of affinity groups. These gamers' experiences suggest there are many things we need to better understand affinity groups, gender, and learning:

- How do affinity groups work? How do they affect learning? What difference does membership in an affinity group make on the quality of one's learning? How does limited connection with an affinity group affect potential learning?
- How does gender function in the formation and maintenance of affinity groups?
- How do technologies mediate affinity groups? How are the social meanings of technology set up to support or exclude certain groups?

Conclusion

As with any technology, video games present differential access and experiences to people occupying different social categories. The gamers discussed in this chapter were middle class, white, heterosexual, educated, and supported by an encouraging and extended family structure. They had easy access to hardware and software. Gender functioned as a factor in the development of learning and literacy practices surrounding their video-gaming practices in a number of ways. First, these gamers had virtually no female role models—they encountered few games with female characters and almost no games with positive, in-control females they could identify with; they knew very few female gamers other than themselves; and even their handheld gaming platform (Game Boy) was gendered male. Second, rather than receiving support or assistance from male gamers they knew well, these young women regularly received the implicit message that gaming was male territory. They thus turned to other female gamers—each other—to play, teach, and learn. Third, the small size of their affinity group and its interrelatedness limited their access to resources. Without support from a larger community structure (either schools or friends, for example) and faced with gendered cultural messages about gaming and gamers (from the princess needing rescue to the geeky white teenage boy), they did not identify themselves as gamers and thus, did not associate themselves with gaming culture. By cutting themselves off and being cut off in this way, they did not access the literacy sources (magazines, informational websites, chatrooms, online gaming communities, discussions with other gamers about the value of different games) or learning strategies of those in the gaming culture discussed by Gee and others in this book. These four gamers persisted in gaming against the gendered stereotypes that attempted to limit their potential as females and, in the process, experienced critical learning processes; critically read and resisted gendered meanings in the gaming environment and community; and functioned as a small affinity group of four which was often disconnected from a larger gaming affinity group. In these ways, their experiences and the sense they make of those experiences, is a comment on the way gender might circulate in what video games can teach us about literacy and learning.

In this chapter, I have focused on one factor important for understanding video games, learning, and literacy. Similarly, we might focus our attention on other factors—race, class, educational level, sexual preference, age level, parental involvement—and talk with the gamers themselves to discover what happens when learners approach video games, learning, and literacy from these different places, viewing the experiences through these different lenses. If we are to build a robust and grounded theory of what we can comprehend about learning and literacy from video games and other new media, it is crucial that learners occupying these different social categories are invited to contribute their perspectives. In that way, we can measure our theories (colored as they are by our own gender/race/generation/educational attainment/sexual identity/religion/other social categories) against what learners do and believe.

Notes

1. I have not edited the girls' contributions to this chapter, allowing them to retain the form of their own language rather than having the character of their responses washed out to match my own standard, academic prose. The majority of the quotes come from our e-mail conversations (kick-started by their responses to my original questionnaire), which can be seen in the structure of their responses (i.e., minimal punctuation, no capitalization, etc.).
2. The generational aspect of understanding video games and recognizing the learning principles experienced through playing them should not be underestimated: "Better theories of learning are embedded in the video games many children in elementary and particularly in high school play than in the schools they attend. Furthermore, the theory of learning in good video games fits better with the modern, high-tech global world today's children and teenagers live in than do the theories (and practices) of learning

that they see in school. Today's world is very different from the world baby boomers like me grew up in and on which we base many of our theories" (p. 7). Most, if not all, of the learning principles Gee articulates should seem familiar to readers of composition pedagogical theory: for example, "All aspects of the learning environment . . . are set up to encourage active and critical, not passive learning," "Learning about and coming to appreciate interrelations within and across multiple sign systems (images, words, actions, symbols, artifacts, etc.) as a complex system is core to the learning experience," "Learning involves active and critical thinking about the relationships of the semiotic domain being learned to other semiotic domains," and "Learners get lots and lots of practice in a context where the practice is not boring" (p. 207). Composition scholars have established these learning principles as central to successful composition pedagogy.

3. Throughout this chapter, I use the terms "video games" and "video gaming" to refer to games played on computer, on gaming consoles (such as PlayStation 2 and Game Cube), and handheld gaming systems (such as Game Boys and Sony Playstation Portables). The girls' experiences with video gaming took place across all of these platforms.

4. It is interesting to think about what kind of cultural work this stereotype is meant to accomplish—it is inseparable from cultural understandings (and stereotypes) of gaming itself as an activity that harms children by exposing them to and encouraging in them violence, apathy, aggression, sexual aggression and oppression, and many other social ills.

5. Gee's thinking about the issues in his book began with observations of his four-year-old son playing interactive video games, a realization that he needed to play the game himself so he could "coach" his son while he played, and a resulting sense of the learning principles involved in video game playing. Like many researchers who happen to also be parents, Gee discovered through his relationship with his son that the literacy practices of young people outside school offer educators and literacy researchers a window onto literacy itself—if we are willing to pay attention. Like Gee, it was through observation of video-game playing among my family members that I first began to think about the questions and concerns I discuss here—both as a parent concerned about teaching my children well and as a writing researcher concerned with teaching other people's children well. In much the same way that conducting this research project has allowed me to understand and connect better with these people I already love, I agree wholeheartedly with Gee that better understanding video gaming will allow us as teachers to understand and connect with our students more successfully.

6. Unless specified in in-text citations, I have relied on three sources for dating these video-game events: "Computer Gaming Timeline," Leonard Herman et al., and Amanda Kudler.

References

About ESRB. (n.d.). *Entertainment Software Rating Board.* Retrieved June 24, 2005, from http://www.esrb.org/about.asp

Cassell, Justine, & Jenkins, Henry (Eds.). (1998). *From Barbie to Mortal Kombat: Gender and computer games.* Cambridge: MIT Press.

Children Now. (2000). Fair play? Violence, gender, and race in video games. Retrieved June 24, 2005, from http://www.childrennow.org/newsroom/news-00/pr-12-12-00.htm

Computer gaming timeline: 1889–2002. *Digiplay Initiative: Research into Computer Gamers and the Industry They Are Part of.* Retrieved June 24, 2005, from http://www.digiplay.org.uk/index2.php

Finders, Margaret. (1997). *Just girls: Hidden literacies and life in junior high.* New York: Teacher's College Press.

Gee, James Paul. (2003). *What video games have to teach us about learning and literacy.* New York: Palgrave Macmillan.

Gilligan, Carol. (1983). *In a different voice. Psychological theory and women's development.* Cambridge, MA: Harvard University Press.

Grisso, Ashley D., & Weiss, David. (2005). What are gURLs talking about? Adolescent girls' construction of sexual identity on gURL.com. In Sharon R. Mazzarella (Ed.), *Girl wide web: Girls, the Internet, and the negotiation of identity.* (pp. 31–49). New York: Peter Lang.

Haddon, Leslie. (1992). Explaining ICT consumption: The case of the home computer. In Roger Silverstone & Eric Hirsch (Eds.), *Consuming technologies: Media and information in domestic spaces* (pp. 82–96). London: Routledge.

Herbst, Claudia. (2004). Lara's lethal and loaded mission: Transposing reproduction and destruction. In Sherrie A. Inness (Ed.), *Action chicks: New images of tough women in popular culture* (pp. 21–45). New York: Palgrave.

Herman, Leonard, Horwitz, Jer, Kent, Steve, & Miller, Skyler. The history of video games. In *Gamespot.* Retrieved June 24, 2005, from http://www.gamespot.com/gamespot/features/video/hov/index.html

Jenkins, Henry. (2001). From Barbie to Mortal Kombat: Further reflections. Retrieved 24 June 2005 from <http://culturalpolicy.uchicago.edu/conf2001/papers/jenkins.html>.

Kubey, Robert, & Larson, Reed. (1990). The use and experience of the new video media among children and young adolescents. *Communication Research, 17,* 107–130

Kudler, Amanda. Timeline: Video games. *Infoplease.* Retrieved June 24, 2005, from http://www.infoplease.com/spot/gamestimeline1.html

McNamee, Sara. (1998). Youth, gender, and video games: Power and control in the home. In Tracey Skelton & Gill Valentine (Eds.), *Cool places: Geographies of youth culture* (pp. 195–206). New York: Routledge.

Provenzo, Eugene. (1991). *Video kids: Making sense of nintendo.* Cambridge, MA: Harvard University Press.

Researchers find gender differences in kids' video use. *Media Literacy Review.* Retrieved June 24, 2005, from http://interact.uoregon.edu/MediaLit/mlr/readings/articles/gender.html

Subrahmanyam, Kaverip, & Greenfield, Patricia. (1998). Computer games for girls: What makes them play? In Justine Cassell & Henry Jenkins (Eds.), *From Barbie to Mortal Kombat: Gender and computer games* (pp. 46–71). Cambridge: MIT Press.

Subrahmanyam, Kaverip, Kraut, Robert E., Greenfield, Patricia, & Gross, Elisheva. (2000). The impact of home computer use on children's activities and development. In Richard Behrman (Ed.), *The Future of Children: Children and Computer Technology, 10,* 127.

Takayoshi, Pamela, Huot, Emily, & Huot, Meghan. (1999). No boys allowed: The world wide web as a clubhouse for girls. *Computers and Composition, 16,* 89–106.

Vygotsky, Lev. (1978). *Mind in society: The development of higher psychological processes.* Cambridge, MA: Harvard University Press.

What Early Gamers Say about Gaming

Paula Boyd

I'm at an all time low in my gaming currently. Maybe it's because I'm a tenured, nearly middle-aged, homeowner. And I no longer have course work or research to avoid. But it's also just tough to pick out games. But I'll do my best. I guess I'll choose those games that currently get the most of my attention, although those don't necessarily reflect the games that have historically been my favorites. But they do fit into the same genres of games that I like. The game I spend the most time playing right now is cribbage, a card game, on my handspring PDA (with Palm OS). I play against a computerized opponent. I don't know if you are familiar with cribbage in general, but it's basically about getting the most points per hand by collecting runs, pairs, suits, or cards that add up to 15; there are points for getting the advantage over your opponent by throwing down cards in pairs, throwing down cards that add up to 15, throwing the last card, etc. The first player to accumulate 121 points wins. It's pretty complicated.

The reason I play this game so much right now is that it is convenient and short. It is a great way to kill short periods of time when waiting at a doctor's office or whatever. I also play at night in bed, the way most people would read. I guess it settles me down. I like playing cribbage specifically because it has so many scoring options and you've got to anticipate a lot and have a little strategy and there's the challenge of computer competition. When I'm tired of cribbage, I play a version of solitaire called "Demon" that I think has one of the lowest win percentages. I also like the challenge of that. Anyway, either way these are very low tech, simple games that are just cards on a monochrome screen. But, like I said, they can be started and finished in a short period of time, and I can carry them around with me.

I used to play cribbage online against live opponents on the Web and for a while I was involved in an online league. That had all the advantages of the cribbage I play on my PDA now, but the opponents were less predictable, and in the league it was a fairly finite community and I could chat with the other player while we played. There was a whole system of finding and playing opponents, reporting outcomes and a ranking system. (I actually was ranked number one once, briefly.) In addition to regular league play they hosted frequent online tournaments in which you played until you lost or were the last one. I eventually lost interest simply because, the way the ranking system worked, you pretty much had to play several matches a day to maintain a decent ranking and you had to find opponents ranked higher than you to move up. It was too time consuming and, even though I like chatting with the other league members, it wasn't any fun for me if I couldn't play enough to have a good rank.

Eva Liestøl

We begin in the game's [*Duke Nukem 3D Atomic Edition*] first episode, "L.A. Meltdown/Hollywood Holocaust," and find ourselves on the roof of a building. Game character Duke has left us in the lurch. His muscular body is not in front of us, and we must tackle this unknown world without any buffer. In front of us we see a hand holding out the weapon we have chosen and the world in which we are supposed to use it. We have no idea of what lies in wait and do not want to take the chance of exploring unarmed. But what should we do? There are no opponents in sight! There is neither visual nor textual information. We see only the flat roof surrounded by a fence made of wire, some uninteresting boxes, and a ventilation fan. The desire to get out of this boring situation leads us to search for a way out, but there are no doors to be seen. As the weapon is our only tool, we shoot at the boxes in the hope that something will happen. Nothing! . . . Irritated at being stuck, we shoot at the ventilation fan. (Liestol, 2003, p. 331)

Brenda Laurel

The truth [is] that from its inception, everything about the computer game industry actively excluded girls. The games were filled with violent action and grisly imagery. They were available only in quintessentially "male" spaces like dark, noisy, smelly arcades or the aisles of computer and electronics stores. Advertisements, commercials, and packaging featured only male players. And that's just the obvious stuff. Given all these barriers, who knew if girls and women would play computer games or not? Were there intrinsic gender differences that caused females to be repelled by computer games? How should we understand the exceptions—games that attracted a higher than usual percentage of female players, like *Pac Man, Mario Brothers,* and *Tetris?* What would it take to design a computer game that a large number of girls really liked?

References

Boyd, Paula. (2004, May 16). Personal interview.

Laurel, Brenda. (2000). Just one of the girls. Retrieved May 29, 2004, from http://www.slmnet.com/signum/Issue6/marrow/girls.html

Liestøl, Eva. (2003). Computer games and the ludic structure of interpretation. In Gunnar Liestøl, Andrew Morrison, & Terje Rasmussen (Eds.), *Digital media revisited* (pp. 327–357). Cambridge: MIT Press.

Afterword: The Return of the Player

Dmitri Williams

In the halls of Congress, in PTA meetings, church groups, and around countless water coolers, the debate over games rages. It is a debate thick with implications for society, literacy and the role of the individual versus the state. The debate rages because academics, pundits, and policy makers are struggling with the issue of games' effects on society and the individual. Some claim that games are creating a nation of trained killers (Grossman, 1995) while others find them potential sources of inspiration and growth (Gee, 2003). But, to put it bluntly, we do not really know much about what games do to or for us. It's still early in the game, so to speak. And of course, this dance is as old as electronic media—television, the Internet, MP3s, games, and on and on are, as usual, alternately praised for their role saving society and damned for destroying it in a pattern that dates back to at least the telegraph (Czitrom, 1982). On one level this debate matters a great deal for public policy. Powerful actors will attempt to control who can watch, play, and read what, just as they always have. But on another level—that of how people actually use these new media—the debate is largely irrelevant. The cat is already out of the bag, the genie out of the bottle, the gamers are off and running and they're not coming back.

In this new century of intimidating, ubiquitous, pervasive, and customizable media, it is still fair to ask about what games are doing *to* us, but it is equally important to ask what they are doing *for* us. It is surprising how seldom that question is asked. From the research agenda to date, you would think that people play little role in these new media, which is ironic given the term "interactivity." Thankfully, some scholars have asked the obvious questions: Do people not have some control over these things? Do they not pick and choose? Do they not have some agency?

One early questioner was Gerard Jones, who wrote *Killing Monsters* (2002) to explore why children played violent games and what they thought about it. Jones's starting assumption was that meaning is made by the game player at least as much as by the game maker. How radical! Well, given the long history of tensions in cultural studies and communication, perhaps it was not that radical. But let's test that sentiment with one of Jones's anecdotes. Who decides what the game means? If a young American Asian boy plays a game napalming a Southeast Asian town, is that an act of sickening depravity and historical unawareness? Or does it mean something totally different to him? Jones suggested that if you want to know the answer, you should talk to the person to find out. And as it turns out, that is a pretty good idea.

That is the powerful contribution of this book—someone took the time to ask these people what they made of their own media use. Rather than judging their play as inherently good or bad, this book asks people to tell their own stories and then analyzes what they said and how it relates to their digital literacy. As always, the results are at once obvious and surprising—obvious because, of course, people are actively engaged with these media, and surprising in that we can rarely predict what an individual will say, do, and think.

In the foreword of this book, James Paul Gee frames this discussion as one of literacy practices embedded within social contexts. In other words, what we get out of our media is dependent on who we are, where we are, what's going on around us, and what we're up to. In my home field of communication, this was originally a controversial thought, but one that more and more scholars have taken up as our media environment becomes more active and less passive. Games are another harbinger of this paradigm shift in media. It is difficult to make the case that gamers are couch potatoes who sit inert, letting programmed meaning wash over and through them. It is not always clear that we can import our older theories and methods to make sense of them. After all, not even the most stringent proponents of effects thinking still subscribe to the stimulus-response model of communication for even more passive media such as television. So it is notable that in this book, none of the players were consumed and programmed by games. They enjoyed reading, exercise, flight training, fishing, sports, and a host of other "more acceptable" pursuits. It is appropriate then that the entire field of communication has moved on to talk about "limited effects" (Lowery & DeFluer, 1995). Some now go so far as to talk about agency among the audience members/viewers/players. It is a good thing, too, or the case studies in this book would seem like portraits from an alien civilization. Our more recent theory-driven labels now say things like "decoding" (Hall, 2000) or "uses and gratifications," (Katz, 1996) depending on your preferred flavor. The point is that the gamer has agency and that researchers are starting to acknowledge it.

What Cynthia Selfe and Gail Hawisher and the contributors here have done is to take this concept a step further. They are not just acknowledging the point. They are chronicling it. And what they have found offers insight into the important issues of agency, social capital, and technoliteracy among gamers. Each of these represents an area unexplored or barely explored by social scientists. Thus, the findings here offer suggestions for theory and hypotheses for testing among survey researchers, experimentalists, and ethnographers as well as literacy researchers.

Studying agency starts by understanding what communication and sociology researchers call context, or what Gee calls "situated meaning." Gamers are not alike, and their social, cultural, and demographic backgrounds have a keen influence on their literacy practices. It makes a great difference if the gamer(s) is encouraged by parents (John, Introduction; Eve, ch. 3), discouraged by teachers (Josh, ch. 1; Danny, ch. 11), are engaged to one another (Josh and Stephanie, ch. 7), is an immigrant (Laxman and Angish, ch. 2), homosexual (Jonathan, ch. 9), elderly (Frank, ch. 12), is a female gamer encouraged by other females (all four women in ch. 13), is a text-based gamer coming from a family that encouraged reading and writing (ch. 4), or comes from a family with problems (Martin, ch. 6). Only with those contextual cues can we make sense of how gamers create meaning from their games at the individual level, and why they are driven to do so.

Once we understand their background, we can explore the appeal of gaming for them. This basic question—what makes things fun to learn?—has been tackled by scholars (Malone, 1980) and, more recently, by introspective game makers themselves (Koster, 2004; Sellers, in press). Their answer has been challenged, which matches what social scientists have found lately (Sherry & Lucas, 2003), and which resonates with the profiles in this book. The gamers in this book liked the process and outcome of mastery. Many of the authors here have noted the keen irony of Gee's observations about games and school: gamers like games because they challenge them to solve problems, while school bores them by not challenging them enough. Students race home from school to engage in problem-solving they cannot get from teachers—what is wrong with this picture? Debra Journet's obsessive puzzle-solving drive in the *Myst* games is an example. It also proved to be a strong way to teach compelling narrative structures. For some, like the four women in chapter 13, gaming was driven by this desire for learning and mastery, and because they frequently did it together, it encouraged a literacy community at the same time. For Frank, the elderly gamer, it was the appealing ability to think and explore on meta levels that gaming allowed him.

Others are compelled by the fact that *they* drive the narrative. It is telling how often the authors and the subjects here mentioned the appeal of the *Dungeons and Dragons* (*D&D*) role-playing game. Indeed, why just watch when you can do? If that paradigm shift makes media moguls', scholars' and policy makers' lives more difficult, too bad. It is real and it is not going away.

That level of cognitive awareness and literacy enabled some (but not all) gamers to fashion meanings that appealed to them, and to read the game texts according to their values. Danny, the young African American player, was keenly aware of the racial roles and stereotypes in *Grand Theft Auto* and chose to play the game in a way that bent the meaning to his values, rather than the developer's. Pamela Takayoshi, in contrast, noted little reading against the intended meaning in the sexual depictions of characters. Her four female gamers bristled at the characters' framing and persisted despite it, but did not reinterpret it to suit their own ideologies. This would appear to be a case in which the developer's framing trumps the players'. Following Mia Consalvo's (2003) early work on sexuality and gaming, Jonathan Alexander et al. spoke with gay gamers and found that games offered them a focal point for gay-centric identity and discussions, and a space to make meaning out of the largely heterosexist game content that exists. That meaning is contested and fluid, and once again, is made by the player as much as by the game maker and the other players. These three examples show Stuart Hall's "decoding" in action (or Gee's "situated learning," if you like), and demonstrate that players are both influenced by the norms and assumptions of the game as well as exerting a fair degree of control over them in his or her own mind.

Gee's literacy communities form what political scientists, sociologists, and communication researchers describe as sites of social capital (Coleman, 1988). These are communities in which the act of consumption and use occurs with others to create some social outcome that benefits the different members of the group. We see the two basic types of social capital—bridging and bonding (Putnam, 2000)—throughout this book. Gamers, especially those playing with others online, were bridging cultures and sidestepping geopolitical boundaries. Josh (ch. 1) and Matt (ch. 8) both made friends in other countries and learned something about those cultures, even as a Nepalese youth (Pandey, ch. 2) reached back to meet American players. The UN should do half as well at promoting internationalism. Meanwhile, it is clear that gaming provides a backdrop for some more supportive, bonding activities as well, if not always clear how often (Williams, 2006, in press). Josh described getting online support after a death in the family through his gaming networks, and the four women of chapter 13 clearly used games as a way to stay connected and supportive of one another.

But of all the outcomes posited by researchers, few seem as obvious or as powerful as technoliteracy. It is increasingly clear that print-only literacy is no longer enough. Digital literacy is now a required skill for survival and competitiveness in a global postmodern society. But do games actually help players acquire digital literacy? In effects research, Sabrina Lin and Mark Lepper (1987) made early claims about the use of games as related to later computer use, but few others have done empirical testing. I have noted elsewhere that the presence of game machines has consistently predated the presence of computers in homes (Williams, in press). But making that connection without survey data or causal evidence is another step. We have not always known exactly how it might occur, yet here are a series of case studies offering welcome evidence.

For Laxman Pandey, and others from less technologically advanced countries, this is an extreme case. For them, gaming was the entrée into skills as taken-for-granted as mousing and keyboard use. For U.S. children, the path is there, but the role of parents and role models appears to matter greatly. Indeed, here is a place where the social context and support networks can play a strong role. For example, Eve, encouraged by her father, became not only comfortable with games, but also established an international career through them. Similarly, the interactive fiction (IF) players of chapter 4 all came from families that could afford technology and also approved of its use—it is no surprise then that the players all ended up working in the IT field. But the key note for the IF players is that they were not only learning about computers, but also learning and mastering literacy at the same time, even if authority figures did not recognize their activities as "writing." IF makes a further contribution by affording a safe place to fail, which Daniel Keller et al. and Gee recognize as Erik Erickson's psychosocial moratorium. Learning is only possible when the learner can fail, and games provide safe spaces for this in a way that few classrooms can duplicate. The appeals of *D&D* for Matt, the rural Kentuckian, worked the same way. His IF was guided by an overall mythology, but then the rest of the literacy came from him. It encouraged him to be literate, independent, and creative, and eventually dovetailed with an interest in computing technology as *D&D* computer games appeared.

The four women of chapter 13 drew inspiration from each other and from other strong female family members. It is not clear if they would have played without such a support network. And although we might have the sense that society is progressing toward women having equal access and rights with technology, the anecdotes here are not encouraging. They support what I have found in the way the press has historically framed these issues (Williams, 2003).

For children, especially ones with learning difficulties, some game play may help them acquire the focus they need to improve their writing and attention to learning tasks. Chris, the Texan student, improved his sentence structure and his knowledge of aviation immediately after his family bought a computer and he began playing *Sim*-style games. His confidence increased, which in turn made him more socially comfortable with his peers. Even more impressively, his grown-up tasks as a political operative may have had some of their basic roots in his early play of *SimCity*. Indeed, Chris's experience provides strong evidence at the case-study level of the broader patterns first suggested by Lin and Lepper nearly 20 years ago, and further supports Gee's claims about identity and learning. As Mathew Bunce and Marjorie Hebert note, gaming is not a panacea for all, but in this case it was clearly a strong positive influence.

Interestingly, they make the generalizability point: not all games work the same. The ones that Chris played encouraged sociability, efficiency, cooperation, and the common good. Bunce and Hebert's analysis suggests that games that promote other less socially desirable outcomes might do harm. And that is an important point to close on—not all games are particularly good. As Journet noted in chapter 5, some games are more compelling and interesting than others. Some are badly made and some are crafted with love and care. Nor are they often even comparable—the meanings, practices, arcs, and linearity of *Grand Theft Auto*, *Microsoft Flight Simulator*, *Halo*, and IF titles are unlikely to be the same. If there is a prediction made by a comparison of the various games here, it is that the more open-ended, less-linear titles may encourage more creativity and digital literacy.

Regardless, games are not the silver-bullet answer to a looming energy crisis, class warfare, and international conflicts. What matters is that their use is affected both by the way they are made and the way they are played. Meaning and use starts with the developer and then is refashioned and recoded by the player. And that, as this book has shown, is a complex and rich process. The case studies here, of course, have their limitations. They are a collection of mostly white, educated subjects including a disproportionately large number of college and graduate students. Thus, the contribution of this book is in uncovering and explaining practices and mechanisms, not in proving how common or likely they are (which Selfe and Hawisher have responsibly put right up front in the introduction). As such, this book lays clear groundwork for others who want to explore the prevalence of the practices shown here. We may not know how common these things are, but we now know they truly exist and have good leverage into how some of them work. This should enable us to continue asking and testing the right range of questions. I defend the practice of asking about the harmful effects of media because they are not mutually exclusive with the positives found here and because, at the end of the day, parents want to know what these things are doing to their kids. However, it is unavoidable that games also have immense positive potential, especially when we account for how different gamers actually use them and think about them.

Perhaps we should simply have heeded the words of Williams Stephenson (1967), who wrote in the aptly named "Play theory of mass communication" almost 40 years ago,

> Social scientists have been busy, since the dawn of mass communication research, trying to prove that the mass media have been sinful where they should have been good. The media have been looked at through the eyes of morality when, instead, what was required was a fresh glance at people existing in their own right for the first time. (p. 45)

That was what Jones was prompting, what Gee was setting up, and what the contributors here have actually done.

References

Coleman, James S. (1988). Social capital in the creation of human capital. *American Journal of Sociology, 94*, S95–S121.

Consalvo, Mia. (2003). Hot dates and fairy-tale romances: Studying sexuality in video games. In M. J. P. Wolf & B. Perron (Eds.), *The video game theory reader* (pp. 171–194). New York: Routledge.

Czitrom, Daniel. (1982). *Media and the American mind: From Morse to McLuhan.* Chapel Hill: University of North Carolina Press.

Gee, James. (2003). *What video games have to teach us about learning and literacy.* New York: Palgrave MacMillan.

Grossman, Dave. (1995). *On killing: The psychological cost of learning to kill in war and society.* Boston: Little, Brown.

Hall, Stuart. (2000). Encoding/Decoding. In P. Marris, & S. Thronham (Eds.), *Media studies: A reader* (Second ed., pp. 51–61). New York: New York University Press.

Jones, Gerard. (2002). *Killing monsters: Why children need superheroes, fantasy games, and make-believe violence.* New York: Basic Books.

Katz, Elihu. (1996). Viewers work. In J. Hay, L. Grossberg, & E. Wartella (Eds.), *The audience and its landscape* (pp. 9–22). Boulder, CO: Westview Press.

Koster, Raph. (2004). *A theory of fun for game design.* Phoenix, AZ: Paraglyph.

Lin, Sabrina, & Lepper, Mark R. (1987). Correlates of children's usage of videogames and computers. *Journal of Applied Social Psychology, 17*(1), 72–93.

Lowery, Shearon, & DeFluer, Melvin. (1995). *Milestones in mass communication research: Media effects.* White Plains, NY: Longman.

Malone, Thomas. (1980). *What makes things fun to learn?* Paper presented at the ACM SIGSMALL, Palo Alto, California.

Putnam, Robert D. (2000). *Bowling alone: The collapse and revival of American community.* New York: Simon & Schuster.

Sellers, Mike. (in press). Designing the experience of interactive play. In P. Vorderer & J. Bryant (Eds.), *Video games: Motivations and consequences of use.* Mahwah, NJ: Erlbaum.

Sherry, John, & Lucas, Kristen. (2003, May). *Video game uses and gratifications as predictors of use and game preference.* Paper presented at the International Communication Association Annual Conference, San Diego, California.

Stephenson, Williams. (1967). *The play theory of mass communication.* Chicago: University of Chicago Press.

Williams, Dmitri. (2003). The video game lightning rod. *Information, Communication & Society, 6*(4), 523–550.

Williams, Dmitri. (in press). Groups and goblins: The social and civic impact an online game. *Journal of Broadcasting and Electronic Media.*

Williams, Dmitri. (2006). A (brief) social history of gaming. In P. Vorderer & J. Bryant (Eds.), *Video games: Motivations and consequences of use.* Mahwah, NJ: Erlbaum.

List of Contributors

Jonathan Alexander is associate professor of English and comparative literature at the University of Cincinnati, where he also serves as director of the English Composition Program. He specializes in both sexuality studies and the teaching of writing with technology. His recent work includes the coedited collection *Bisexuality and Transgenderism: InterSEXions of the Others* (Harrington Park Press, 2004), the coauthored book *Argument Now* (Longman, 2004), the coedited collection *Role Play: Distance Learning and the Teaching of English* (Hampton, 2005), and *Digital Youth: Emerging Literacies on the World Wide Web* (Hampton, 2005).

Paul Ardis, who studied computer science and mathematics at Purdue University, was born on the University of Illinois campus in 1983 but spent the first half of his life on the East Coast before moving to Naperville, Illinois. Ten years there declared him a "Midwesterner," though he would meet and fall in love with a girl from Massachusetts while studying at Purdue. His current plans include marriage, graduate school, and finding an interesting job (though not necessarily in that order).

Jessica Lyn Bannon is a doctoral student in writing studies at the University of Illinois in Urbana-Champaign. Her research centers on literacy studies and policy, with a particular focus on the connections between public perceptions of literacy and federal adult education policy since the 1960s. While her nephew keeps her up-to-date on the newest video game technologies, she prefers the more familiar Atari and Super Nintendo.

Matthew Barnes is a graphic designer at Elizabethtown, Kentucky's *The News-Enterprise*. His hobbies include drawing, reading, and playing computer and video games.

Samantha Blackmon is a native of Detroit, Michigan, and a recent transplant to West Lafayette, Indiana, where she serves as assistant professor of English at Purdue University. She earned her PhD in rhetoric and composition from Wayne State University in Detroit, in 2001. Her research and teaching interests are in minority rhetoric and computers and composition. Her more recent research projects look at how issues of race play out in the computerized writing environment and race and network theory. She has published in *Kairos, Teaching Writing with Computers,* and *Modern Fiction Studies,* and has articles forthcoming in *JAC, Enculturation,* and several edited collections.

John Branscum is a doctoral student at the University of Cincinnati. His special interests include the use of dreamsharing in the composition classroom, multimodal texts, creative writing, and religious rhetoric. He sometimes suspects that he may be a virtual character in a cosmic video game.

Matthew Bunce is in the Rhetoric and Technical Communication Department at Michigan Technological University. His current research interests look at how learning-different students engage with the many literacy challenges that face them in school and employment. He was the recipient of the NCTE (National Council of Teachers of English)/ACE (Assembly on Computers in English) K-12 Participation Award at the 2004 Computers and Writing conference.

Brynn Carlson is currently in the second grade in Lake Bluff, Illinois. She is the best writer in her class and likes to play games of all kinds, not just computer games. She is very good at them.

Kylie Carlson is currently in the sixth grade in Lake Bluff, Illinois. She excels in school, in winning games, and is especially talented in gymnastics.

J. Christopher Collins graduated with his BA in communication from St. Edward's University in Austin, Texas. He currently serves as an intern for Representative Eddie Rodriguez at the Texas State Capitol and is a licensed pilot.

Vivienne Dunstan is currently a PhD student at the University of Dundee, Scotland, researching reading habits in Scotland in the eighteenth and nineteenth centuries. Before converting to history, she was a computer science student, undergraduate and postgraduate, at the University of St. Andrews, and has played computer games for well over 20 years.

Stephanie Owen Fleischer is a doctoral candidate in rhetoric and composition at the University of Louisville. Her scholarly interests are literacy studies, particularly multimodal and popular culture literacies; identity theory; narrative theory; ecocriticism; and nineteenth-century literature. She currently works as an editorial assistant at the *Henry James Review* and as an assistant director of the Writing Centers Research Project at the university.

Josh Gardiner was born and lives in a small town in Upper Michigan. He was introduced to technology at a very young age. Eventually moving into Web design, then into game design, he has always been fascinated with creating things out of his own free will. Keeping mainly to a few simple strategy games in his younger years, Josh has moved into first-person shooters over the past several years. He has always taken a leadership role, such as captain or team leader, in such games.

James Paul Gee is the Tashia Morgridge Professor of Reading at the University of Wisconsin-Madison. He is the author of, among other books, *Social Linguistics* *and Literacies; The Social Mind; The New Work Order; What Video Games Have to Teach Us about Learning and Literacy;* and *Situated Language and Learning,* as well as numerous articles in sociolinguistics, discourse analysis, literacy studies, and on games and learning.

JoAnn Griffin is a doctoral student at the University of Louisville. Her research interests are in writing center effectiveness and the humor of nineteenth-century women writers and speakers. Her other interests include a large family of dogs and horses.

Gail E. Hawisher is professor of English and founding director of the Center for Writing Studies at the University of Illinois, Urbana-Champaign. Her published work includes books, articles, and chapters that have grown out of her interest in computers as new media for written and visual communication. With Cynthia Selfe, she edits *Computers and Composition: An International Journal,* and is also coeditor, with Selfe, of *Global Literacies and the World Wide Web* and *Passions, Pedagogies, and 21st Century Technologies,* which won the Distinguished Book Award at Computers and Writing 2000. Her most recent coauthored project is *Literate Lives in the Information Age: Narratives of Literacy from the United States* (2004).

Marjorie Hebert is in the Rhetoric and Technical Communication Program at Michigan Technological University. Her current research interest is the development of sustainable technology practices in composition classrooms. She has also served Michigan Technological University as lab consultant for five years and as the associate Director of Electronic Communication across the Curriculum for the past two years.

Rachel Henry is a stay-at-home mom who lives in Massachusetts with her husband and two young sons. She grew up playing games (from Nintendo to Crystal Caverns) with her family and reading everything in sight (from Walter Farley to Tolkien). She rediscovered text adventures while a student at MIT, and she hopes to someday finish writing her own game, which combines formal gardens, origami, lots of animals, and a ghost story. In the meantime, she works hard to pass on her love of both gaming and reading to the next generation.

Debra Journet is professor of English at the University of Louisville, where she teaches a variety of courses in rhetoric and composition. Her research has examined the rhetorical and epistemological functions of narrative, genre, and interdisciplinarity and appears in such journals as *Written Communication, Social Epistemology,* and *Technical Communication Quarterly.* She has won the NCTE Award for Research in Technical Communication three times and has received awards from the National Endowment for Humanities (NEH), National Science Foundation (NSF), and Fulbright Commission. Currently, she is completing a book on narrative rhetoric in evolutionary biology.

Dan Keller is a doctoral student in rhetoric and composition at the University of Louisville.

Samantha Looker received her BA in English linguistics at Arizona State University and is currently working on her PhD in writing studies at the University of Illinois, Urbana-Champaign. She teaches in Illinois's Academic Writing Program, which has fostered her interests in basic writing pedagogy and diversity in the composition classroom.

Anne Mareck is a graduate student of humanities at Michigan Technological University where she is pursuing a PhD in technology studies and rhetoric.

Mack McCoy has worked with computers since 1991. During his career, he has been part of and led teams working on everything from communication satellites or laser printers to healthcare management systems and DSL deployments. Mack holds a bachelor's degree in computer information systems from Colorado State University, Pueblo, and has been gaming online for nearly a decade.

Deanna McGaughey-Summers holds a master's degree in sociology from Ohio University, a master's degree in Administration of Justice from the University of Louisville, and is currently pursuing a PhD in rhetoric and composition from the University of Louisville. Her research interests include transdisciplinary studies concerning sexuality, justice, technology, and social inequality. She has collaborated on articles that have appeared in *Gender and Society,* the *Journal of Gay, Lesbian, and Bisexual Identity, Sociological Spectrum,* and *American Journal of Criminal Justice.*

Iswari P. Pandey is a doctoral student in rhetoric and composition at the University of Louisville. His interests include literacies in the transnational interface, literary theory (especially postcolonial), immigrant writings, and cultural issues in rhetoric and composition. He has published articles in literary and rhetorical studies in Nepal and the United States.

Laxman Pandey graduated with an MBA from the University of Dayton in 2004. He is currently working as a mortgage consultant for SAI Mortgage, Inc., in Virginia.

Beth Powell is a doctoral student at the University of Louisville. Her special interests include technology and new media texts in composition and sociolinguistic research in the composition class. She has always enjoyed playing video games, and she enjoys learning about new games from her 16-year-old brother.

Frank Quickert runs the financial advisory firm, Investment Strategies, as well as a number of investment clubs. Formerly a state representative and director of law for the city of Louisville, he maintains a keen interest in law and government. He has given up sleeping for playing video games.

Cynthia L. Selfe is Humanities Distinguished Professor in the Department of English at The Ohio State University and the coeditor, with Gail Hawisher, of

Computers and Composition: An International Journal. In 1996, Selfe was recognized as an EDUCOM Medal award winner for innovative computer use in higher education—the first woman and the first English teacher ever to receive this award. Along with long-time collaborator Gail Hawisher, Selfe was presented in 2000 with the Outstanding Technology Innovator award. She has also served as the chair of the Conference on College Composition and Communication and the chair of the college section of the NCTE.

Erin Smith is assistant professor of New Media and Technical Communication in the Humanities Department at Michigan Technological University. Her research centers on the rhetorical and intellectual possibilities of new technologies, as well as on the disciplinary issues related to digital technology, film, and composition studies. She has published in *Kairos* and has a forthcoming publication in the *International Handbook of Virtual Learning Environments* on the place of Donna Haraway's work in the field of composition studies.

Angish Shreshtha completed his MBA from the University of Findlay in 2005 and started working as an intern financial analyst for an investment banking company, Oppenheimer & Co, Inc., in Washington D.C.

Russell Summers is employed in maintenance and security at a local residential complex. He spends his spare time moderating online gaming communities, playing video games, and writing short stories.

Pamela Takayoshi is associate professor of English at Kent State University. In addition to publications that have appeared in numerous journals and edited collections, her collection with Brian Huot, *Teaching Writing with Computers,* won the 2003 Computers and Composition Distinguished Book Award. She believes that as writing technologies become more a part of everyday life, they are affecting the ways people interact with literacy, text, and communication. Her research projects explore this intersection between literacy, writing, communication, and technologies. She is currently studying the ways young people use synchronous communications technologies (such as instant messaging and chat rooms), and completing a book-length study of a high school English teacher's first year in the classroom.

Daniel Terrell is currently in a residential vocational program in Wisconsin where he is finishing his high school education and training to be an electrician. He continues to be an avid gamer and would love to develop video games one day.

Adam Thornton was born in 1971 and grew up 30 miles west of Atlanta. He graduated with a BA in Ancient Mediterranean History from Rice University in 1994 and went to Princeton to pursue a PhD in the history of science, specifically the history of computing. In 1998 with an MA in hand, he left graduate school to play with computers rather than write stories about people who played with computers. Today, for fun, he plays ancient video games and writes games for obsolete systems.

Derek Van Ittersum is a doctoral student in writing studies at the University of Illinois, Urbana-Champaign. His research combines historical and qualitative approaches to the study of computers and the activity of writing, and he is especially interested in why some devices, such as the mouse and keyboard, became central to writing while other devices, such as Douglas Engelbart's chord keyset, has had little impact.

Carlos Velez, a native of central Florida, is an active composer and flutist, pursuing his musical studies in Cincinnati, Ohio. He is also an avid PC gamer and a very fun-loving person in general.

Dmitri Williams is assistant professor of speech communication at the University of Illinois, Urbana-Champaign, where he teaches, among other courses, a play and technology seminar. His current research investigates the effects of online video game play, including its impact on family and community, social networks, aggression, health, and perceptions. An offshoot of his research is the development and use of scales to measure social capital in online and offline contexts. He was honored in 2005 by the National Communication Association (NCA) with of the Gerald R. Miller Outstanding Doctoral Dissertation Award for his "Trouble in River City: The Social Impact of Video Games."

Brett Witty is a 20-something mathematics PhD student in Canberra, Australia. His hobbies are writing, programming, and interactive fiction.

Susan Wright is a doctoral candidate at the University of Louisville who enjoys reading, writing, and playing video games.

Index

Printed in the United States
101665LV00002B/139-324/P

9 781403 972200